ALSO AVAILABLE FROM ⊕TOKYOPOP®

PRIEST
PRINCESS AI
PSYCHIC ACADEMY
RAGNAROK
RAVE MASTER
REALITY CHECK
REBIRTH
REBOUND
REMOTE
RISING STARS OF MANGA
SABER MARIONETTE J
SAILOR MOON
SAINT TAIL
SAYUKI
SAMURAI DEEPER KYO
SAMURAI GIRL REAL BOUT HIGH SCHOOL
SCRYED
SEIKAI TRILOGY, THE
SGT. FROG
SHAOLIN SISTERS
SHIRAHIME-SYO: SNOW GODDESS TALES
SHUTTERBOX
SKULL MAN, THE
SMUGGLER
SNOW DROP
SORCERER HUNTERS
STONE
SUIKODEN III
SUKI
THREADS OF TIME
TOKYO BABYLON
TOKYO MEW MEW
TOKYO TRIBES
TRAMPS LIKE US
UNDER THE GLASS MOON
VAMPIRE GAME
VISION OF ESCAFLOWNE, THE
WARRIORS OF TAO
WILD ACT
WISH
WORLD OF HARTZ
X-DAY
ZODIAC P.I.

MANGA

CLAMP SCHOOL PARANORMAL INVESTIGATORS
KARMA CLUB
SAILOR MOON
SLAYERS

ART BOOKS

ART OF CARDCAPTOR SAKURA
ART OF MAGIC KNIGHT RAYEARTH, THE
PEACH: MIWA UEDA ILLUSTRATIONS

ANIME GUIDES

COWBOY BEBOP
GUNDAM TECHNICAL MANUALS
SAILOR MOON SCOUT GUIDES

TOKYOPOP KIDS

STRAY SHEEP

CINE-MANGA™

ALADDIN
ASTRO BOY
CARDCAPTORS
CONFESSIONS OF A TEENAGE DRAMA QUEEN
DUEL MASTERS
FAIRLY ODDPARENTS, THE
FAMILY GUY
FINDING NEMO
G.I. JOE SPY TROOPS
JACKIE CHAN ADVENTURES
JIMMY NEUTRON: BOY GENIUS, THE ADVENTURES OF
KIM POSSIBLE
LILO & STITCH
LIZZIE MCGUIRE
LIZZIE MCGUIRE MOVIE, THE
MALCOLM IN THE MIDDLE
POWER RANGERS: NINJA STORM
SHREK 2
SPONGEBOB SQUAREPANTS
SPY KIDS 2
SPY KIDS 3-D: GAME OVER
TEENAGE MUTANT NINJA TURTLES
THAT'S SO RAVEN
TRANSFORMERS: ARMADA
TRANSFORMERS: ENERGON

For more
information visit
www.TOKYOPOP.com

03.01.04T

ALSO AVAILABLE FROM **TOKYOPOP**

03.01.04T

Translator - Nan Rymer
English Adaptation - Stuart Hazleton
Retouch and Lettering - Maitreya Andrews
Cover Layout - Patrick Hook
Graphic Designer - John Lo

Editor - Nora Wong
Digital Imaging Manager - Chris Buford
Pre-Press Manager - Antonio DePietro
Production Managers - Jennifer Miller, Mutsumi Miyazaki
Art Director - Matt Alford
Managing Editor - Jill Freshney
VP of Production - Ron Klamert
President & C.O.O. - John Parker
Publisher & C.E.O. - Stuart Levy

E-mail: info@TOKYOPOP.com

Come visit us online at www.TOKYOPOP.com

A  Manga

TOKYOPOP Inc.
5900 Wilshire Blvd. Suite 2000
Los Angeles, CA 90036

Crescent Moon Vol. 1

Crescent Moon Volume 1 (originally published as Mikan no Tsuki) © Haruko IIDA 2000 © RED 2000.
First published in Japan 2000 by KADOKAWA SHOTEN PUBLISHING CO., LTD., Tokyo.
English translation rights arranged with KADOKAWA SHOTEN PUBLISHING CO., LTD., Tokyo
through TUTTLE-MORI AGENCY, INC., Tokyo.

English text copyright ©2004 TOKYOPOP Inc.

ISBN: 1-59182-792-2

First TOKYOPOP printing: May 2004

10 9 8 7 6 5 4

Printed in the USA

Crescent Moon

Haruko Iida. Original Works:

Red Company/Takamura Matsuda Volume 1

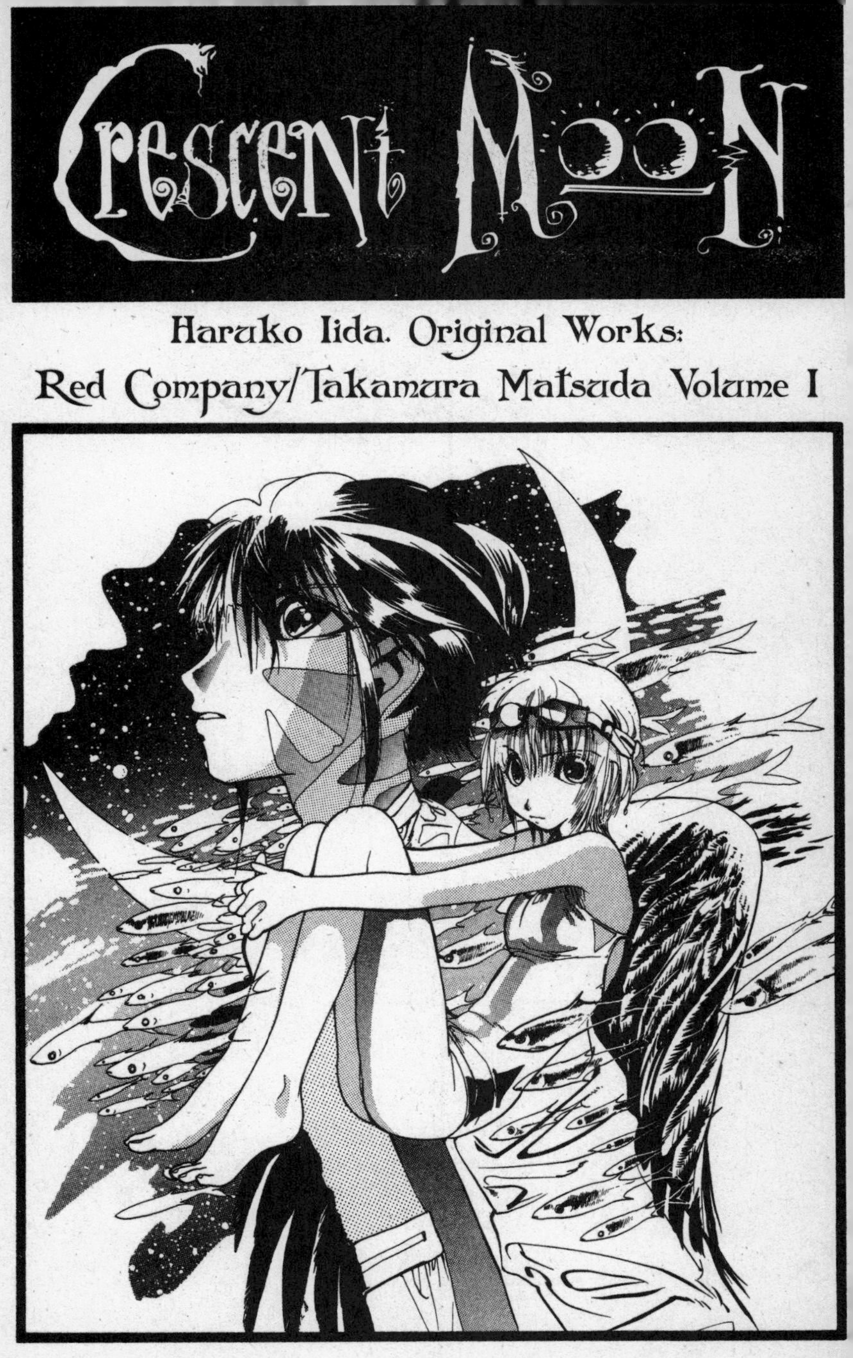

Crescent Moon

Contents

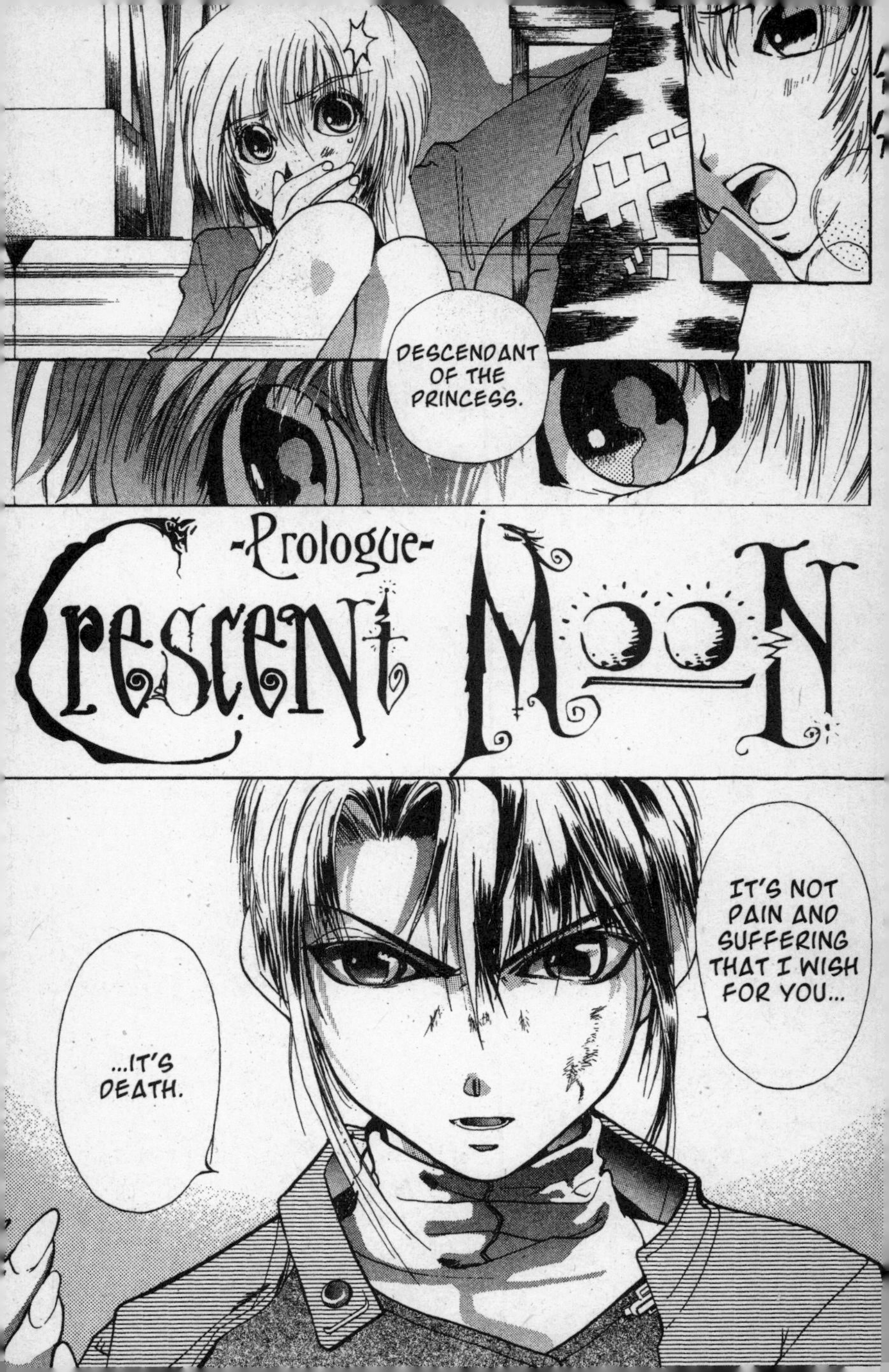
DESCENDANT OF THE PRINCESS.
-Prologue-
Crescent Moon
IT'S NOT PAIN AND SUFFERING THAT I WISH FOR YOU...
...IT'S DEATH.

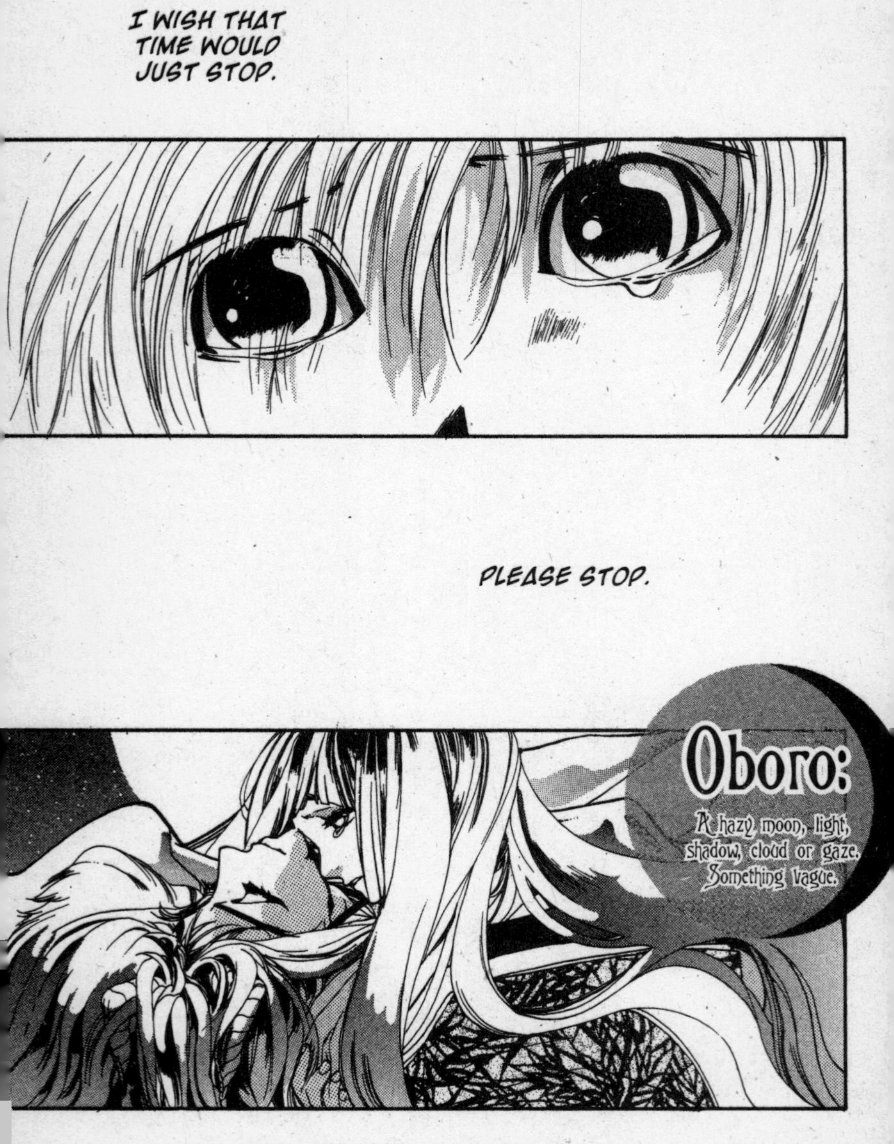
I WISH THAT TIME WOULD JUST STOP.
PLEASE STOP.
Oboro:
A hazy moon, light, shadow, cloud or gaze. Something vague.

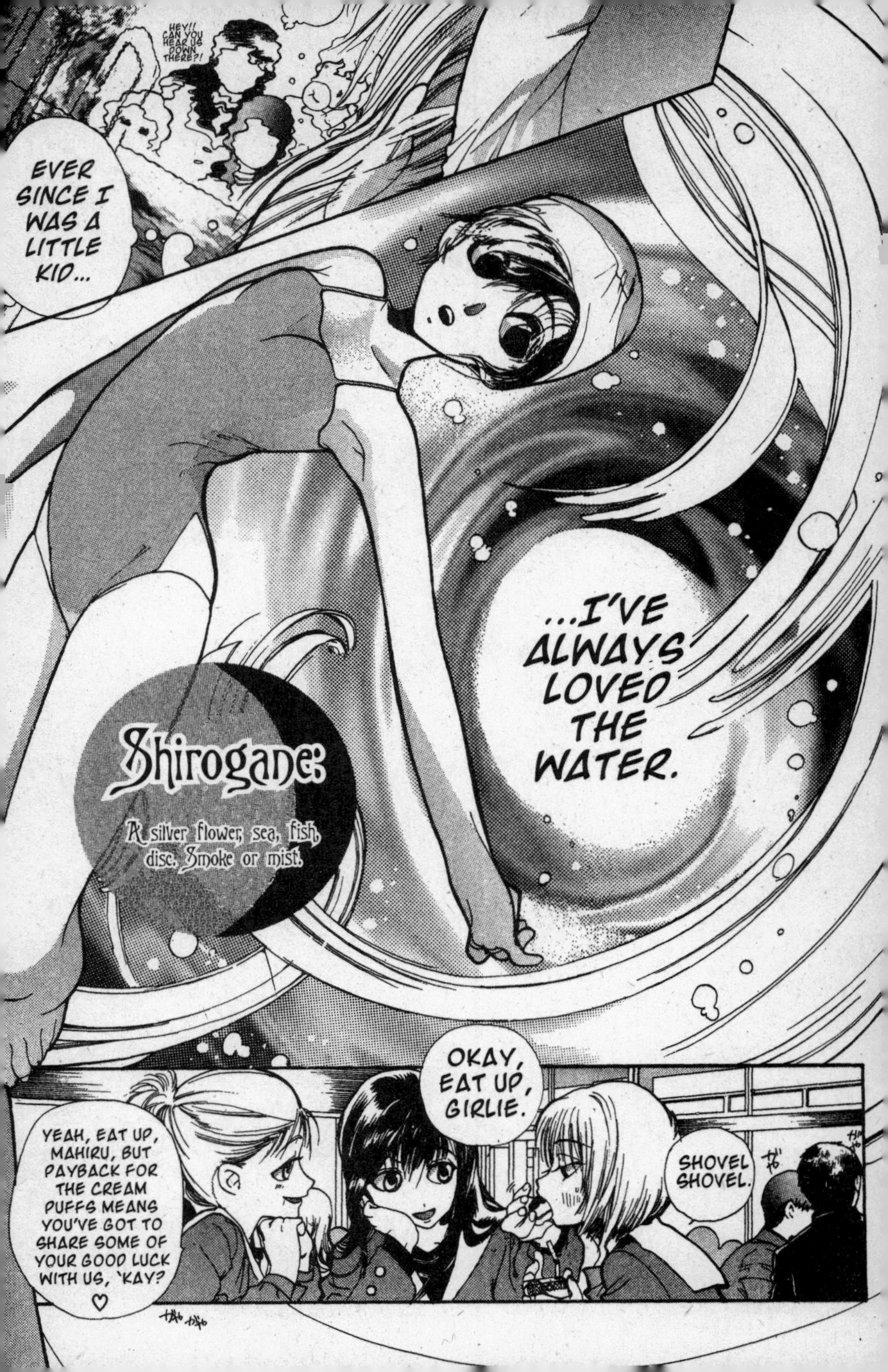
HEY!! CAN YOU HEAR US DOWN THERE?!
EVER SINCE I WAS A LITTLE KID...
...I'VE ALWAYS LOVED THE WATER.
Shirogane:
A silver flower, sea, fish, disc. Smoke or mist.
SHOVEL SHOVEL.
OKAY, EAT UP, GIRLIE.
YEAH, EAT UP, MAHIRU, BUT PAYBACK FOR THE CREAM PUFFS MEANS YOU'VE GOT TO SHARE SOME OF YOUR GOOD LUCK WITH US, 'KAY? ♡

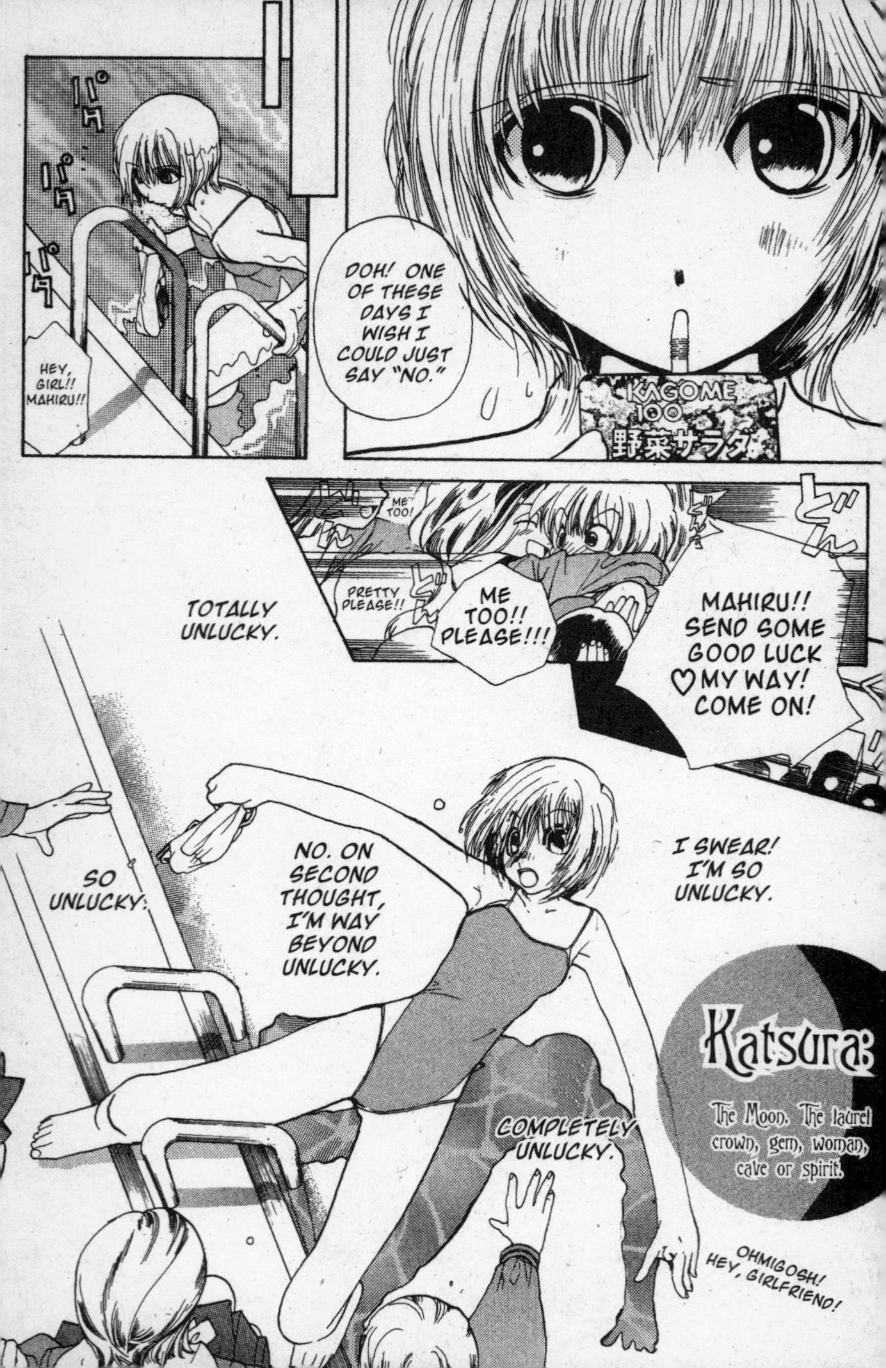

DOH! ONE OF THESE DAYS I WISH I COULD JUST SAY "NO."
KAGOME 100
野菜サラダ
パタ
パタ
パタ
HEY, GIRL!! MAHIRU!!
どん
MAHIRU!! SEND SOME GOOD LUCK ♡ MY WAY! COME ON!
ME TOO!! PLEASE!!!
PRETTY PLEASE!!
ME TOO!
TOTALLY UNLUCKY.
I SWEAR! I'M SO UNLUCKY.
Katsura:
The Moon. The laurel crown, gem, woman, cave or spirit.
NO. ON SECOND THOUGHT, I'M WAY BEYOND UNLUCKY.
SO UNLUCKY.
COMPLETELY UNLUCKY.
OHMIGOSH! HEY, GIRLFRIEND!

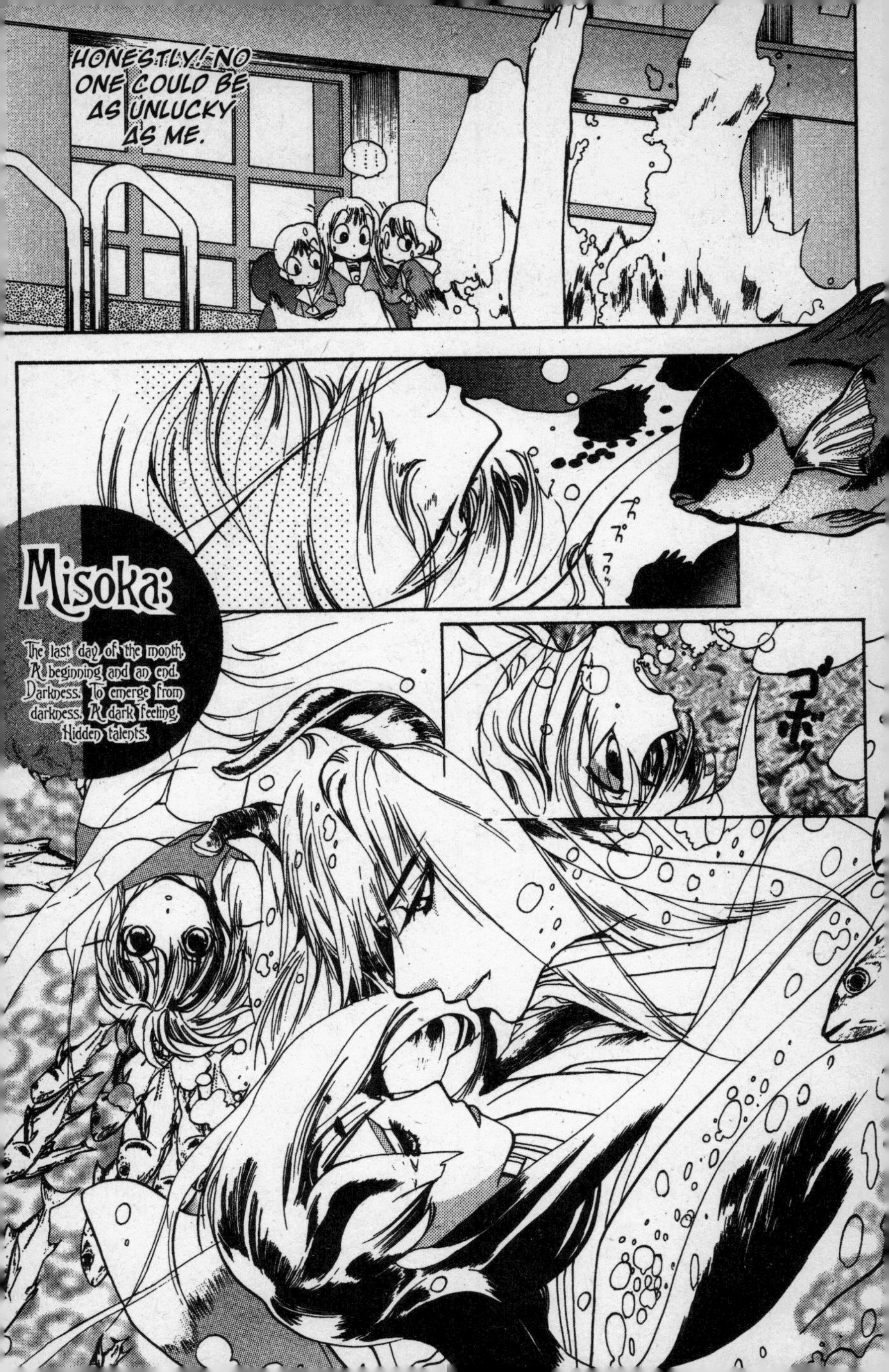
HONESTLY! NO ONE COULD BE AS UNLUCKY AS ME.
Misoka:
The last day of the month. A beginning and an end. Darkness. To emerge from darkness. A dark feeling. Hidden talents.

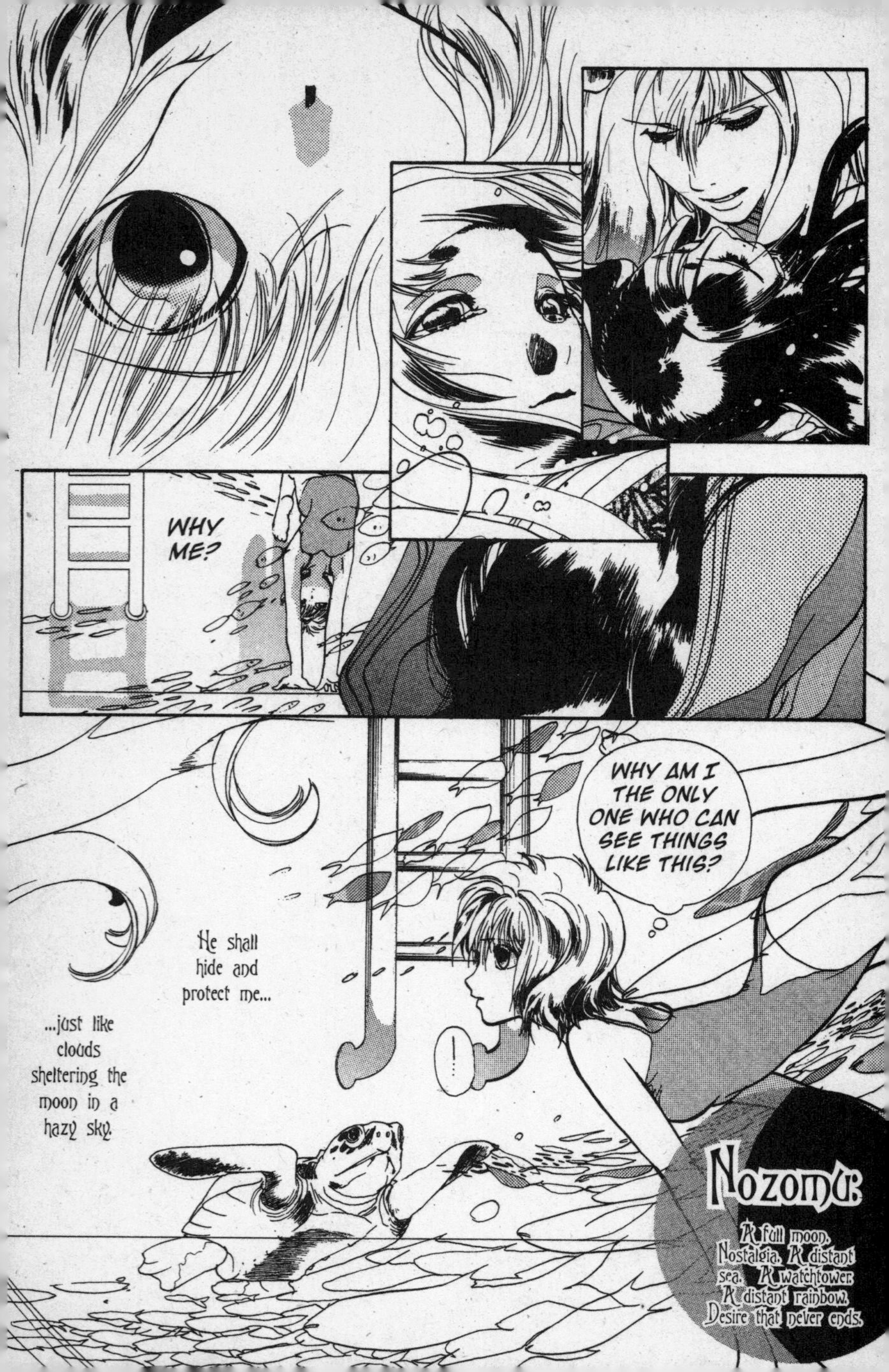
WHY ME?
WHY AM I THE ONLY ONE WHO CAN SEE THINGS LIKE THIS?
He shall hide and protect me...
!...
...just like clouds sheltering the moon in a hazy sky.
Nozomu:
A full moon. Nostalgia. A distant sea. A watchtower. A distant rainbow. Desire that never ends.

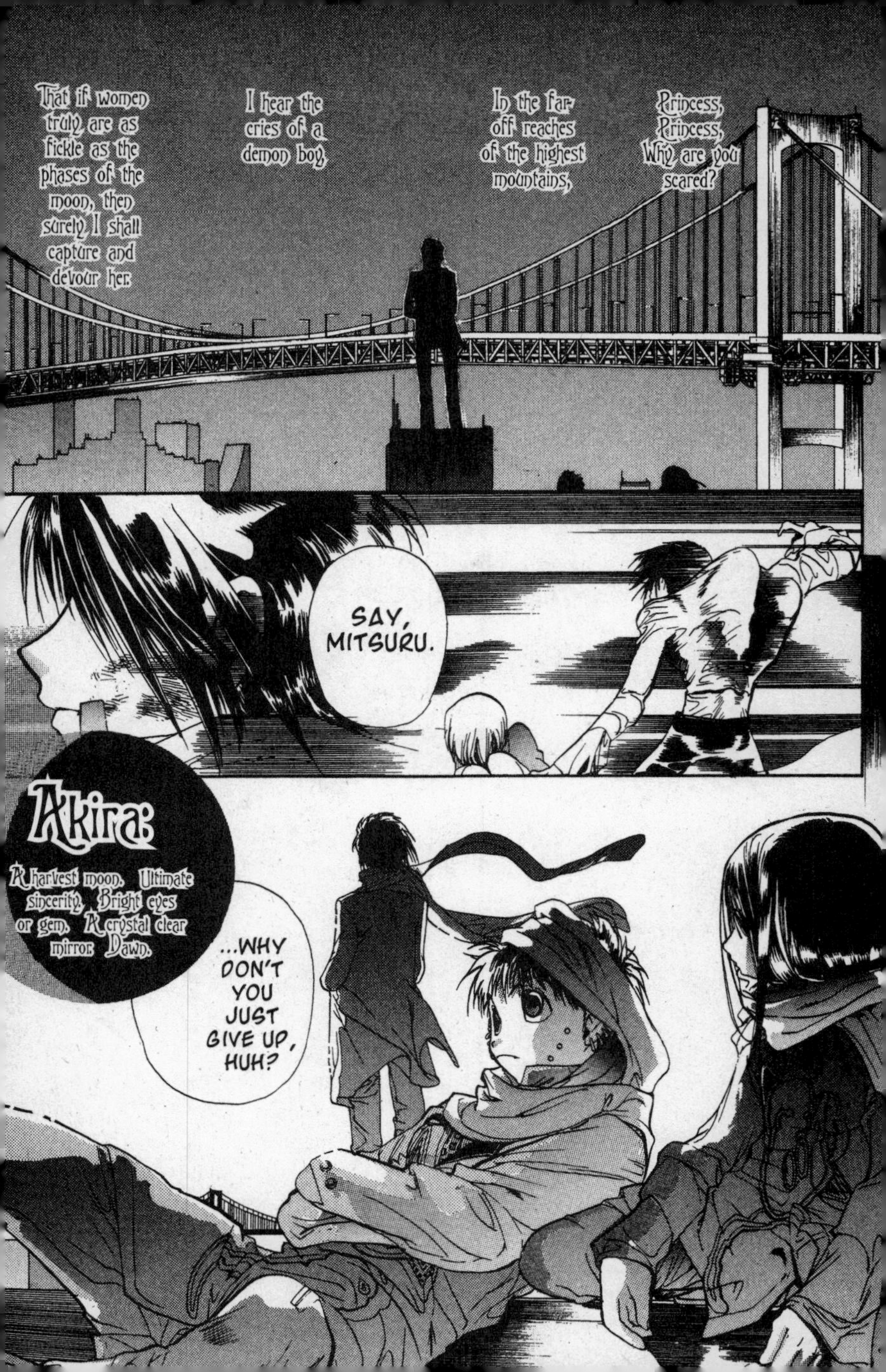
Princess, Princess, Why are you scared?
In the far-off reaches of the highest mountains,
I hear the cries of a demon boy,
That if women truly are as fickle as the phases of the moon, then surely I shall capture and devour her.
SAY, MITSURU.
Akira:
A harvest moon. Ultimate sincerity. Bright eyes or gem. A crystal clear mirror. Dawn.
...WHY DON'T YOU JUST GIVE UP, HUH?

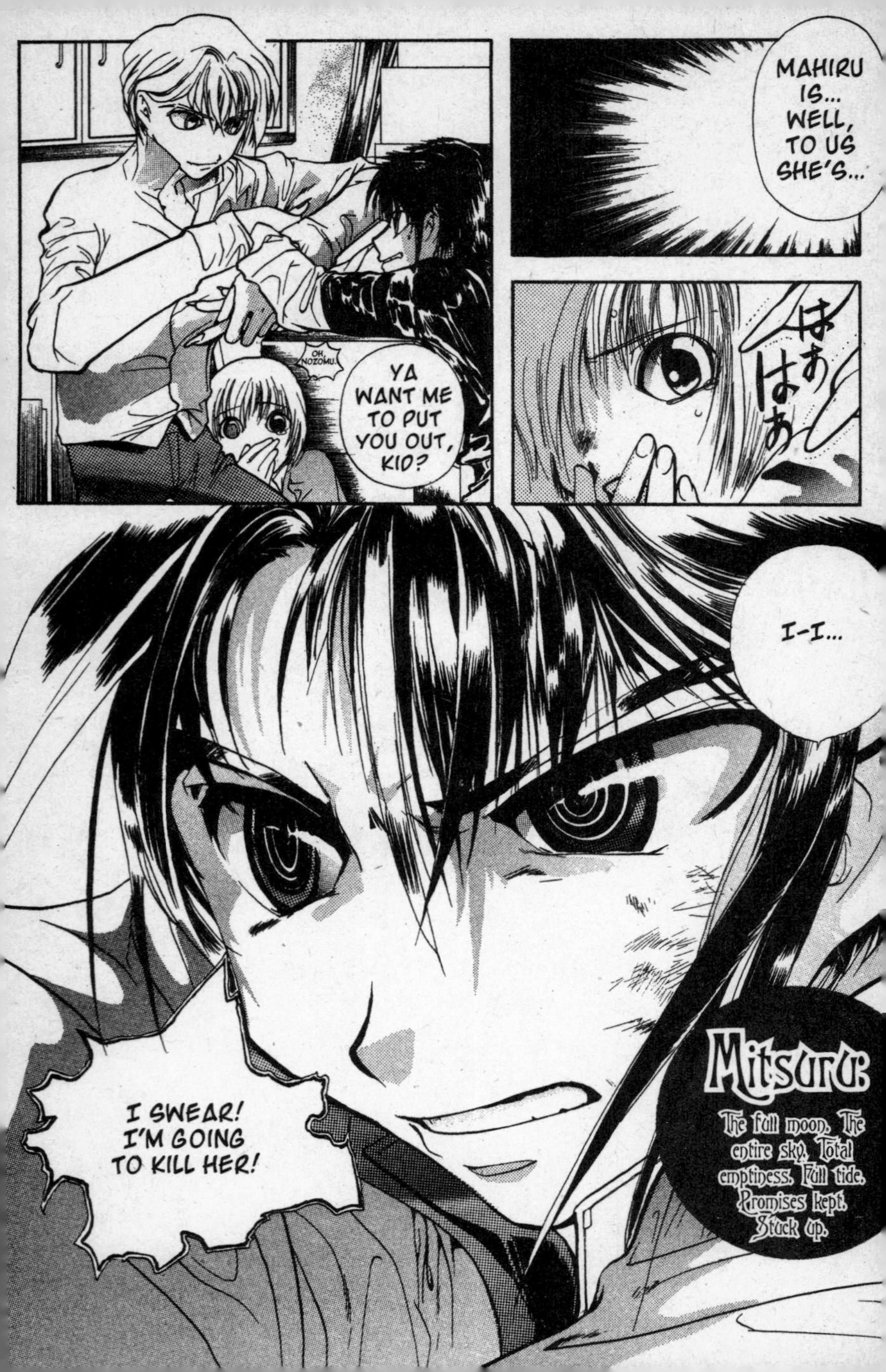
MAHIRU IS... WELL, TO US SHE'S...
はぁ はぁ
YA WANT ME TO PUT YOU OUT, KID?
OH, NOZOMU!
I-I...
I SWEAR! I'M GOING TO KILL HER!
Mitsuru:
The full moon. The entire sky. Total emptiness. Full tide. Promises kept. Stuck up.

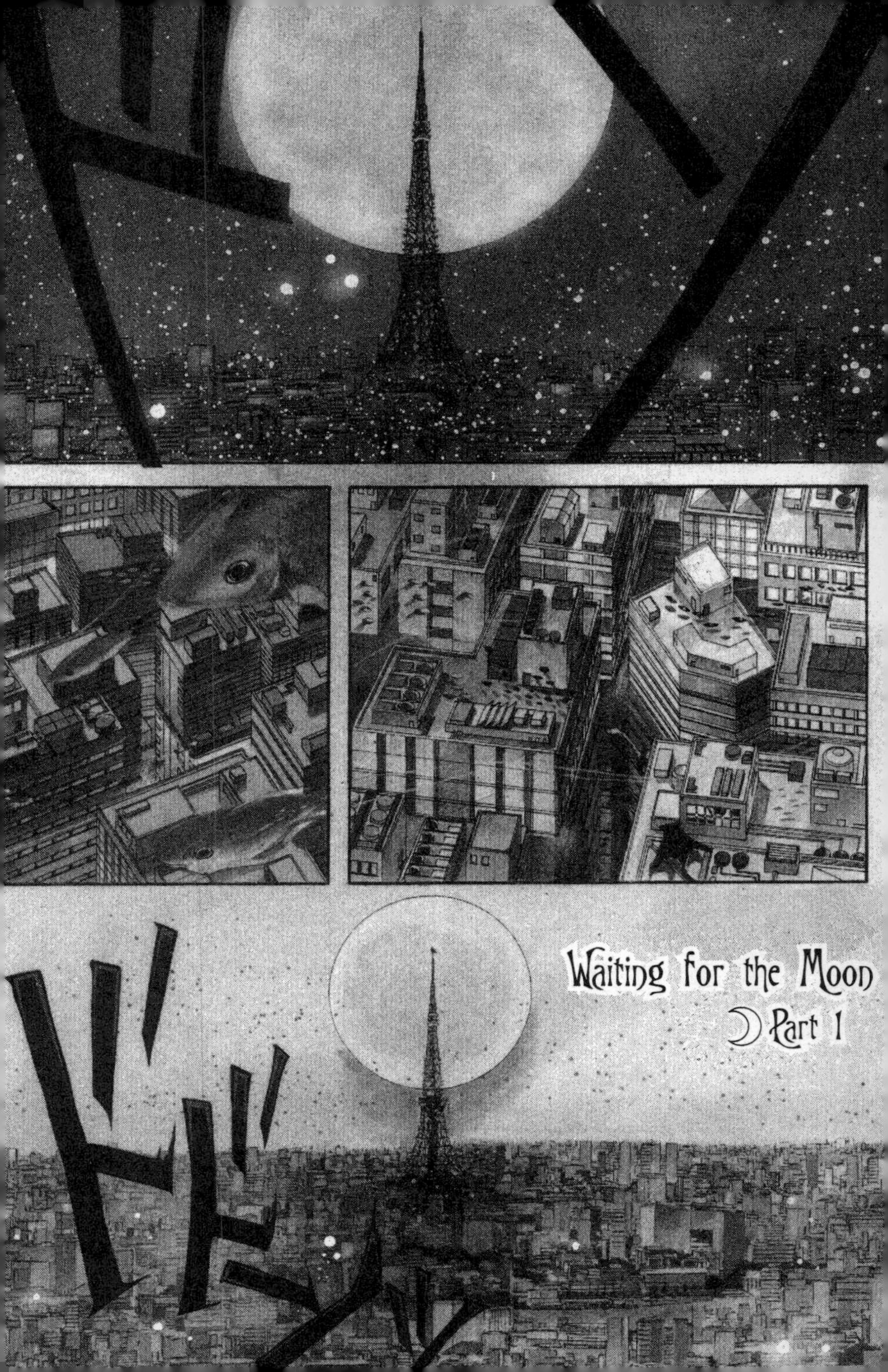
Waiting for the Moon
Part 1

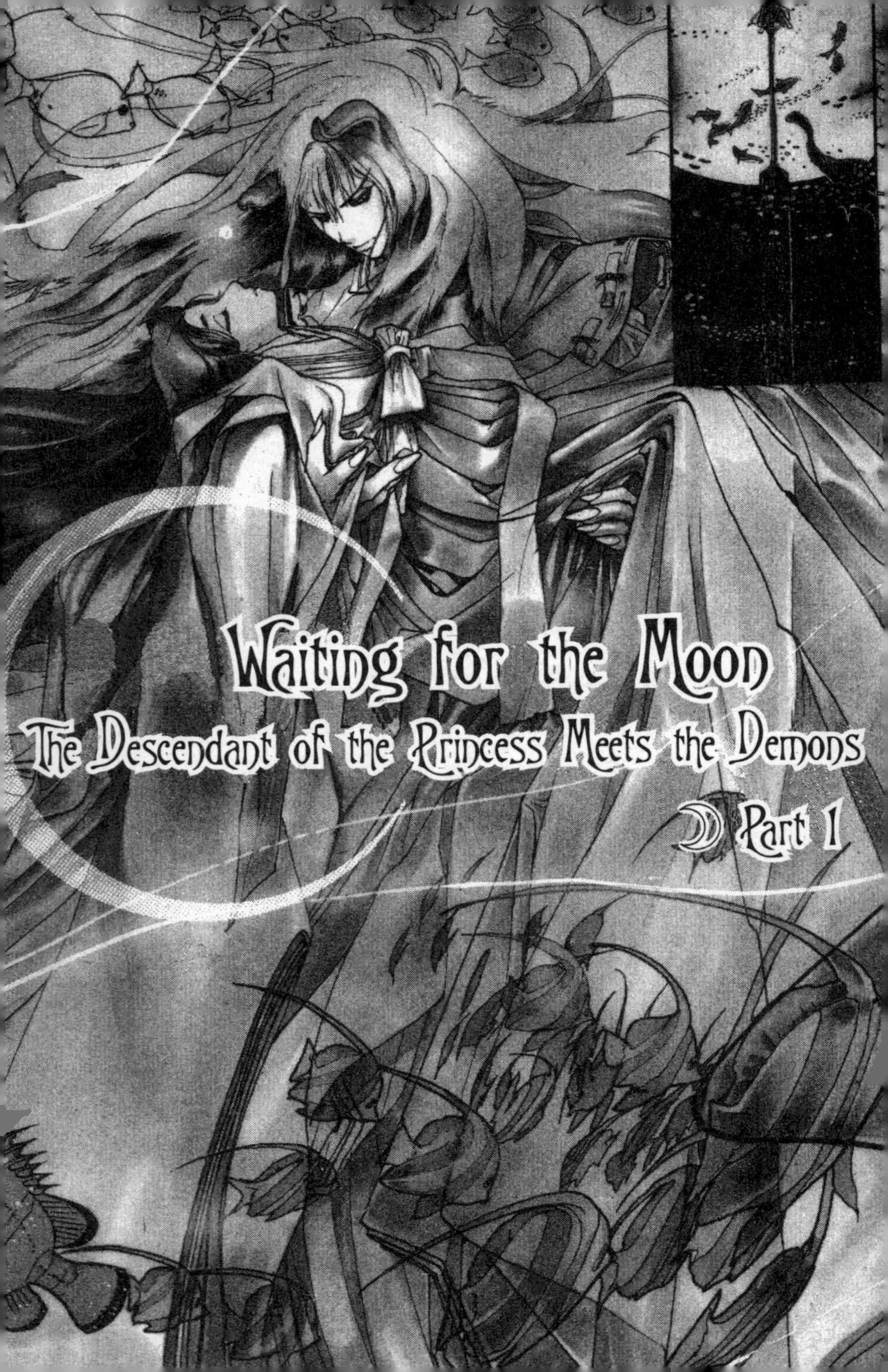
Waiting for the Moon
The Descendant of the Princess Meets the Demons
Part 1

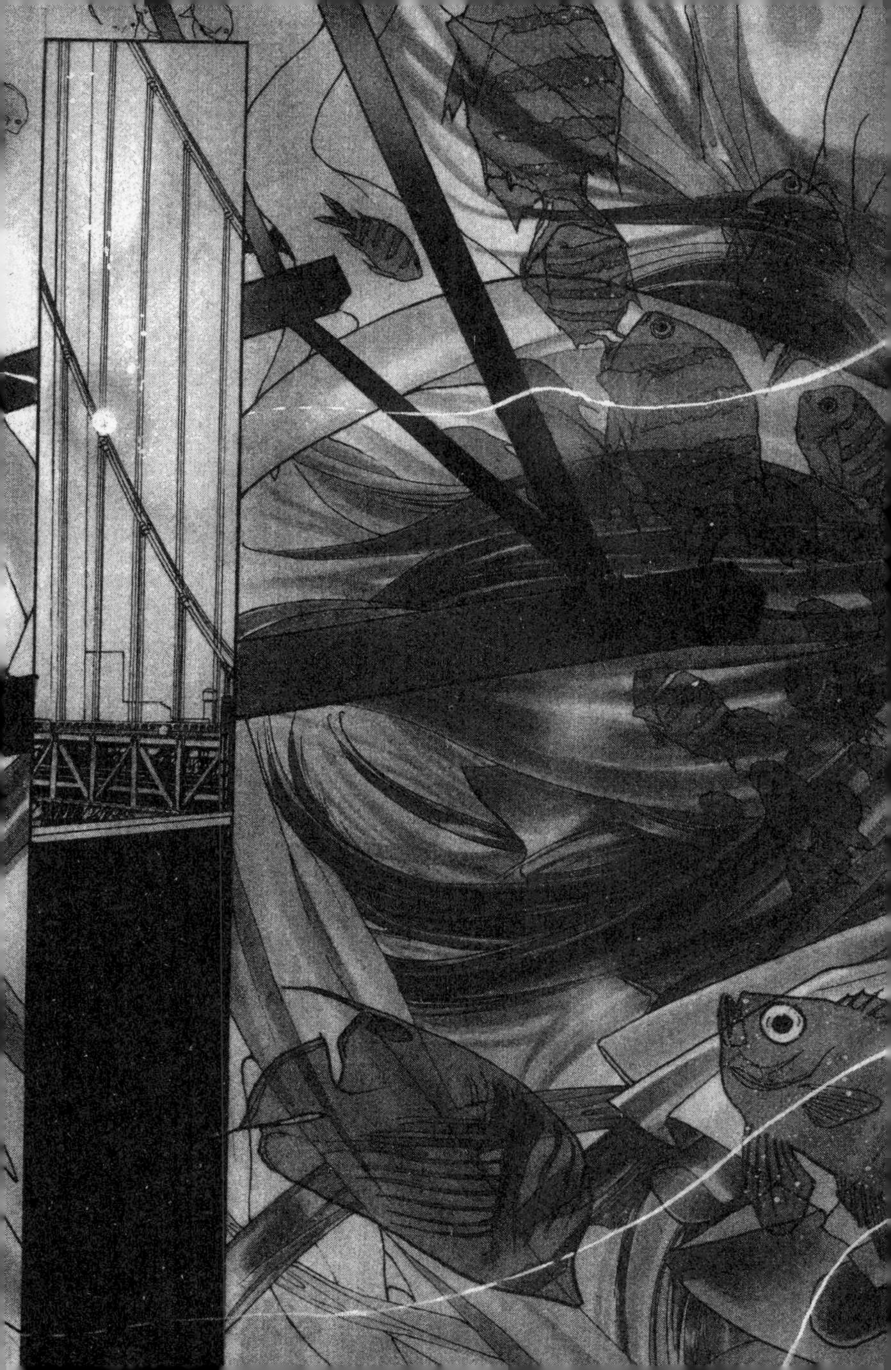

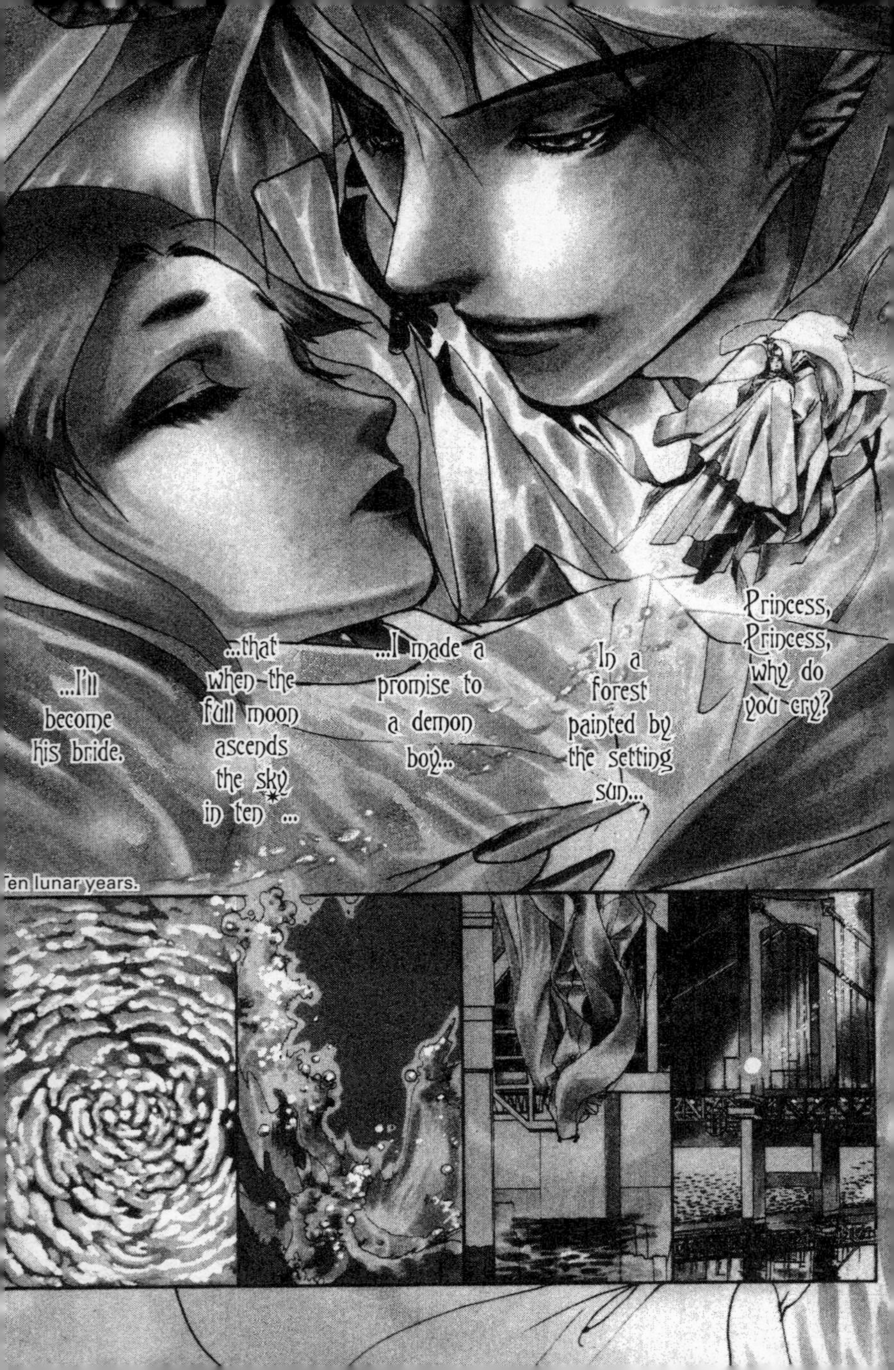
Princess, Princess, why do you cry?
In a forest painted by the setting sun...
...I made a promise to a demon boy...
...that when the full moon ascends the sky in ten*...
...I'll become his bride.
*Ten lunar years.

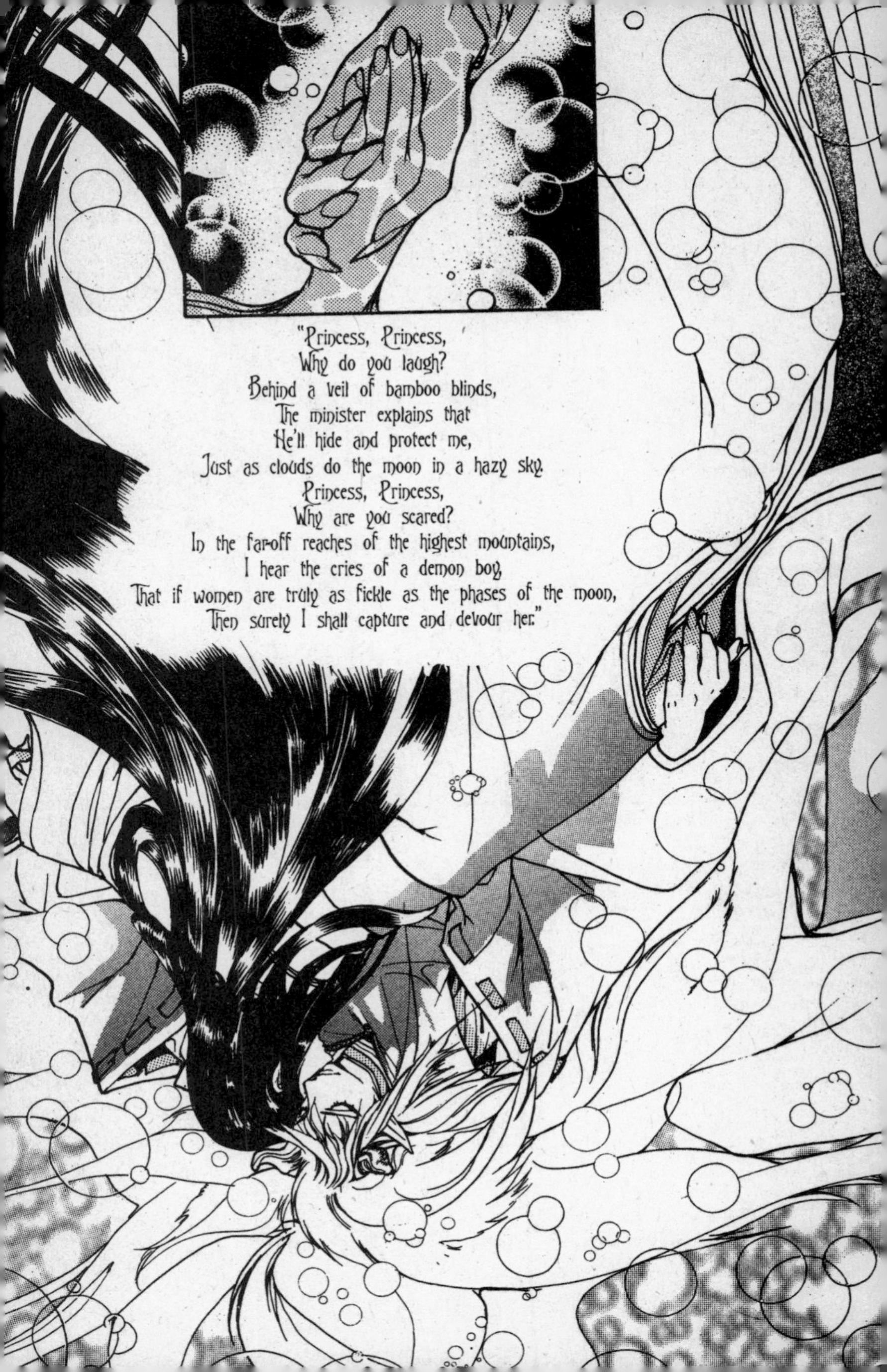
"Princess, Princess,
Why do you laugh?
Behind a veil of bamboo blinds,
The minister explains that
He'll hide and protect me,
Just as clouds do the moon in a hazy sky.
Princess, Princess,
Why are you scared?
In the far-off reaches of the highest mountains,
I hear the cries of a demon boy,
That if women are truly as fickle as the phases of the moon,
Then surely I shall capture and devour her."

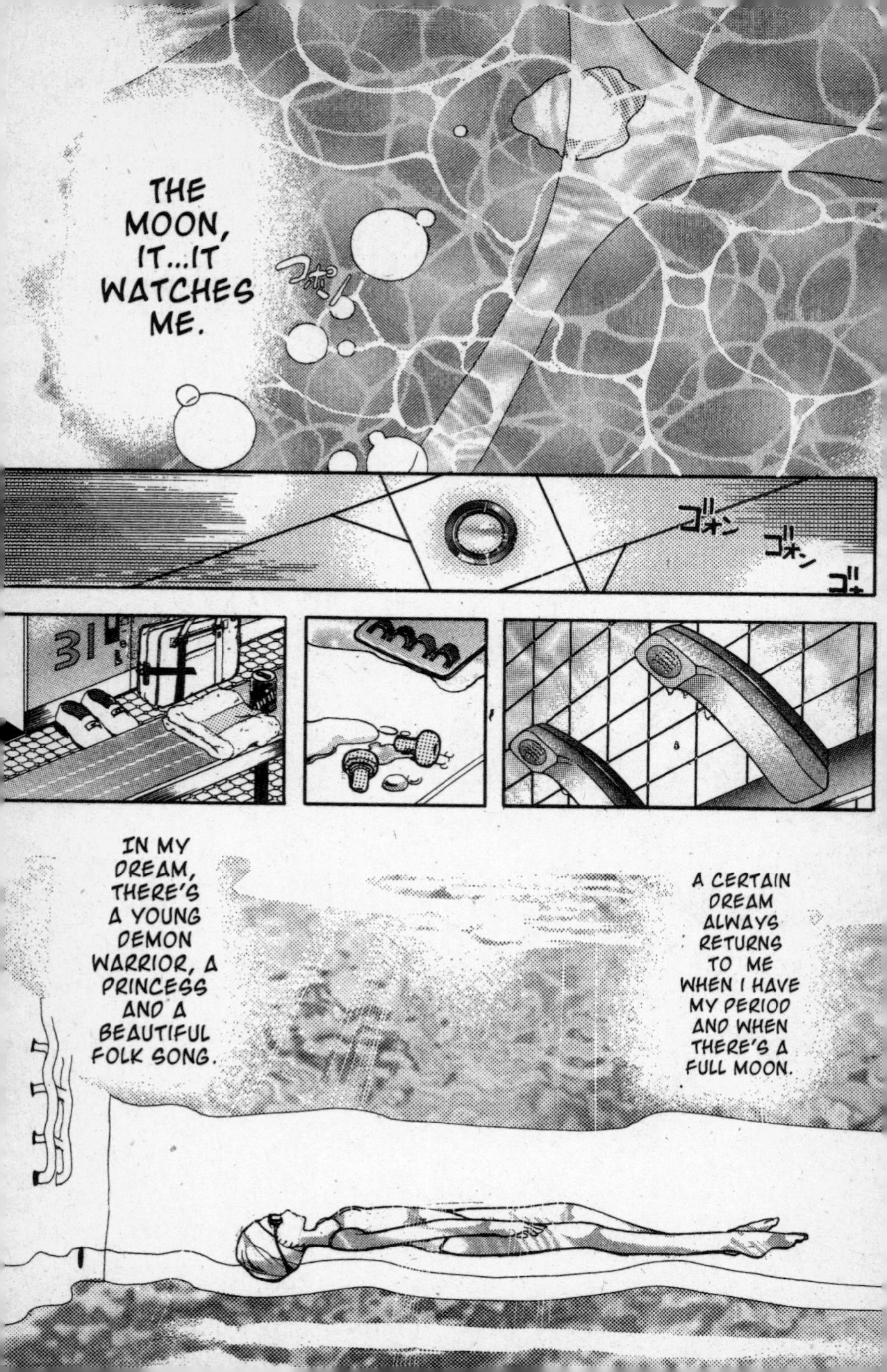
THE MOON, IT...IT WATCHES ME.
ゴォン
ゴォン
ゴォ
A CERTAIN DREAM ALWAYS RETURNS TO ME WHEN I HAVE MY PERIOD AND WHEN THERE'S A FULL MOON.
IN MY DREAM, THERE'S A YOUNG DEMON WARRIOR, A PRINCESS AND A BEAUTIFUL FOLK SONG.

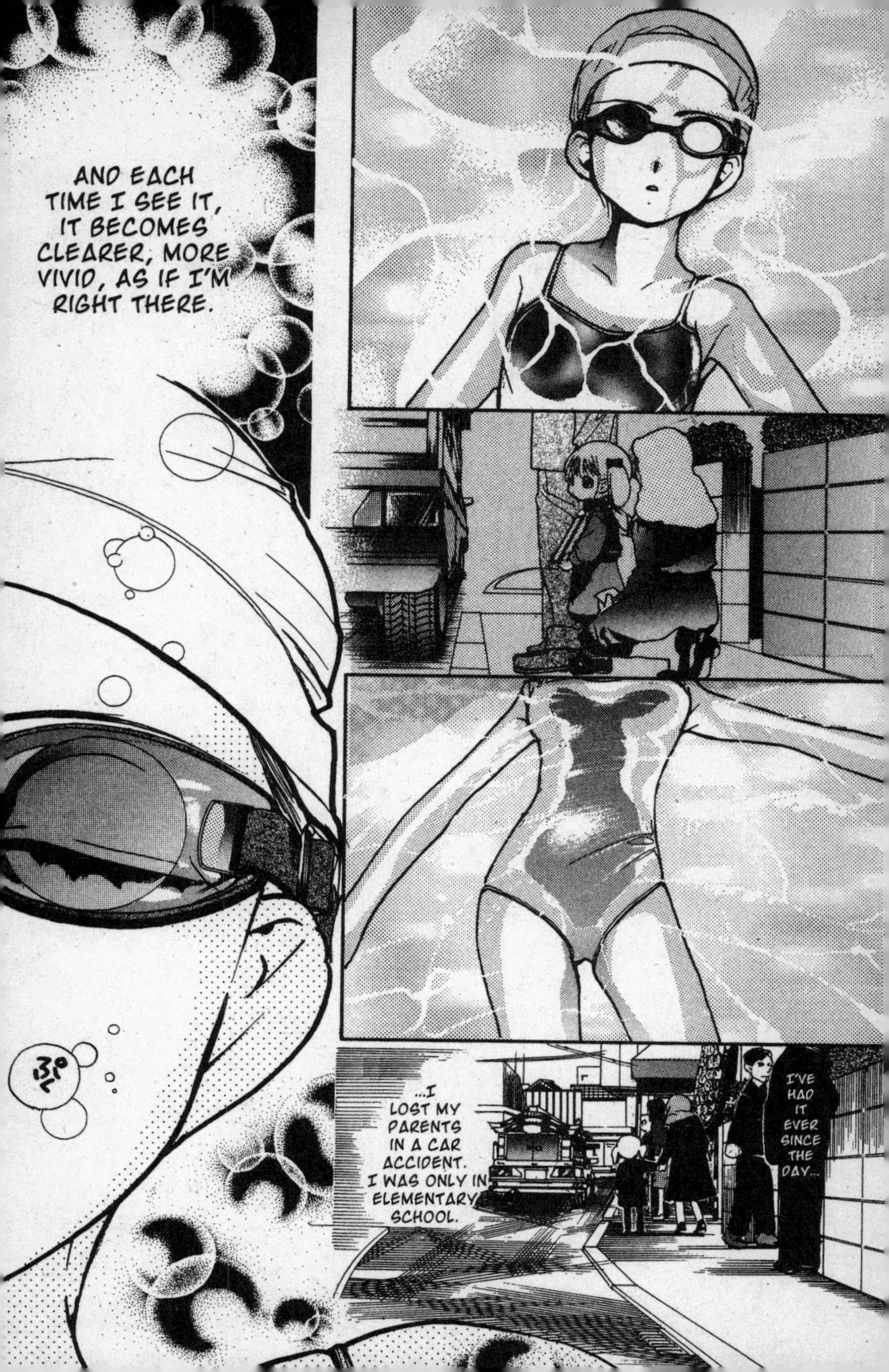
I'VE HAD IT EVER SINCE THE DAY...
...I LOST MY PARENTS IN A CAR ACCIDENT. I WAS ONLY IN ELEMENTARY SCHOOL.
AND EACH TIME I SEE IT, IT BECOMES CLEARER, MORE VIVID, AS IF I'M RIGHT THERE.
ぷく

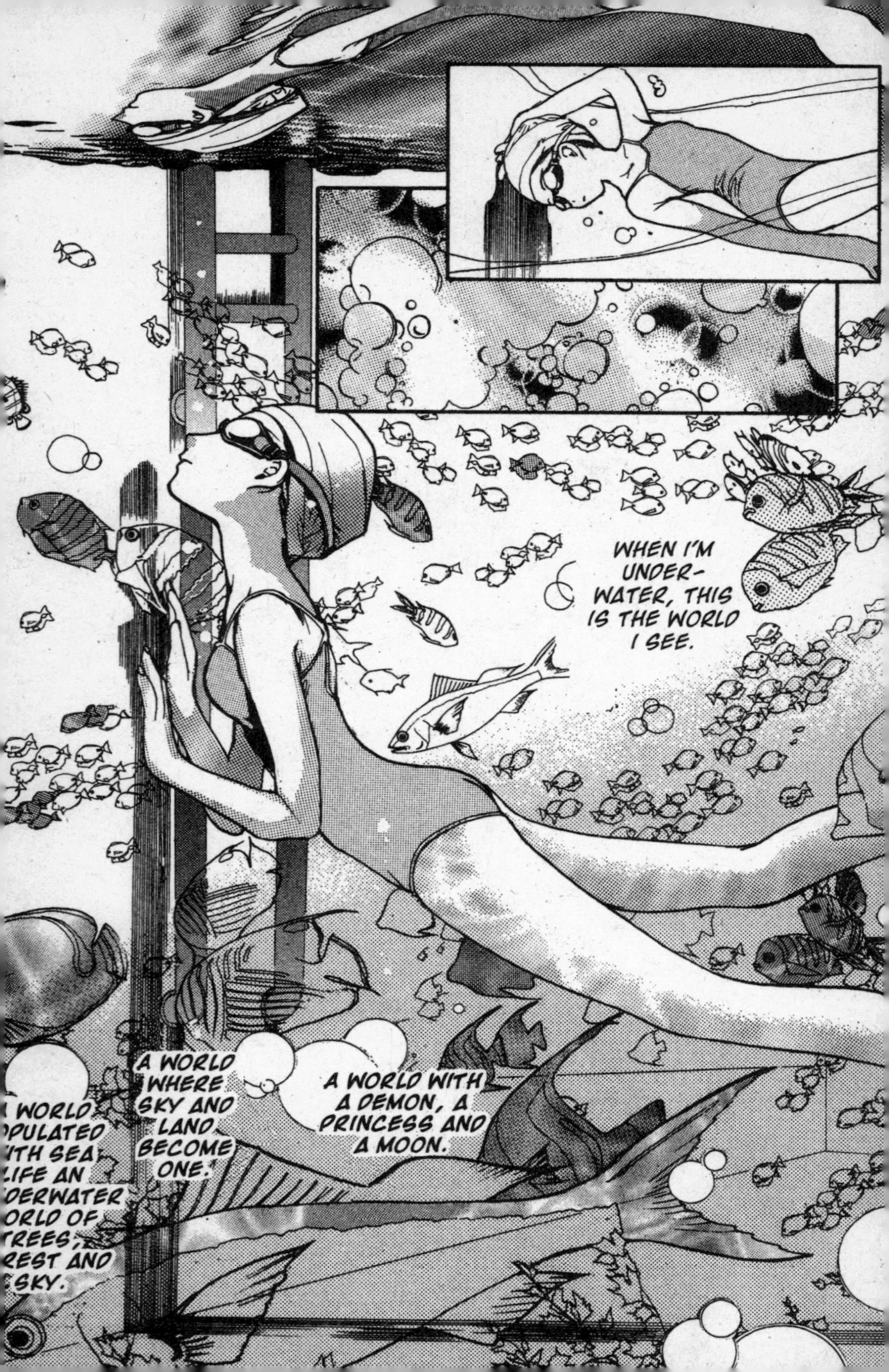

WHEN I'M UNDER-WATER, THIS IS THE WORLD I SEE.
A WORLD WITH A DEMON, A PRINCESS AND A MOON.
A WORLD WHERE SKY AND LAND BECOME ONE.*
WORLD OPULATED ITH SEA LIFE AN DERWATER ORLD OF TREES, REST AND SKY.

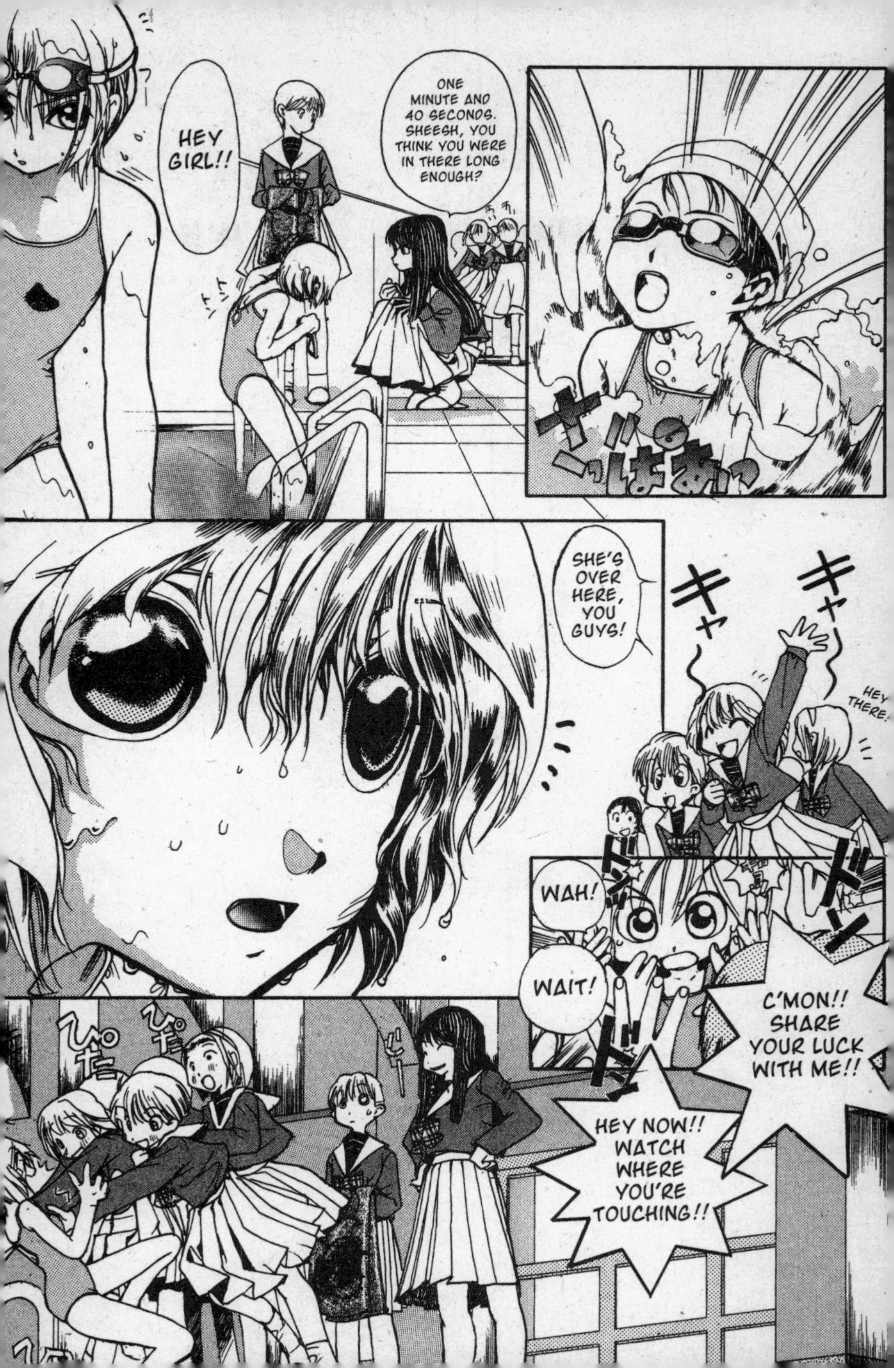
ONE MINUTE AND 40 SECONDS. SHEESH, YOU THINK YOU WERE IN THERE LONG ENOUGH?
HEY GIRL!!
キャ キャ
SHE'S OVER HERE, YOU GUYS!
HEY THERE.
WAH!
WAIT!
C'MON!! SHARE YOUR LUCK WITH ME!!
HEY NOW!! WATCH WHERE YOU'RE TOUCHING!!

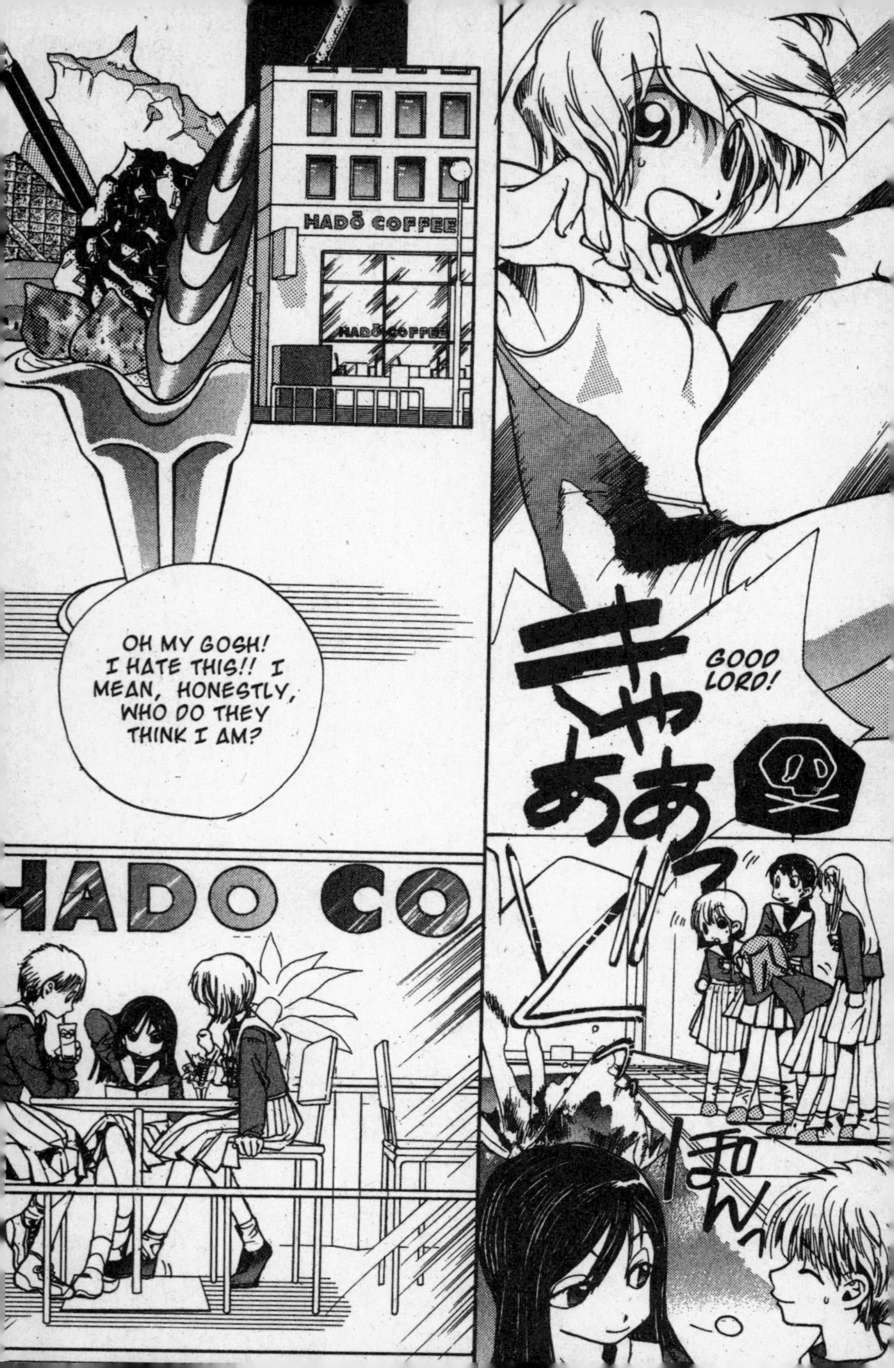
きゃああっ
GOOD LORD!
HADŌ COFFEE
HADŌ COFFEE
OH MY GOSH! I HATE THIS!! I MEAN, HONESTLY, WHO DO THEY THINK I AM?
ぽん
HADO CO

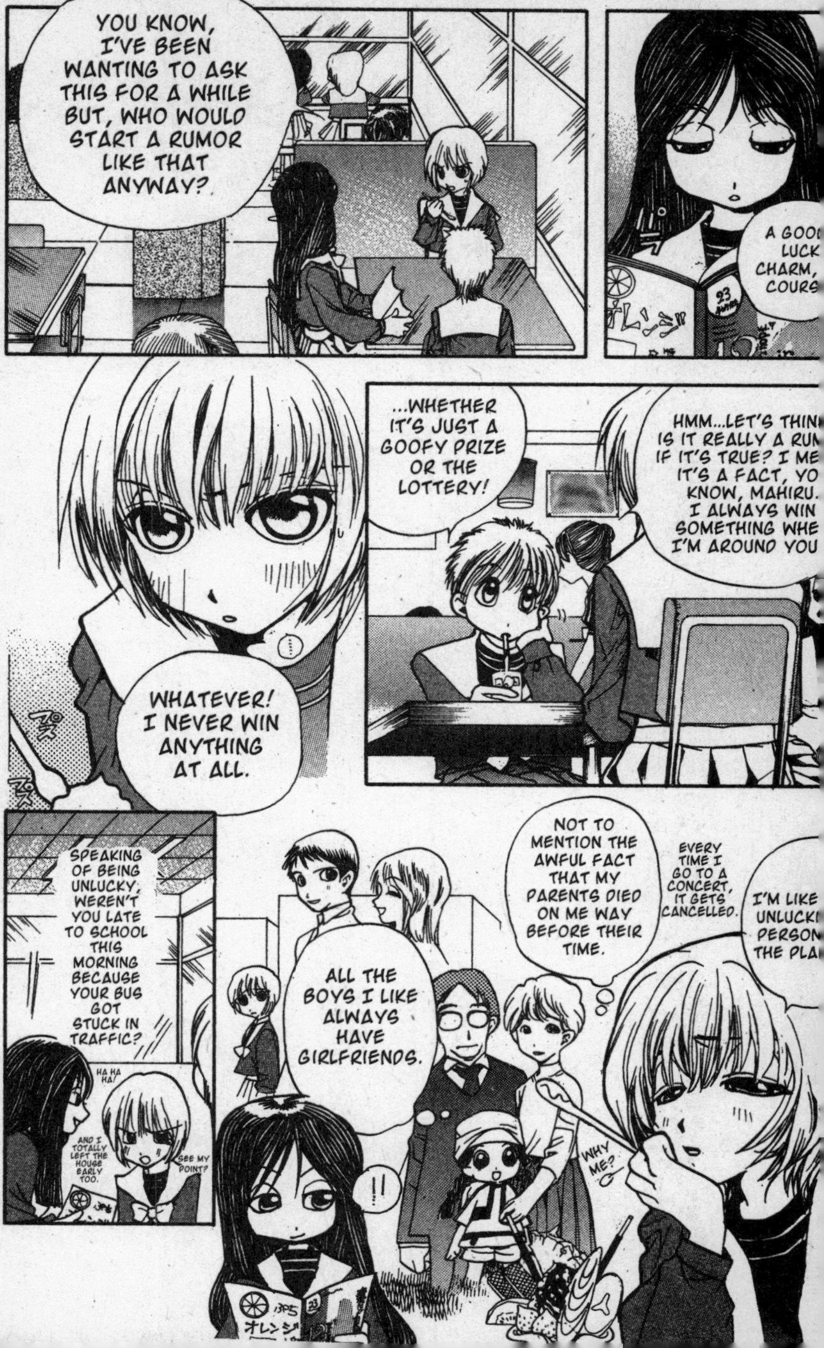
A GOOD
LUCK
CHARM,
COURS
YOU KNOW, I'VE BEEN WANTING TO ASK THIS FOR A WHILE BUT, WHO WOULD START A RUMOR LIKE THAT ANYWAY?
HMM...LET'S THIN
IS IT REALLY A RUM
IF IT'S TRUE? I ME
IT'S A FACT, YO
KNOW, MAHIRU.
I ALWAYS WIN
SOMETHING WHE
I'M AROUND YOU
...WHETHER IT'S JUST A GOOFY PRIZE OR THE LOTTERY!
WHATEVER! I NEVER WIN ANYTHING AT ALL.
I'M LIKE
UNLUCKI
PERSON
THE PLA
EVERY TIME I GO TO A CONCERT, IT GETS CANCELLED.
NOT TO MENTION THE AWFUL FACT THAT MY PARENTS DIED ON ME WAY BEFORE THEIR TIME.
ALL THE BOYS I LIKE ALWAYS HAVE GIRLFRIENDS.
WHY ME?
!!
SPEAKING OF BEING UNLUCKY, WEREN'T YOU LATE TO SCHOOL THIS MORNING BECAUSE YOUR BUS GOT STUCK IN TRAFFIC?
HA HA HA!
AND I TOTALLY LEFT THE HOUSE EARLY TOO.
SEE MY POINT?

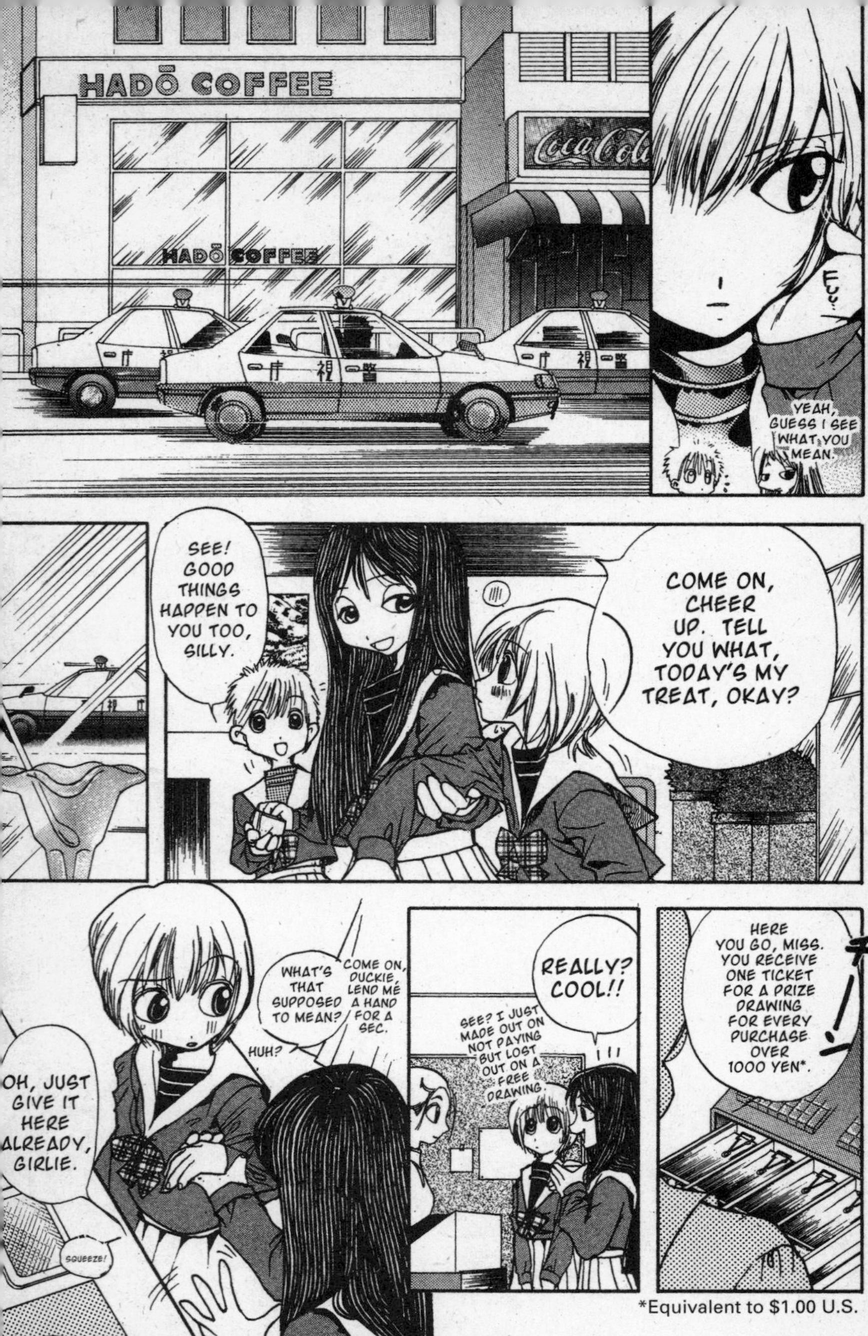
YEAH, GUESS I SEE WHAT YOU MEAN.
HADŌ COFFEE
Coca-Cola
HADŌ COFFEE
COME ON, CHEER UP. TELL YOU WHAT, TODAY'S MY TREAT, OKAY?
SEE! GOOD THINGS HAPPEN TO YOU TOO, SILLY.
HERE YOU GO, MISS. YOU RECEIVE ONE TICKET FOR A PRIZE DRAWING FOR EVERY PURCHASE OVER 1000 YEN*.
REALLY? COOL!!
SEE? I JUST MADE OUT ON NOT PAYING BUT LOST OUT ON A FREE DRAWING.
COME ON, DUCKIE, LEND ME A HAND FOR A SEC.
WHAT'S THAT SUPPOSED TO MEAN?
HUH?
OH, JUST GIVE IT HERE ALREADY, GIRLIE.
SQUEEZE!

*Equivalent to $1.00 U.S.

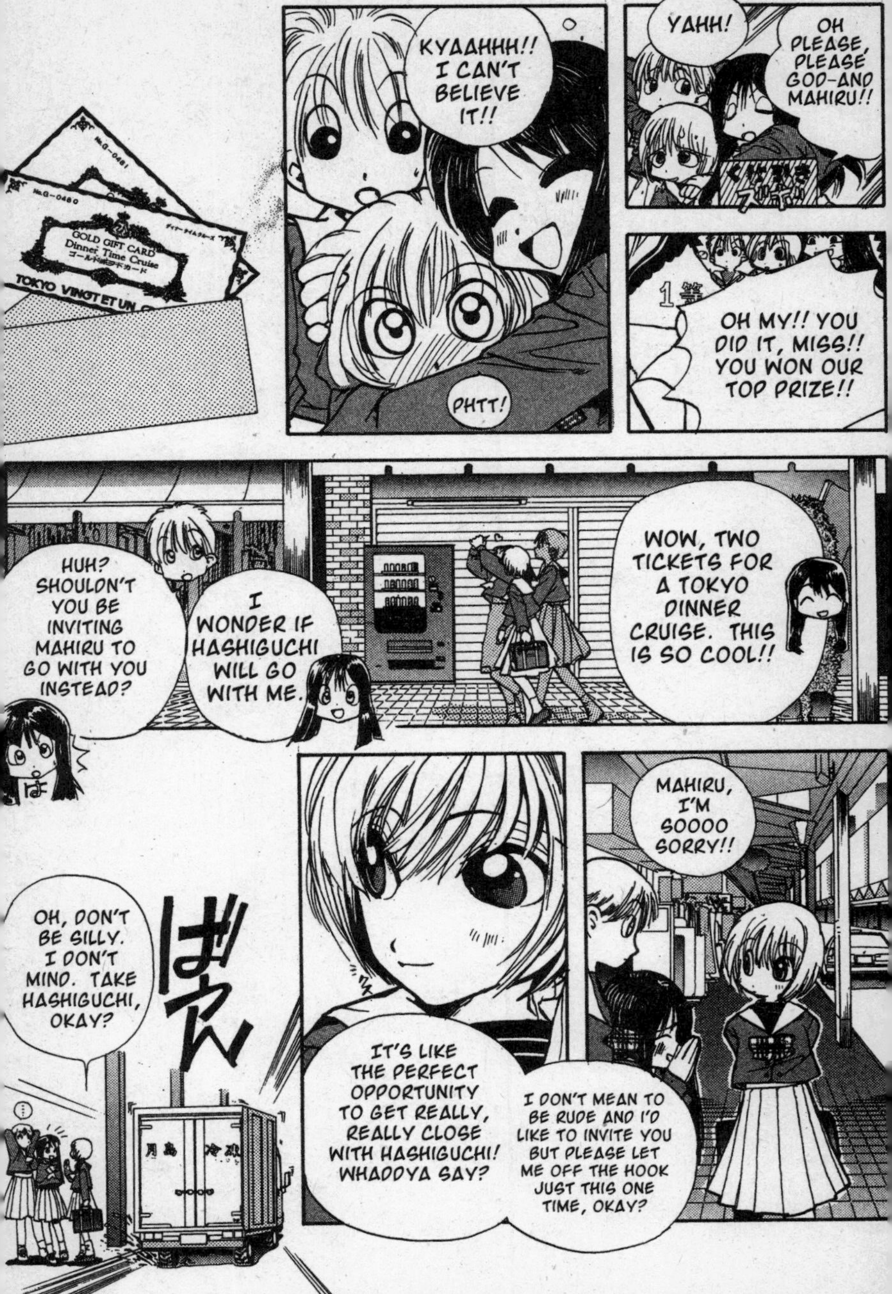
OH PLEASE, PLEASE GOD–AND MAHIRU!!
YAHH!
OH MY!! YOU DID IT, MISS!! YOU WON OUR TOP PRIZE!!
KYAAHHH!! I CAN'T BELIEVE IT!!
PHTT!
GOLD GIFT CARD
Dinner Time Cruise
WOW, TWO TICKETS FOR A TOKYO DINNER CRUISE. THIS IS SO COOL!!
I WONDER IF HASHIGUCHI WILL GO WITH ME.
HUH? SHOULDN'T YOU BE INVITING MAHIRU TO GO WITH YOU INSTEAD?
は
MAHIRU, I'M SOOOO SORRY!!
I DON'T MEAN TO BE RUDE AND I'D LIKE TO INVITE YOU BUT PLEASE LET ME OFF THE HOOK JUST THIS ONE TIME, OKAY?
IT'S LIKE THE PERFECT OPPORTUNITY TO GET REALLY, REALLY CLOSE WITH HASHIGUCHI! WHADDYA SAY?
OH, DON'T BE SILLY. I DON'T MIND. TAKE HASHIGUCHI, OKAY?
ぱぁん
...

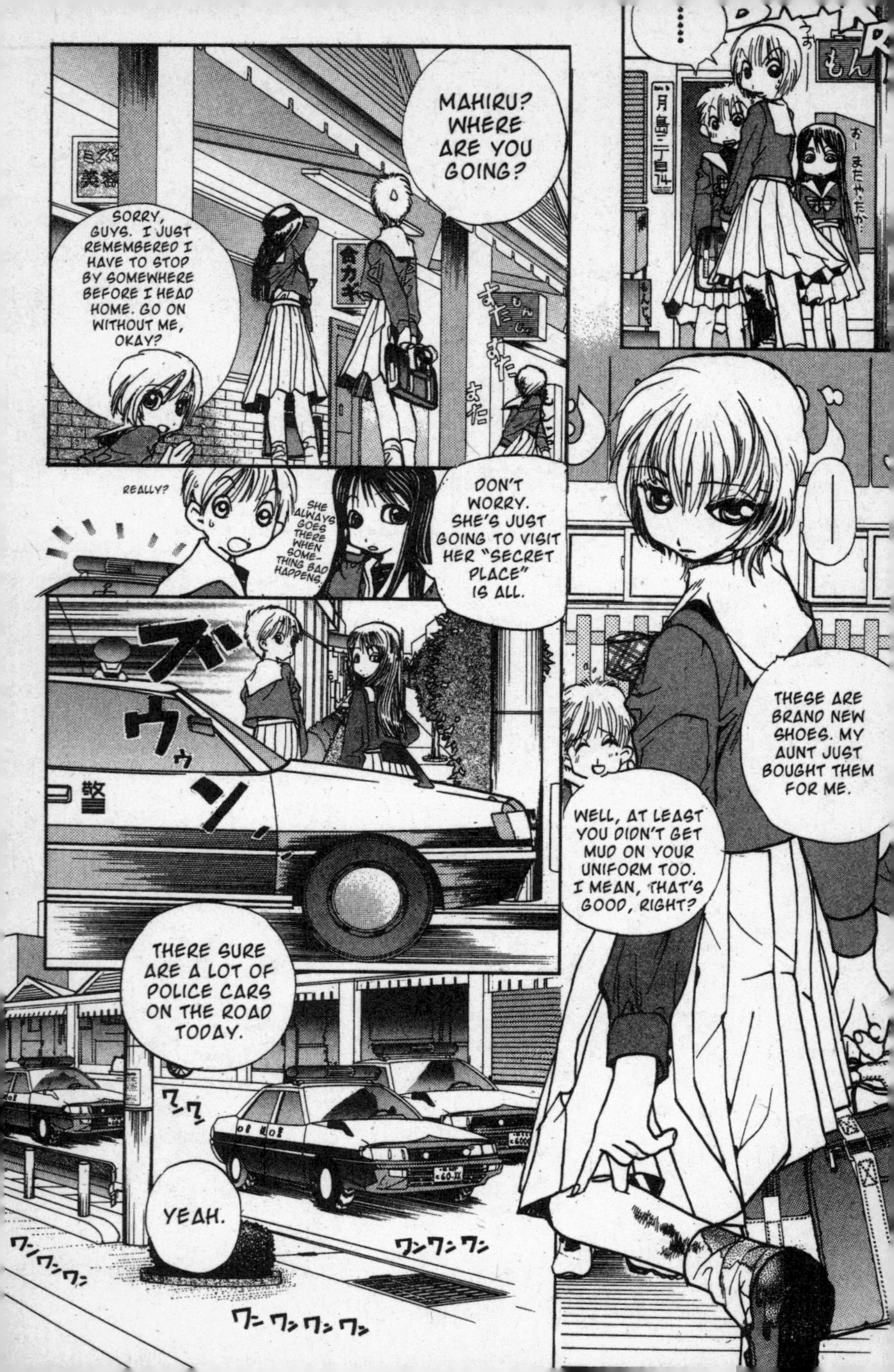

THESE ARE BRAND NEW SHOES. MY AUNT JUST BOUGHT THEM FOR ME.
WELL, AT LEAST YOU DIDN'T GET MUD ON YOUR UNIFORM TOO. I MEAN, THAT'S GOOD, RIGHT?
MAHIRU? WHERE ARE YOU GOING?
SORRY, GUYS. I JUST REMEMBERED I HAVE TO STOP BY SOMEWHERE BEFORE I HEAD HOME. GO ON WITHOUT ME, OKAY?
DON'T WORRY. SHE'S JUST GOING TO VISIT HER "SECRET PLACE" IS ALL.
SHE ALWAYS GOES THERE WHEN SOMETHING BAD HAPPENS.
REALLY?
THERE SURE ARE A LOT OF POLICE CARS ON THE ROAD TODAY.
YEAH.

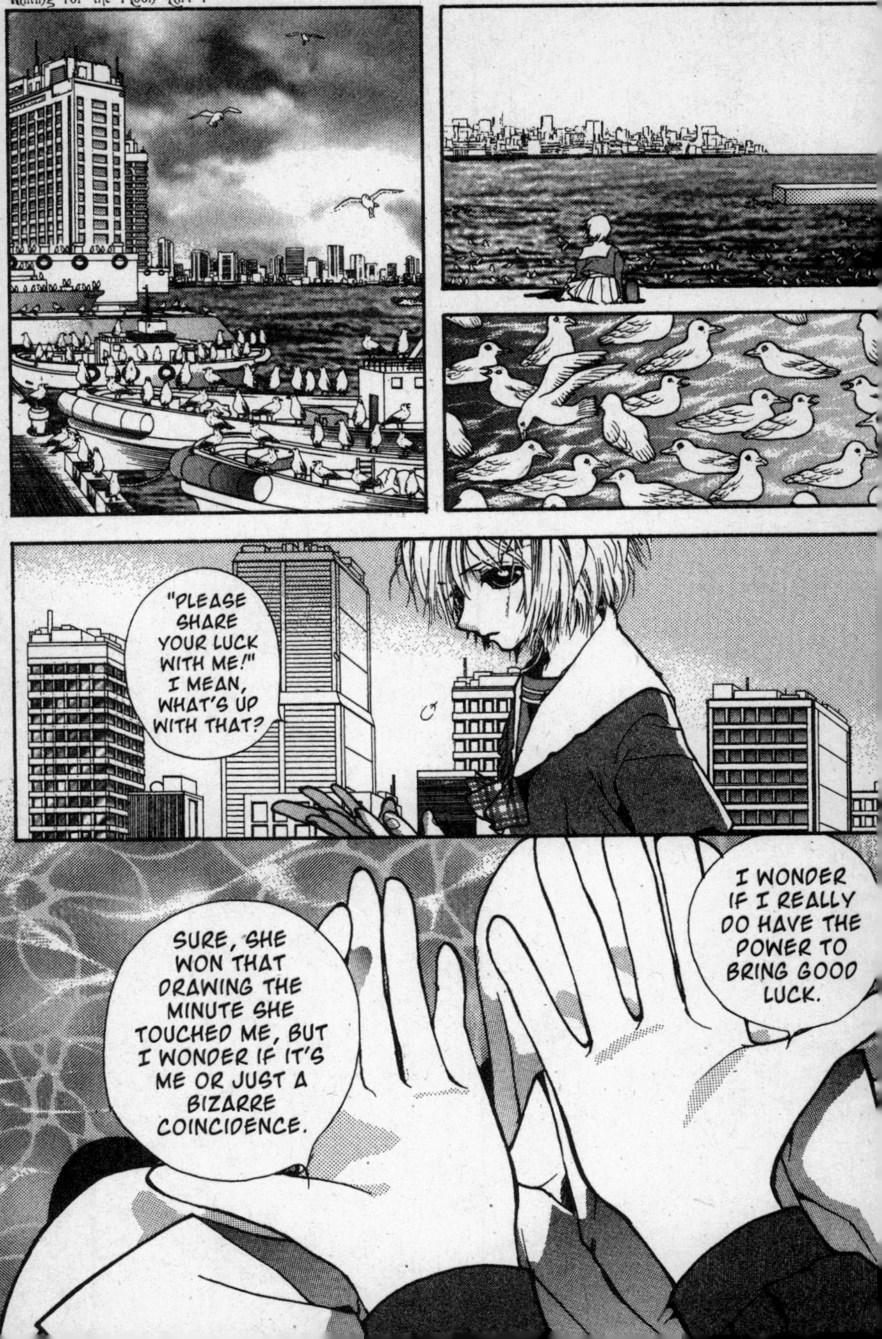
"PLEASE SHARE YOUR LUCK WITH ME!" I MEAN, WHAT'S UP WITH THAT?
I WONDER IF I REALLY DO HAVE THE POWER TO BRING GOOD LUCK.
SURE, SHE WON THAT DRAWING THE MINUTE SHE TOUCHED ME, BUT I WONDER IF IT'S ME OR JUST A BIZARRE COINCIDENCE.

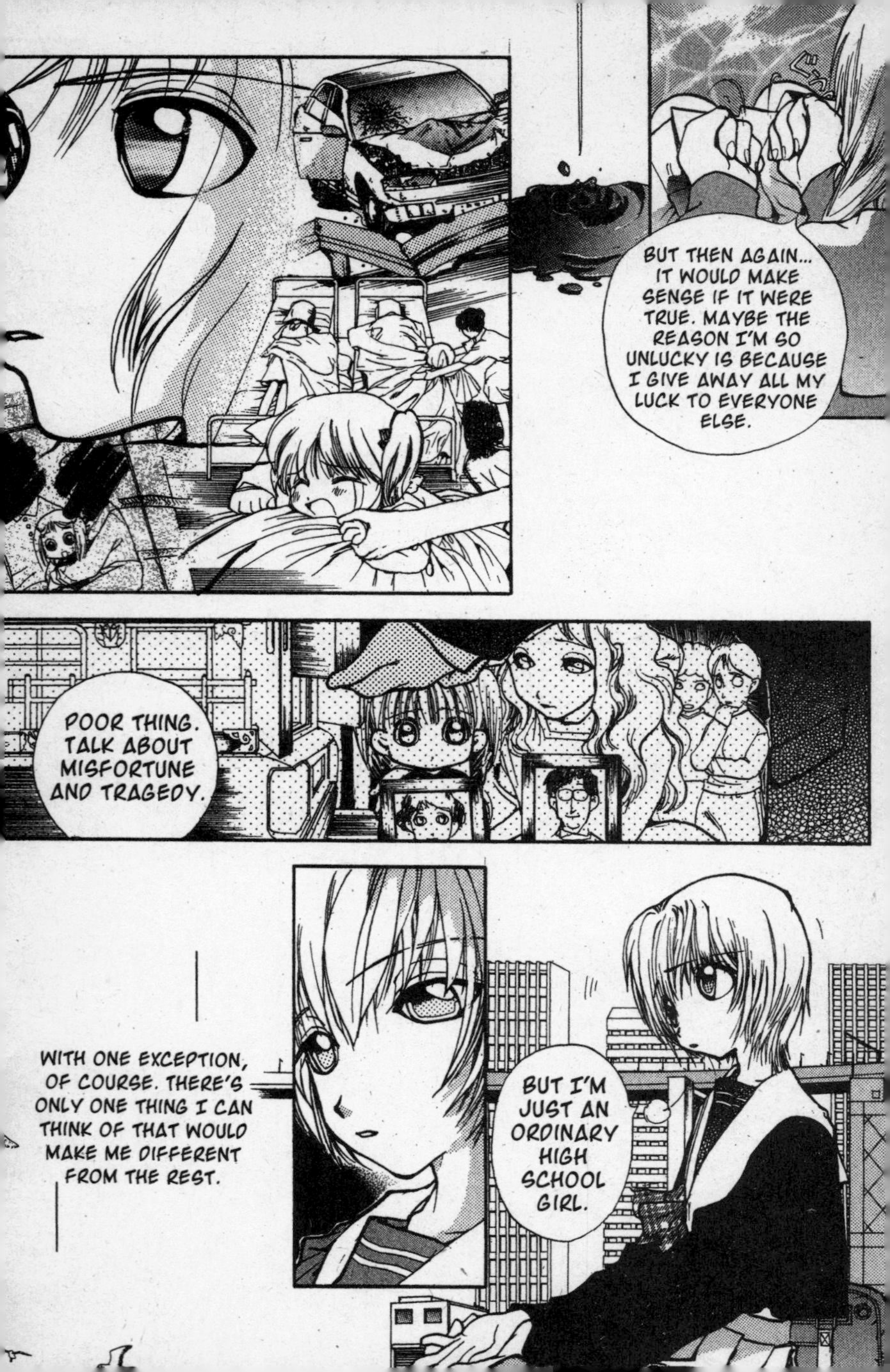
BUT THEN AGAIN... IT WOULD MAKE SENSE IF IT WERE TRUE. MAYBE THE REASON I'M SO UNLUCKY IS BECAUSE I GIVE AWAY ALL MY LUCK TO EVERYONE ELSE.
POOR THING. TALK ABOUT MISFORTUNE AND TRAGEDY.
BUT I'M JUST AN ORDINARY HIGH SCHOOL GIRL.
WITH ONE EXCEPTION, OF COURSE. THERE'S ONLY ONE THING I CAN THINK OF THAT WOULD MAKE ME DIFFERENT FROM THE REST.

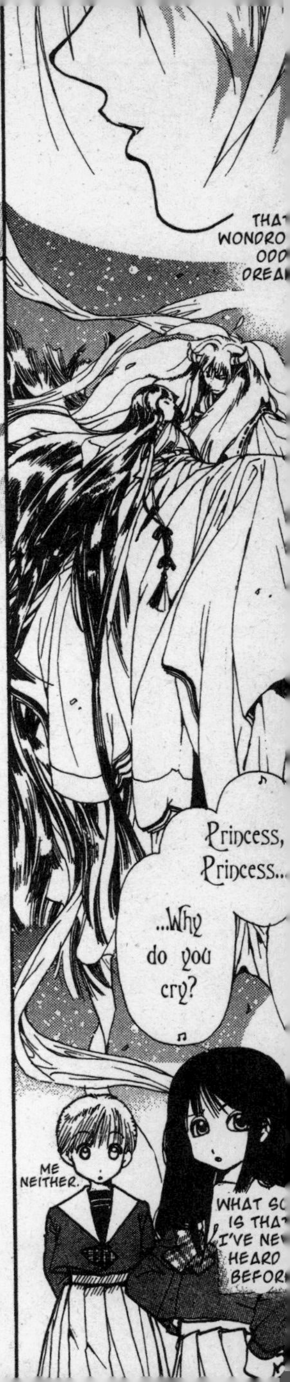
THAT
WONDRO
ODD
DREA
Princess, Princess...
...Why do you cry?
WHAT SO
IS THAT
I'VE NE
HEARD
BEFOR
ME NEITHER.

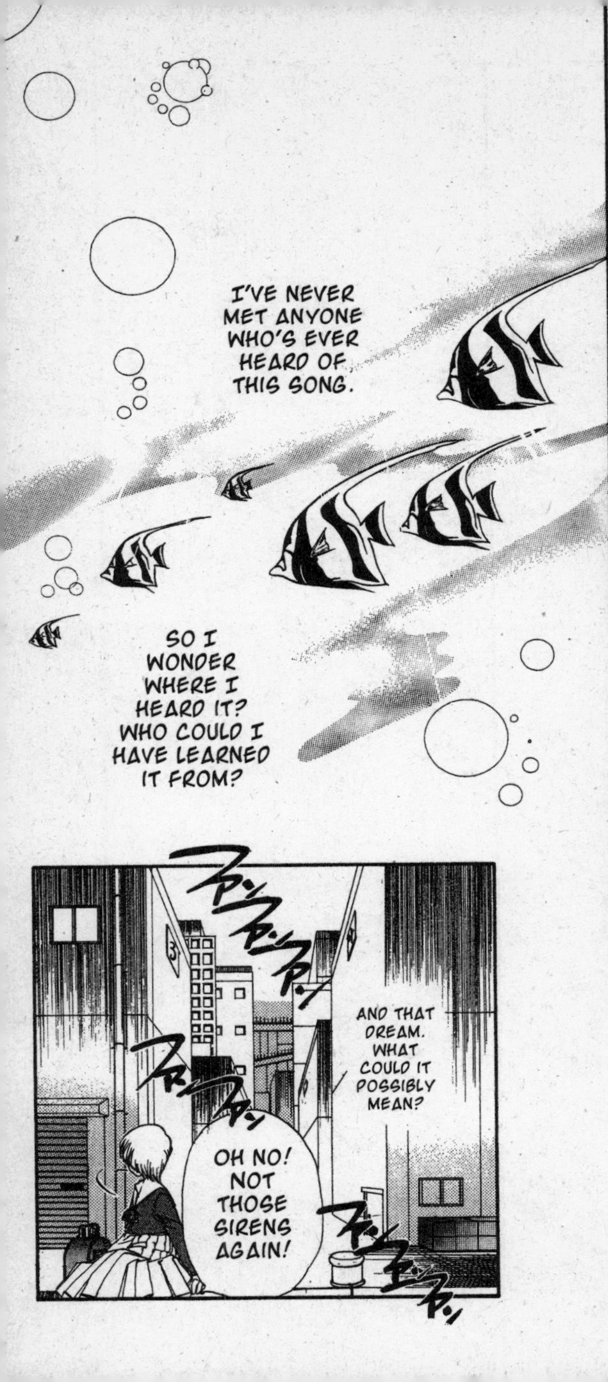
I'VE NEVER MET ANYONE WHO'S EVER HEARD OF THIS SONG.
SO I WONDER WHERE I HEARD IT? WHO COULD I HAVE LEARNED IT FROM?
AND THAT DREAM. WHAT COULD IT POSSIBLY MEAN?
OH NO! NOT THOSE SIRENS AGAIN!

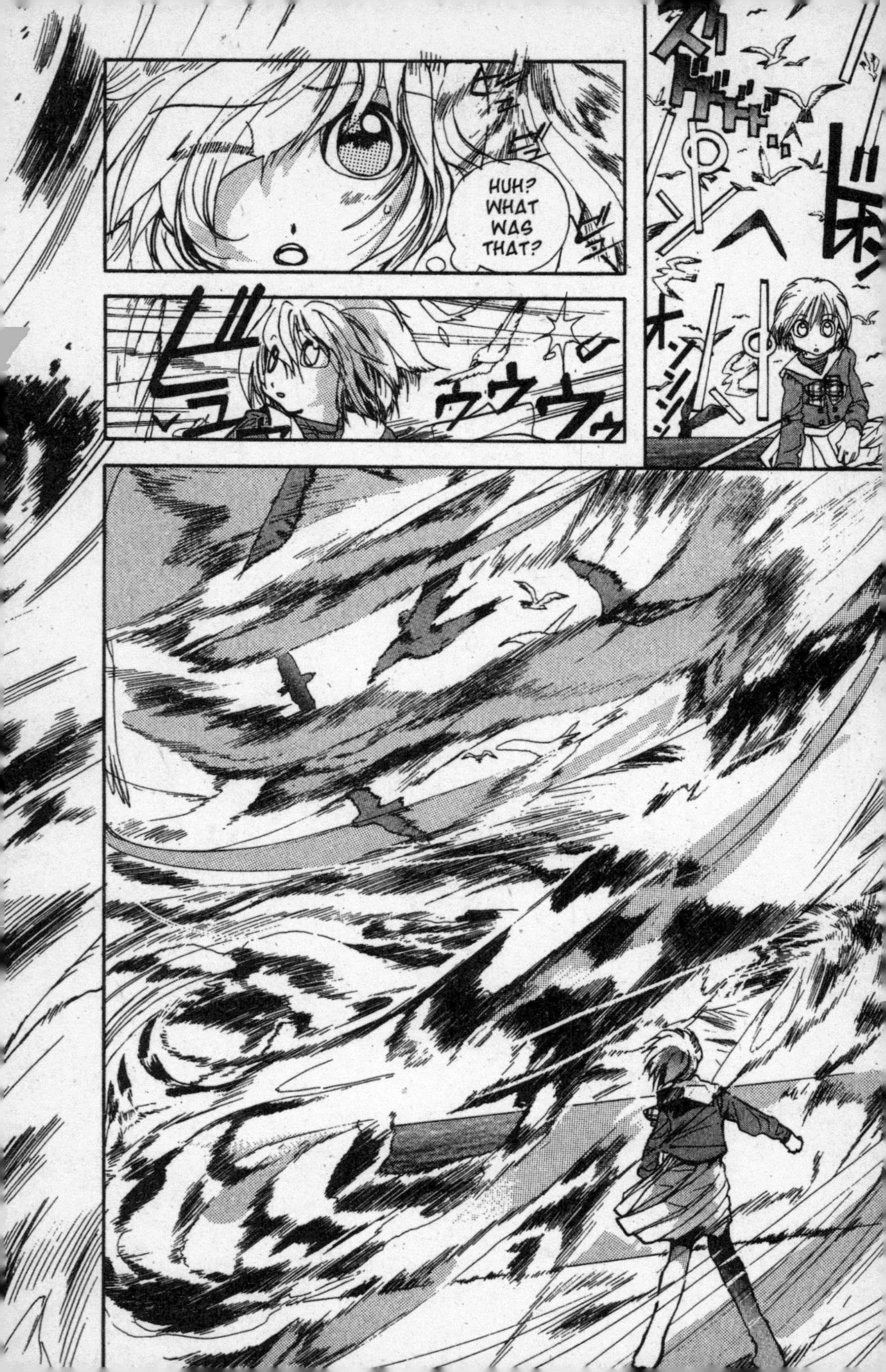
HUH? WHAT WAS THAT?

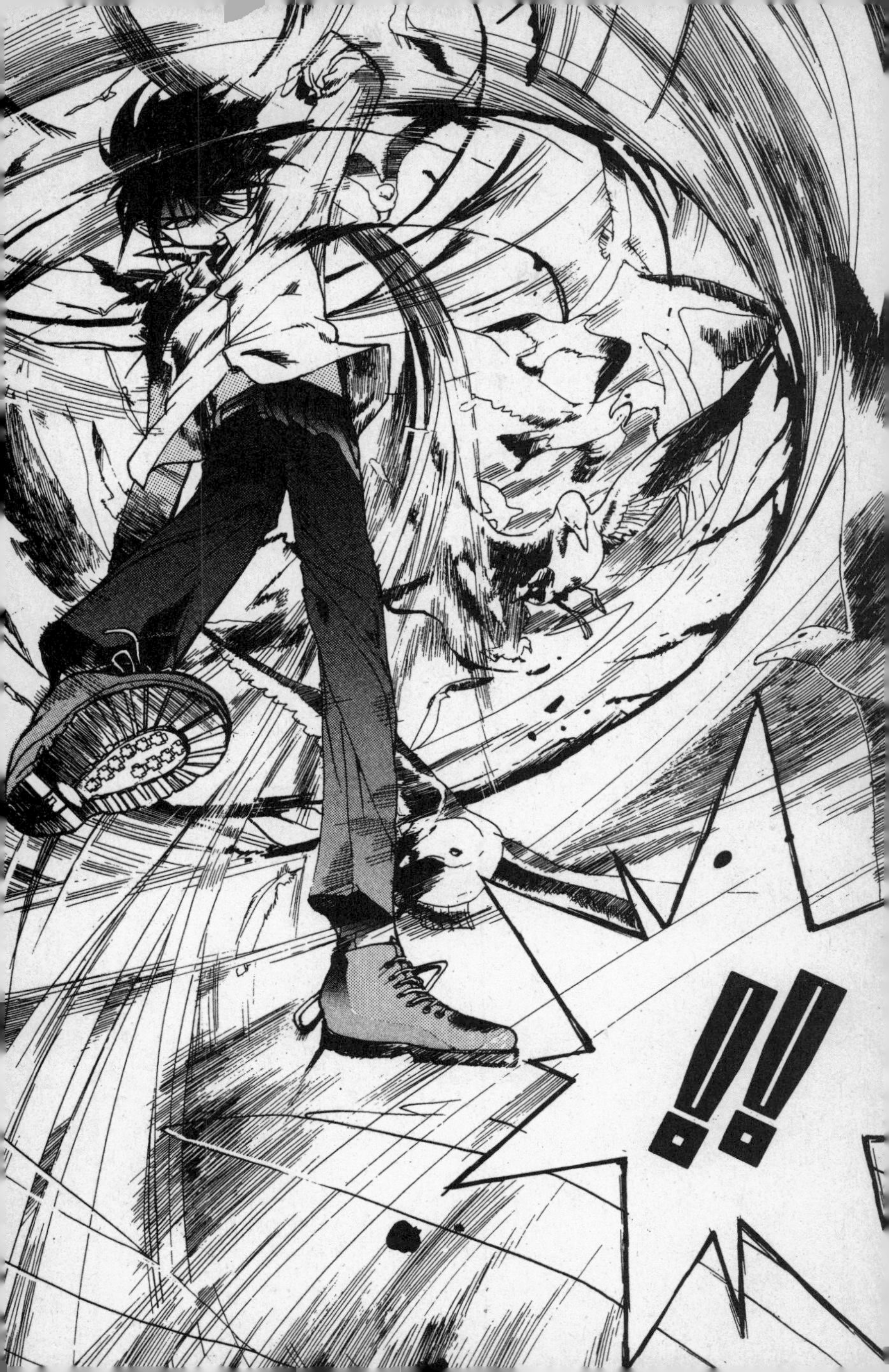
!!

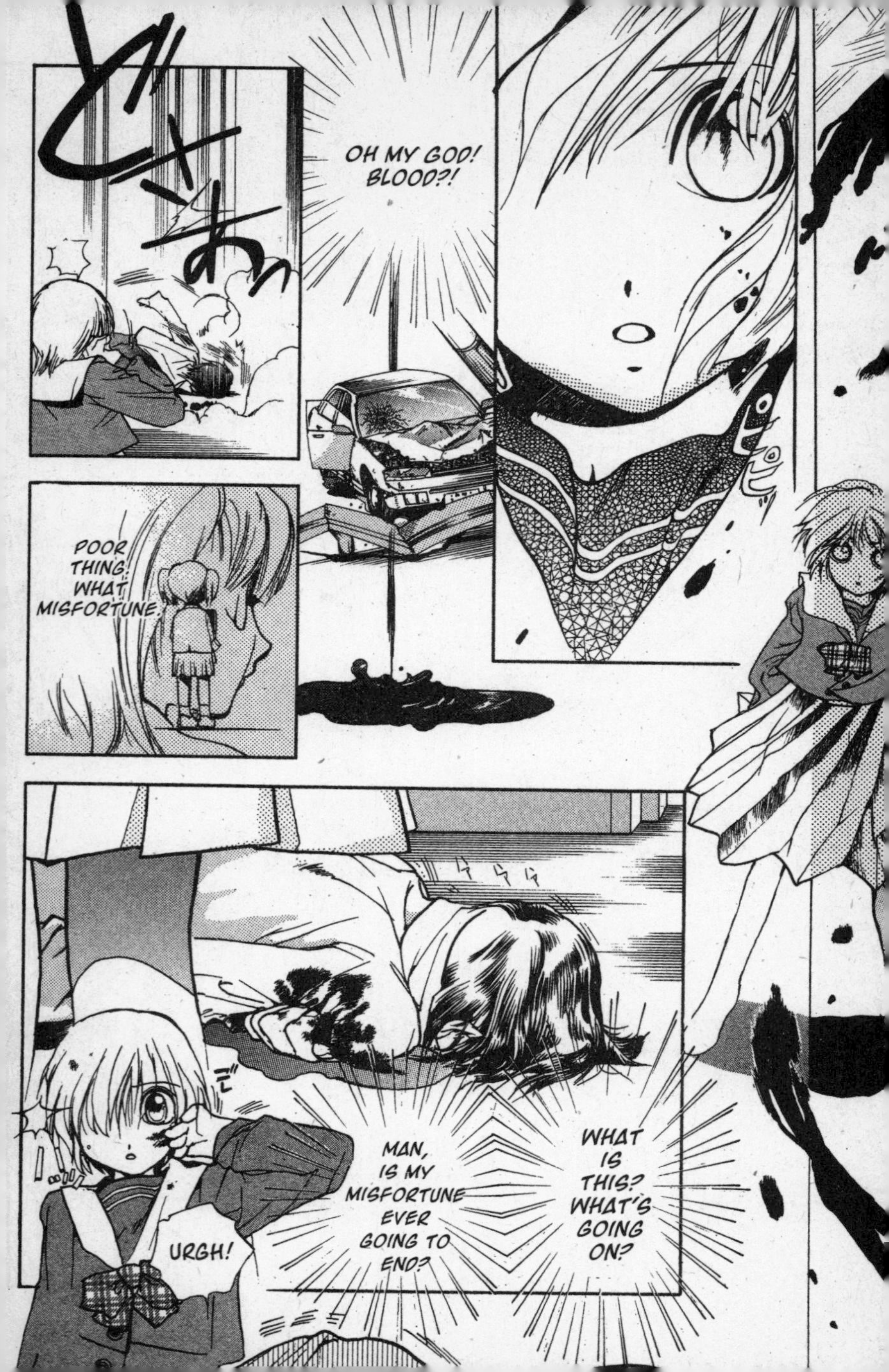
OH MY GOD! BLOOD?!
POOR THING. WHAT MISFORTUNE.
WHAT IS THIS? WHAT'S GOING ON?
MAN, IS MY MISFORTUNE EVER GOING TO END?
URGH!

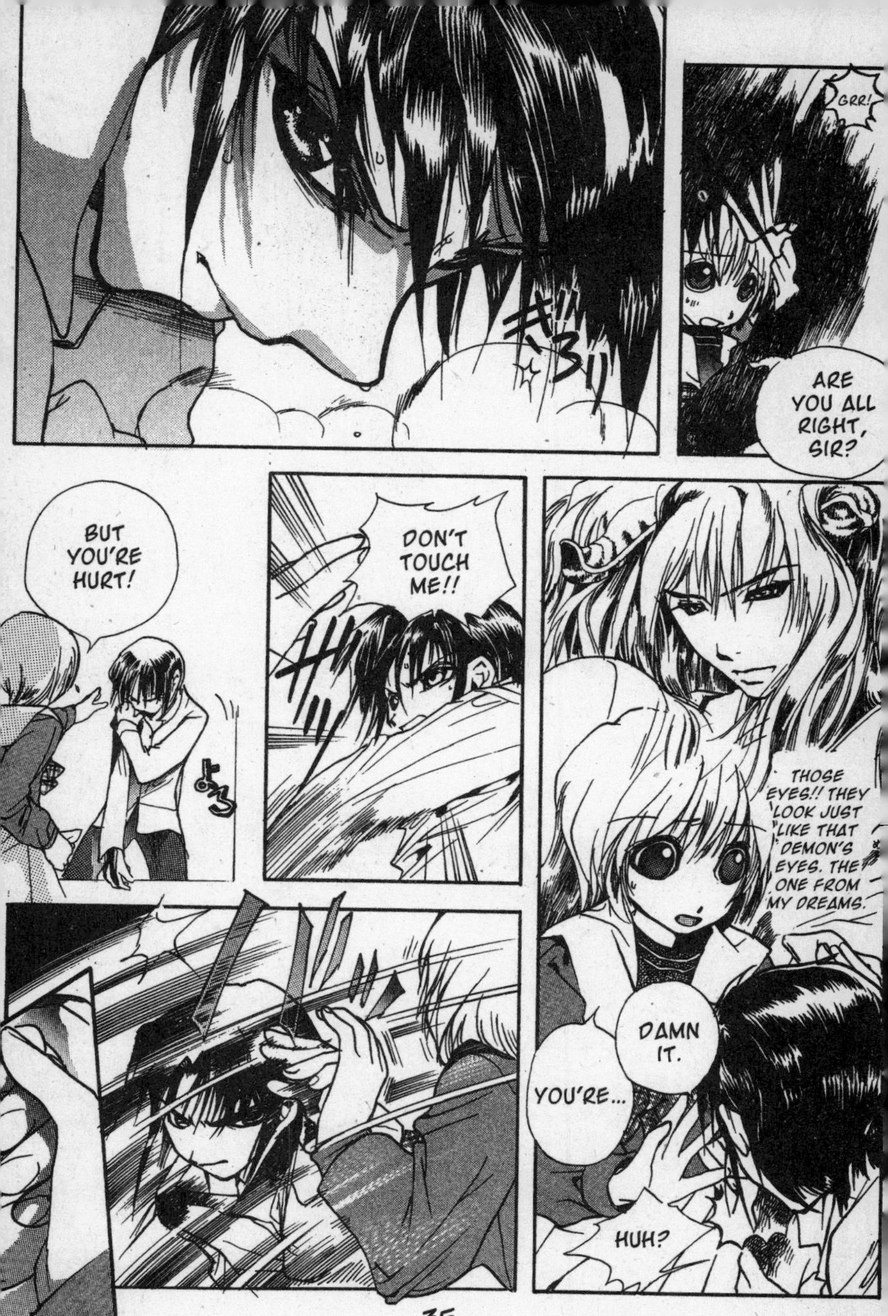
GRR!
ARE YOU ALL RIGHT, SIR?
THOSE EYES!! THEY LOOK JUST LIKE THAT DEMON'S EYES. THE ONE FROM MY DREAMS.
YOU'RE...
DAMN IT.
HUH?
DON'T TOUCH ME!!
BUT YOU'RE HURT!

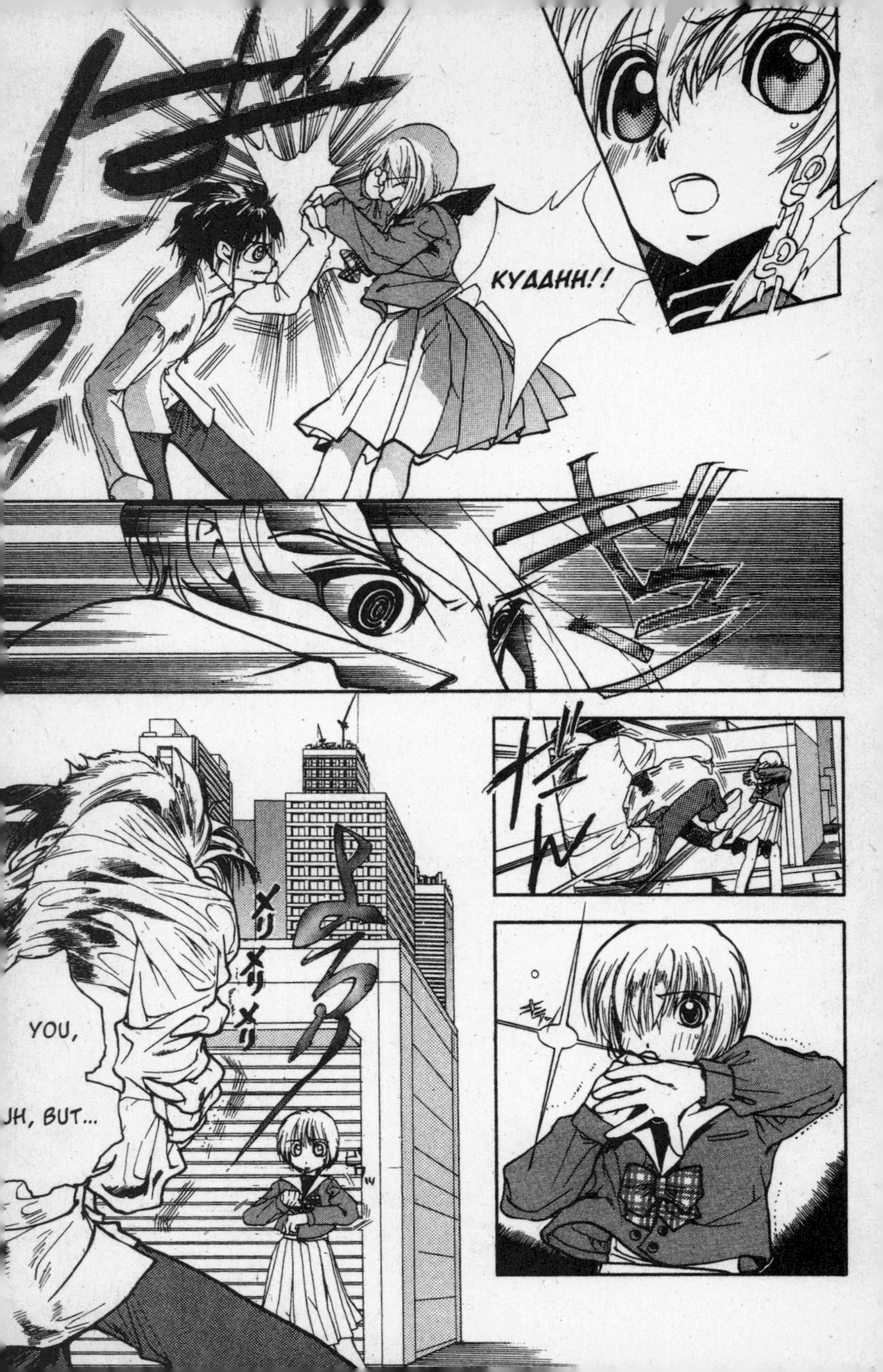
KYAAHH!!
YOU,
UH, BUT...

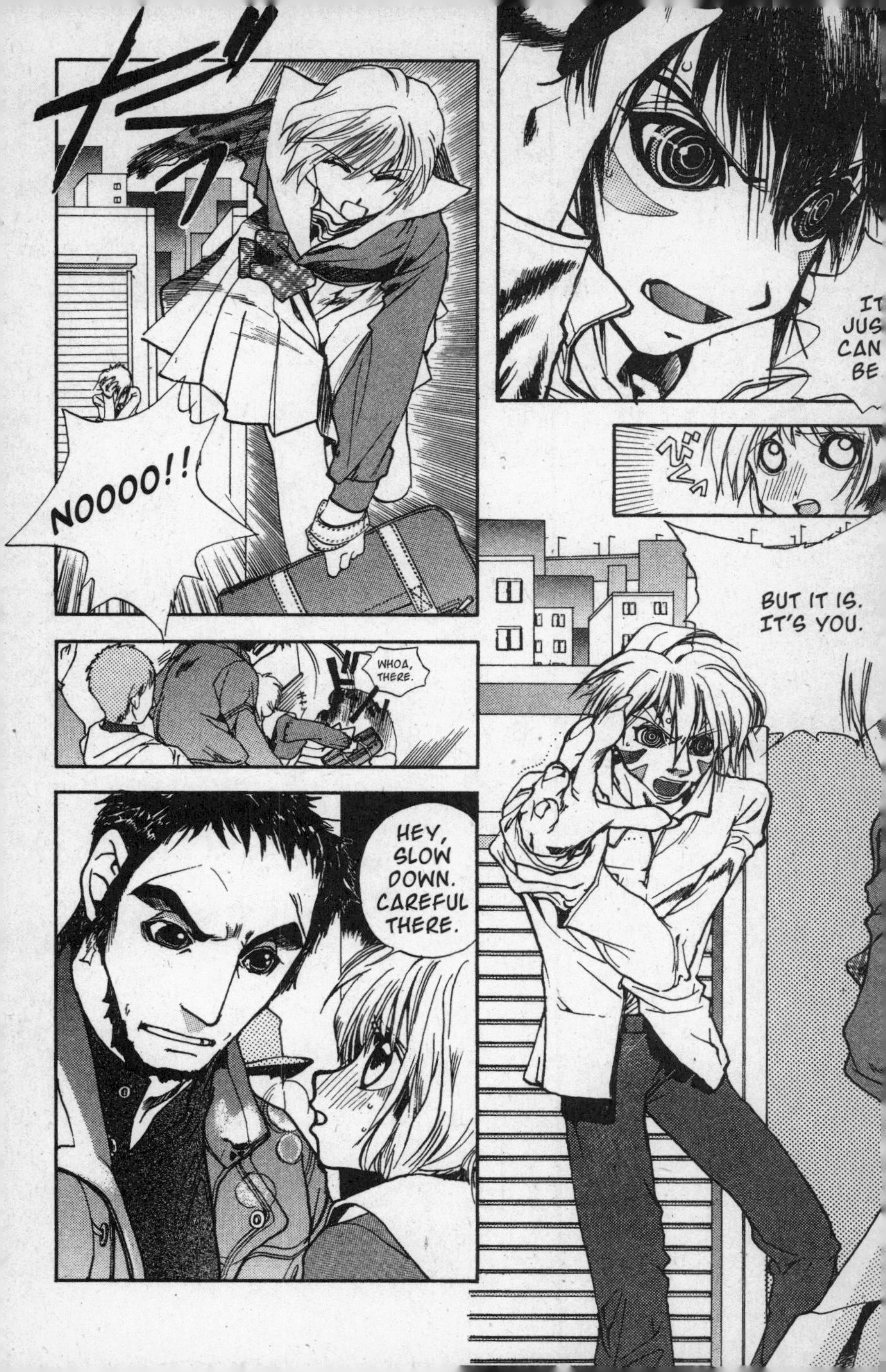
IT JUS CAN BE
BUT IT IS. IT'S YOU.
NOOOO!!
WHOA, THERE.
HEY, SLOW DOWN. CAREFUL THERE.

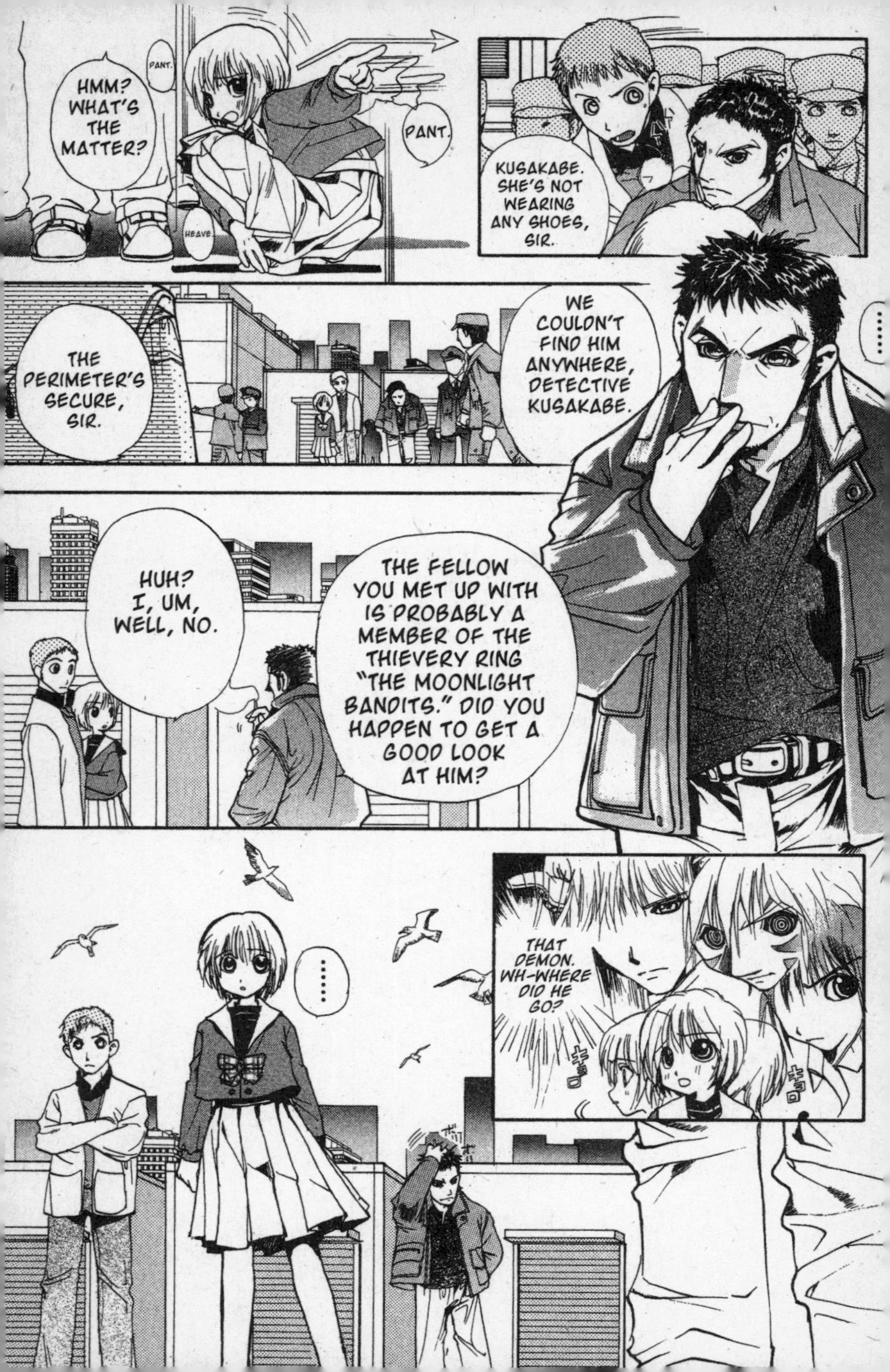
KUSAKABE. SHE'S NOT WEARING ANY SHOES, SIR.
PANT.
PANT.
HMM? WHAT'S THE MATTER?
HEAVE.
......
WE COULDN'T FIND HIM ANYWHERE, DETECTIVE KUSAKABE.
THE PERIMETER'S SECURE, SIR.
THE FELLOW YOU MET UP WITH IS PROBABLY A MEMBER OF THE THIEVERY RING "THE MOONLIGHT BANDITS." DID YOU HAPPEN TO GET A GOOD LOOK AT HIM?
HUH? I, UM, WELL, NO.
THAT DEMON. WH-WHERE DID HE GO?
......

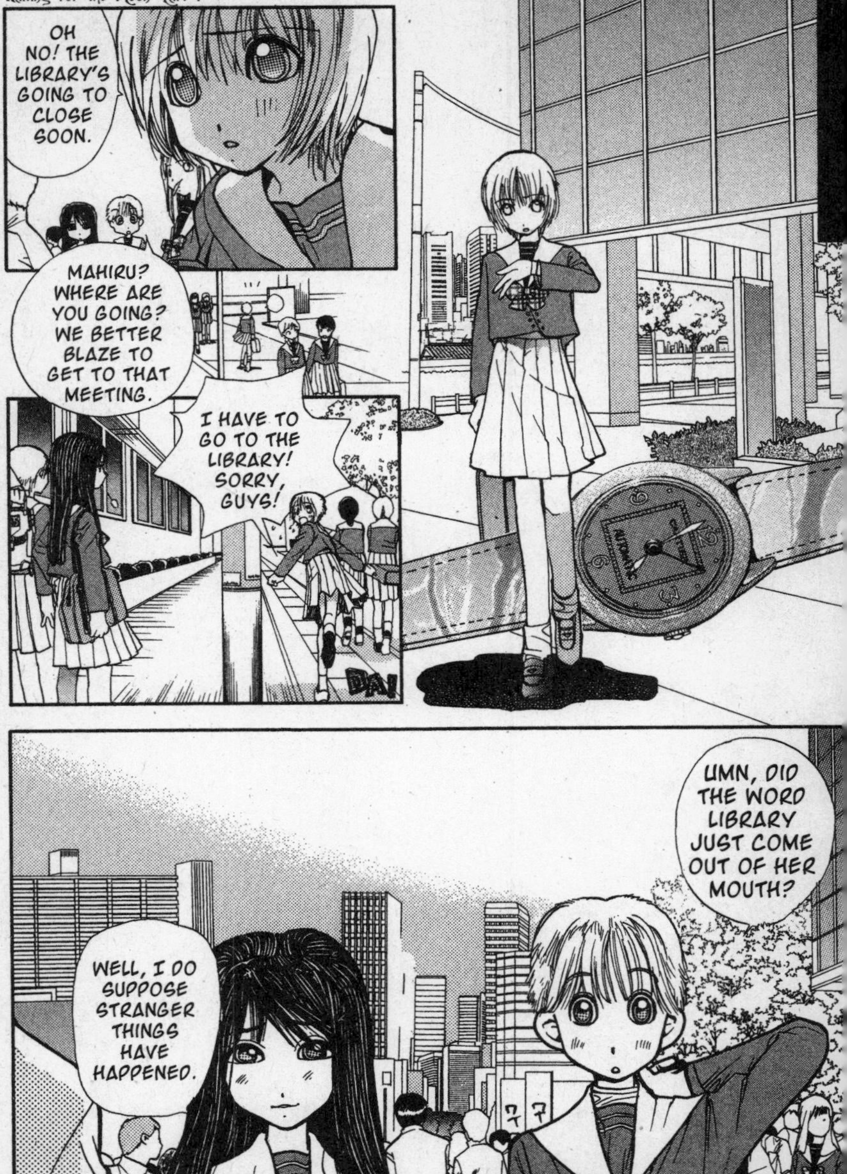
OH NO! THE LIBRARY'S GOING TO CLOSE SOON.
MAHIRU? WHERE ARE YOU GOING? WE BETTER BLAZE TO GET TO THAT MEETING.
I HAVE TO GO TO THE LIBRARY! SORRY, GUYS!
DA!
UMN, DID THE WORD LIBRARY JUST COME OUT OF HER MOUTH?
WELL, I DO SUPPOSE STRANGER THINGS HAVE HAPPENED.

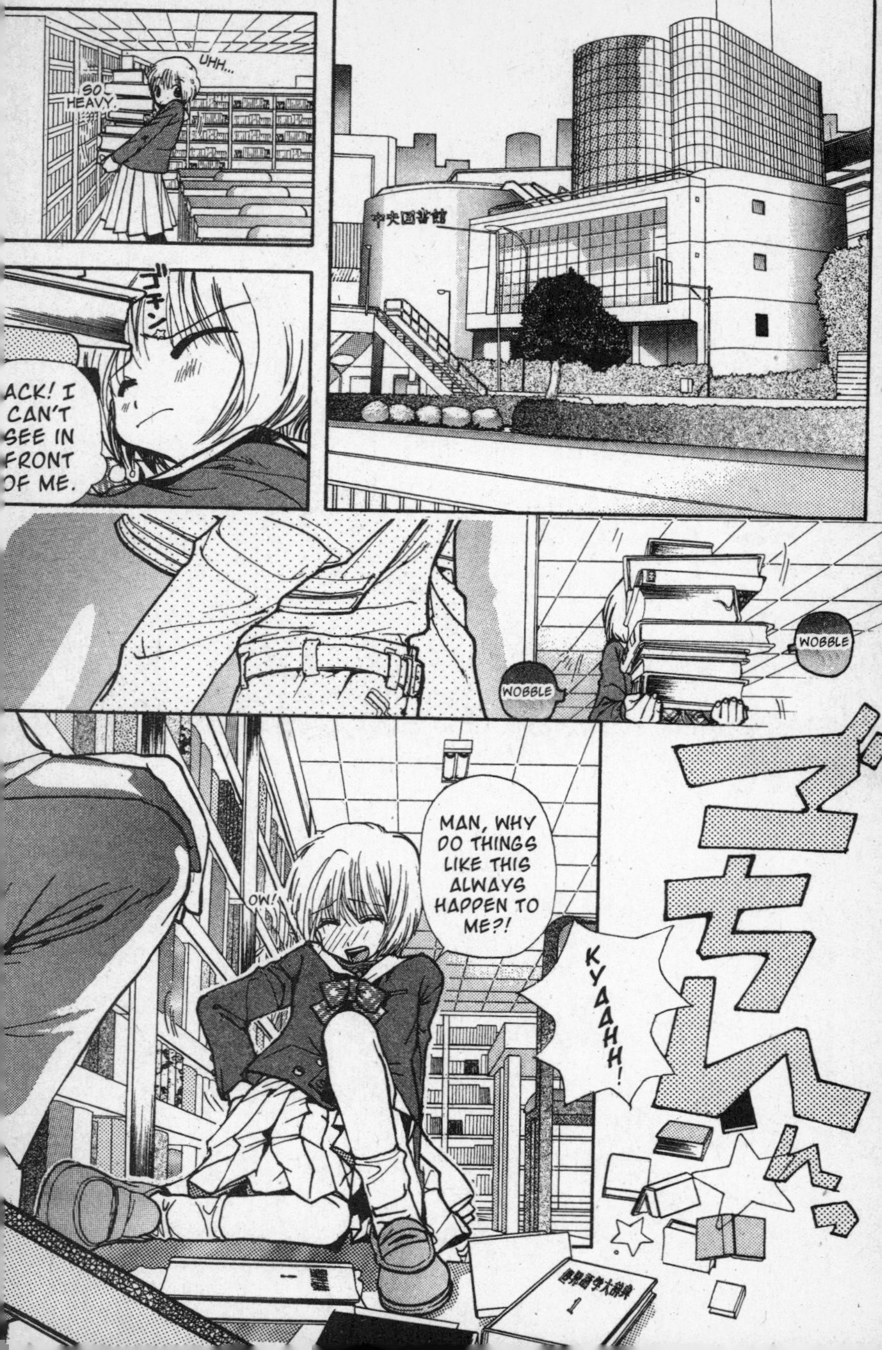
中央図書館
UHH...
SO HEAVY.
ゴチン
ACK! I CAN'T SEE IN FRONT OF ME.
WOBBLE
WOBBLE
KYAAHH!
MAN, WHY DO THINGS LIKE THIS ALWAYS HAPPEN TO ME?!
OW!

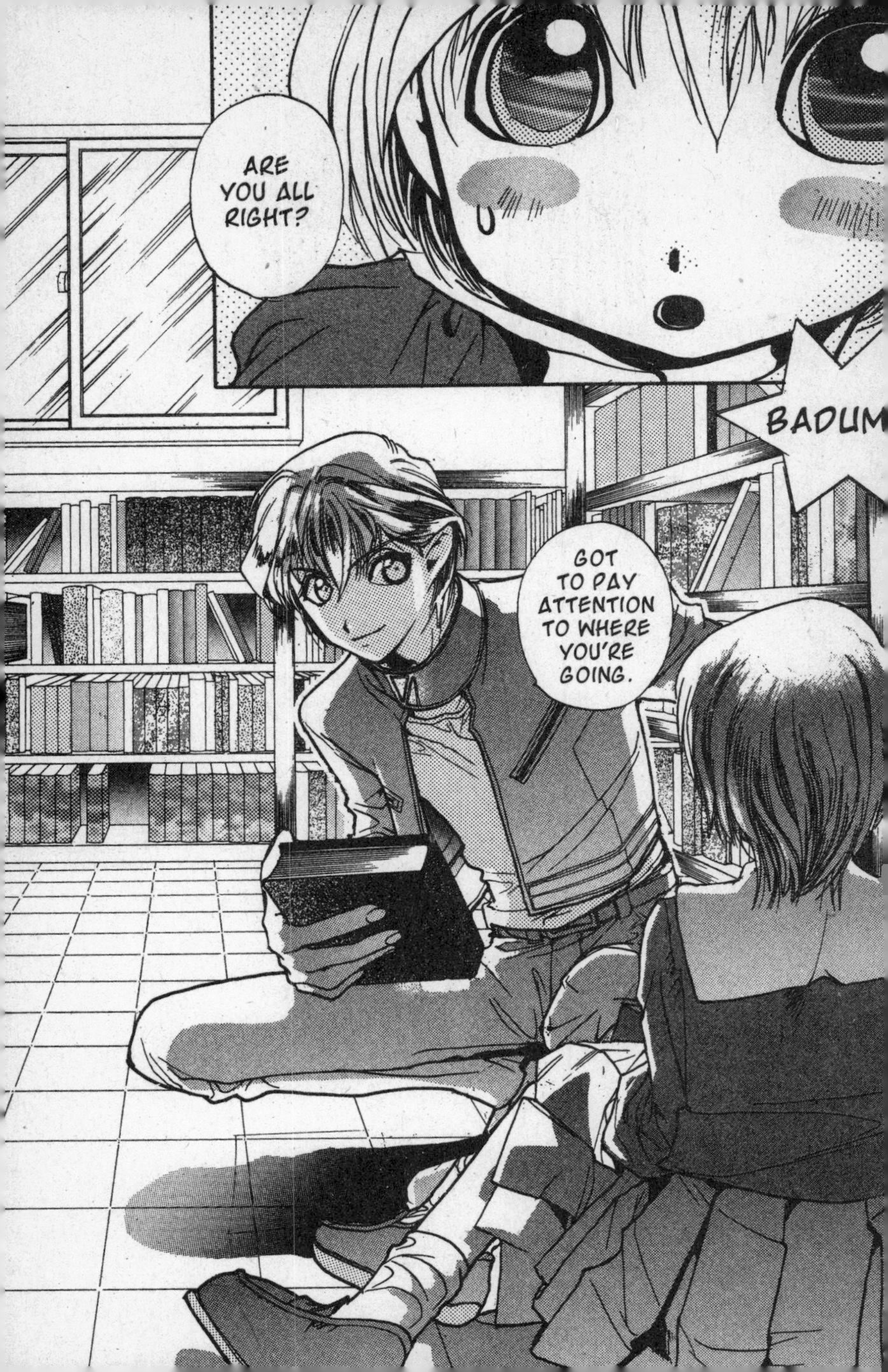
ARE YOU ALL RIGHT?
BADUM
GOT TO PAY ATTENTION TO WHERE YOU'RE GOING.

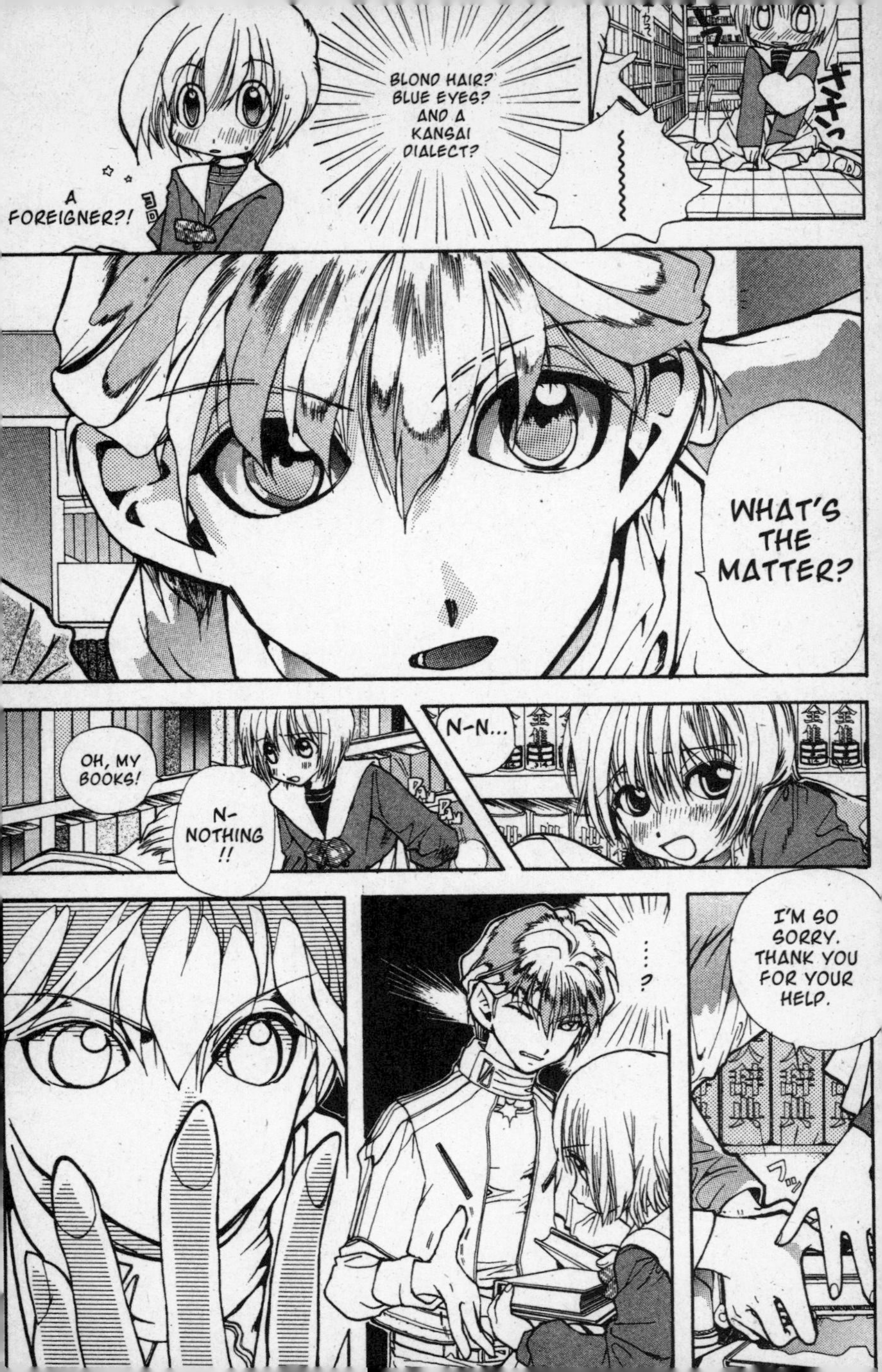
BLOND HAIR? BLUE EYES? AND A KANSAI DIALECT?
A FOREIGNER?!
WHAT'S THE MATTER?
N-N...
N-NOTHING!!
OH, MY BOOKS!
I'M SO SORRY. THANK YOU FOR YOUR HELP.
...?

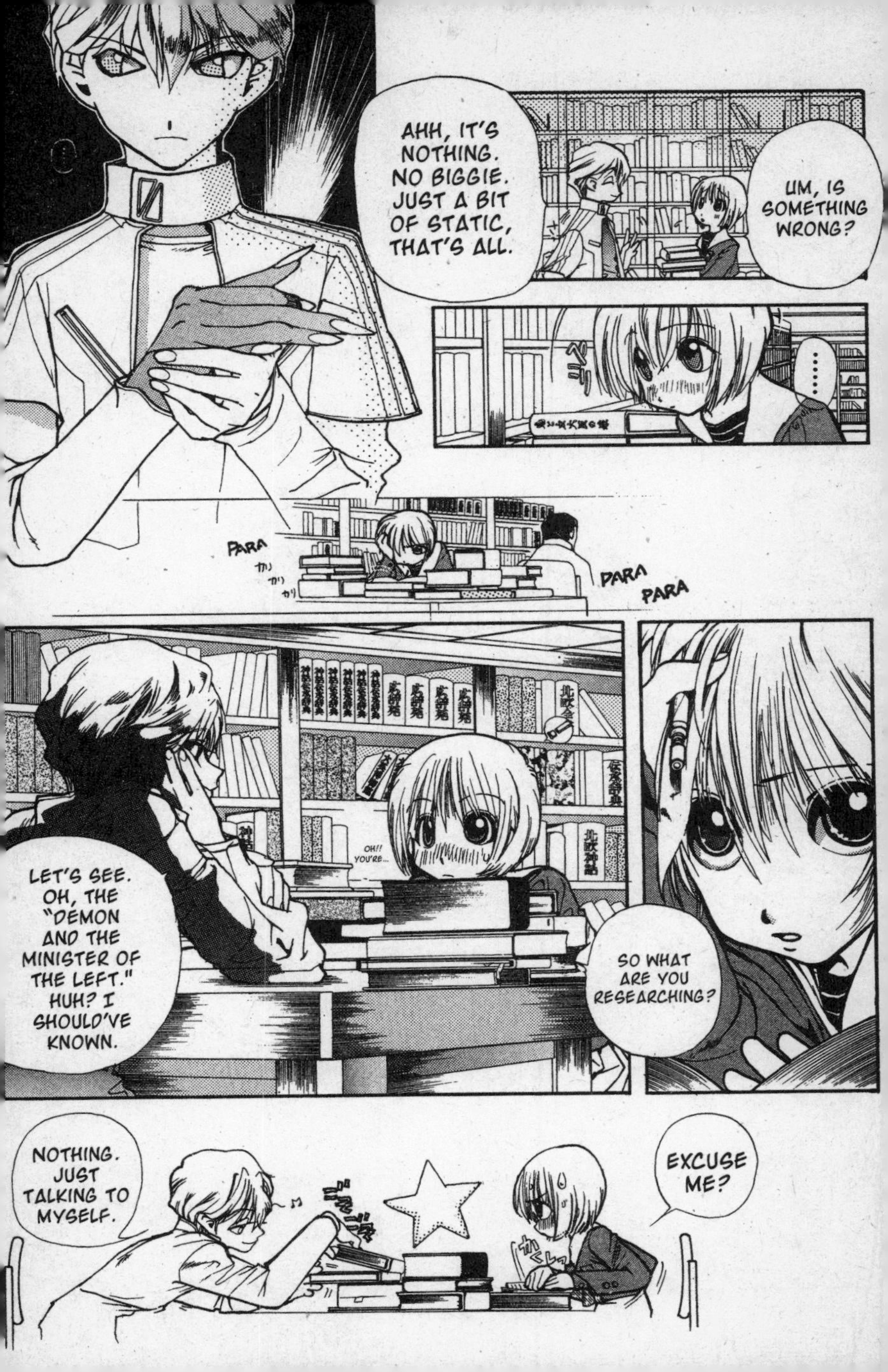
UM, IS SOMETHING WRONG?
AHH, IT'S NOTHING. NO BIGGIE. JUST A BIT OF STATIC, THAT'S ALL.
.....
PARA
PARA
PARA
SO WHAT ARE YOU RESEARCHING?
OH!! YOU'RE...
LET'S SEE. OH, THE "DEMON AND THE MINISTER OF THE LEFT." HUH? I SHOULD'VE KNOWN.
EXCUSE ME?
NOTHING. JUST TALKING TO MYSELF.

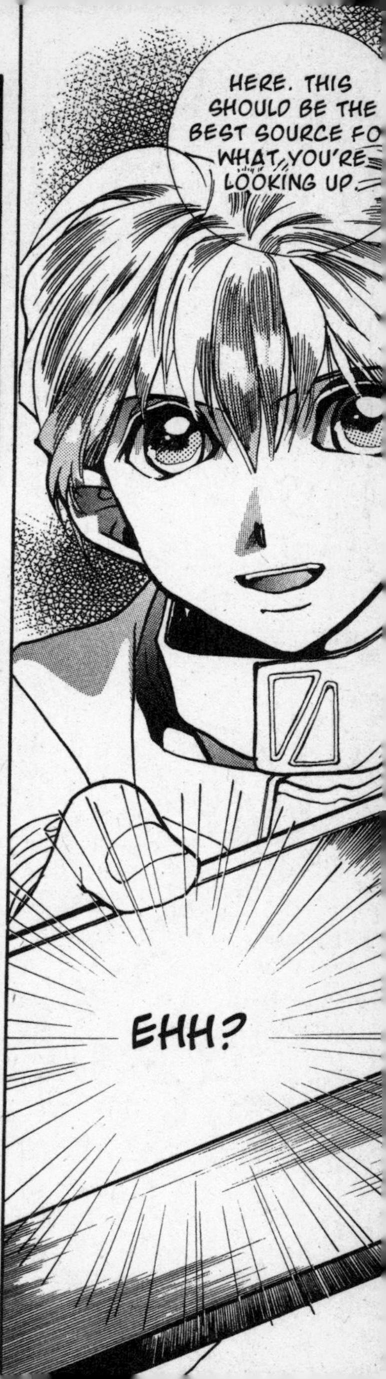
HERE. THIS SHOULD BE THE BEST SOURCE FO WHAT YOU'RE LOOKING UP.
EHH?

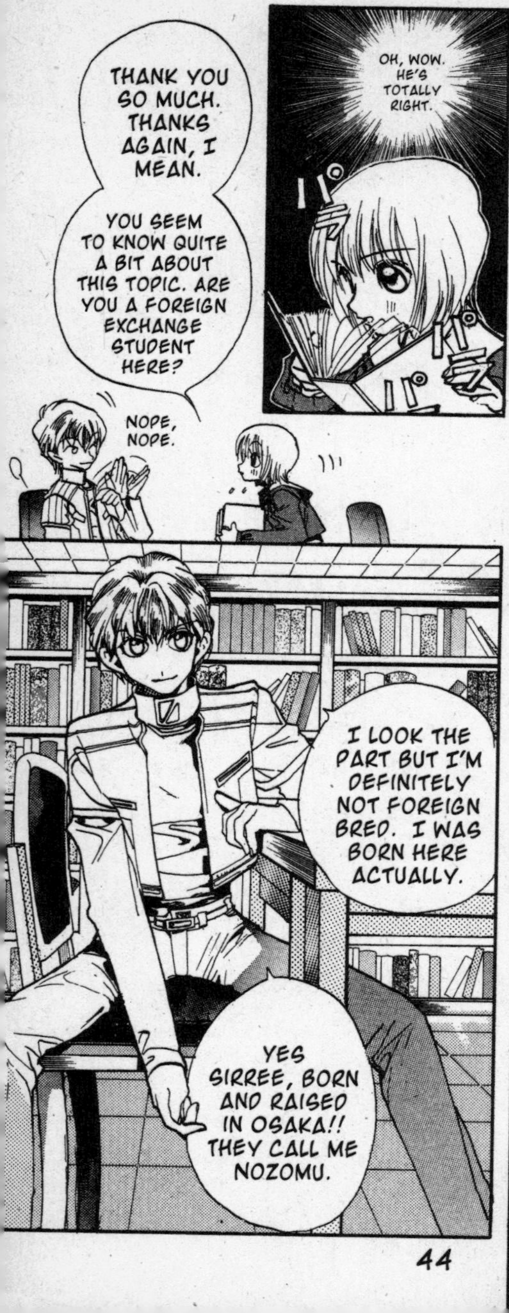
OH, WOW. HE'S TOTALLY RIGHT.
THANK YOU SO MUCH. THANKS AGAIN, I MEAN.
YOU SEEM TO KNOW QUITE A BIT ABOUT THIS TOPIC. ARE YOU A FOREIGN EXCHANGE STUDENT HERE?
NOPE, NOPE.
I LOOK THE PART BUT I'M DEFINITELY NOT FOREIGN BRED. I WAS BORN HERE ACTUALLY.
YES SIRREE, BORN AND RAISED IN OSAKA!! THEY CALL ME NOZOMU.

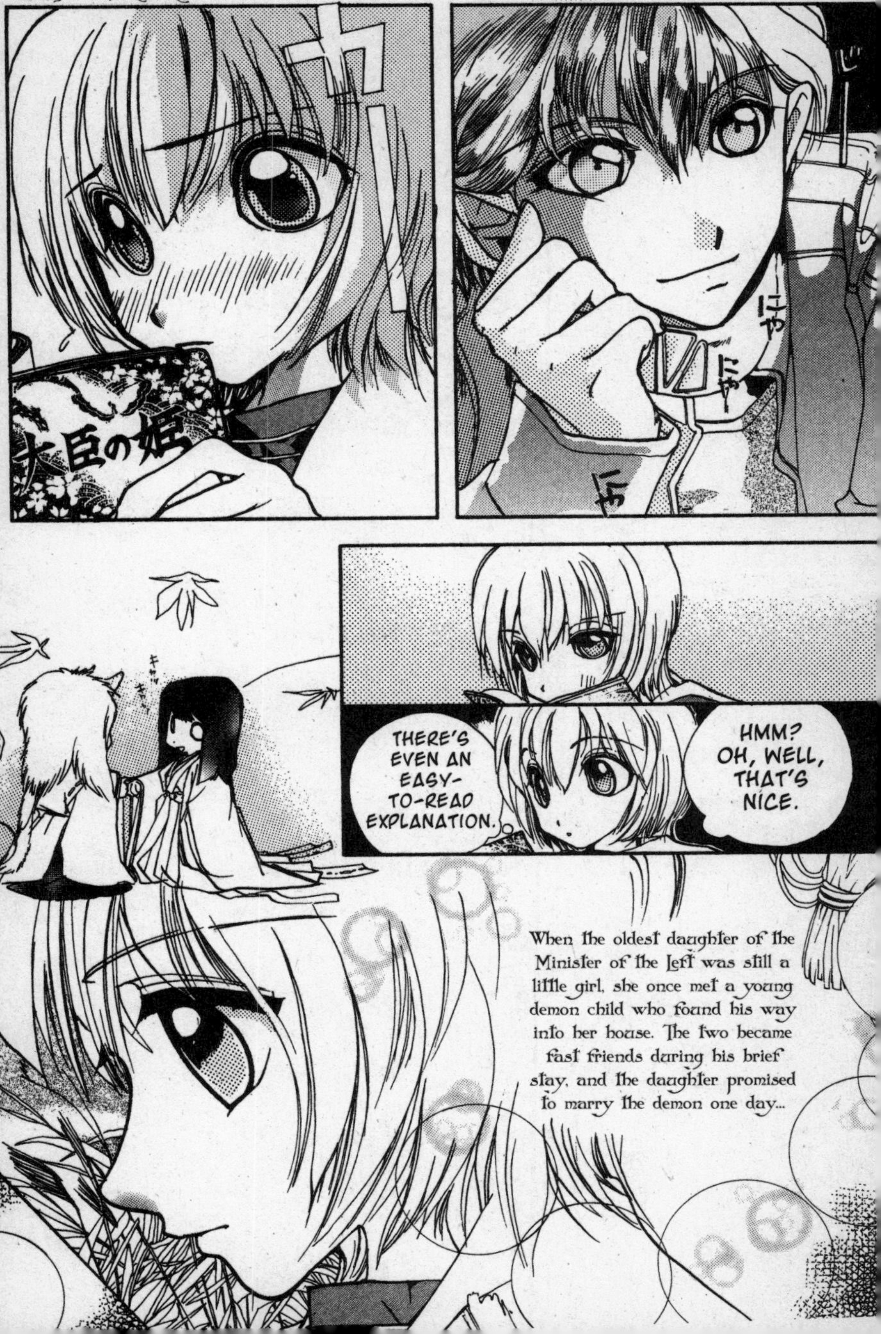
にゃ
にゃ
大臣の姫
HMM? OH, WELL, THAT'S NICE.
THERE'S EVEN AN EASY-TO-READ EXPLANATION.
When the oldest daughter of the Minister of the Left was still a little girl, she once met a young demon child who found his way into her house. The two became fast friends during his brief stay, and the daughter promised to marry the demon one day...

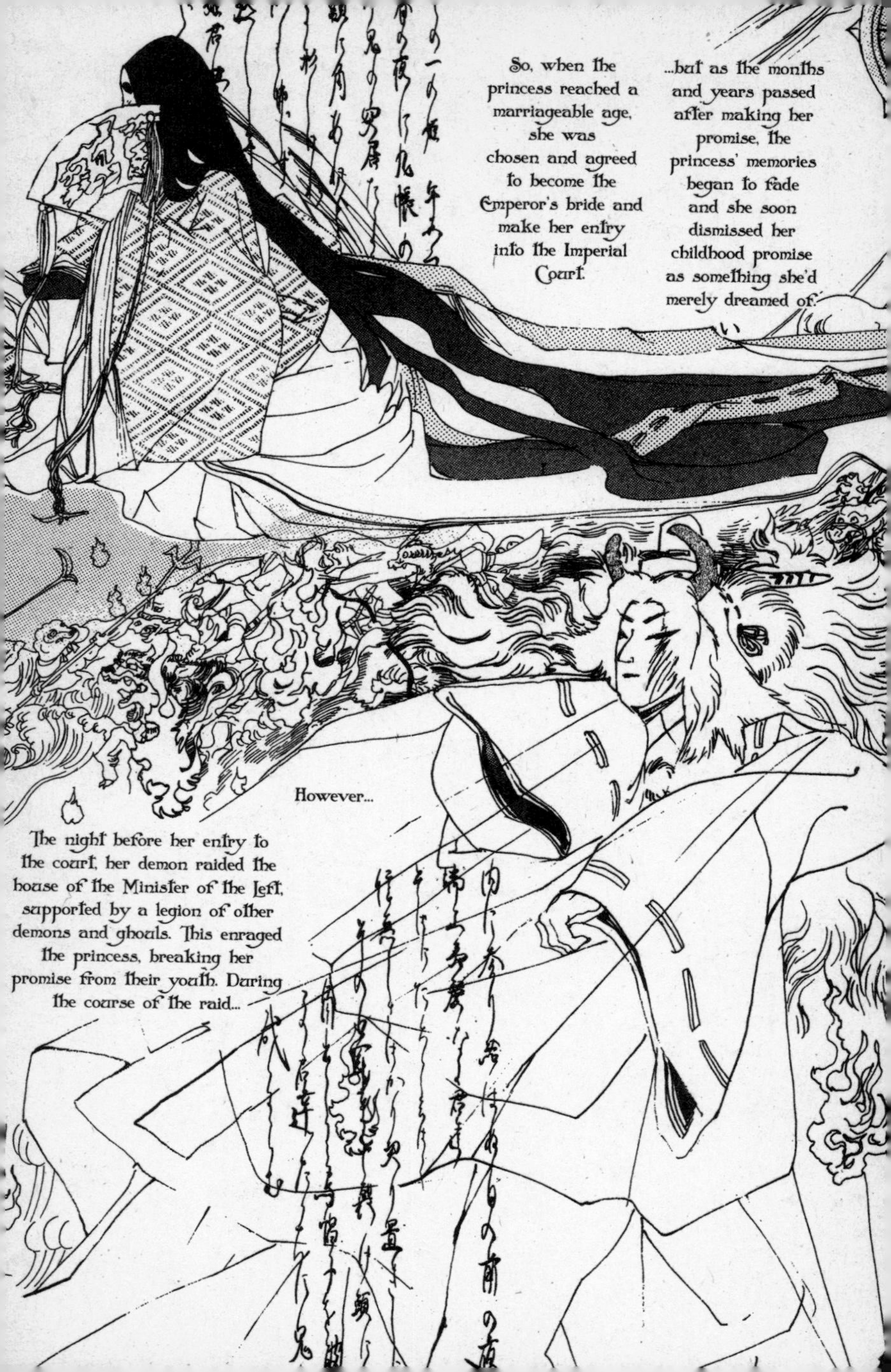

...but as the months and years passed after making her promise, the princess' memories began to fade and she soon dismissed her childhood promise as something she'd merely dreamed of.
So, when the princess reached a marriageable age, she was chosen and agreed to become the Emperor's bride and make her entry into the Imperial Court.
However...
The night before her entry to the court, her demon raided the house of the Minister of the Left, supported by a legion of other demons and ghouls. This enraged the princess, breaking her promise from their youth. During the course of the raid...

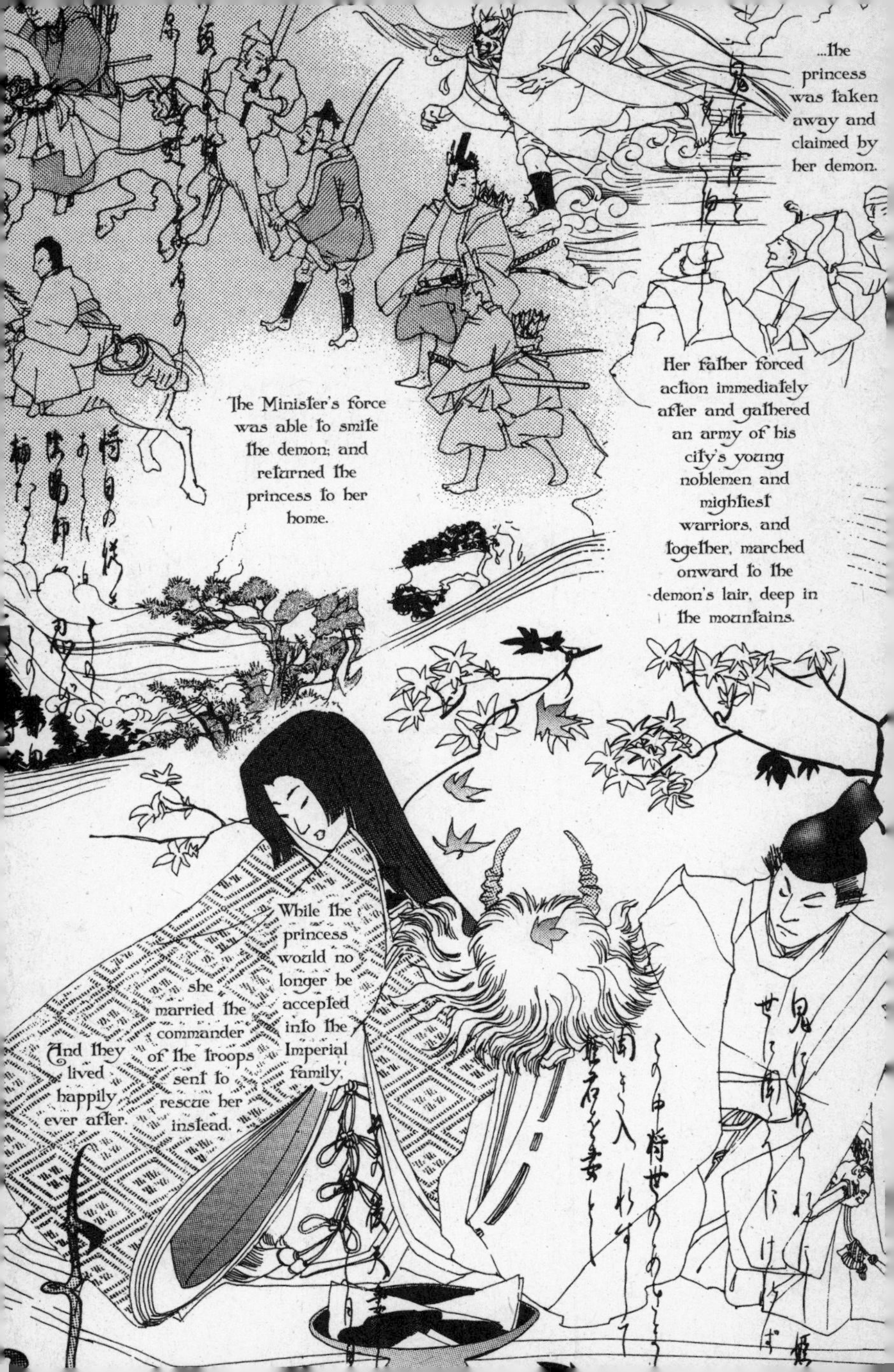

...the princess was taken away and claimed by her demon.
Her father forced action immediately after and gathered an army of his city's young noblemen and mightiest warriors, and together, marched onward to the demon's lair, deep in the mountains.
The Minister's force was able to smite the demon; and returned the princess to her home.
While the princess would no longer be accepted into the Imperial family,
she married the commander of the troops sent to rescue her instead.
And they lived happily ever after.

*It was said that even though it seems like a dream, don't sell your soul to the devil.

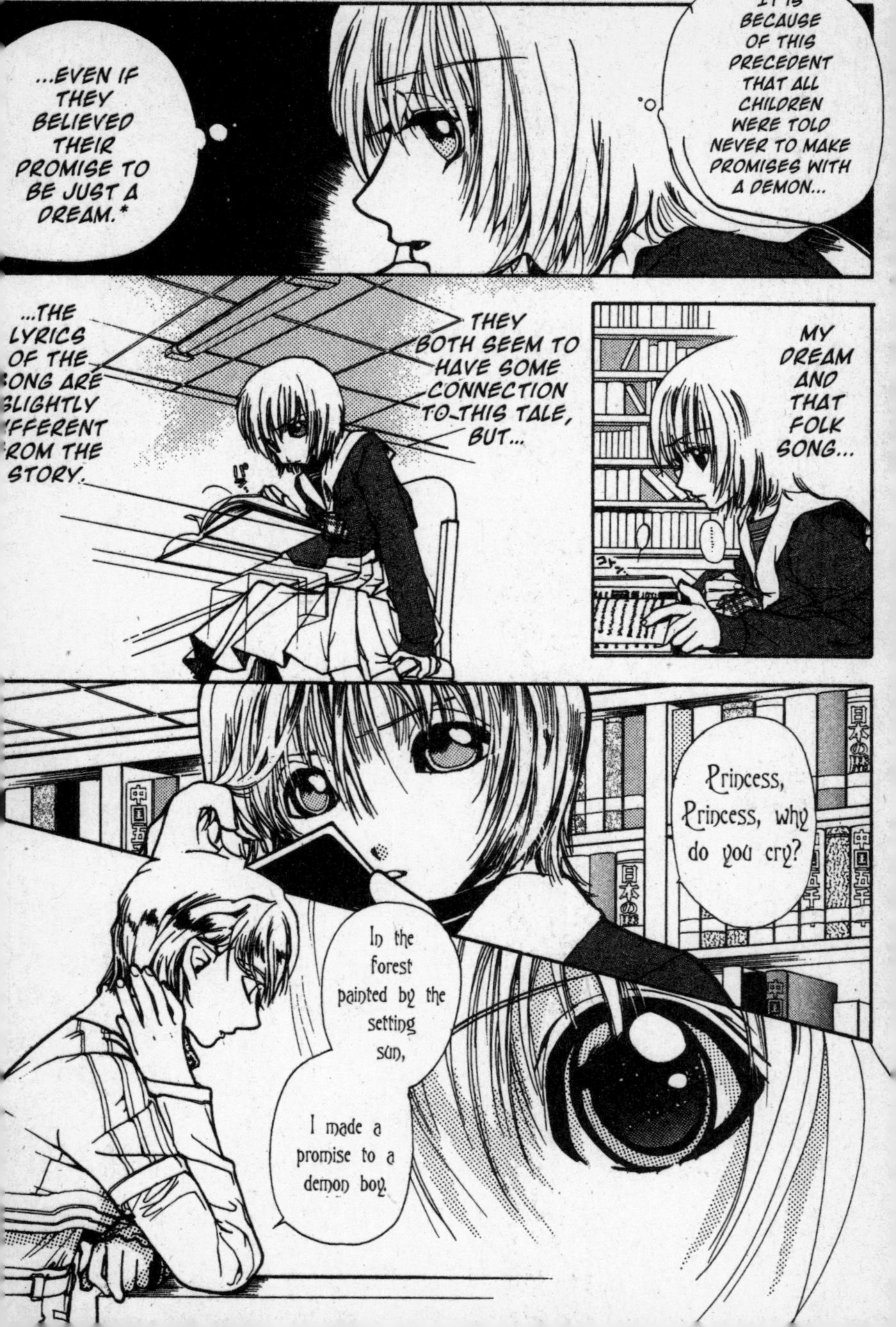
IT IS BECAUSE OF THIS PRECEDENT THAT ALL CHILDREN WERE TOLD NEVER TO MAKE PROMISES WITH A DEMON...
...EVEN IF THEY BELIEVED THEIR PROMISE TO BE JUST A DREAM.*
MY DREAM AND THAT FOLK SONG...
......
THEY BOTH SEEM TO HAVE SOME CONNECTION TO THIS TALE, BUT...
...THE LYRICS OF THE ONG ARE LIGHTLY IFFERENT ROM THE STORY.
Princess, Princess, why do you cry?
In the forest painted by the setting sun,
I made a promise to a demon boy.

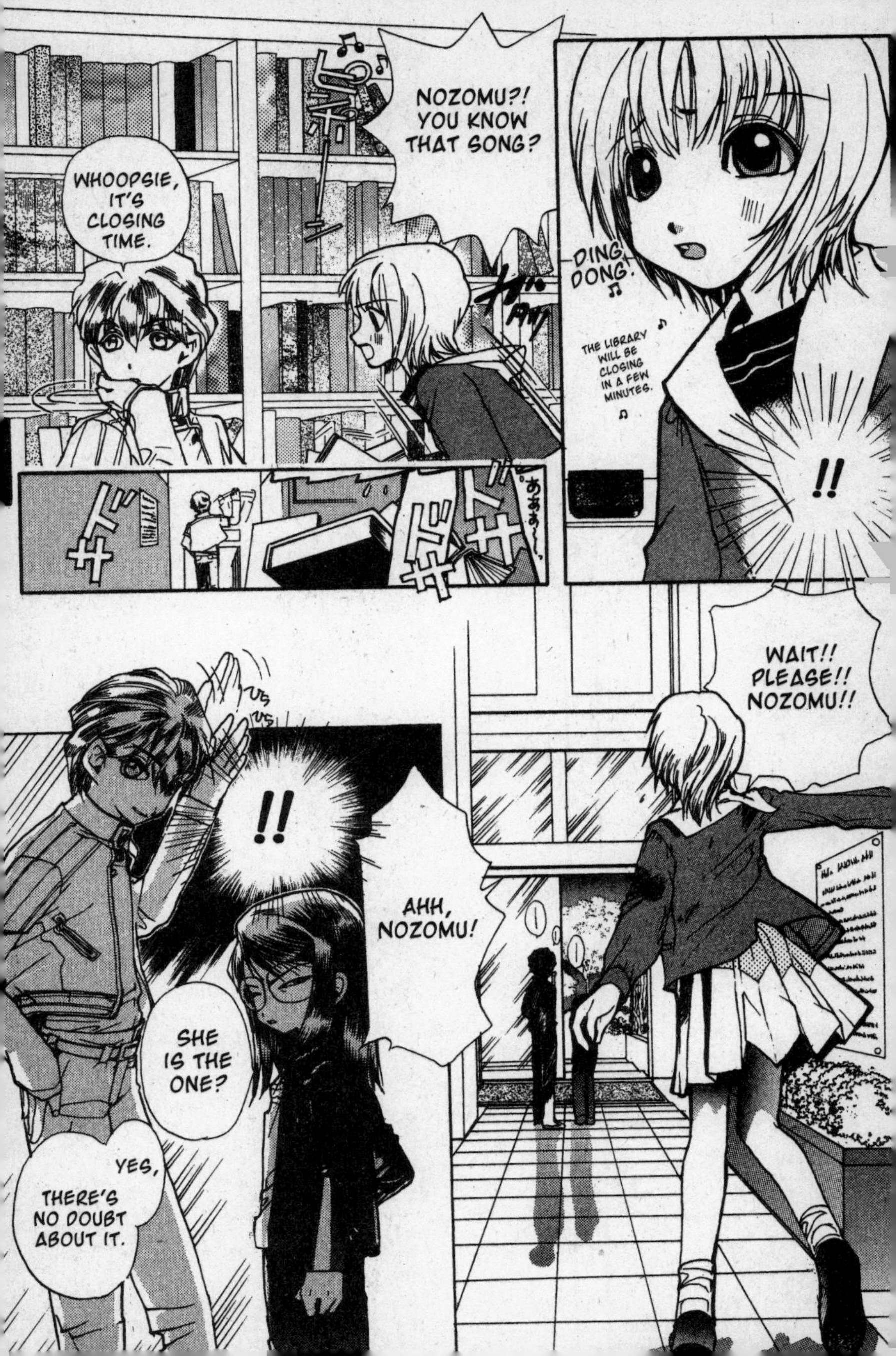
DING DONG ♫
THE LIBRARY WILL BE CLOSING IN A FEW MINUTES. ♫
!!
NOZOMU?! YOU KNOW THAT SONG?
WHOOPSIE, IT'S CLOSING TIME.
WAIT!! PLEASE!! NOZOMU!!
AHH, NOZOMU!
!!
SHE IS THE ONE?
YES, THERE'S NO DOUBT ABOUT IT.

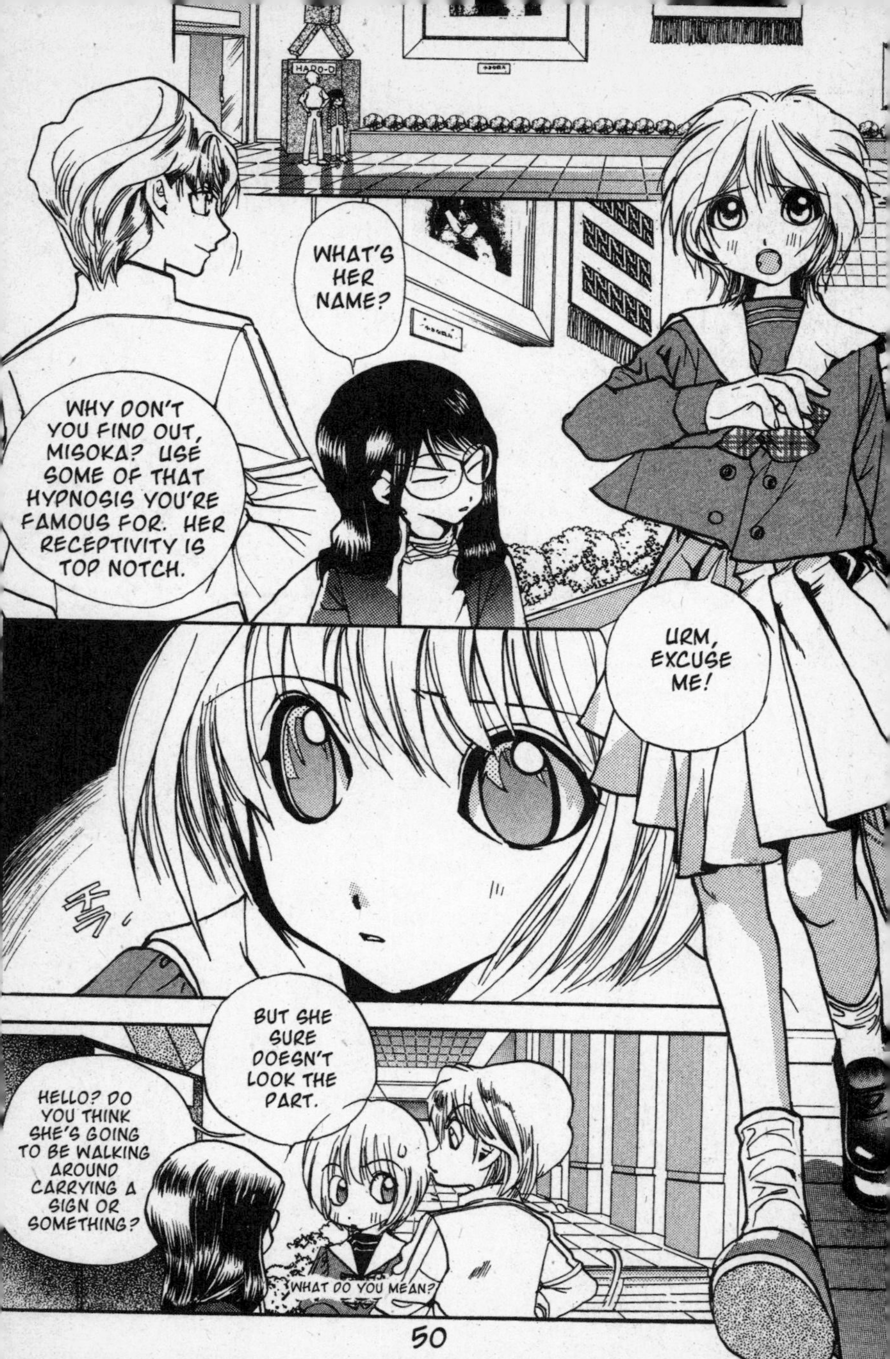
URM, EXCUSE ME!
WHAT'S HER NAME?
WHY DON'T YOU FIND OUT, MISOKA? USE SOME OF THAT HYPNOSIS YOU'RE FAMOUS FOR. HER RECEPTIVITY IS TOP NOTCH.
BUT SHE SURE DOESN'T LOOK THE PART.
HELLO? DO YOU THINK SHE'S GOING TO BE WALKING AROUND CARRYING A SIGN OR SOMETHING?
WHAT DO YOU MEAN?

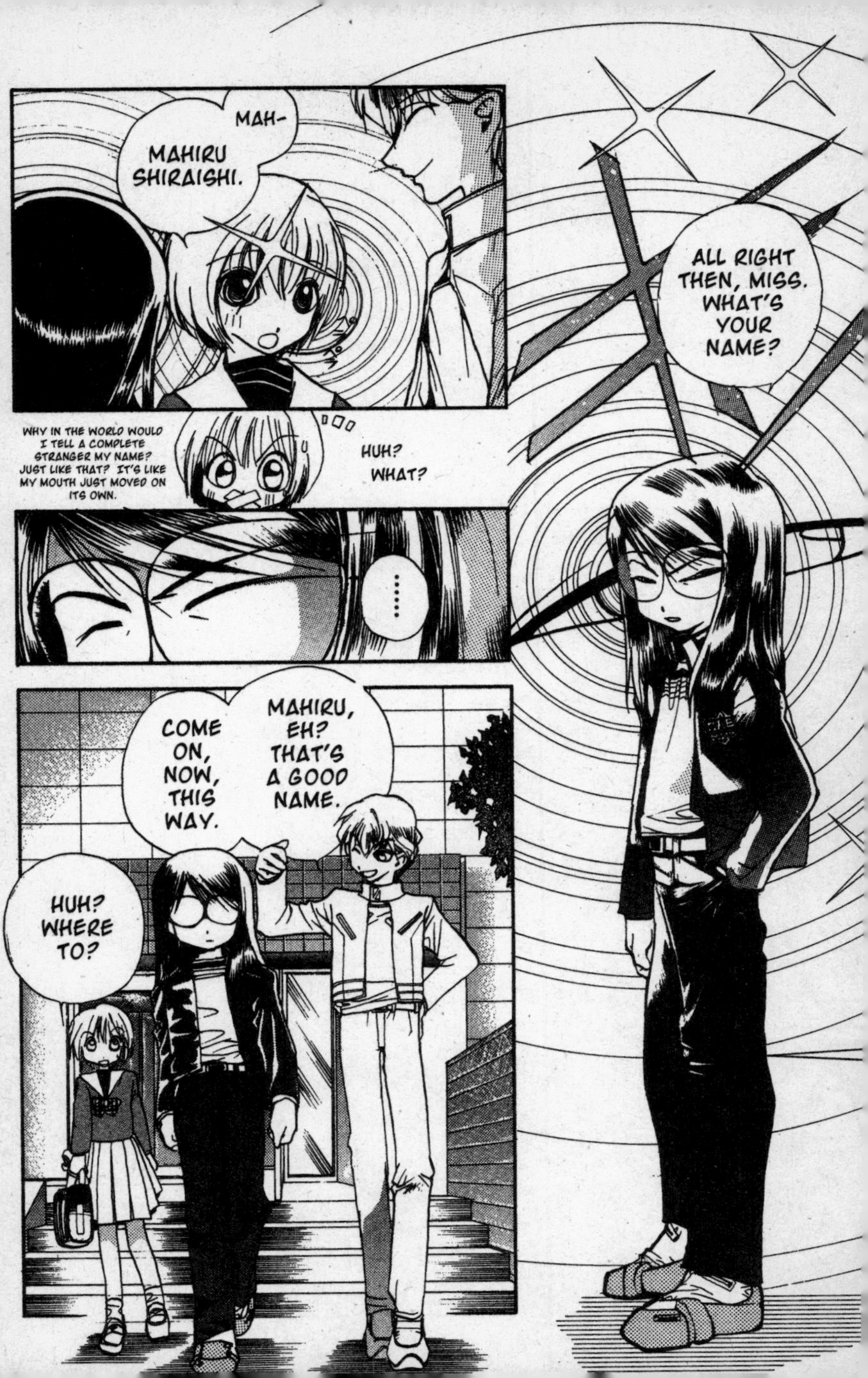
ALL RIGHT THEN, MISS. WHAT'S YOUR NAME?
MAH-
MAHIRU SHIRAISHI.
HUH? WHAT?
WHY IN THE WORLD WOULD I TELL A COMPLETE STRANGER MY NAME? JUST LIKE THAT? IT'S LIKE MY MOUTH JUST MOVED ON ITS OWN.
......
MAHIRU, EH? THAT'S A GOOD NAME.
COME ON, NOW, THIS WAY.
HUH? WHERE TO?

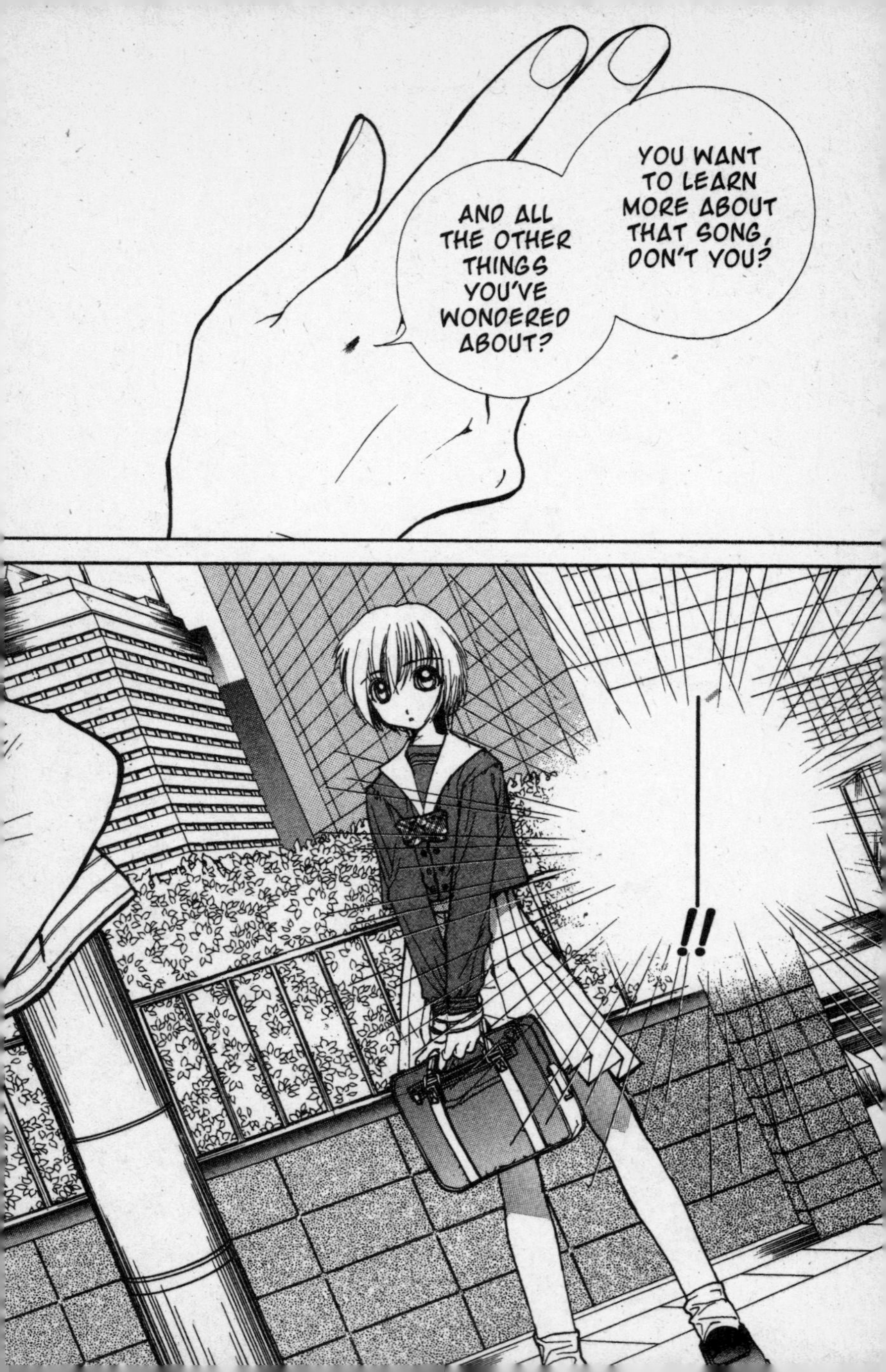
YOU WANT TO LEARN MORE ABOUT THAT SONG, DON'T YOU?
AND ALL THE OTHER THINGS YOU'VE WONDERED ABOUT?
—!!

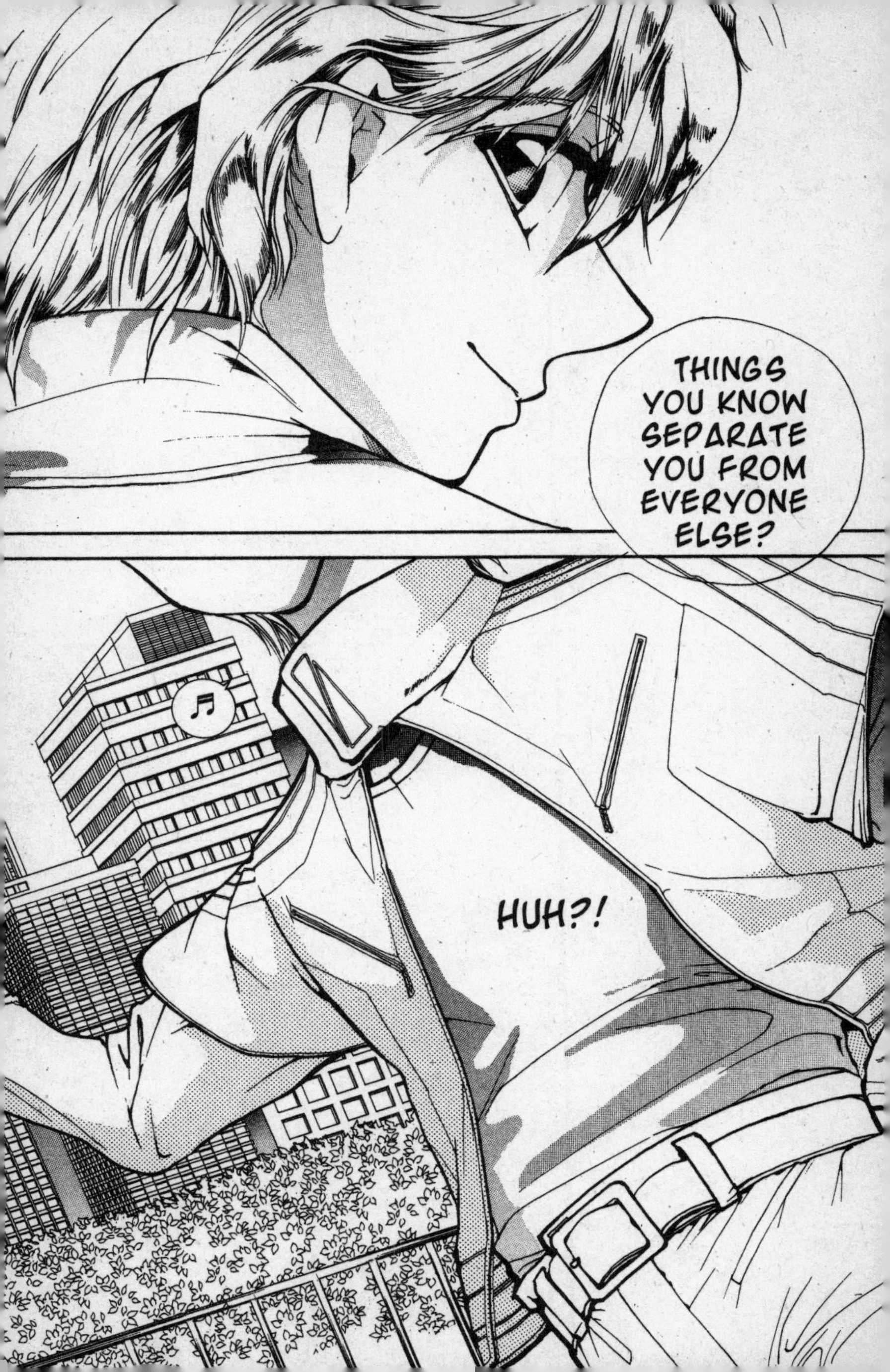
THINGS YOU KNOW SEPARATE YOU FROM EVERYONE ELSE?
HUH?!

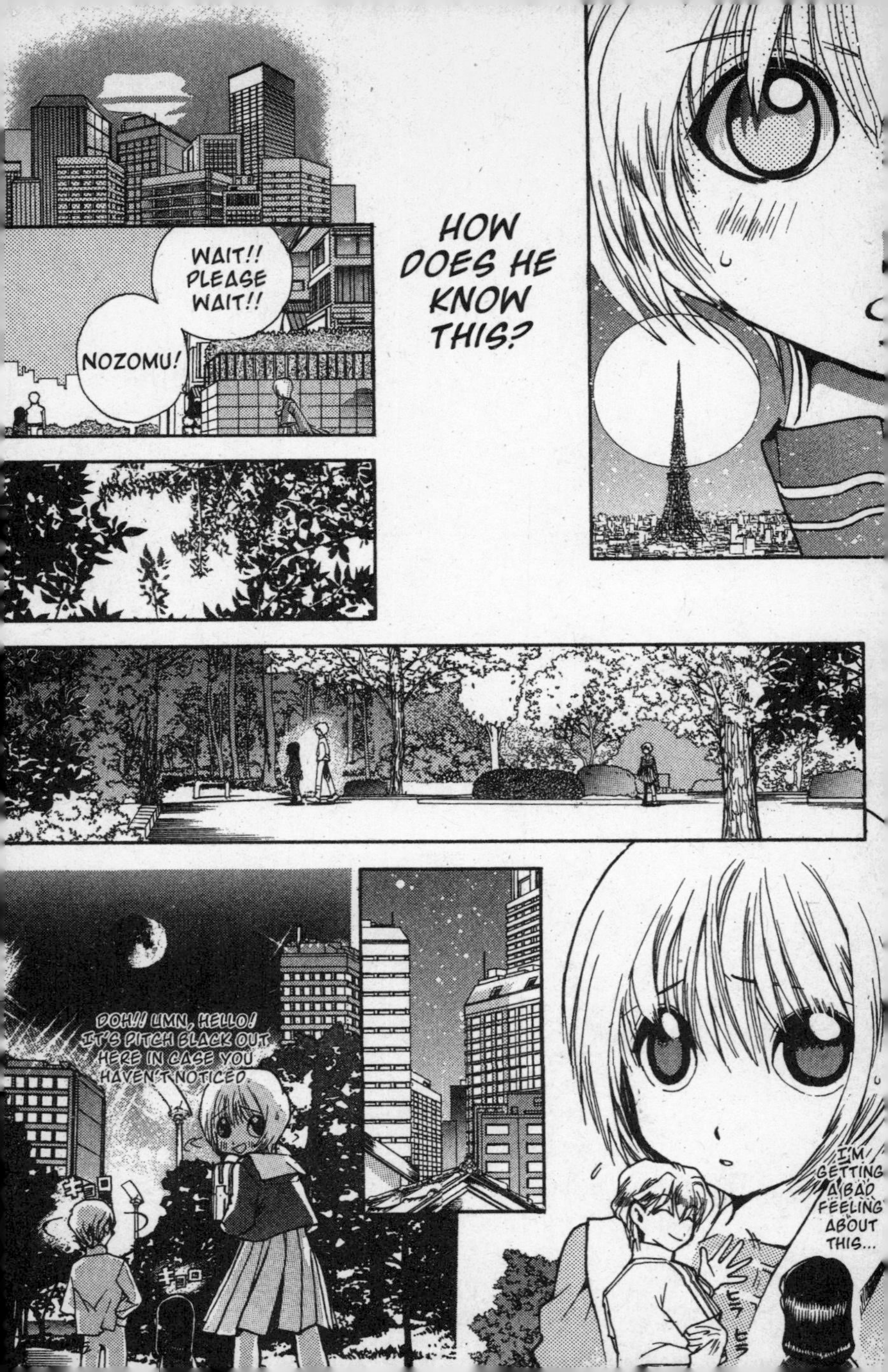
HOW DOES HE KNOW THIS?
WAIT!! PLEASE WAIT!!
NOZOMU!
I'M GETTING A BAD FEELING ABOUT THIS...
DOH!! UMN, HELLO! IT'S PITCH BLACK OUT HERE IN CASE YOU HAVEN'T NOTICED

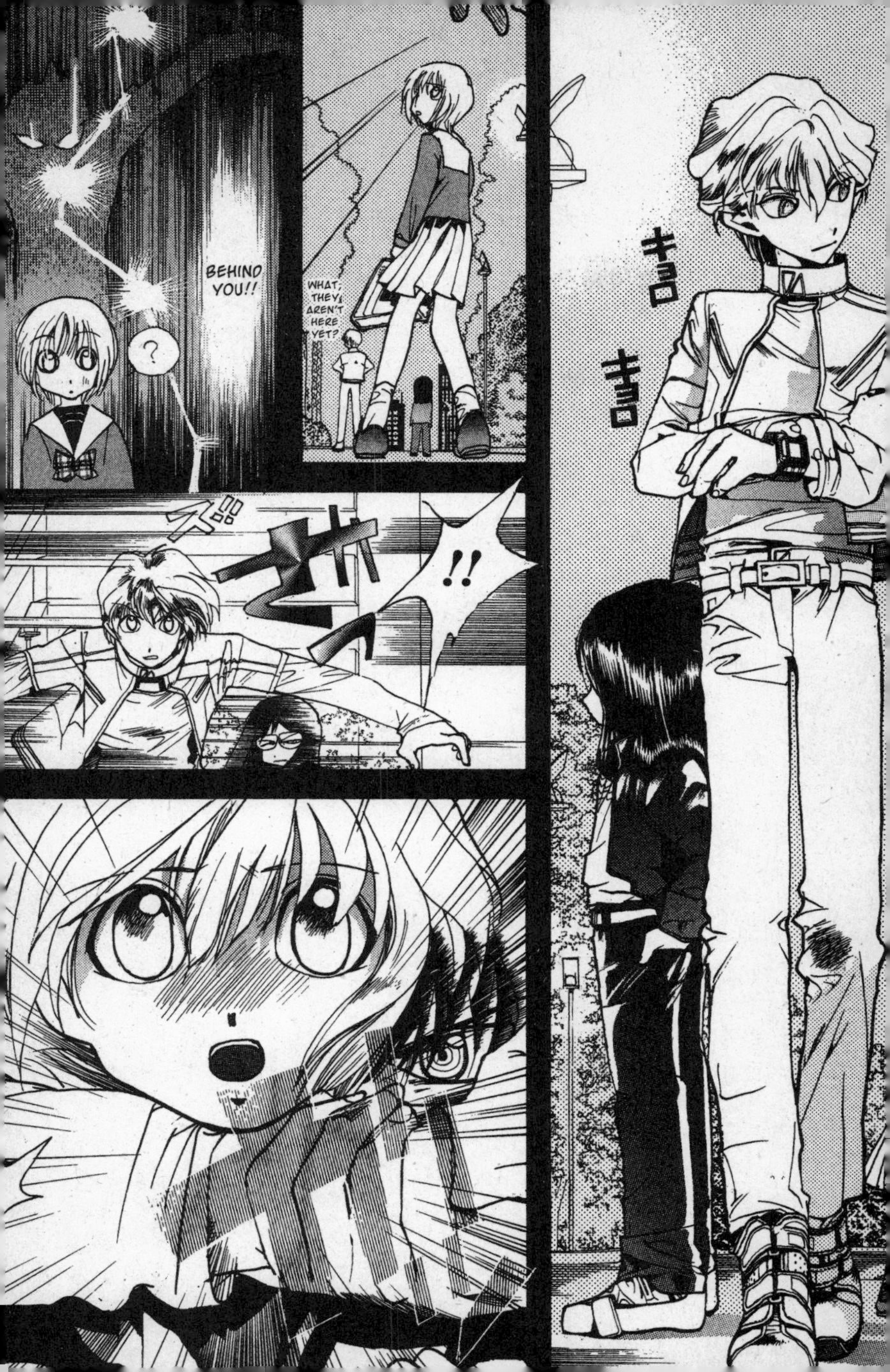
キョロ
キョロ
WHAT, THEY AREN'T HERE YET?
BEHIND YOU!!
?
!!

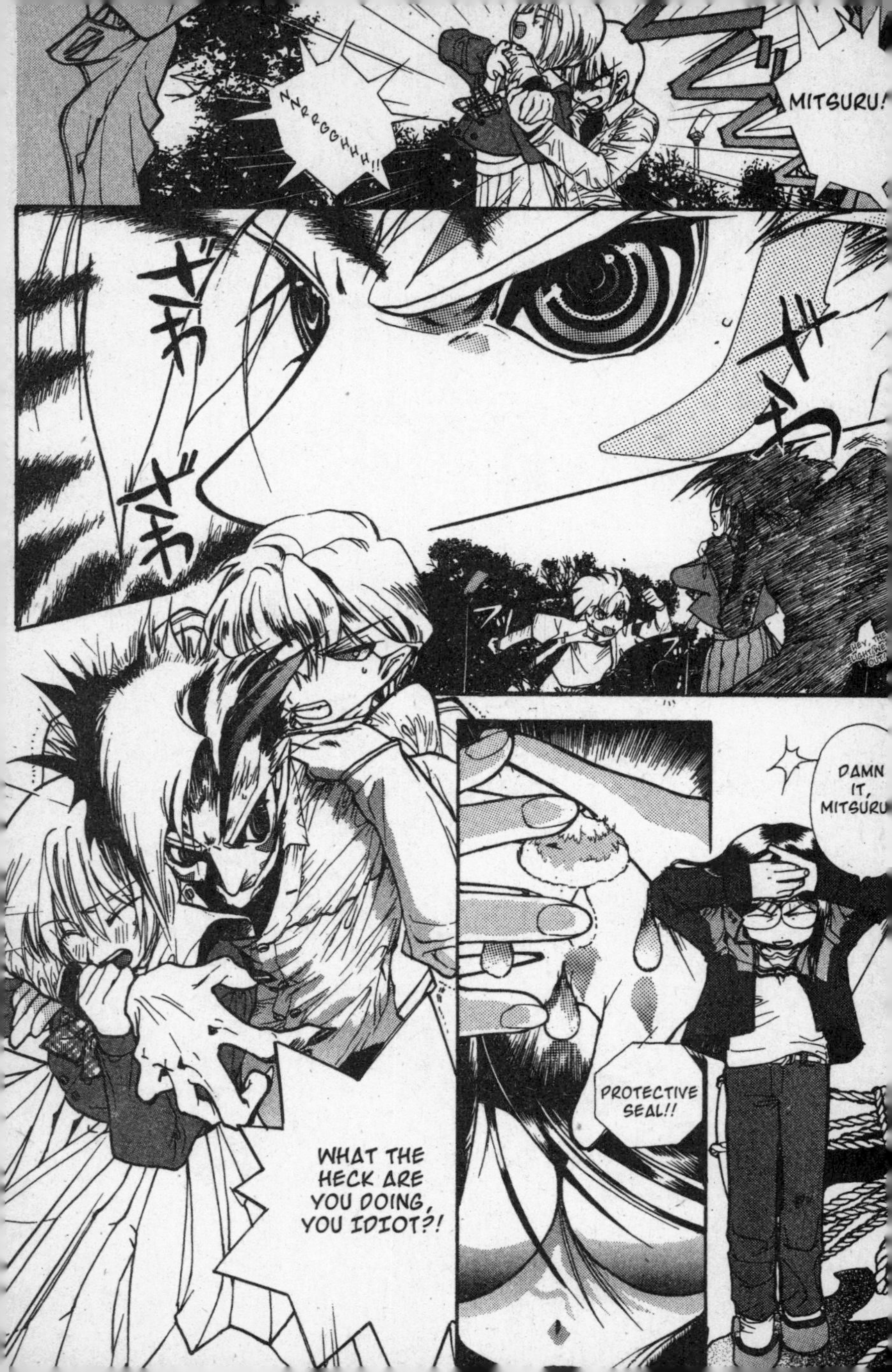
MITSURU!
NNNRRGGHHH!!
ざわ
ざわ
ざわ
HEY, THE LIGHTS WE OUT!
DAMN IT, MITSURU
PROTECTIVE SEAL!!
WHAT THE HECK ARE YOU DOING, YOU IDIOT?!

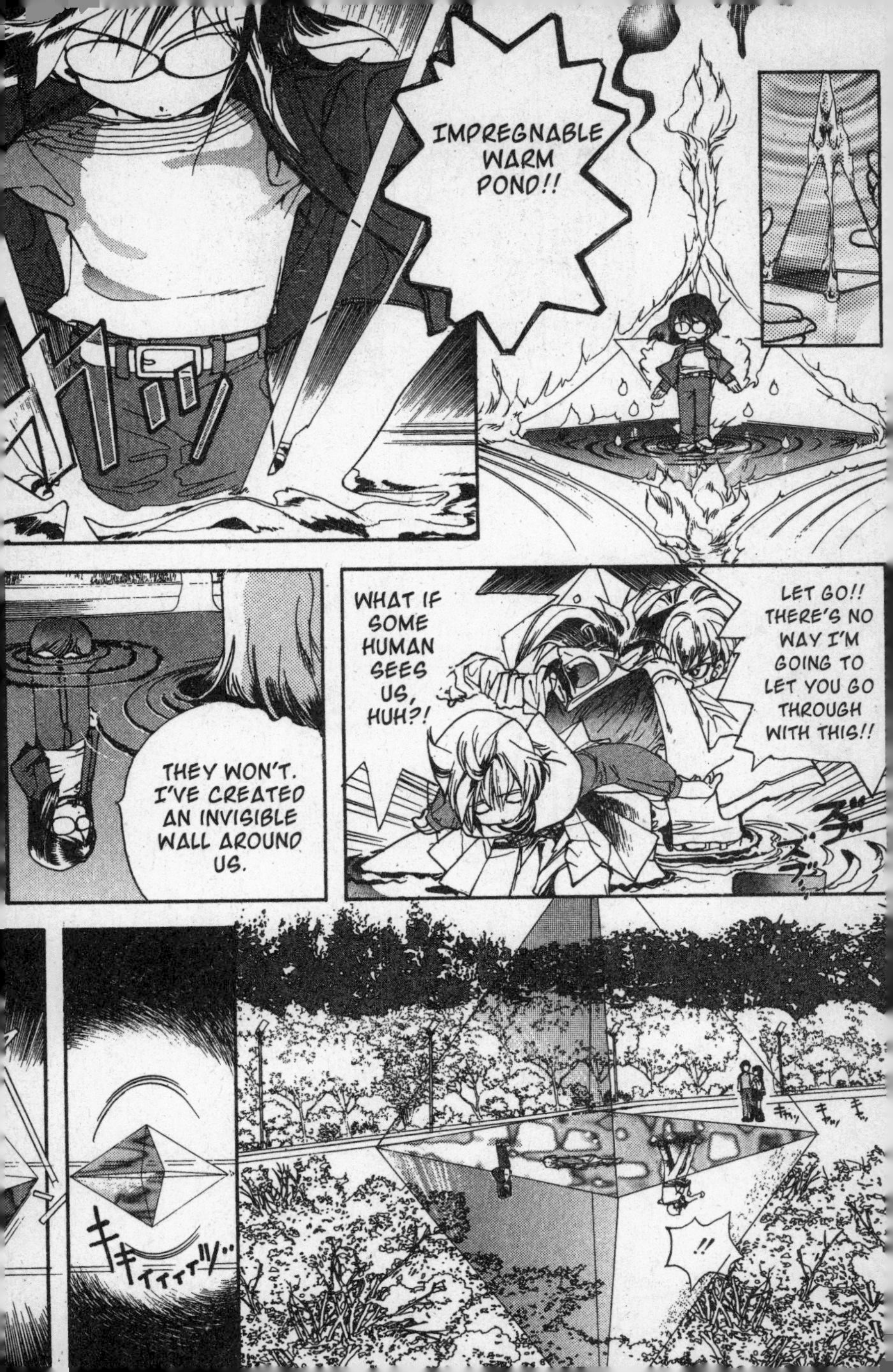
IMPREGNABLE WARM POND!!
LET GO!! THERE'S NO WAY I'M GOING TO LET YOU GO THROUGH WITH THIS!!
WHAT IF SOME HUMAN SEES US, HUH?!
THEY WON'T. I'VE CREATED AN INVISIBLE WALL AROUND US.
!!

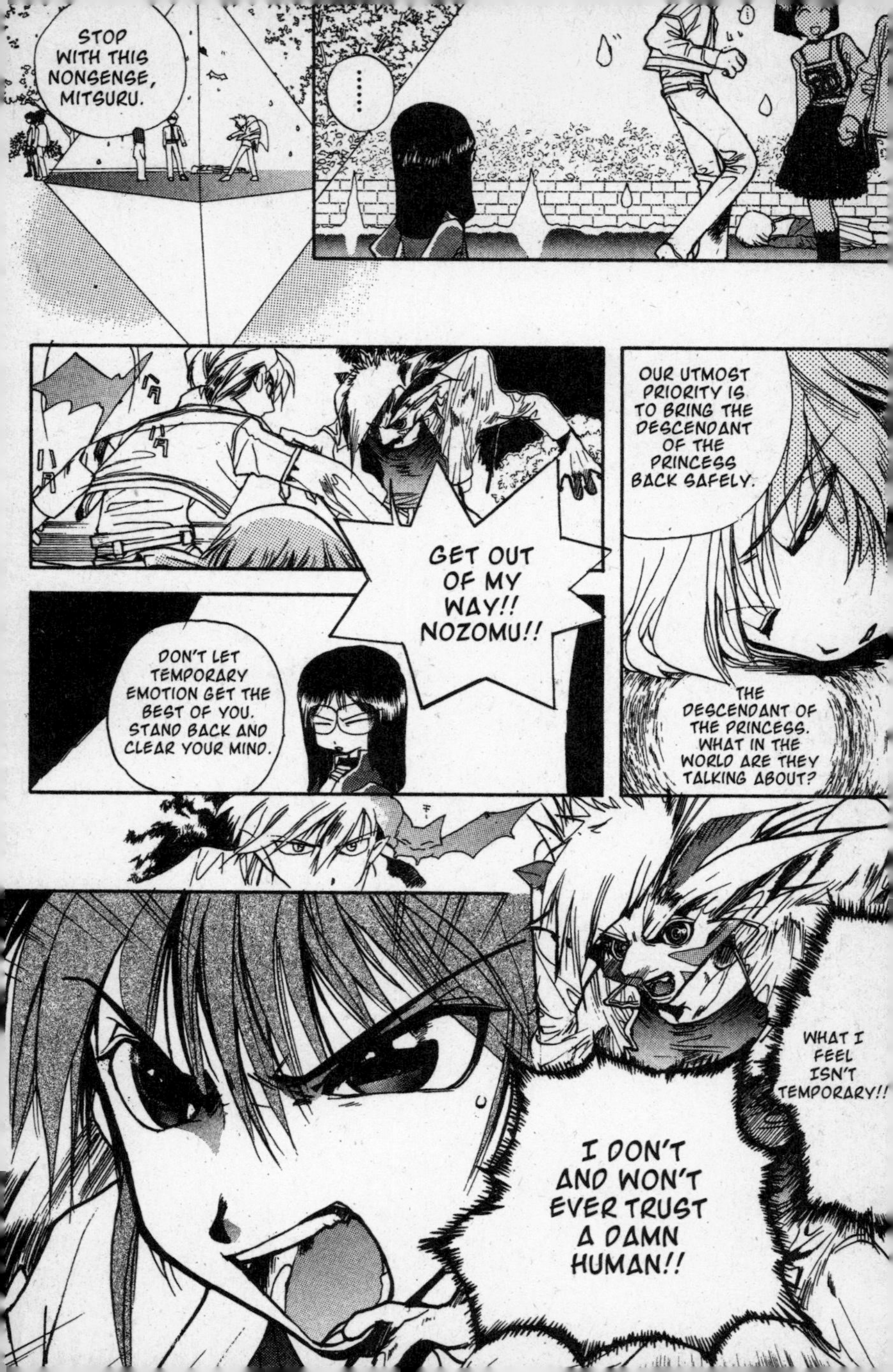
......
STOP WITH THIS NONSENSE, MITSURU.
OUR UTMOST PRIORITY IS TO BRING THE DESCENDANT OF THE PRINCESS BACK SAFELY.
THE DESCENDANT OF THE PRINCESS. WHAT IN THE WORLD ARE THEY TALKING ABOUT?
GET OUT OF MY WAY!! NOZOMU!!
DON'T LET TEMPORARY EMOTION GET THE BEST OF YOU. STAND BACK AND CLEAR YOUR MIND.
WHAT I FEEL ISN'T TEMPORARY!!
I DON'T AND WON'T EVER TRUST A DAMN HUMAN!!

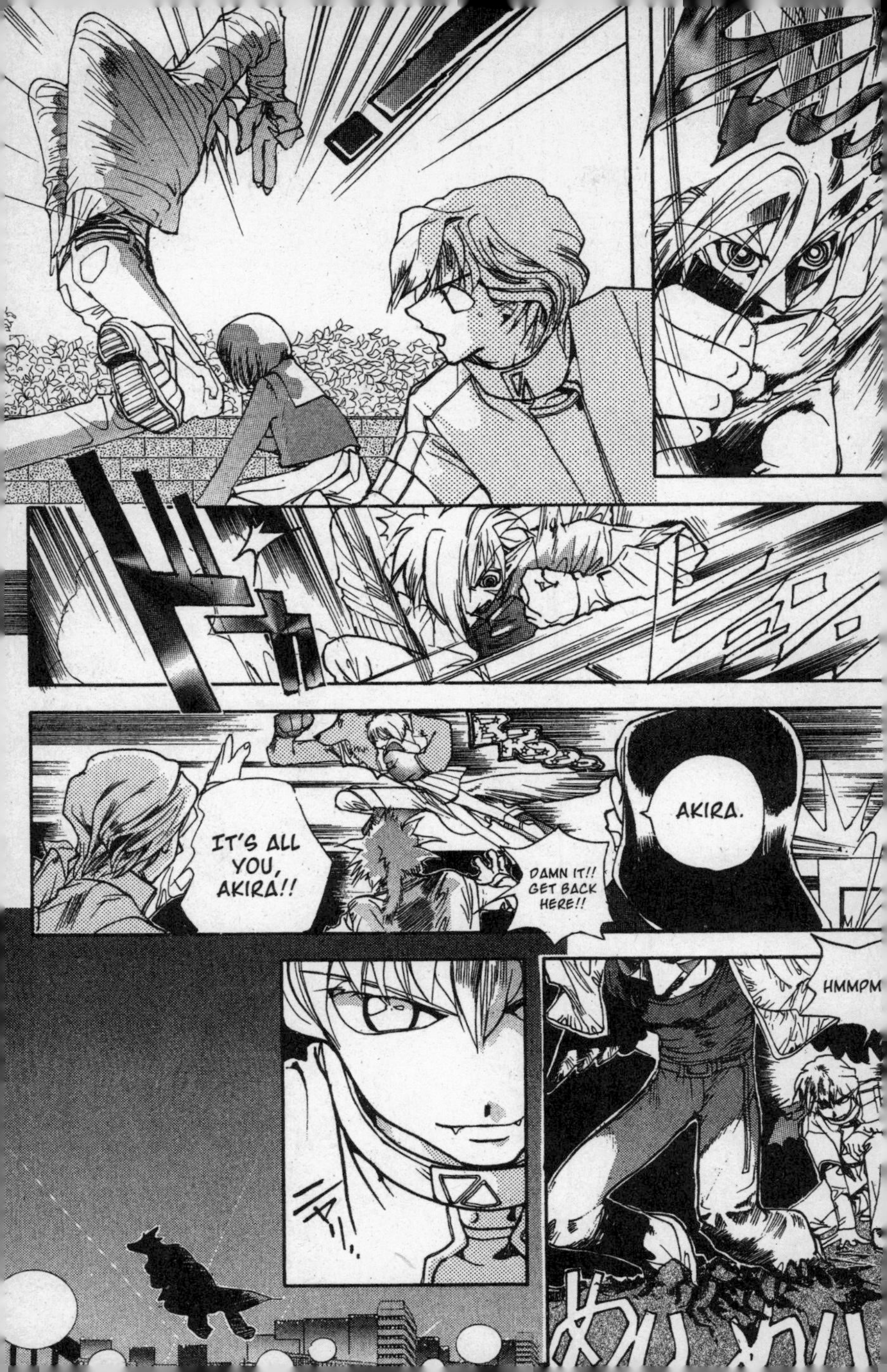
AKIRA.
DAMN IT!! GET BACK HERE!!
IT'S ALL YOU, AKIRA!!
HMMPM

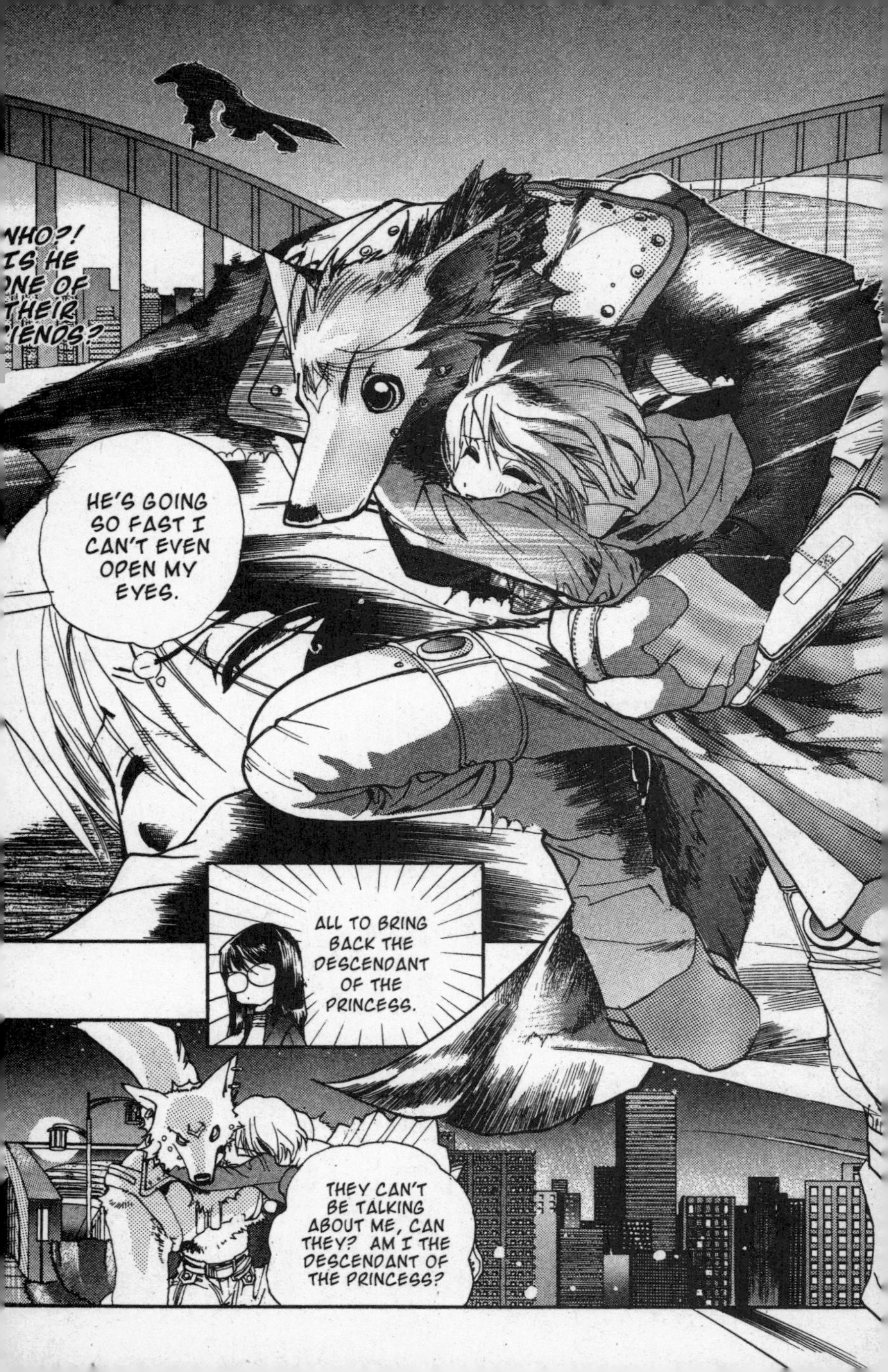
WHO?! IS HE ONE OF THEIR FRIENDS?
HE'S GOING SO FAST I CAN'T EVEN OPEN MY EYES.
ALL TO BRING BACK THE DESCENDANT OF THE PRINCESS.
THEY CAN'T BE TALKING ABOUT ME, CAN THEY? AM I THE DESCENDANT OF THE PRINCESS?

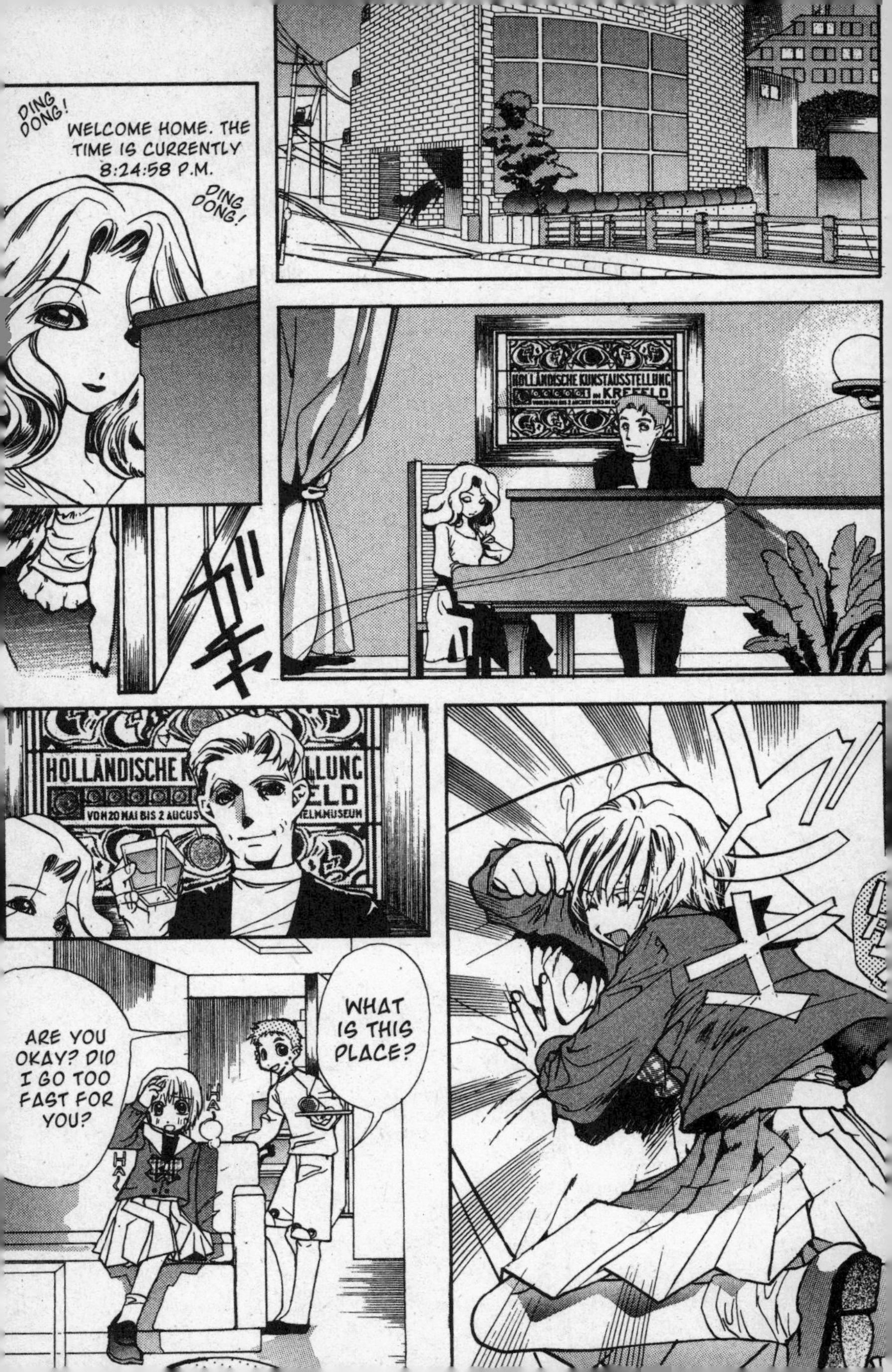
DING DONG!
WELCOME HOME. THE TIME IS CURRENTLY 8:24:58 P.M.
DING DONG!
HOLLÄNDISCHE KUNSTAUSSTELLUNG
KREFELD
ガチャ
WHAT IS THIS PLACE?
ARE YOU OKAY? DID I GO TOO FAST FOR YOU?
HA
HA

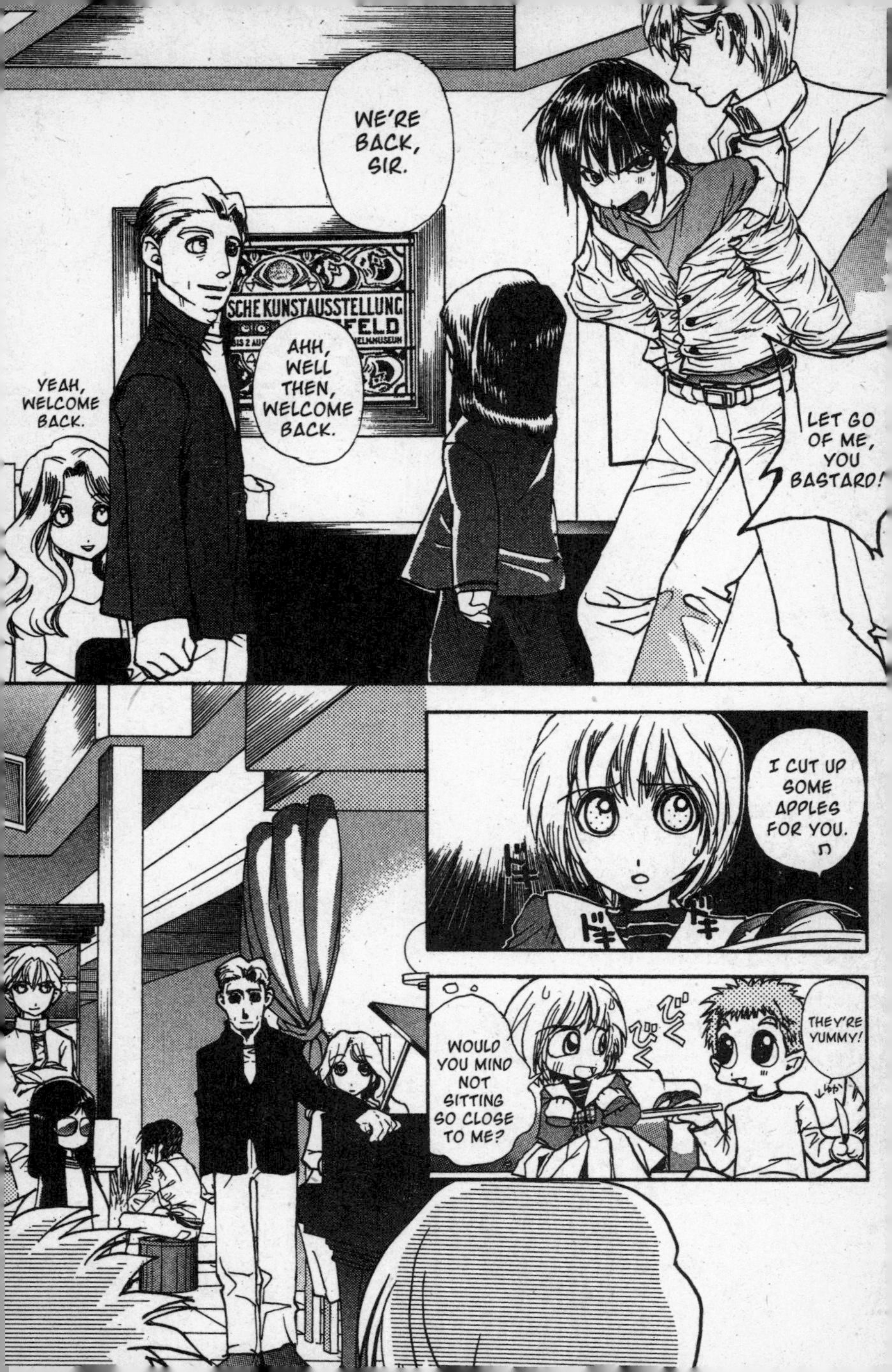
WE'RE BACK, SIR.
SCHE KUNSTAUSSTELLUNG
FELD
LET GO OF ME, YOU BASTARD!
AHH, WELL THEN, WELCOME BACK.
YEAH, WELCOME BACK.
I CUT UP SOME APPLES FOR YOU. ♫
ドキドキ
THEY'RE YUMMY!
びくびく
WOULD YOU MIND NOT SITTING SO CLOSE TO ME?

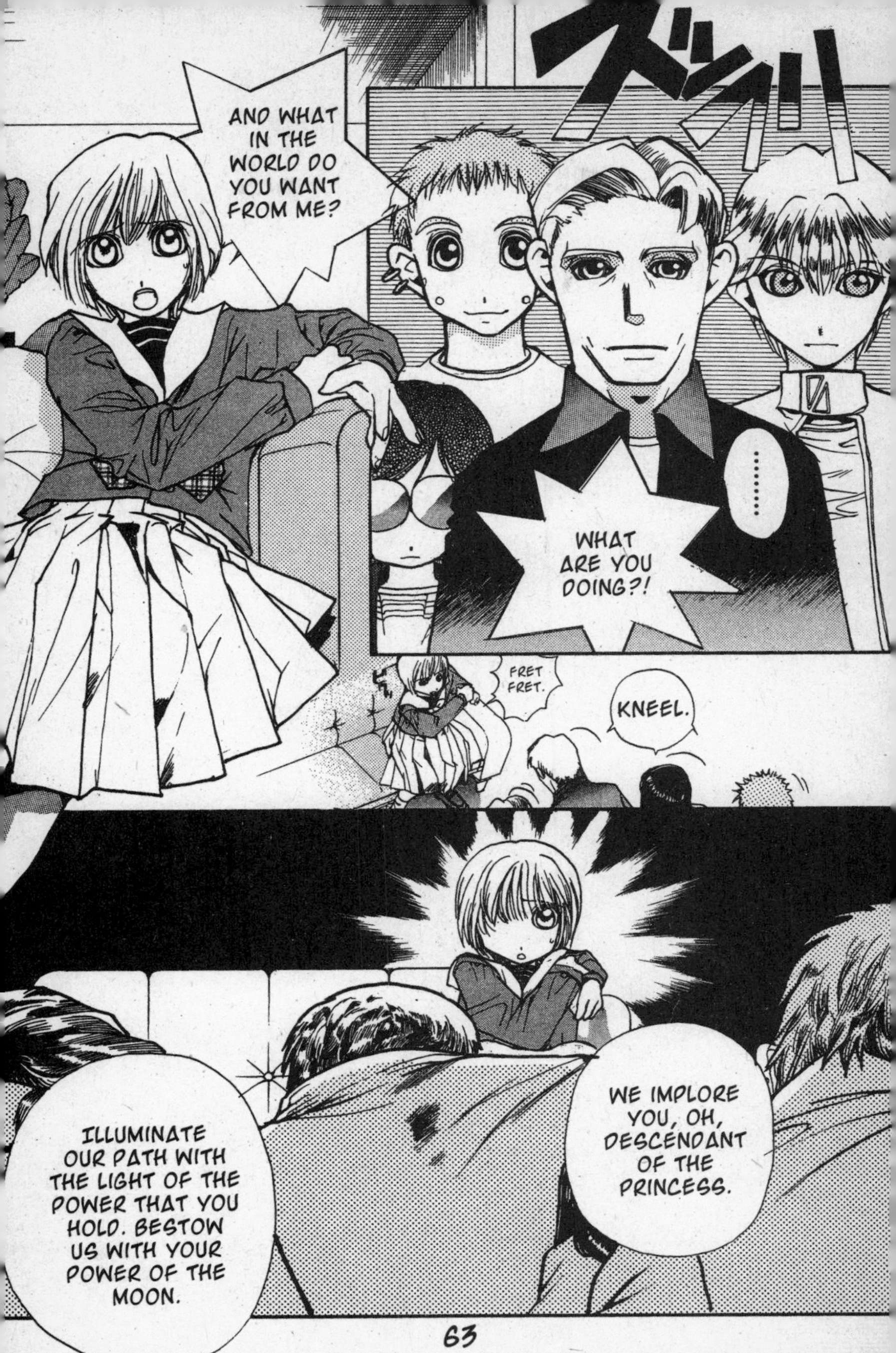
ズッ
......
WHAT ARE YOU DOING?!
KNEEL.
FRET FRET.
AND WHAT IN THE WORLD DO YOU WANT FROM ME?
WE IMPLORE YOU, OH, DESCENDANT OF THE PRINCESS.
ILLUMINATE OUR PATH WITH THE LIGHT OF THE POWER THAT YOU HOLD. BESTOW US WITH YOUR POWER OF THE MOON.

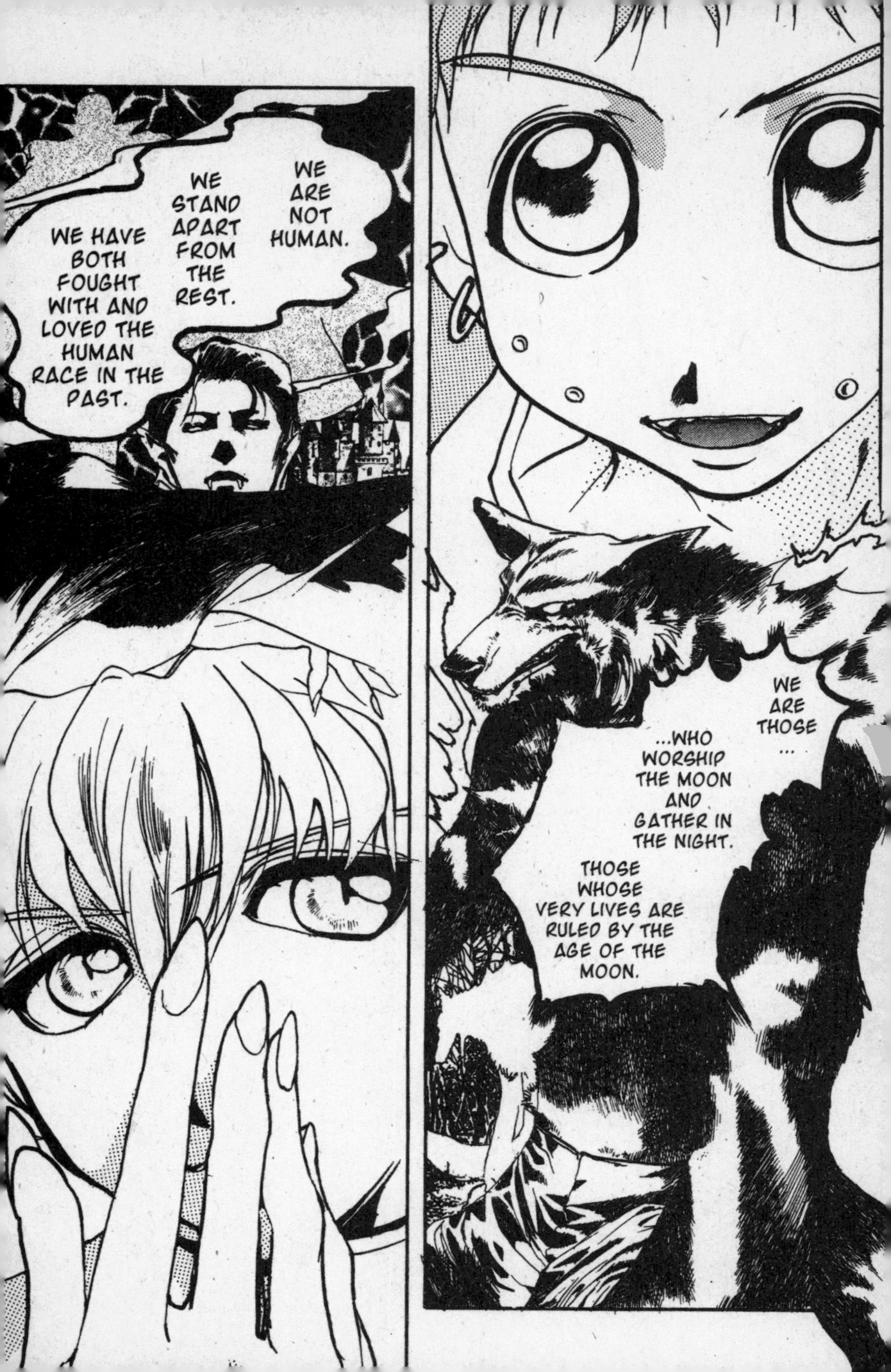
WE ARE THOSE ...
...WHO WORSHIP THE MOON AND GATHER IN THE NIGHT.
THOSE WHOSE VERY LIVES ARE RULED BY THE AGE OF THE MOON.
WE ARE NOT HUMAN.
WE STAND APART FROM THE REST.
WE HAVE BOTH FOUGHT WITH AND LOVED THE HUMAN RACE IN THE PAST.

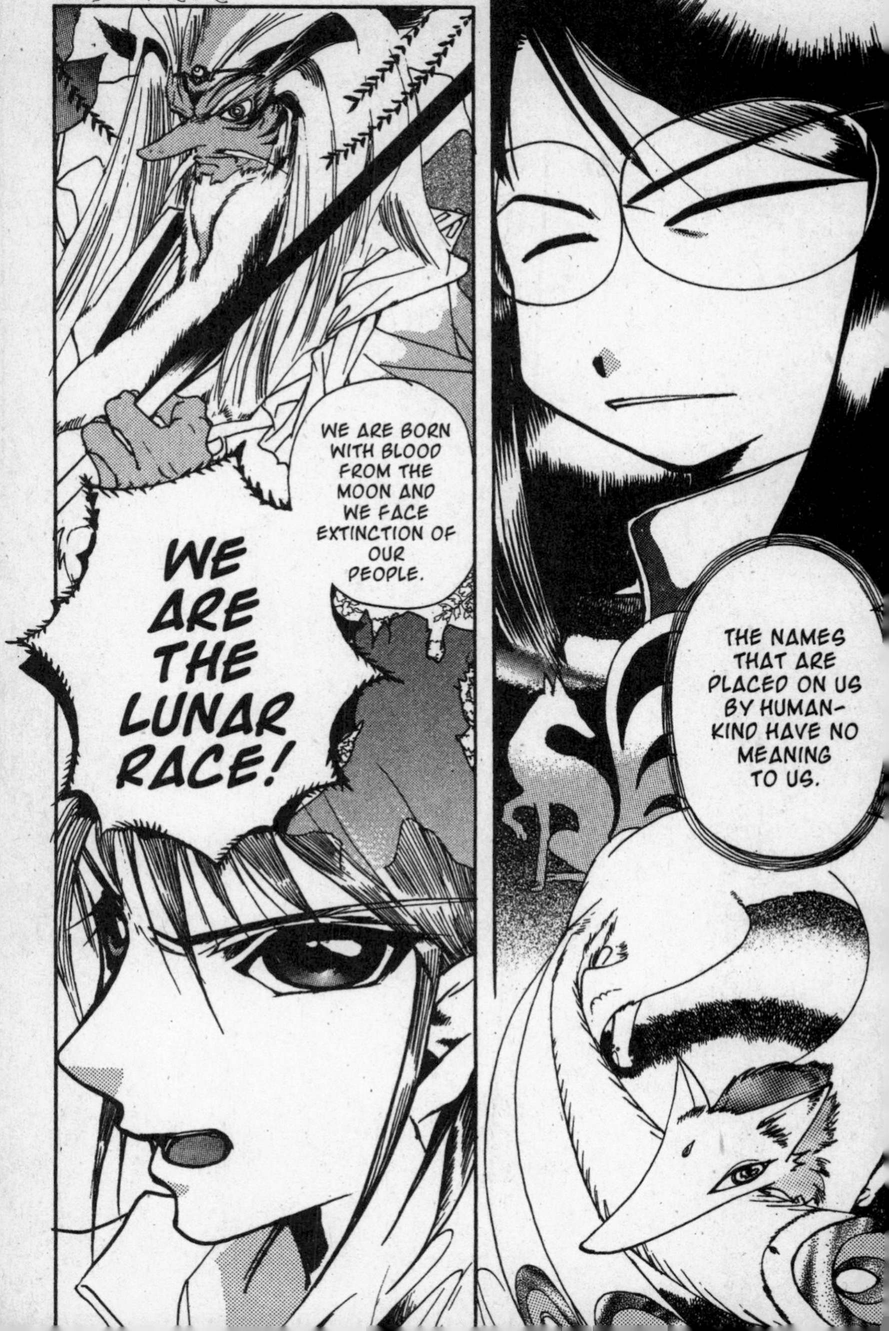
THE NAMES THAT ARE PLACED ON US BY HUMAN-KIND HAVE NO MEANING TO US.
WE ARE BORN WITH BLOOD FROM THE MOON AND WE FACE EXTINCTION OF OUR PEOPLE.
WE ARE THE LUNAR RACE!

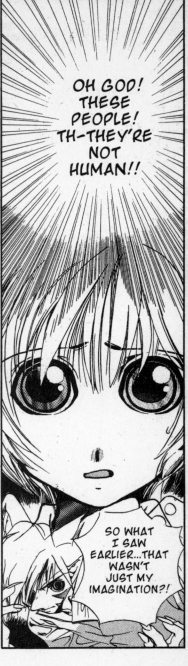

OH GOD! THESE PEOPLE! TH-THEY'RE NOT HUMAN!!

SO WHAT I SAW EARLIER...THAT WASN'T JUST MY IMAGINATION?!

MAHIRU?!

WAIT!!

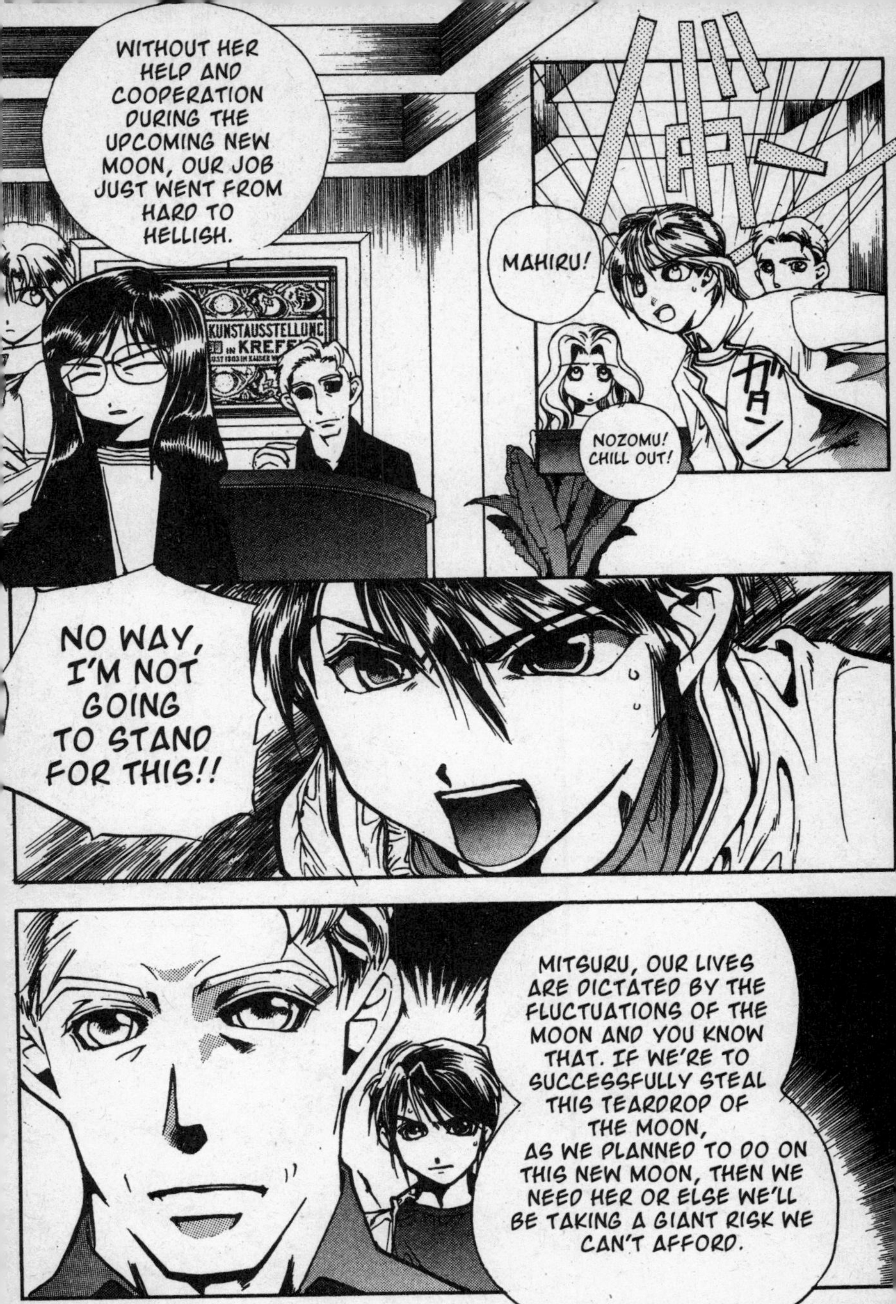
MAHIRU!
NOZOMU! CHILL OUT!
WITHOUT HER HELP AND COOPERATION DURING THE UPCOMING NEW MOON, OUR JOB JUST WENT FROM HARD TO HELLISH.
KUNSTAUSSTELLUNG
NO WAY, I'M NOT GOING TO STAND FOR THIS!!
MITSURU, OUR LIVES ARE DICTATED BY THE FLUCTUATIONS OF THE MOON AND YOU KNOW THAT. IF WE'RE TO SUCCESSFULLY STEAL THIS TEARDROP OF THE MOON, AS WE PLANNED TO DO ON THIS NEW MOON, THEN WE NEED HER OR ELSE WE'LL BE TAKING A GIANT RISK WE CAN'T AFFORD.

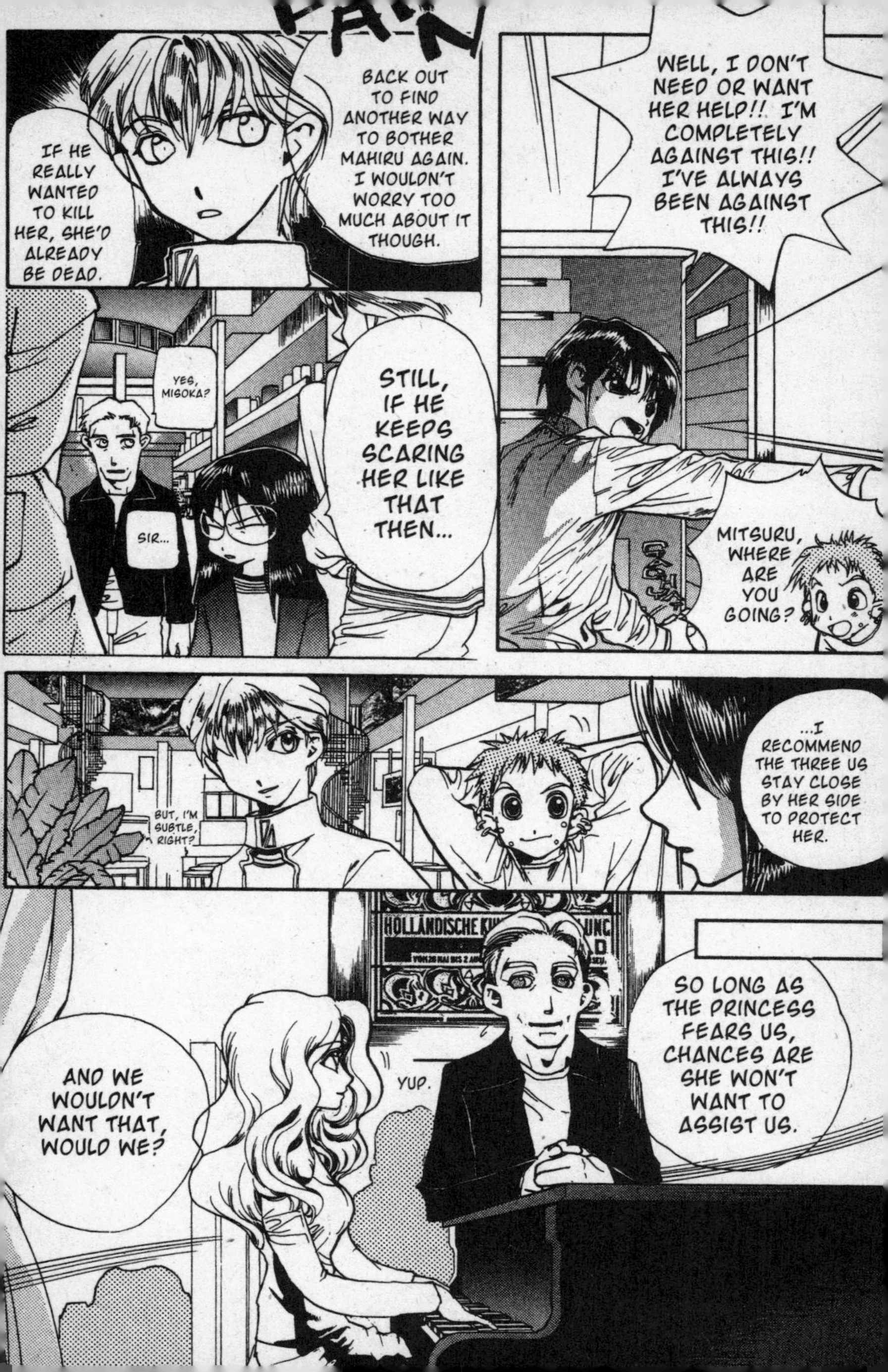
WELL, I DON'T NEED OR WANT HER HELP!! I'M COMPLETELY AGAINST THIS!! I'VE ALWAYS BEEN AGAINST THIS!!
BACK OUT TO FIND ANOTHER WAY TO BOTHER MAHIRU AGAIN. I WOULDN'T WORRY TOO MUCH ABOUT IT THOUGH.
IF HE REALLY WANTED TO KILL HER, SHE'D ALREADY BE DEAD.
MITSURU, WHERE ARE YOU GOING?
STILL, IF HE KEEPS SCARING HER LIKE THAT THEN...
YES, MISOKA?
SIR...
...I RECOMMEND THE THREE US STAY CLOSE BY HER SIDE TO PROTECT HER.
BUT, I'M SUBTLE, RIGHT?
SO LONG AS THE PRINCESS FEARS US, CHANCES ARE SHE WON'T WANT TO ASSIST US.
YUP.
AND WE WOULDN'T WANT THAT, WOULD WE?

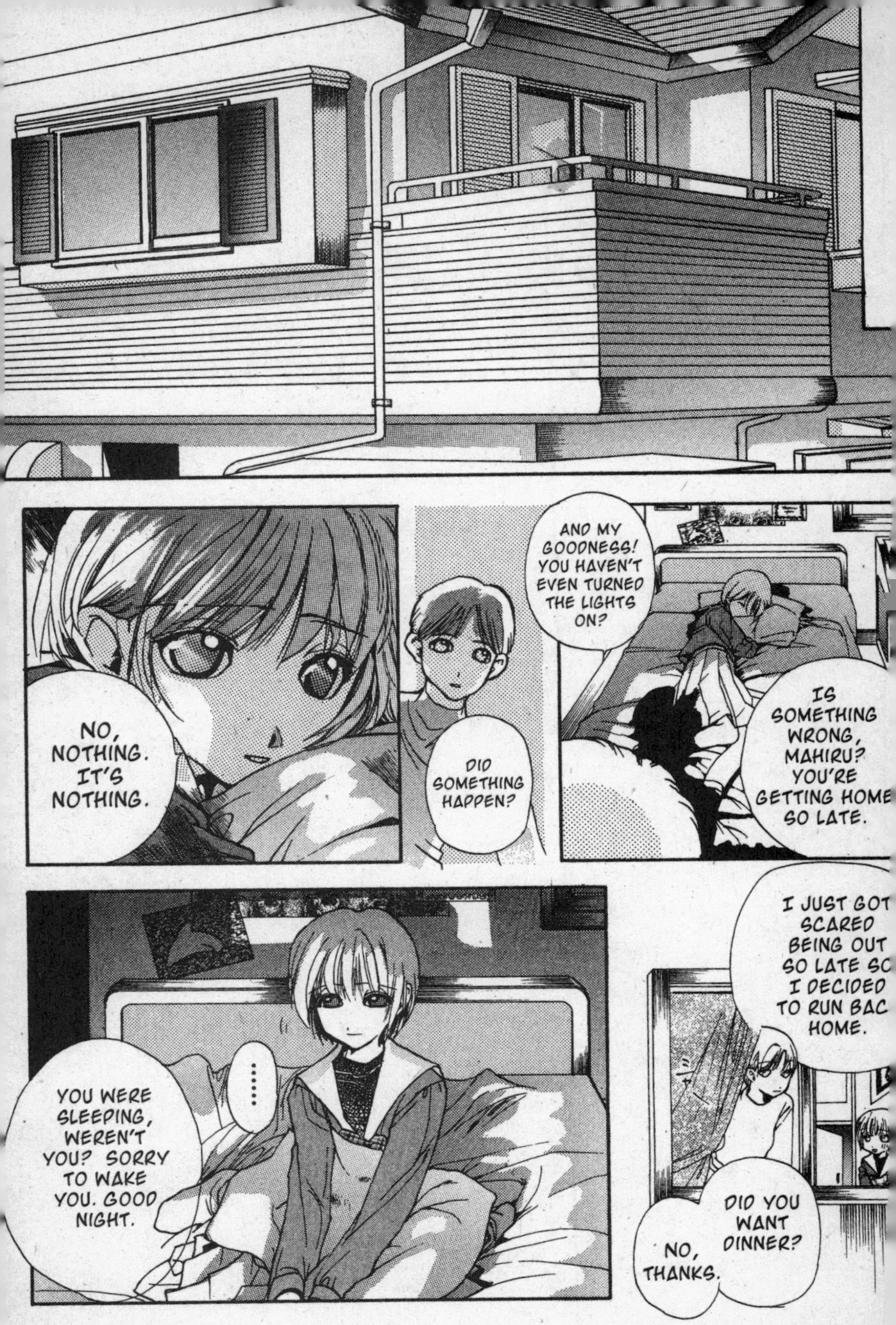
IS SOMETHING WRONG, MAHIRU? YOU'RE GETTING HOME SO LATE.
AND MY GOODNESS! YOU HAVEN'T EVEN TURNED THE LIGHTS ON?
DID SOMETHING HAPPEN?
NO, NOTHING. IT'S NOTHING.
I JUST GOT SCARED BEING OUT SO LATE SO I DECIDED TO RUN BACK HOME.
DID YOU WANT DINNER?
NO, THANKS.
......
YOU WERE SLEEPING, WEREN'T YOU? SORRY TO WAKE YOU. GOOD NIGHT.

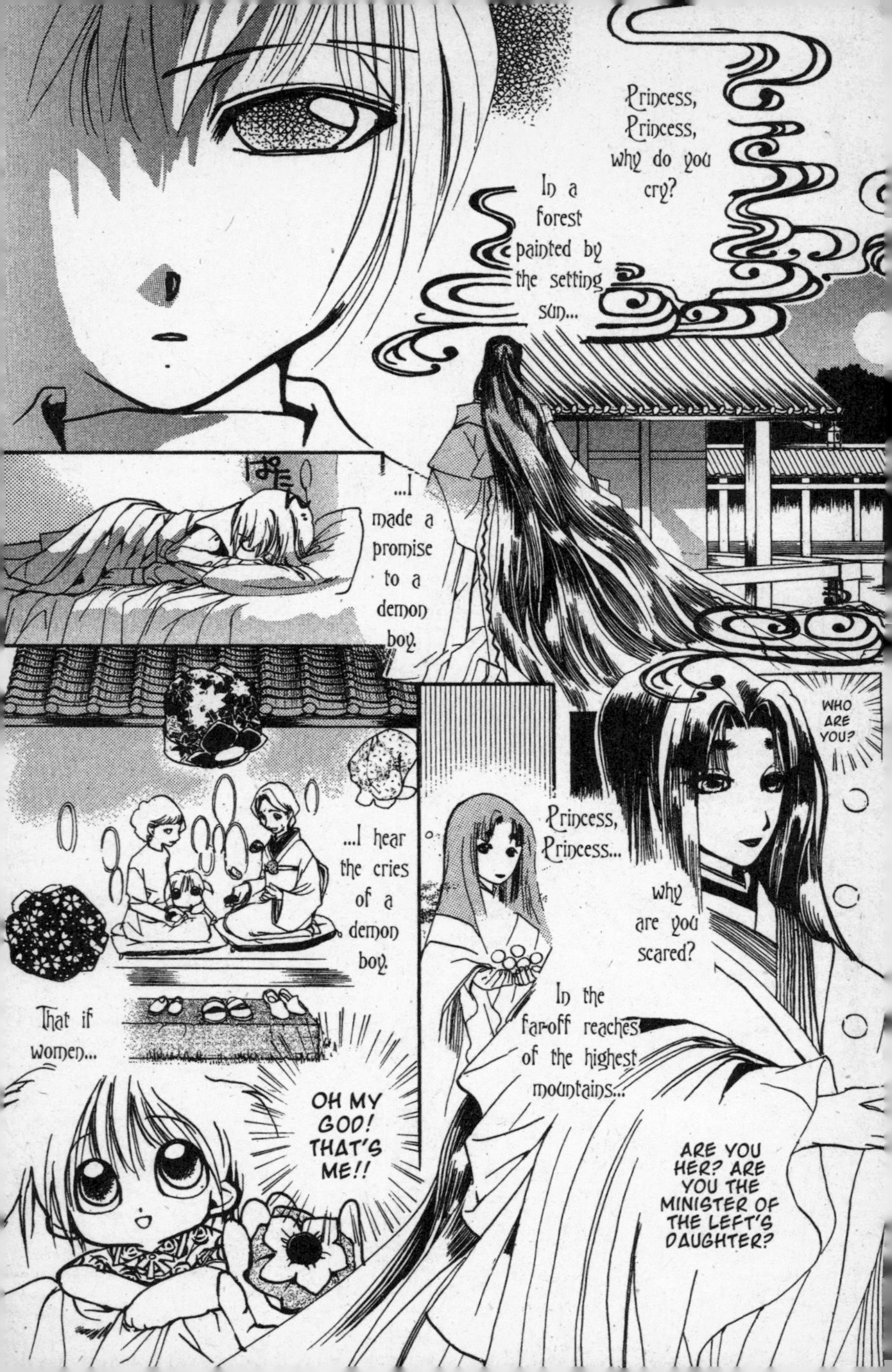
Princess, Princess, why do you cry?
In a forest painted by the setting sun...
ぱた
...I made a promise to a demon boy.
WHO ARE YOU?
Princess, Princess...
why are you scared?
In the far-off reaches of the highest mountains...
ARE YOU HER? ARE YOU THE MINISTER OF THE LEFT'S DAUGHTER?
...I hear the cries of a demon boy.
That if women...
OH MY GOD! THAT'S ME!!

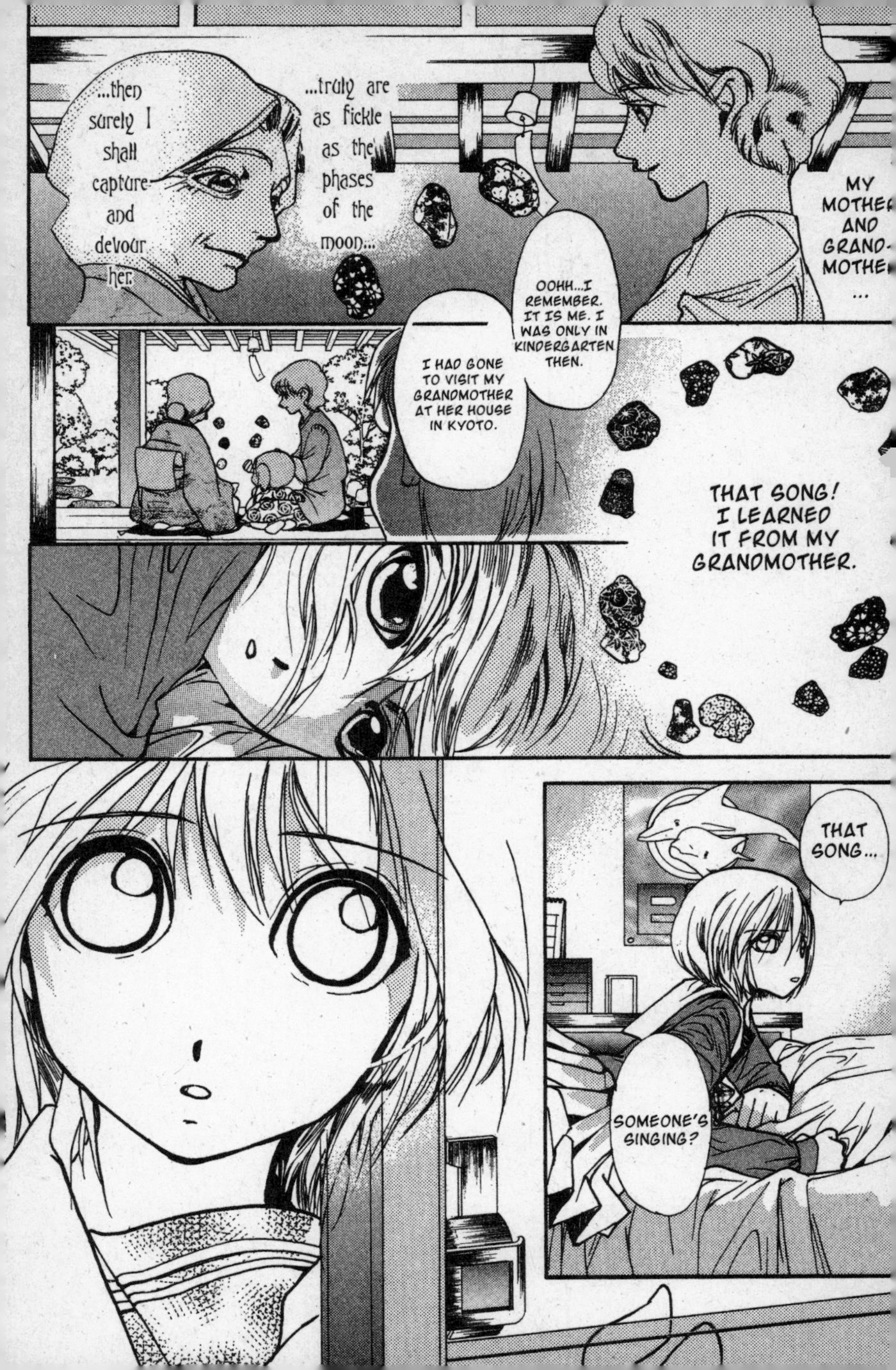
MY MOTHER AND GRAND-MOTHER...
...truly are as fickle as the phases of the moon...
...then surely I shall capture and devour her.
OOHH...I REMEMBER. IT IS ME. I WAS ONLY IN KINDERGARTEN THEN.
I HAD GONE TO VISIT MY GRANDMOTHER AT HER HOUSE IN KYOTO.
THAT SONG! I LEARNED IT FROM MY GRANDMOTHER.
THAT SONG...
SOMEONE'S SINGING?

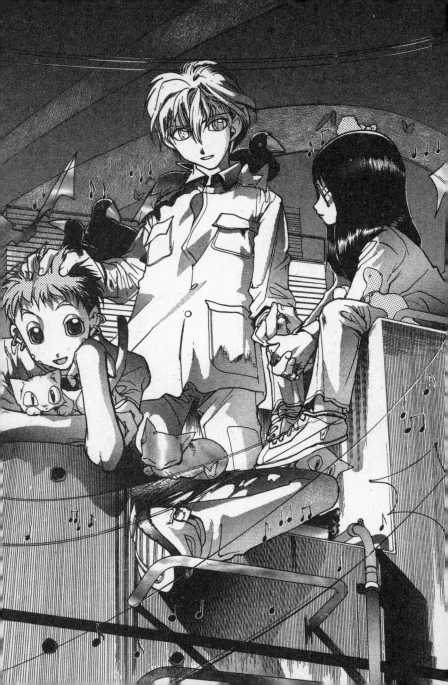

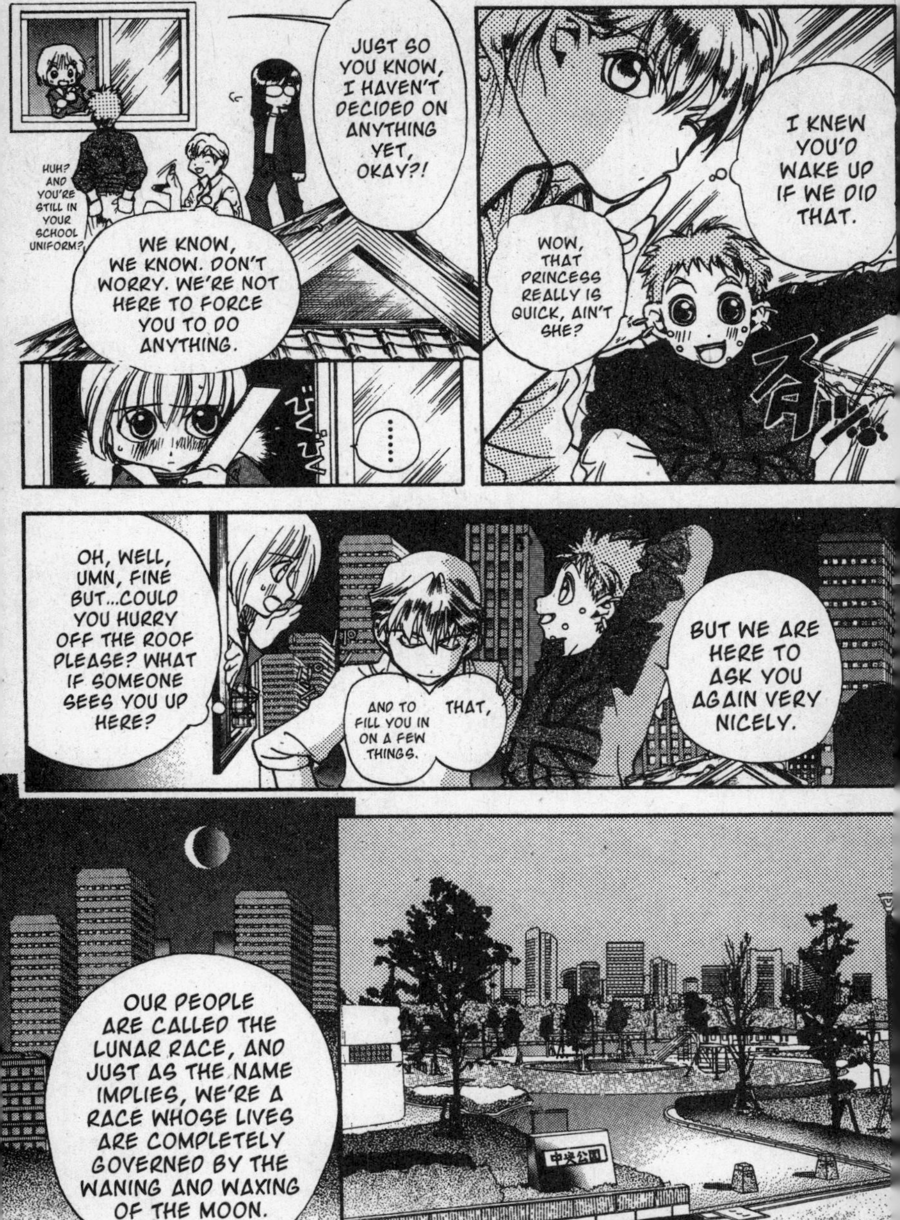
I KNEW YOU'D WAKE UP IF WE DID THAT.
WOW, THAT PRINCESS REALLY IS QUICK, AIN'T SHE?
JUST SO YOU KNOW, I HAVEN'T DECIDED ON ANYTHING YET, OKAY?!
HUH? AND YOU'RE STILL IN YOUR SCHOOL UNIFORM?
WE KNOW, WE KNOW. DON'T WORRY. WE'RE NOT HERE TO FORCE YOU TO DO ANYTHING.
......
BUT WE ARE HERE TO ASK YOU AGAIN VERY NICELY.
THAT, AND TO FILL YOU IN ON A FEW THINGS.
OH, WELL, UMN, FINE BUT...COULD YOU HURRY OFF THE ROOF PLEASE? WHAT IF SOMEONE SEES YOU UP HERE?
中央公園
OUR PEOPLE ARE CALLED THE LUNAR RACE, AND JUST AS THE NAME IMPLIES, WE'RE A RACE WHOSE LIVES ARE COMPLETELY GOVERNED BY THE WANING AND WAXING OF THE MOON.

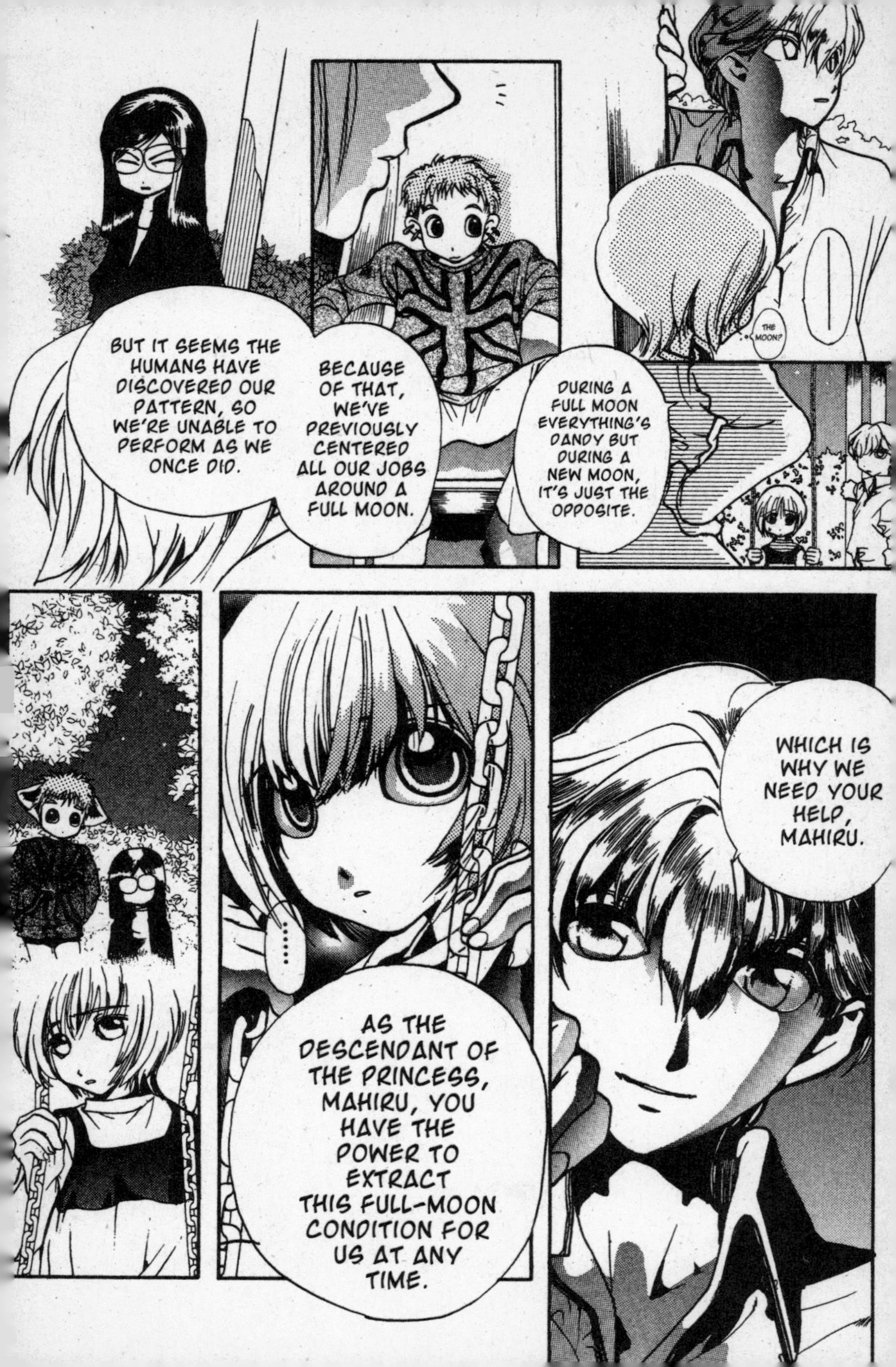
THE MOON?
DURING A FULL MOON EVERYTHING'S DANDY BUT DURING A NEW MOON, IT'S JUST THE OPPOSITE.
BECAUSE OF THAT, WE'VE PREVIOUSLY CENTERED ALL OUR JOBS AROUND A FULL MOON.
BUT IT SEEMS THE HUMANS HAVE DISCOVERED OUR PATTERN, SO WE'RE UNABLE TO PERFORM AS WE ONCE DID.
WHICH IS WHY WE NEED YOUR HELP, MAHIRU.
AS THE DESCENDANT OF THE PRINCESS, MAHIRU, YOU HAVE THE POWER TO EXTRACT THIS FULL-MOON CONDITION FOR US AT ANY TIME.

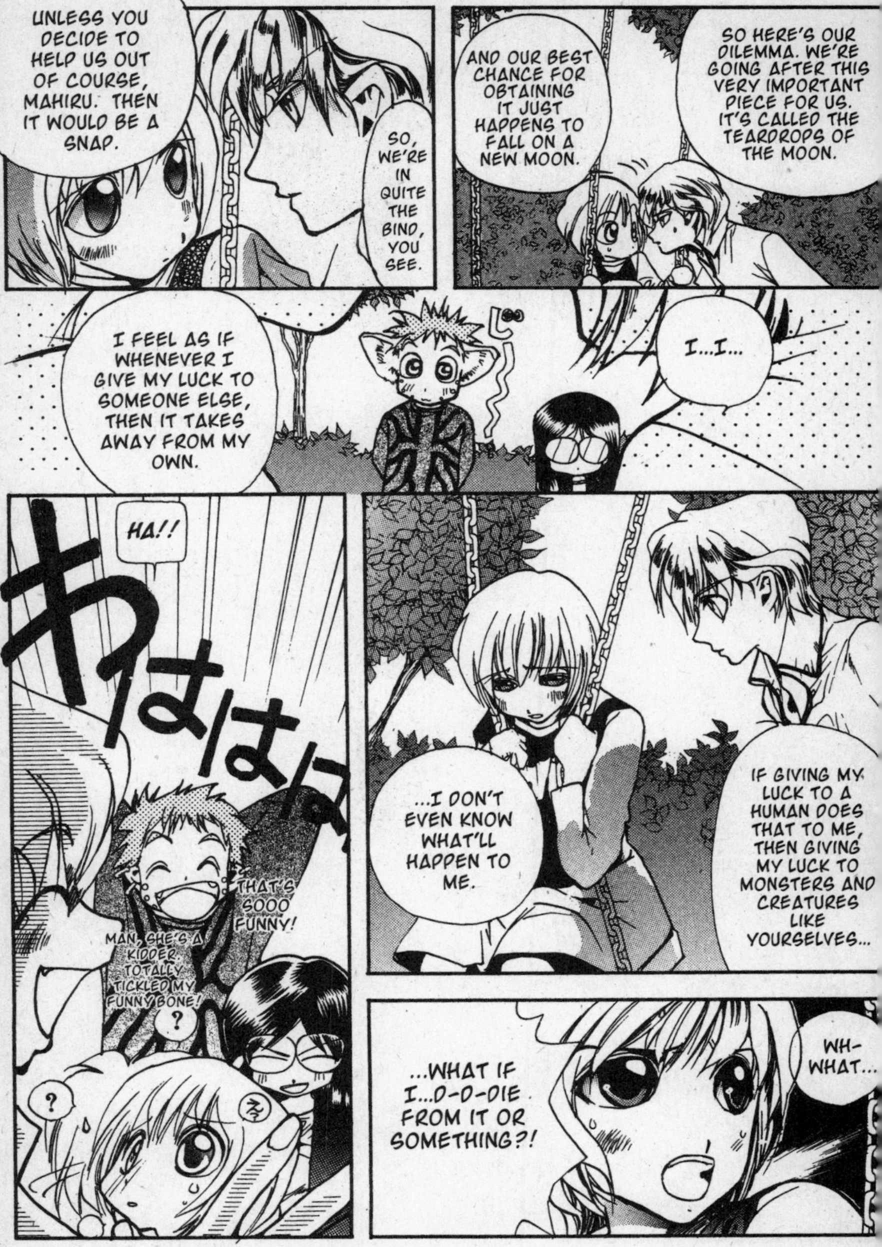
SO HERE'S OUR DILEMMA. WE'RE GOING AFTER THIS VERY IMPORTANT PIECE FOR US. IT'S CALLED THE TEARDROPS OF THE MOON.
AND OUR BEST CHANCE FOR OBTAINING IT JUST HAPPENS TO FALL ON A NEW MOON.
SO, WE'RE IN QUITE THE BIND, YOU SEE.
UNLESS YOU DECIDE TO HELP US OUT OF COURSE, MAHIRU. THEN IT WOULD BE A SNAP.
I...I...
じ
I FEEL AS IF WHENEVER I GIVE MY LUCK TO SOMEONE ELSE, THEN IT TAKES AWAY FROM MY OWN.
IF GIVING MY LUCK TO A HUMAN DOES THAT TO ME, THEN GIVING MY LUCK TO MONSTERS AND CREATURES LIKE YOURSELVES...
...I DON'T EVEN KNOW WHAT'LL HAPPEN TO ME.
WH-WHAT...
...WHAT IF I...D-D-DIE FROM IT OR SOMETHING?!
やはは
HA!!
THAT'S SOOO FUNNY!
MAN, SHE'S A KIDDER. TOTALLY TICKLED MY FUNNY BONE!
?
?

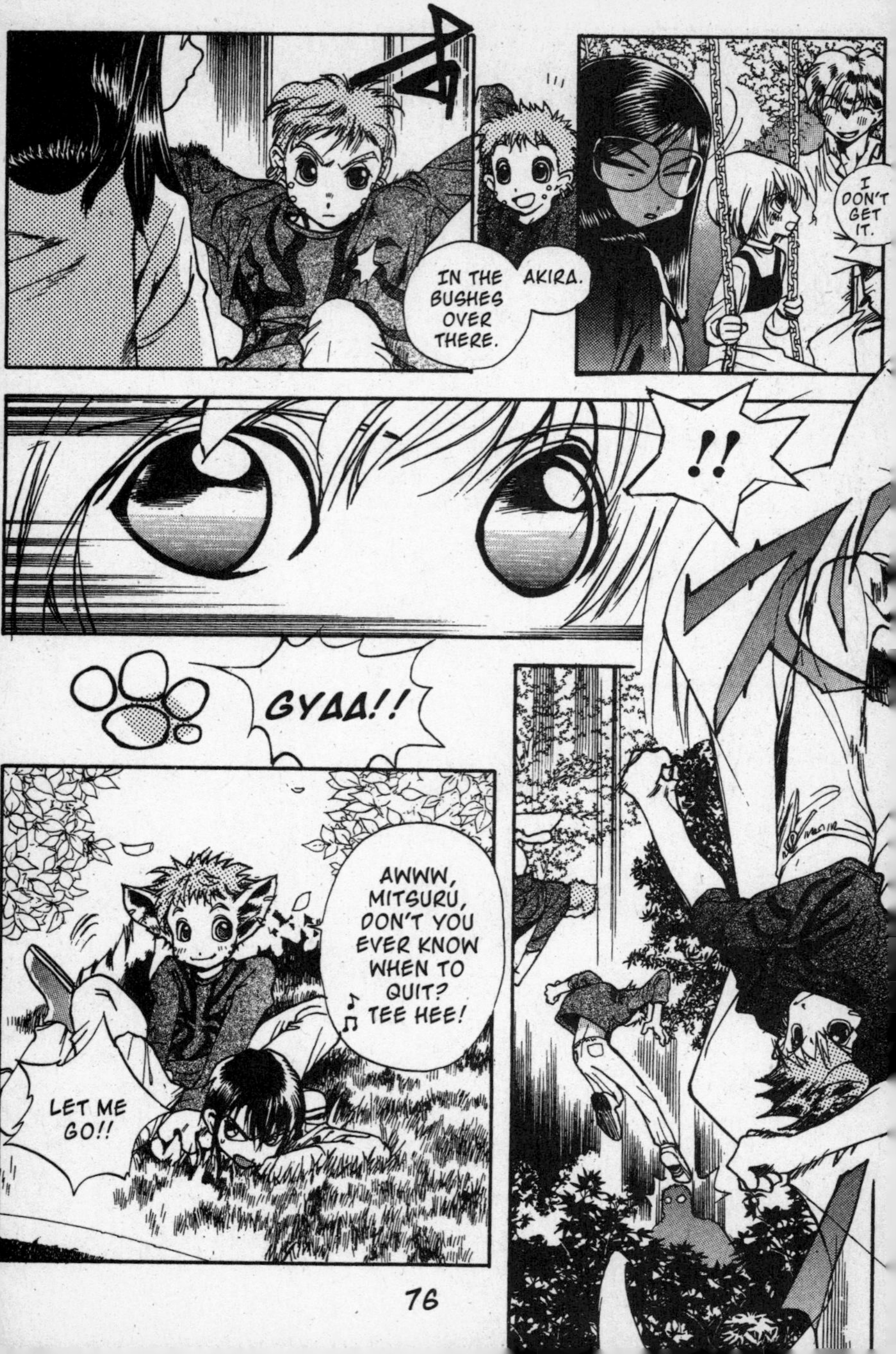
I DON'T GET IT.
AKIRA.
IN THE BUSHES OVER THERE.
!!
GYAA!!
AWWW, MITSURU, DON'T YOU EVER KNOW WHEN TO QUIT? ♪ TEE HEE!
LET ME GO!!

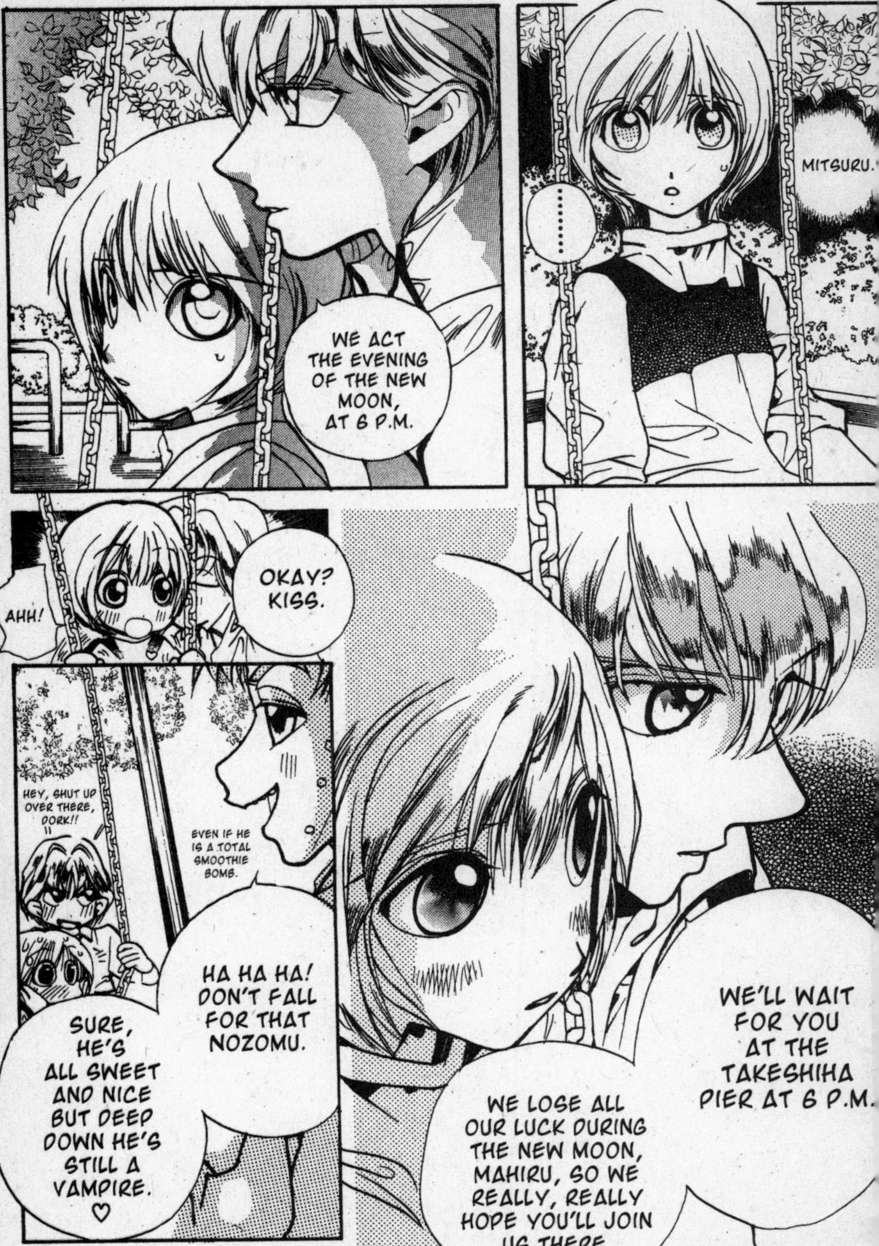

......
MITSURU.
WE ACT THE EVENING OF THE NEW MOON, AT 6 P.M.
WE'LL WAIT FOR YOU AT THE TAKESHIHA PIER AT 6 P.M.
WE LOSE ALL OUR LUCK DURING THE NEW MOON, MAHIRU, SO WE REALLY, REALLY HOPE YOU'LL JOIN US THERE.
OKAY? KISS.
AHH!
HA HA HA! DON'T FALL FOR THAT NOZOMU.
EVEN IF HE IS A TOTAL SMOOTHIE BOMB.
SURE, HE'S ALL SWEET AND NICE BUT DEEP DOWN HE'S STILL A VAMPIRE. ♡
HEY, SHUT UP OVER THERE, DORK!!

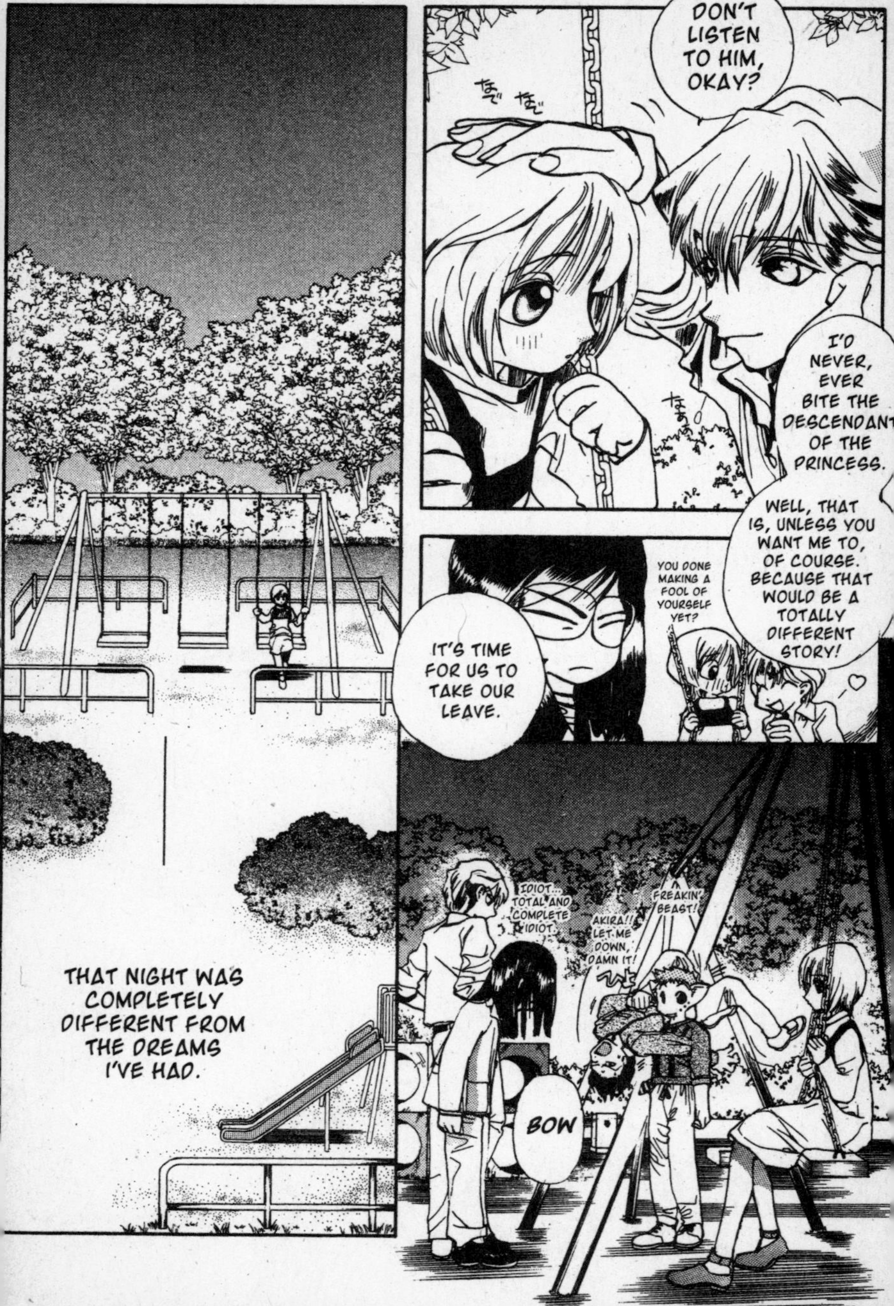
DON'T LISTEN TO HIM, OKAY?
I'D NEVER, EVER BITE THE DESCENDANT OF THE PRINCESS.
WELL, THAT IS, UNLESS YOU WANT ME TO, OF COURSE. BECAUSE THAT WOULD BE A TOTALLY DIFFERENT STORY!
YOU DONE MAKING A FOOL OF YOURSELF YET?
IT'S TIME FOR US TO TAKE OUR LEAVE.
FREAKIN' BEAST!
IDIOT... TOTAL AND COMPLETE IDIOT.
AKIRA!! LET ME DOWN, DAMN IT!
BOW
THAT NIGHT WAS COMPLETELY DIFFERENT FROM THE DREAMS I'VE HAD.

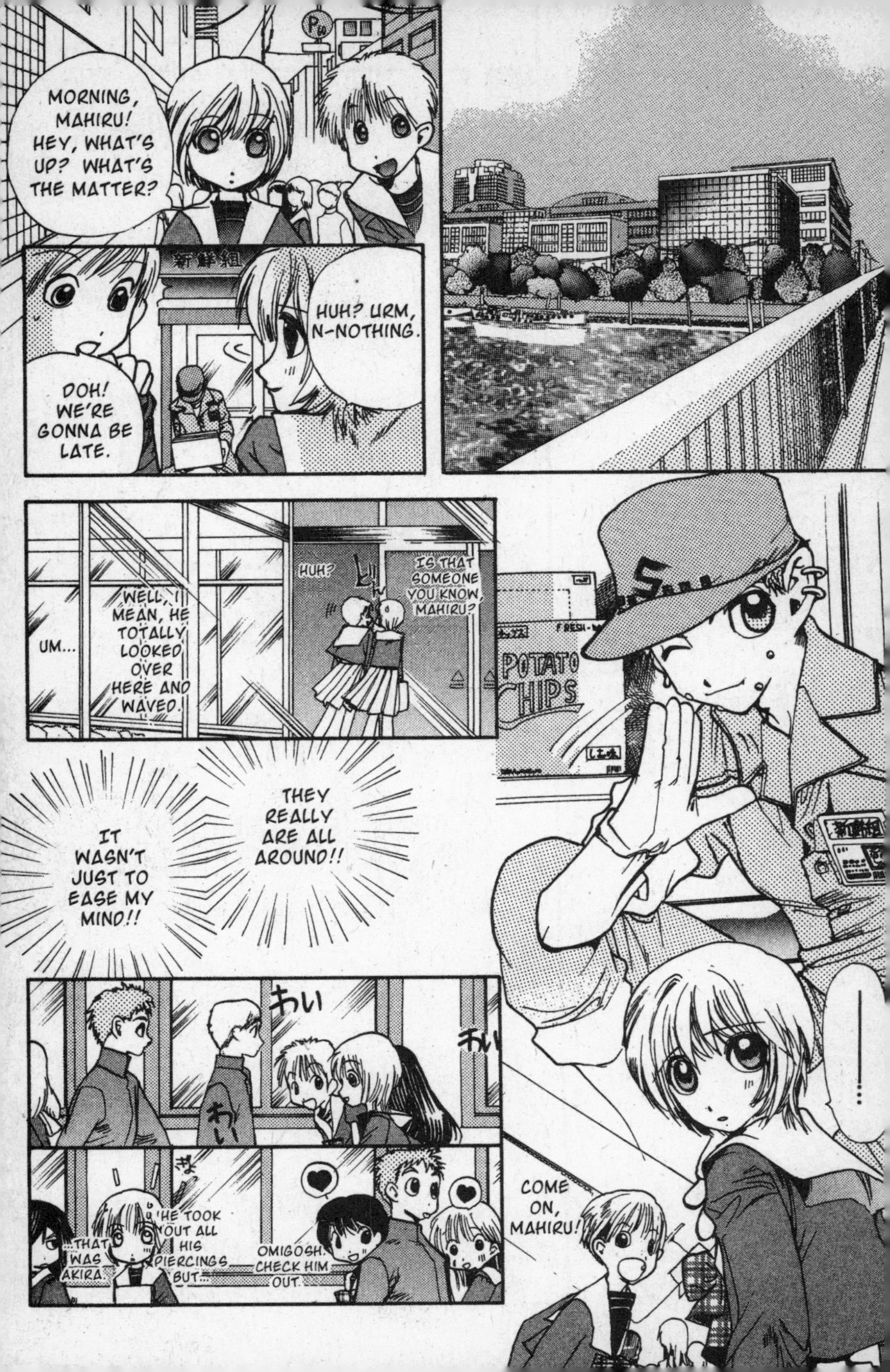

MORNING, MAHIRU! HEY, WHAT'S UP? WHAT'S THE MATTER?
新鮮組
HUH? URM, N-NOTHING.
DOH! WE'RE GONNA BE LATE.
POTATO CHIPS
......
COME ON, MAHIRU!
IS THAT SOMEONE YOU KNOW, MAHIRU?
HUH?
WELL, I MEAN, HE TOTALLY LOOKED OVER HERE AND WAVED.
UM...
THEY REALLY ARE ALL AROUND!!
IT WASN'T JUST TO EASE MY MIND!!
わい
わい
わい
OMIGOSH. CHECK HIM OUT.
HE TOOK OUT ALL HIS PIERCINGS BUT...
...THAT WAS AKIRA.

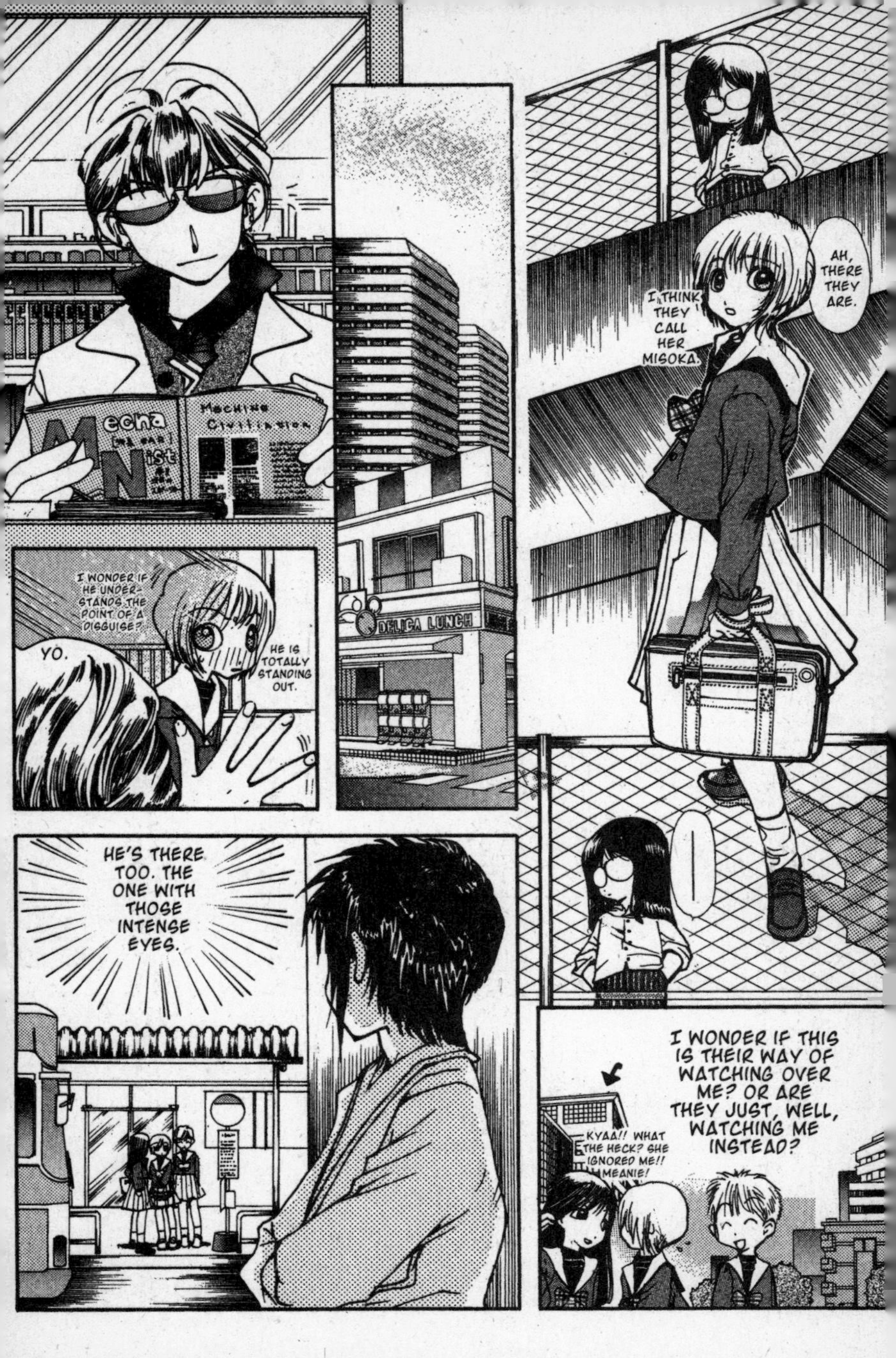

AH, THERE THEY ARE.
I THINK THEY CALL HER MISOKA.
DELICA LUNCH
I WONDER IF HE UNDERSTANDS THE POINT OF A DISGUISE?
YO.
HE IS TOTALLY STANDING OUT.
I WONDER IF THIS IS THEIR WAY OF WATCHING OVER ME? OR ARE THEY JUST, WELL, WATCHING ME INSTEAD?
KYAA!! WHAT THE HECK? SHE IGNORED ME!! MEANIE!
HE'S THERE TOO. THE ONE WITH THOSE INTENSE EYES.

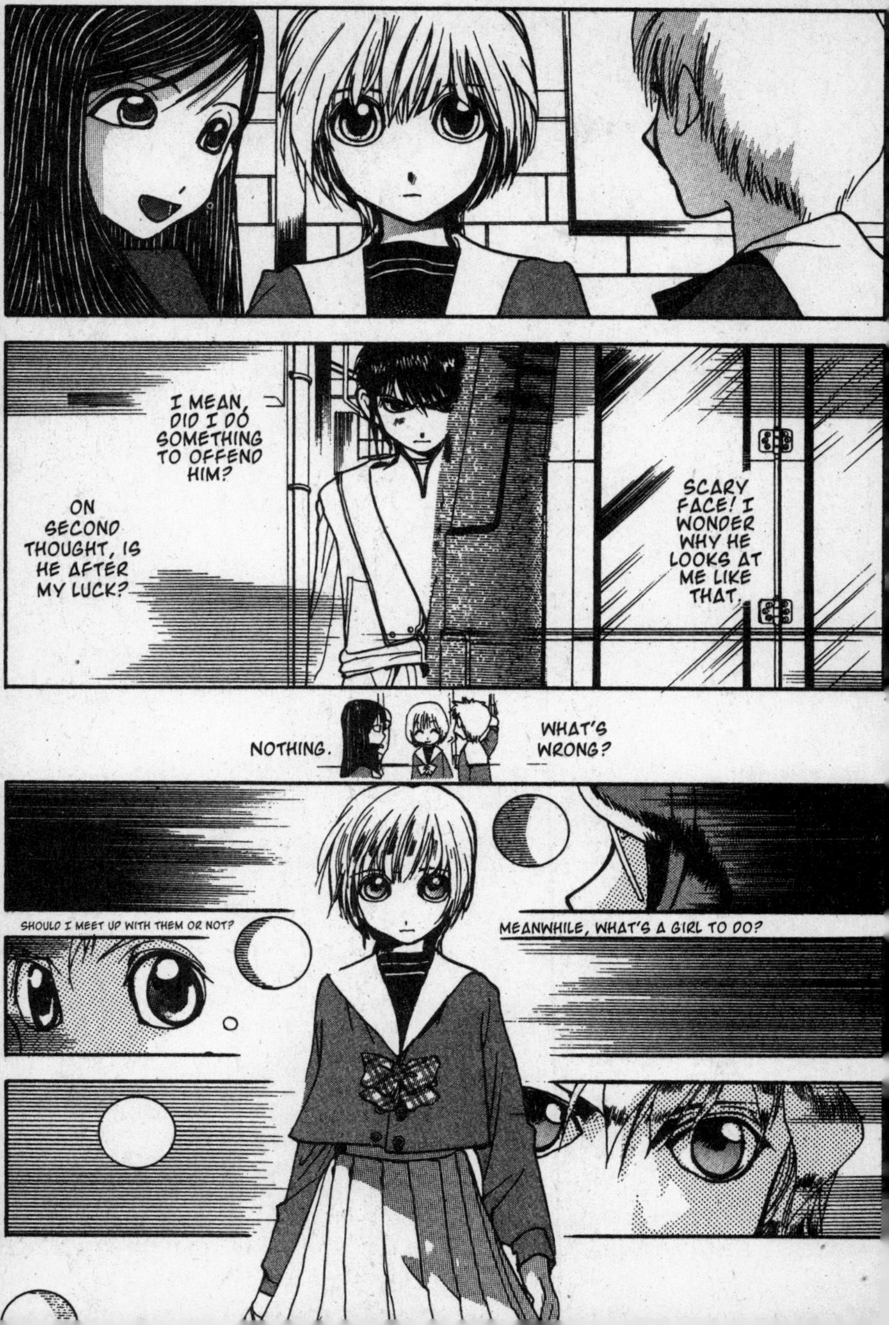
SCARY FACE! I WONDER WHY HE LOOKS AT ME LIKE THAT.
I MEAN, DID I DO SOMETHING TO OFFEND HIM?
ON SECOND THOUGHT, IS HE AFTER MY LUCK?
WHAT'S WRONG?
NOTHING.
MEANWHILE, WHAT'S A GIRL TO DO?
SHOULD I MEET UP WITH THEM OR NOT?

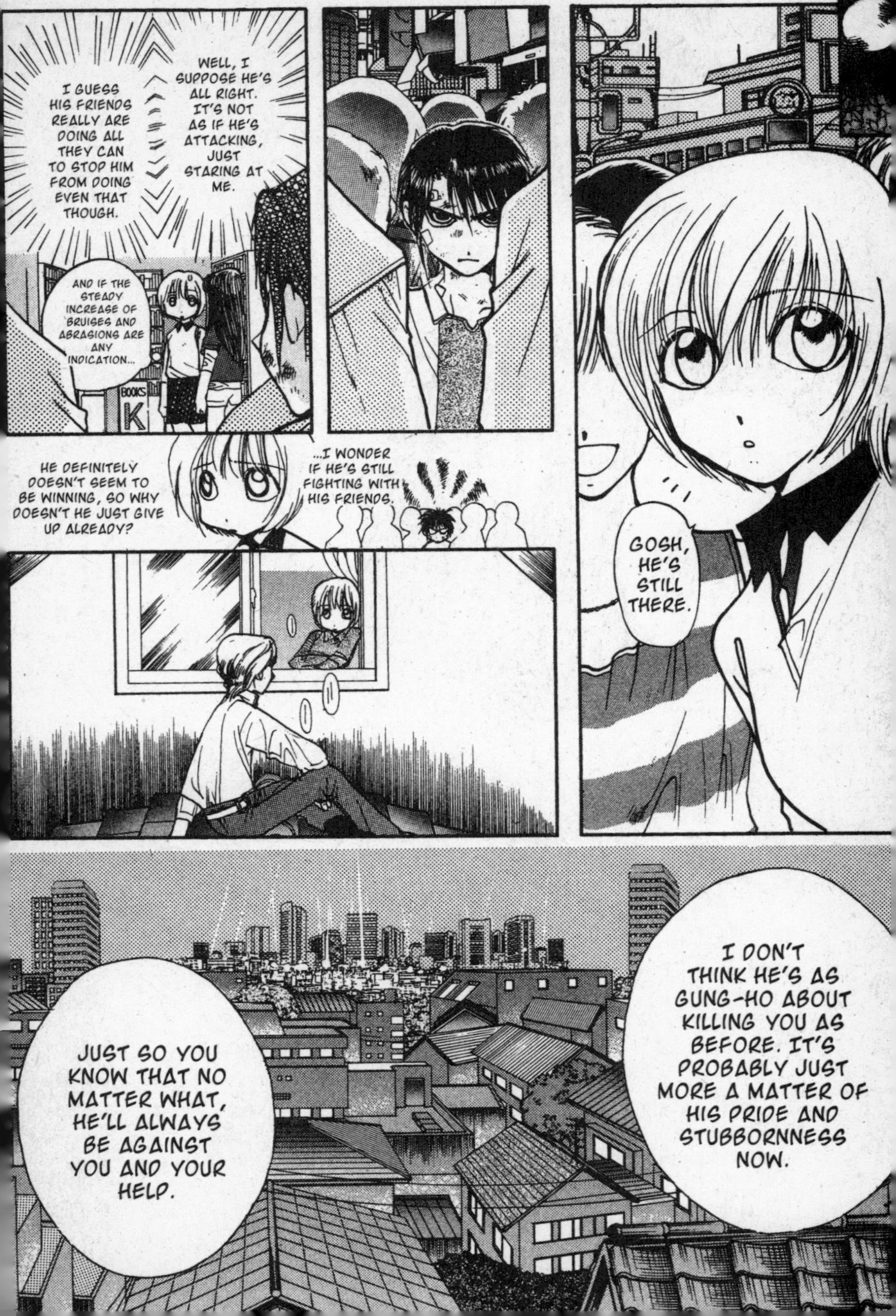
GOSH, HE'S STILL THERE.
WELL, I SUPPOSE HE'S ALL RIGHT. IT'S NOT AS IF HE'S ATTACKING, JUST STARING AT ME.
I GUESS HIS FRIENDS REALLY ARE DOING ALL THEY CAN TO STOP HIM FROM DOING EVEN THAT THOUGH.
AND IF THE STEADY INCREASE OF BRUISES AND ABRASIONS ARE ANY INDICATION...
BOOKS
K
...I WONDER IF HE'S STILL FIGHTING WITH HIS FRIENDS.
HE DEFINITELY DOESN'T SEEM TO BE WINNING, SO WHY DOESN'T HE JUST GIVE UP ALREADY?
I DON'T THINK HE'S AS GUNG-HO ABOUT KILLING YOU AS BEFORE. IT'S PROBABLY JUST MORE A MATTER OF HIS PRIDE AND STUBBORNNESS NOW.
JUST SO YOU KNOW THAT NO MATTER WHAT, HE'LL ALWAYS BE AGAINST YOU AND YOUR HELP.

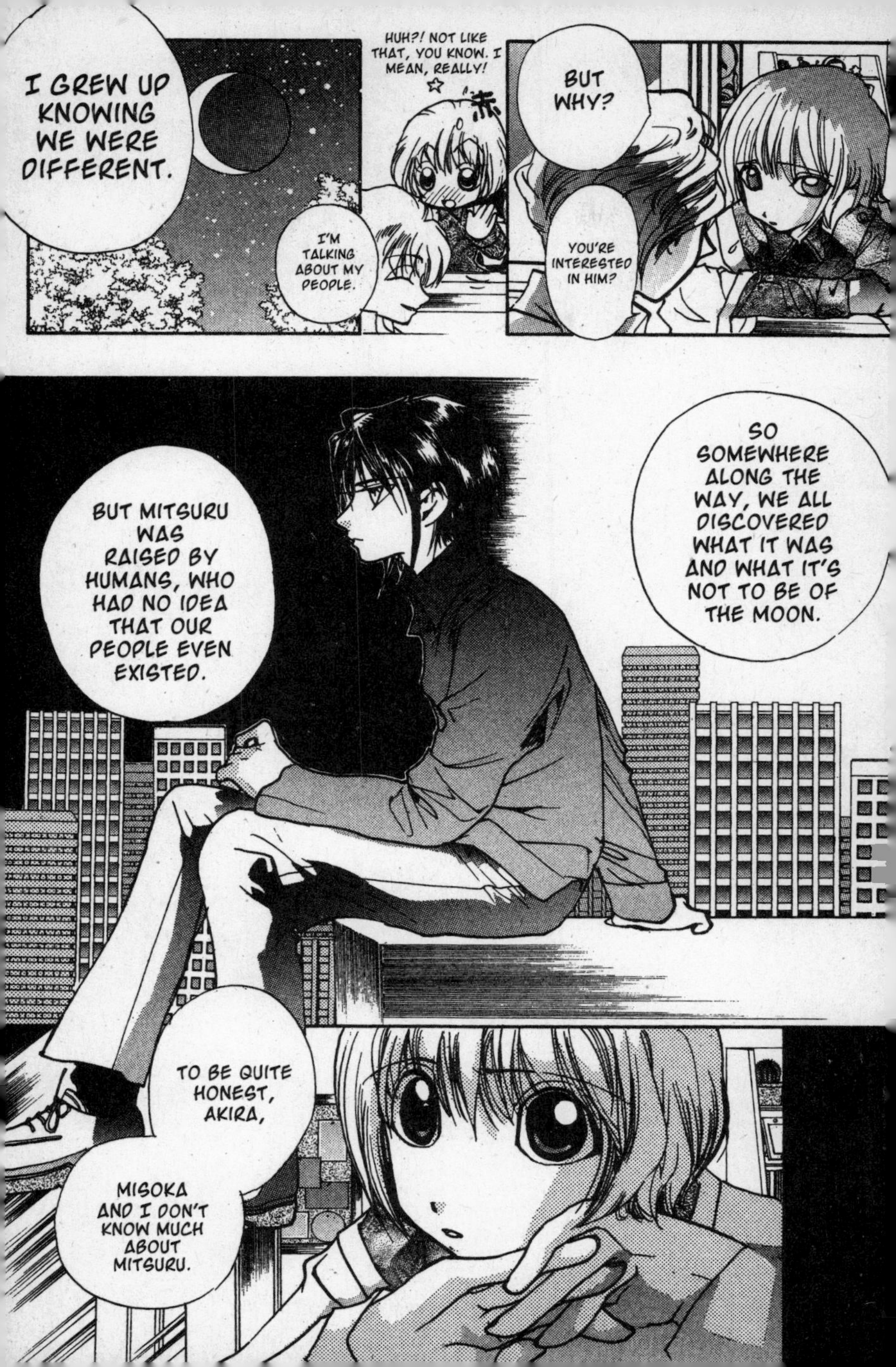
BUT WHY?
YOU'RE INTERESTED IN HIM?
HUH?! NOT LIKE THAT, YOU KNOW. I MEAN, REALLY!
I'M TALKING ABOUT MY PEOPLE.
I GREW UP KNOWING WE WERE DIFFERENT.
SO SOMEWHERE ALONG THE WAY, WE ALL DISCOVERED WHAT IT WAS AND WHAT IT'S NOT TO BE OF THE MOON.
BUT MITSURU WAS RAISED BY HUMANS, WHO HAD NO IDEA THAT OUR PEOPLE EVEN EXISTED.
TO BE QUITE HONEST, AKIRA,
MISOKA AND I DON'T KNOW MUCH ABOUT MITSURU.

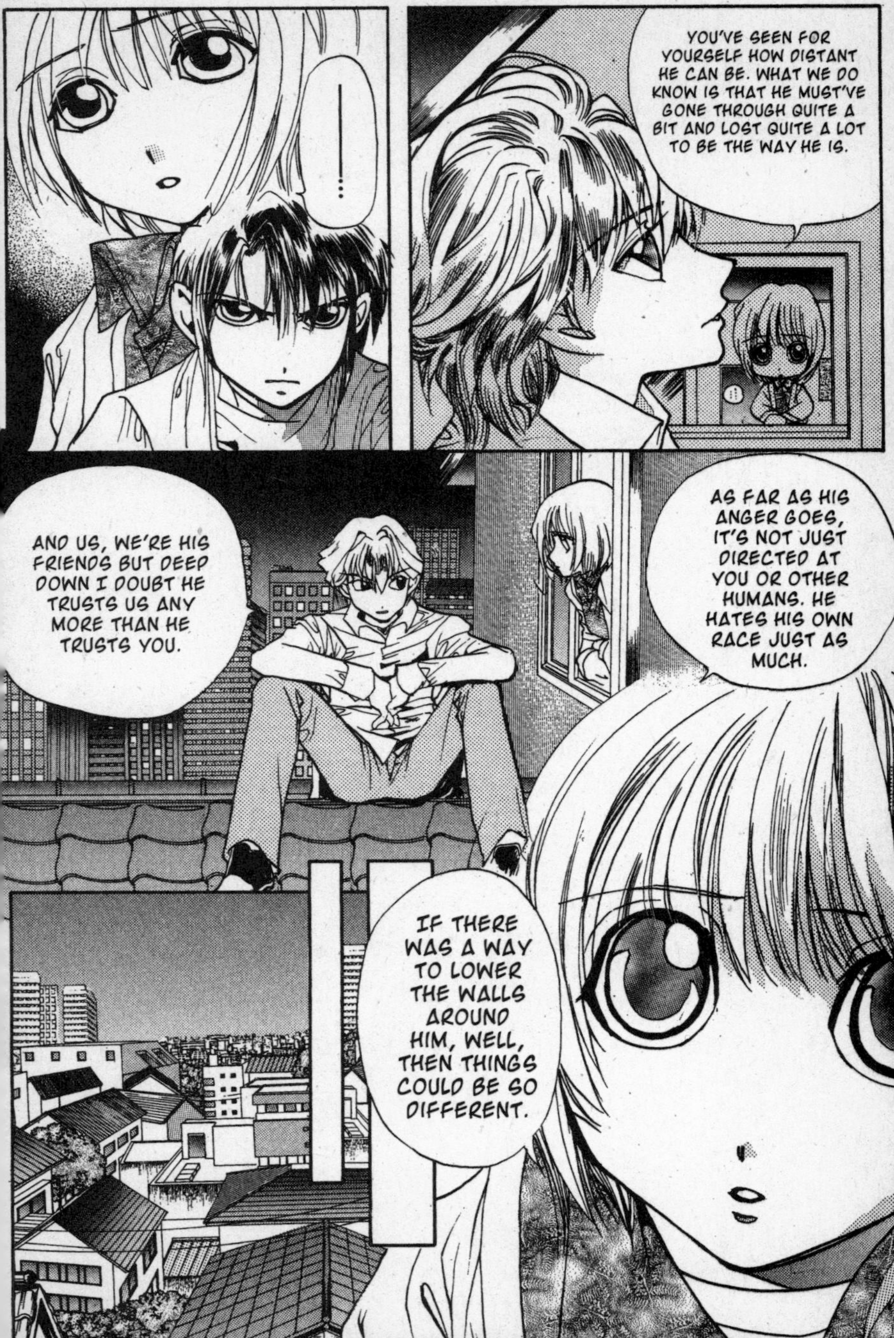
YOU'VE SEEN FOR YOURSELF HOW DISTANT HE CAN BE. WHAT WE DO KNOW IS THAT HE MUST'VE GONE THROUGH QUITE A BIT AND LOST QUITE A LOT TO BE THE WAY HE IS.
AS FAR AS HIS ANGER GOES, IT'S NOT JUST DIRECTED AT YOU OR OTHER HUMANS. HE HATES HIS OWN RACE JUST AS MUCH.
AND US, WE'RE HIS FRIENDS BUT DEEP DOWN I DOUBT HE TRUSTS US ANY MORE THAN HE TRUSTS YOU.
IF THERE WAS A WAY TO LOWER THE WALLS AROUND HIM, WELL, THEN THINGS COULD BE SO DIFFERENT.

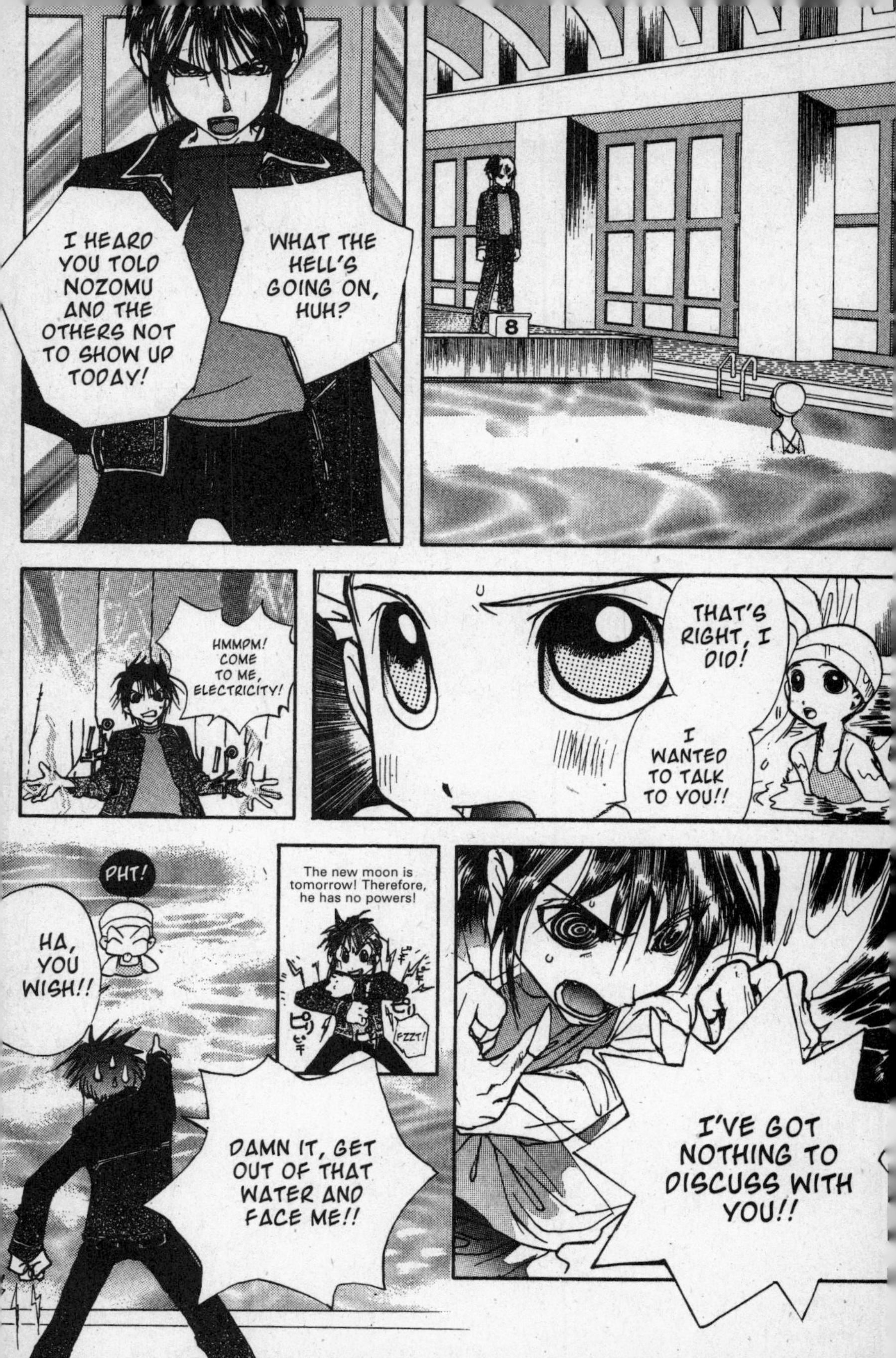
WHAT THE HELL'S GOING ON, HUH?
I HEARD YOU TOLD NOZOMU AND THE OTHERS NOT TO SHOW UP TODAY!
THAT'S RIGHT, I DID!
I WANTED TO TALK TO YOU!!
HMMPM! COME TO ME, ELECTRICITY!
I'VE GOT NOTHING TO DISCUSS WITH YOU!!
The new moon is tomorrow! Therefore, he has no powers!
FZZT!
PHT!
HA, YOU WISH!!
DAMN IT, GET OUT OF THAT WATER AND FACE ME!!

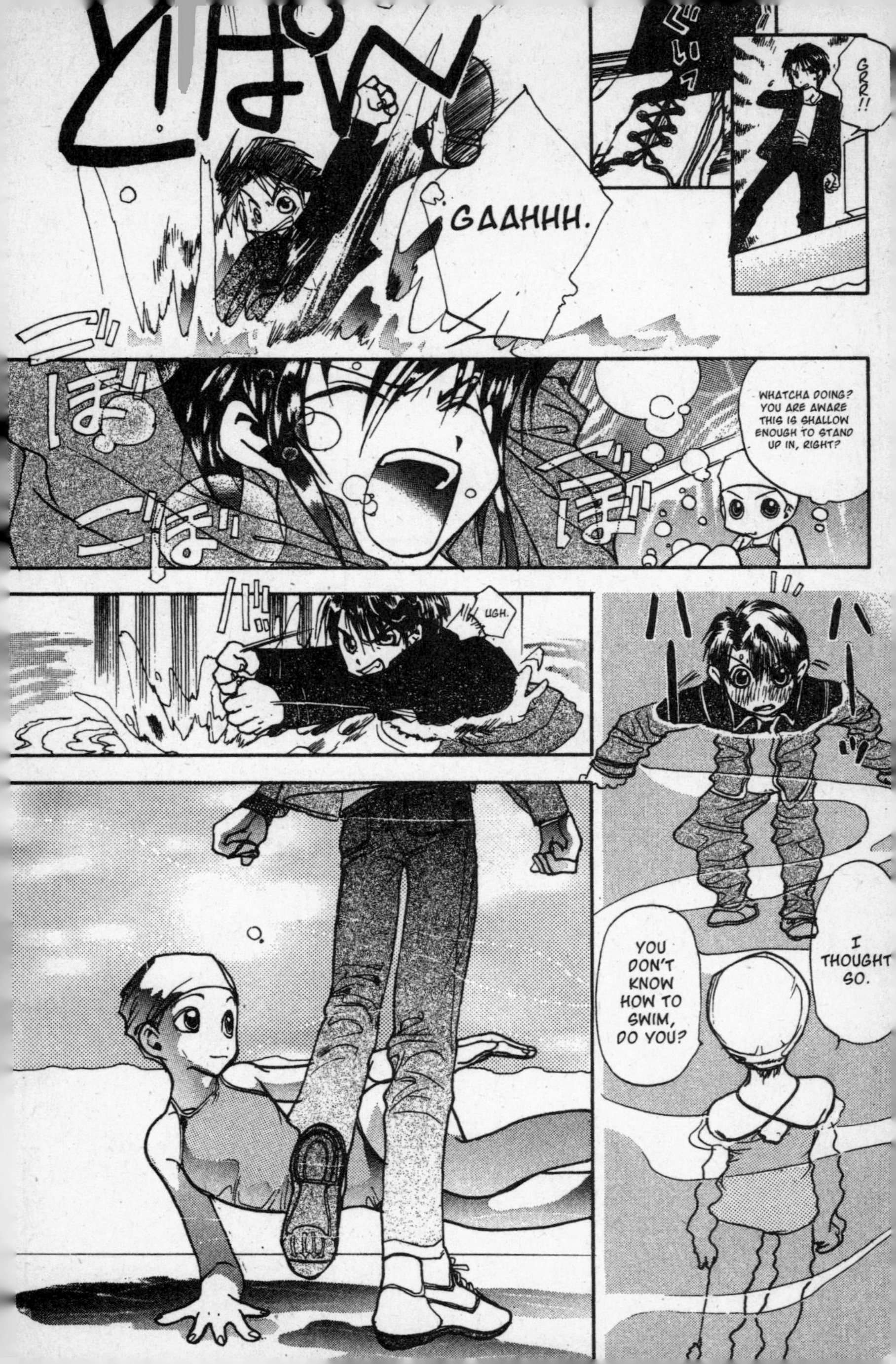
GRR!!
GAAHHH.
WHATCHA DOING? YOU ARE AWARE THIS IS SHALLOW ENOUGH TO STAND UP IN, RIGHT?
UGH.
I THOUGHT SO.
YOU DON'T KNOW HOW TO SWIM, DO YOU?

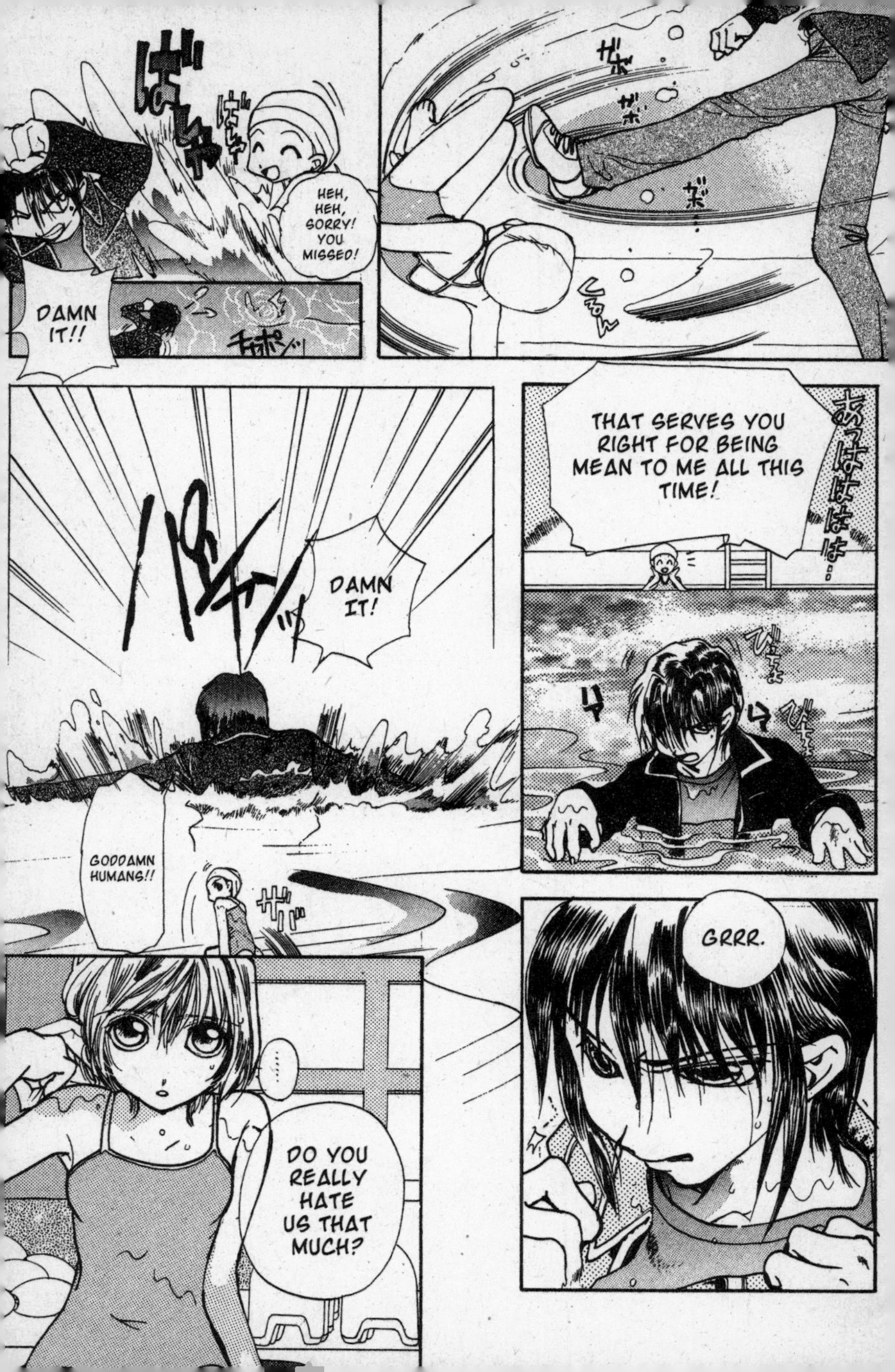

ザボ
ザボ
ザブ
くるん
ばしゃ
HEH, HEH, SORRY! YOU MISSED!
DAMN IT!!
チャポン
THAT SERVES YOU RIGHT FOR BEING MEAN TO ME ALL THIS TIME!
あっははははは!
DAMN IT!
GODDAMN HUMANS!!
ザバ
GRRR.
......
DO YOU REALLY HATE US THAT MUCH?

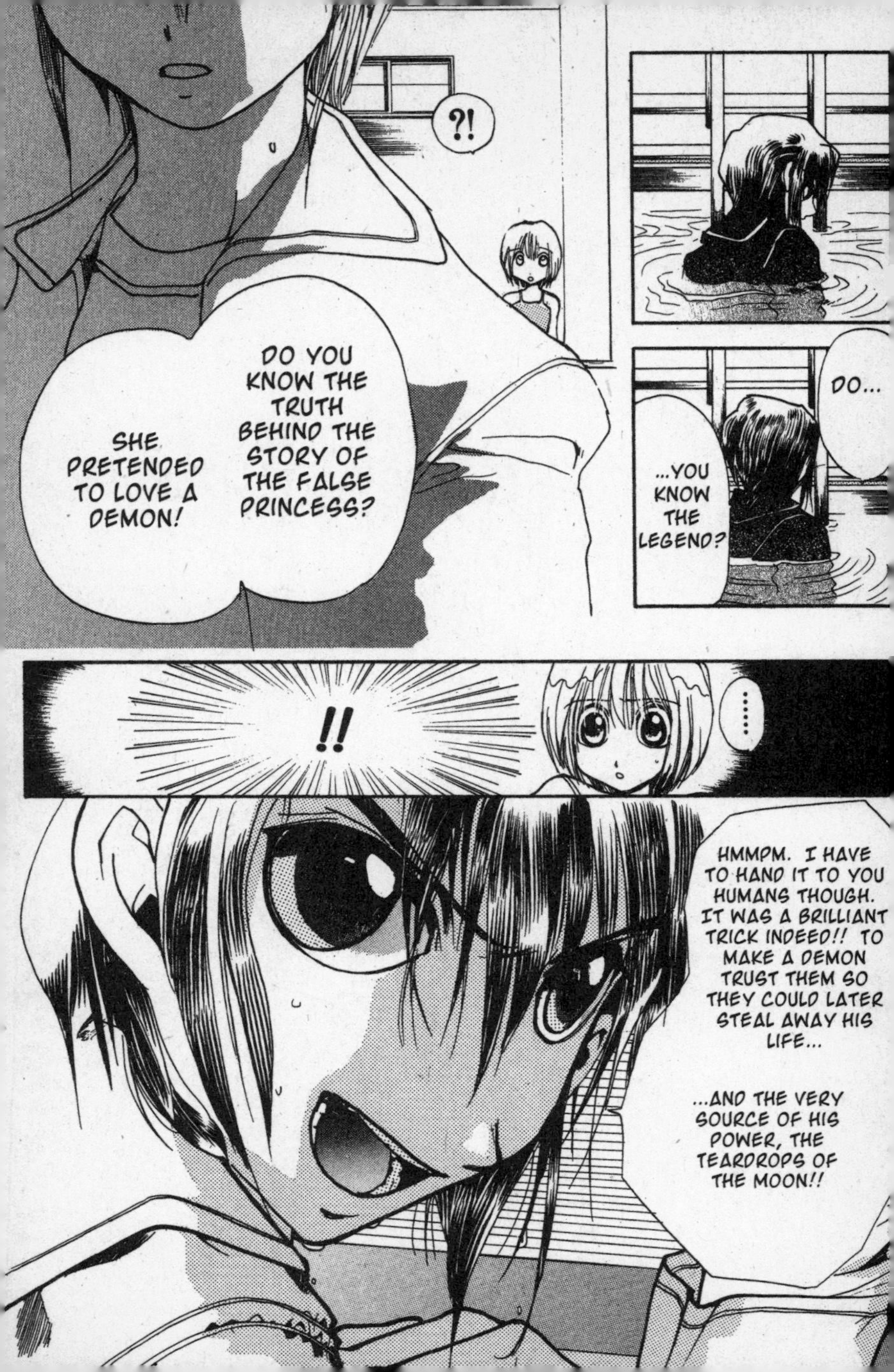
DO...
...YOU KNOW THE LEGEND?
?!
DO YOU KNOW THE TRUTH BEHIND THE STORY OF THE FALSE PRINCESS?
SHE PRETENDED TO LOVE A DEMON!
......
!!
HMMPM. I HAVE TO HAND IT TO YOU HUMANS THOUGH. IT WAS A BRILLIANT TRICK INDEED!! TO MAKE A DEMON TRUST THEM SO THEY COULD LATER STEAL AWAY HIS LIFE...
...AND THE VERY SOURCE OF HIS POWER, THE TEARDROPS OF THE MOON!!

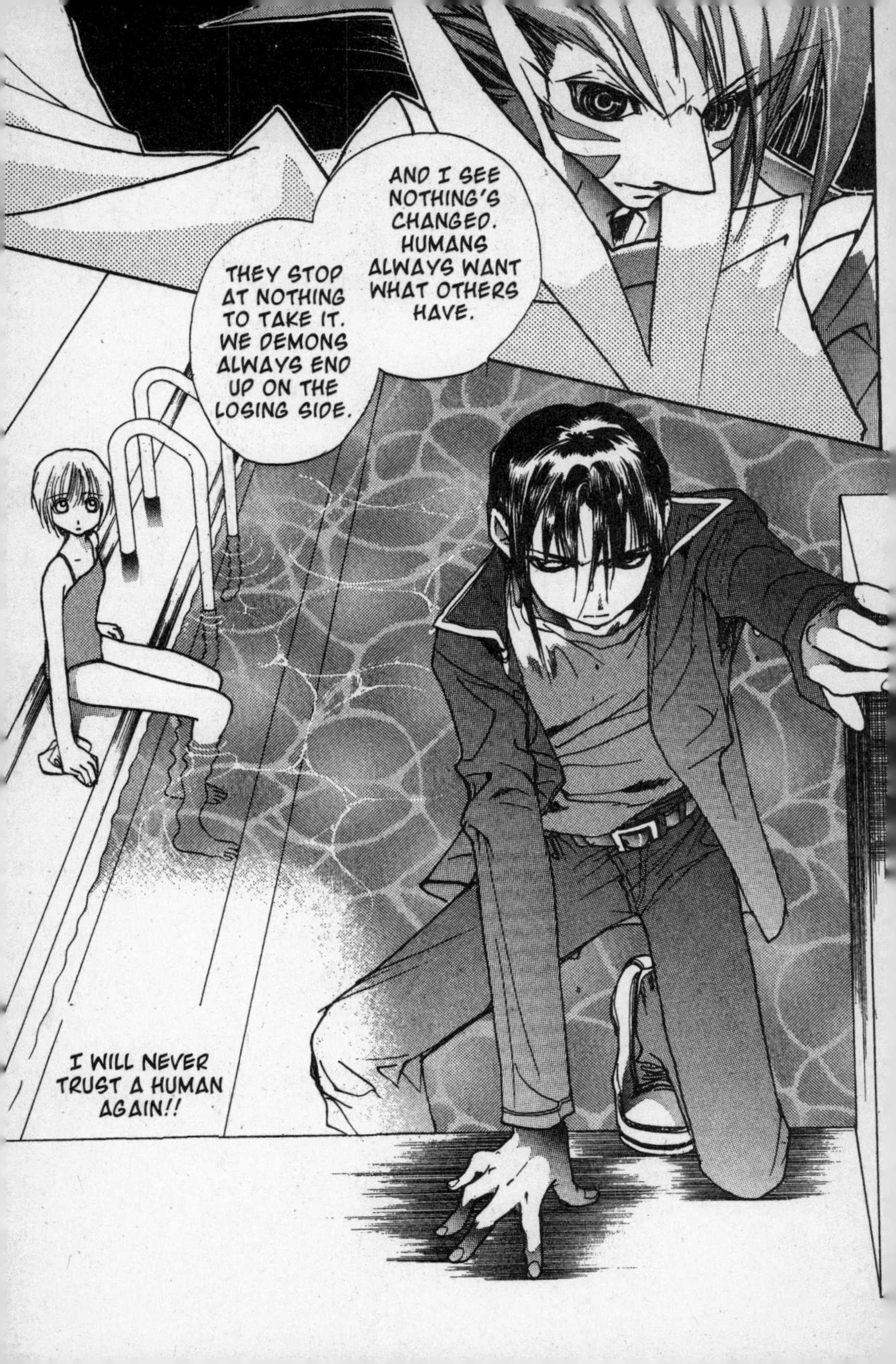
AND I SEE NOTHING'S CHANGED. HUMANS ALWAYS WANT WHAT OTHERS HAVE.
THEY STOP AT NOTHING TO TAKE IT. WE DEMONS ALWAYS END UP ON THE LOSING SIDE.
I WILL NEVER TRUST A HUMAN AGAIN!!

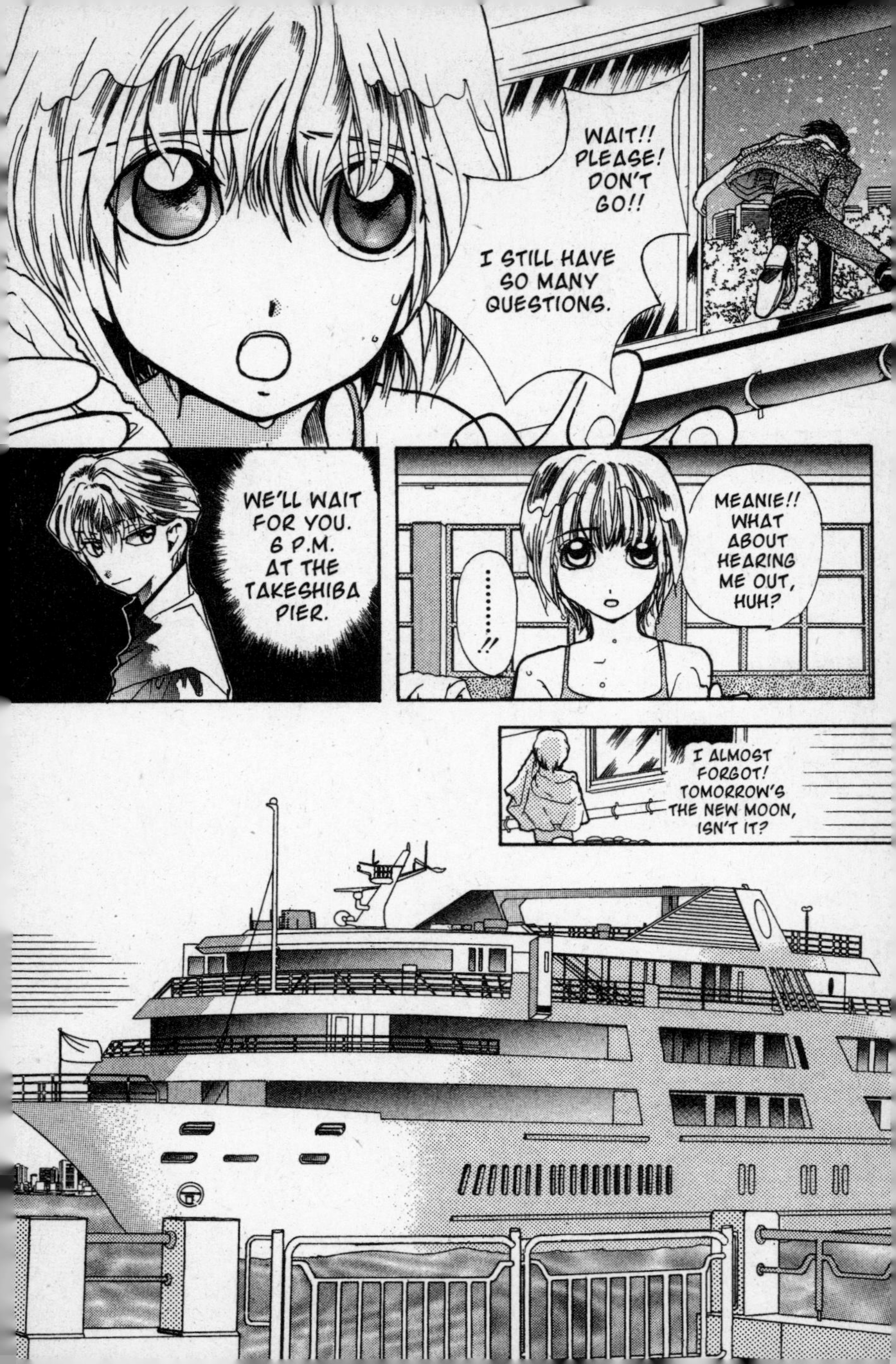
WAIT!! PLEASE! DON'T GO!!
I STILL HAVE SO MANY QUESTIONS.
MEANIE!! WHAT ABOUT HEARING ME OUT, HUH?
......!!
WE'LL WAIT FOR YOU. 6 P.M. AT THE TAKESHIBA PIER.
I ALMOST FORGOT! TOMORROW'S THE NEW MOON, ISN'T IT?

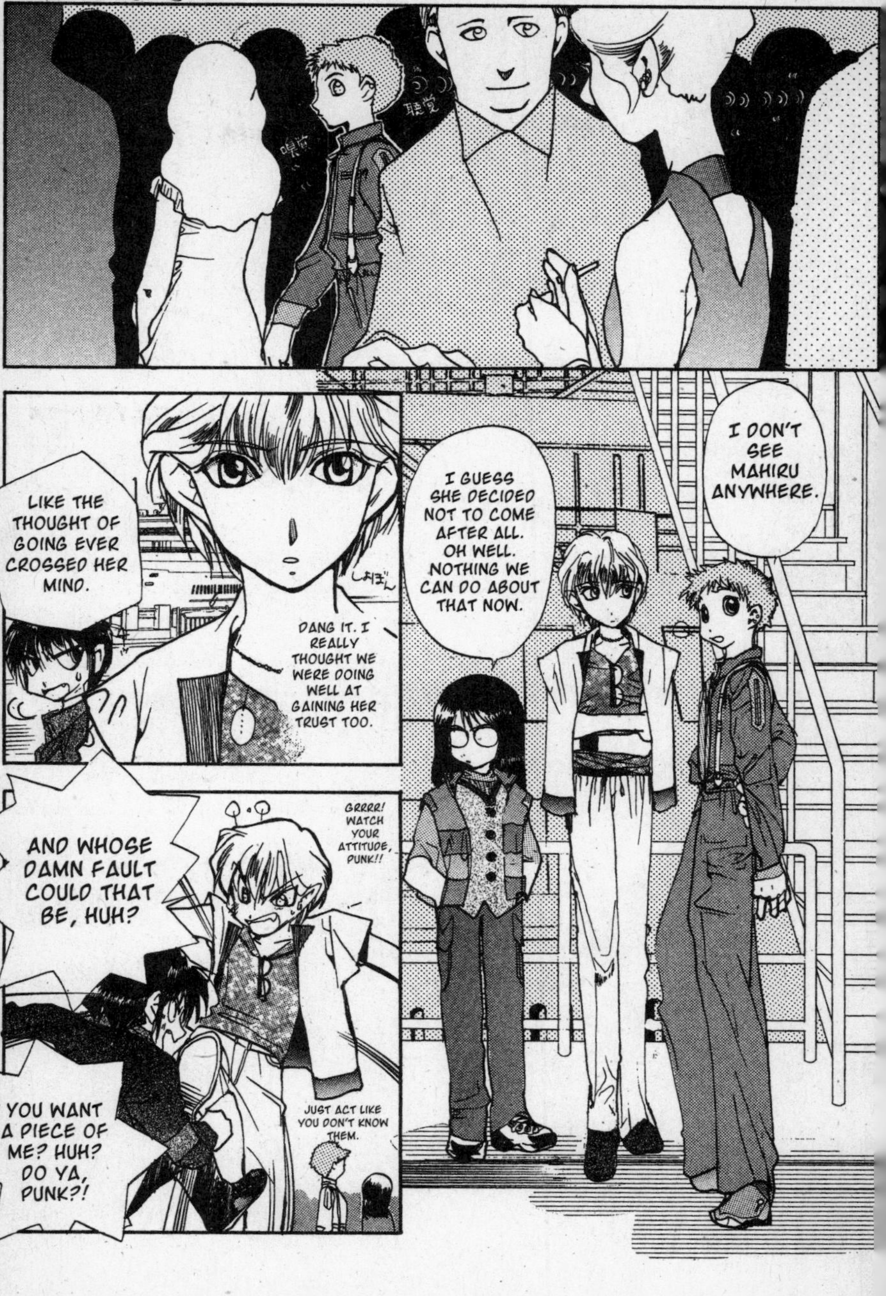
聴覚
嗅覚
I DON'T SEE MAHIRU ANYWHERE.
I GUESS SHE DECIDED NOT TO COME AFTER ALL. OH WELL. NOTHING WE CAN DO ABOUT THAT NOW.
DANG IT. I REALLY THOUGHT WE WERE DOING WELL AT GAINING HER TRUST TOO.
LIKE THE THOUGHT OF GOING EVER CROSSED HER MIND.
GRRRR! WATCH YOUR ATTITUDE, PUNK!!
AND WHOSE DAMN FAULT COULD THAT BE, HUH?
JUST ACT LIKE YOU DON'T KNOW THEM.
YOU WANT A PIECE OF ME? HUH? DO YA, PUNK?!

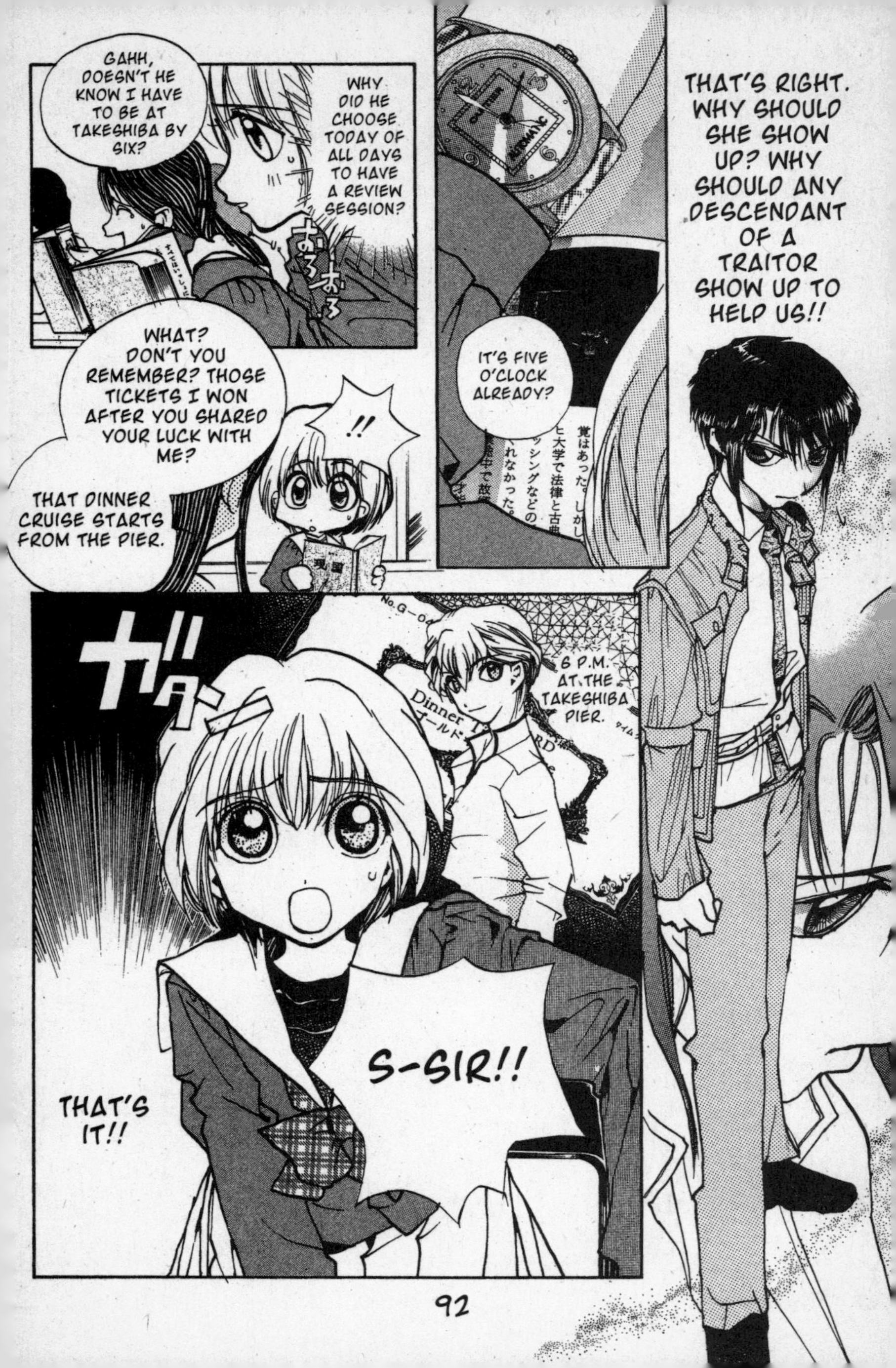
THAT'S RIGHT. WHY SHOULD SHE SHOW UP? WHY SHOULD ANY DESCENDANT OF A TRAITOR SHOW UP TO HELP US!!
IT'S FIVE O'CLOCK ALREADY?
GAHH, DOESN'T HE KNOW I HAVE TO BE AT TAKESHIBA BY SIX?
WHY DID HE CHOOSE TODAY OF ALL DAYS TO HAVE A REVIEW SESSION?
WHAT? DON'T YOU REMEMBER? THOSE TICKETS I WON AFTER YOU SHARED YOUR LUCK WITH ME?
!!
THAT DINNER CRUISE STARTS FROM THE PIER.
6 P.M. AT THE TAKESHIBA PIER.
S-SIR!!
THAT'S IT!!

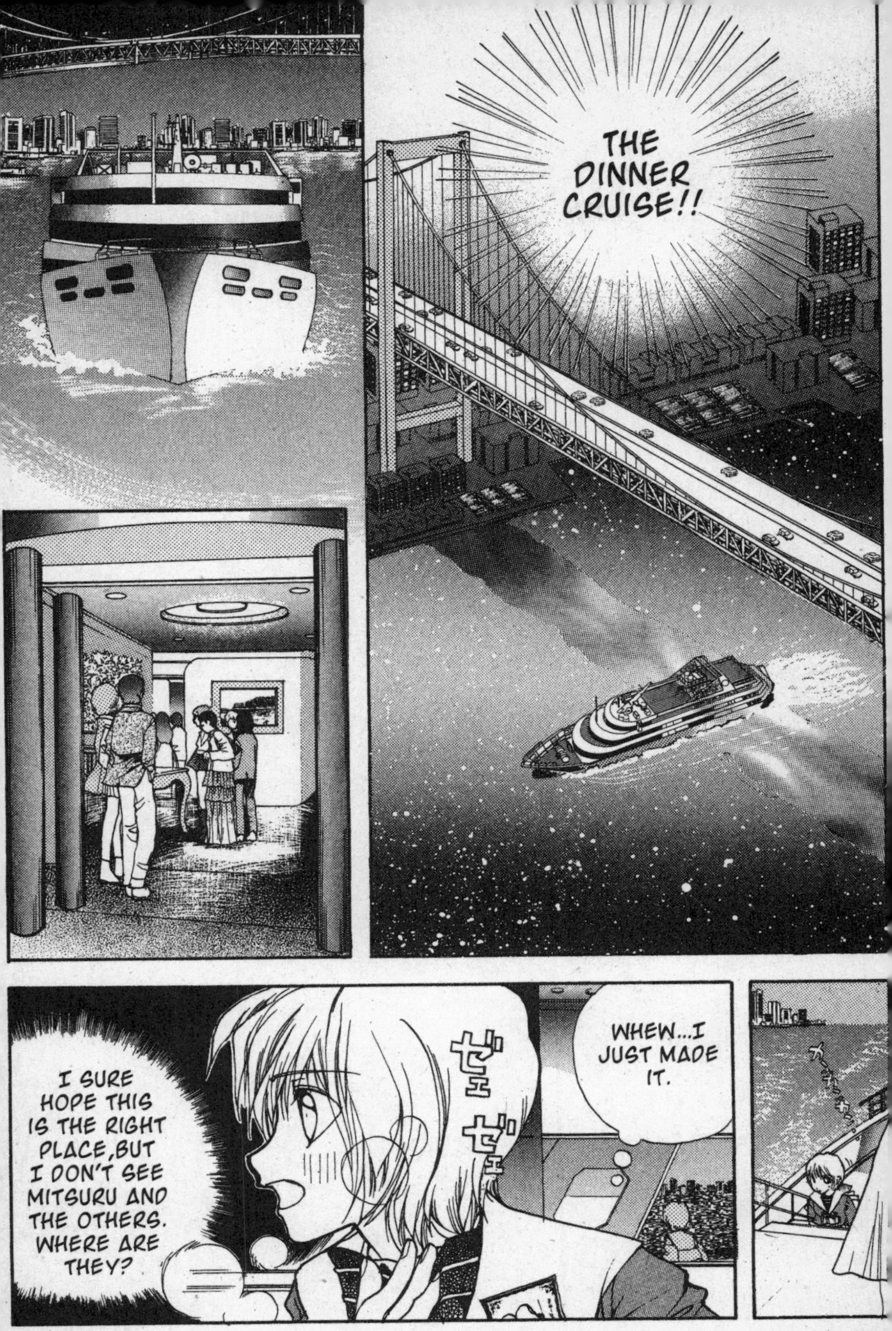
THE DINNER CRUISE!!
ゼェ ゼェ
WHEW...I JUST MADE IT.
I SURE HOPE THIS IS THE RIGHT PLACE, BUT I DON'T SEE MITSURU AND THE OTHERS. WHERE ARE THEY?

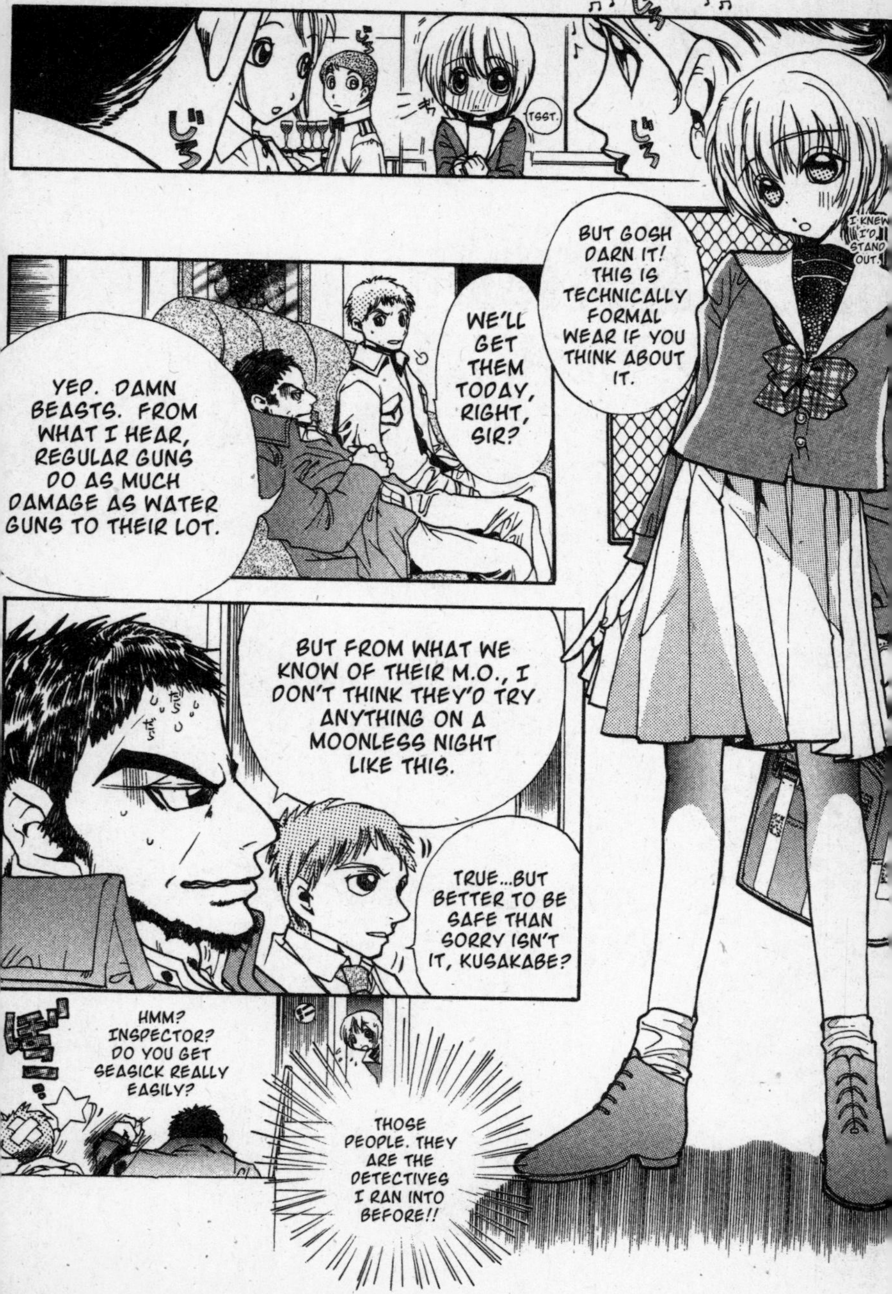
TSST.
BUT GOSH DARN IT! THIS IS TECHNICALLY FORMAL WEAR IF YOU THINK ABOUT IT.
I KNEW I'D STAND OUT.
WE'LL GET THEM TODAY, RIGHT, SIR?
YEP. DAMN BEASTS. FROM WHAT I HEAR, REGULAR GUNS DO AS MUCH DAMAGE AS WATER GUNS TO THEIR LOT.
BUT FROM WHAT WE KNOW OF THEIR M.O., I DON'T THINK THEY'D TRY ANYTHING ON A MOONLESS NIGHT LIKE THIS.
TRUE...BUT BETTER TO BE SAFE THAN SORRY ISN'T IT, KUSAKABE?
HMM? INSPECTOR? DO YOU GET SEASICK REALLY EASILY?
THOSE PEOPLE. THEY ARE THE DETECTIVES I RAN INTO BEFORE!!

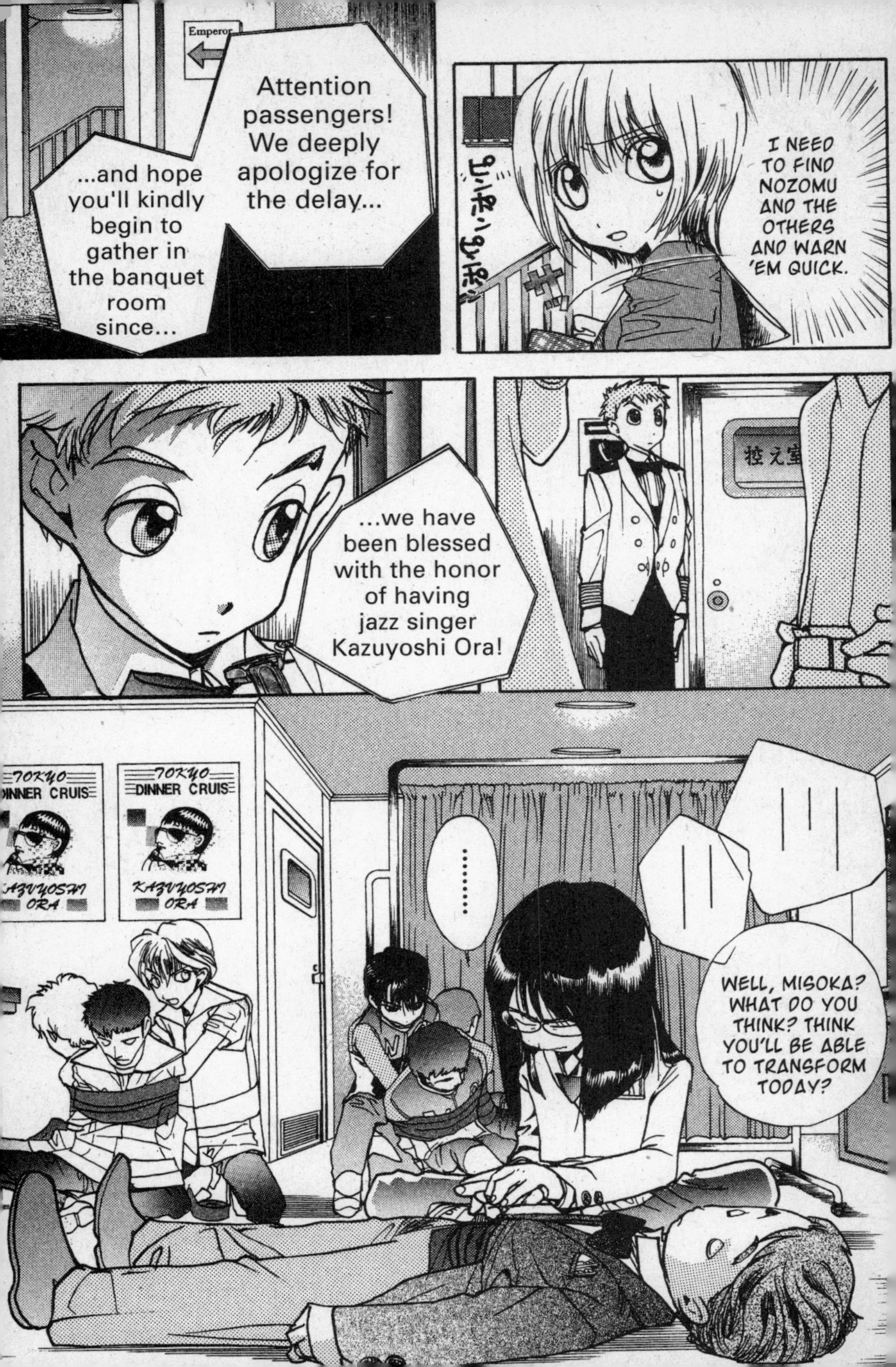
ピンポンピンポン
I NEED TO FIND NOZOMU AND THE OTHERS AND WARN 'EM QUICK.
Emperor
Attention passengers! We deeply apologize for the delay...
...and hope you'll kindly begin to gather in the banquet room since...
控え
...we have been blessed with the honor of having jazz singer Kazuyoshi Ora!
WELL, MISOKA? WHAT DO YOU THINK? THINK YOU'LL BE ABLE TO TRANSFORM TODAY?
......
TOKYO DINNER CRUIS
KAZUYOSHI ORA
TOKYO DINNER CRUIS
KAZUYOSHI ORA

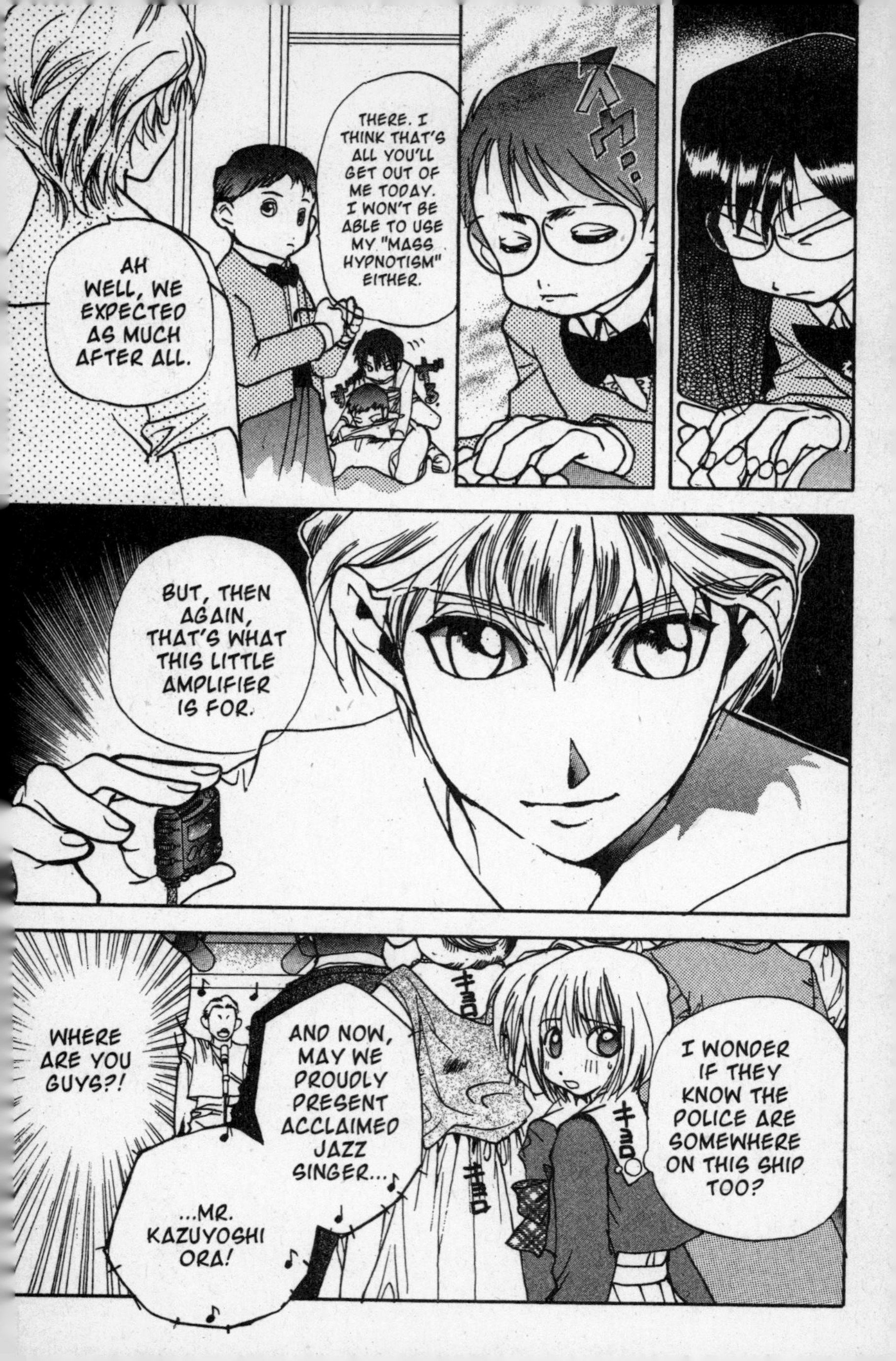
THERE. I THINK THAT'S ALL YOU'LL GET OUT OF ME TODAY. I WON'T BE ABLE TO USE MY "MASS HYPNOTISM" EITHER.
AH WELL, WE EXPECTED AS MUCH AFTER ALL.
BUT, THEN AGAIN, THAT'S WHAT THIS LITTLE AMPLIFIER IS FOR.
I WONDER IF THEY KNOW THE POLICE ARE SOMEWHERE ON THIS SHIP TOO?
AND NOW, MAY WE PROUDLY PRESENT ACCLAIMED JAZZ SINGER...
WHERE ARE YOU GUYS?!
...MR. KAZUYOSHI ORA!

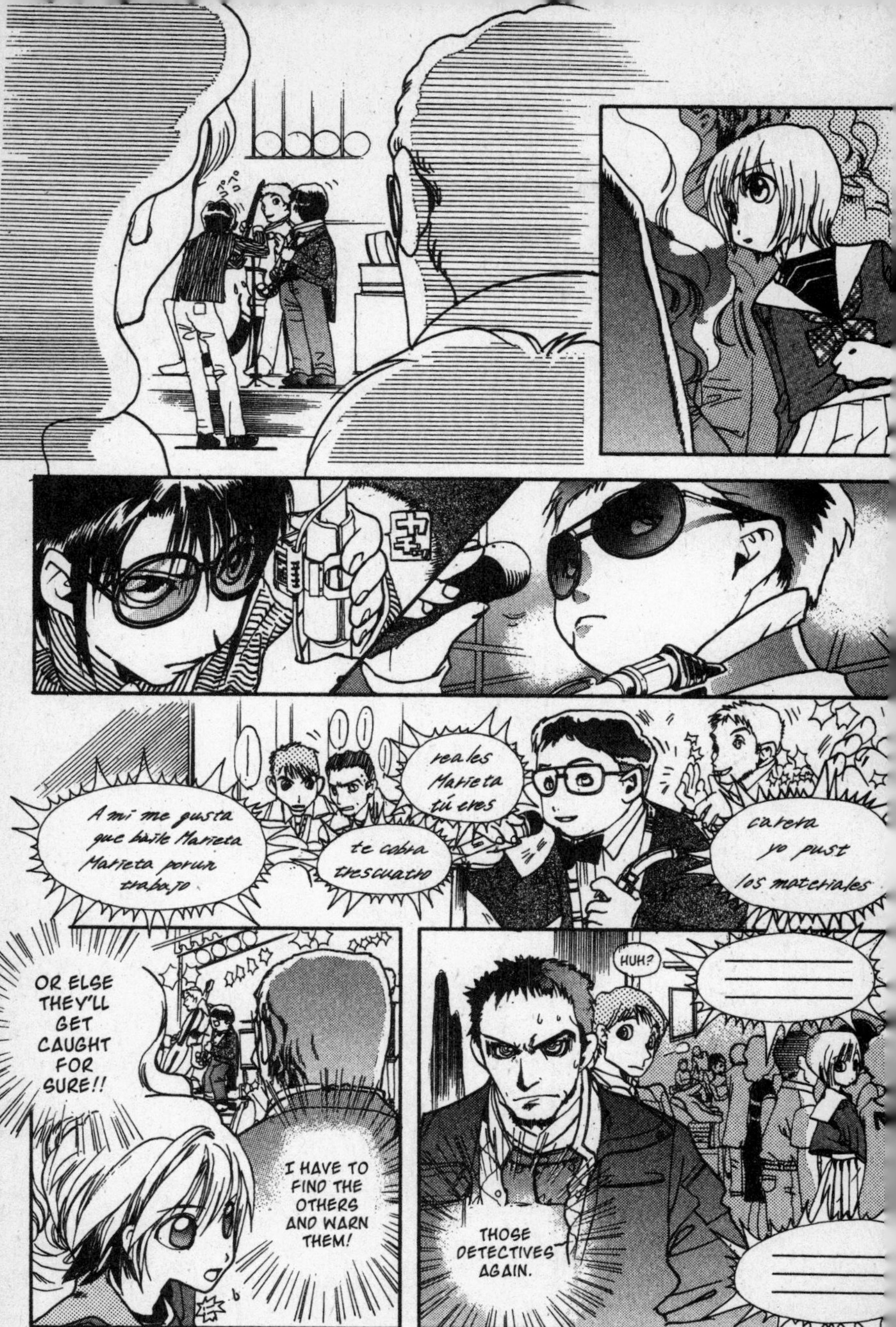

careta yo pust los materiales
reales Marieta tú eres
te cobra trescuatro
A mi me gusta que baile Marieta Marieta porun trabajo
HUH?
THOSE DETECTIVES AGAIN.
I HAVE TO FIND THE OTHERS AND WARN THEM!
OR ELSE THEY'LL GET CAUGHT FOR SURE!!

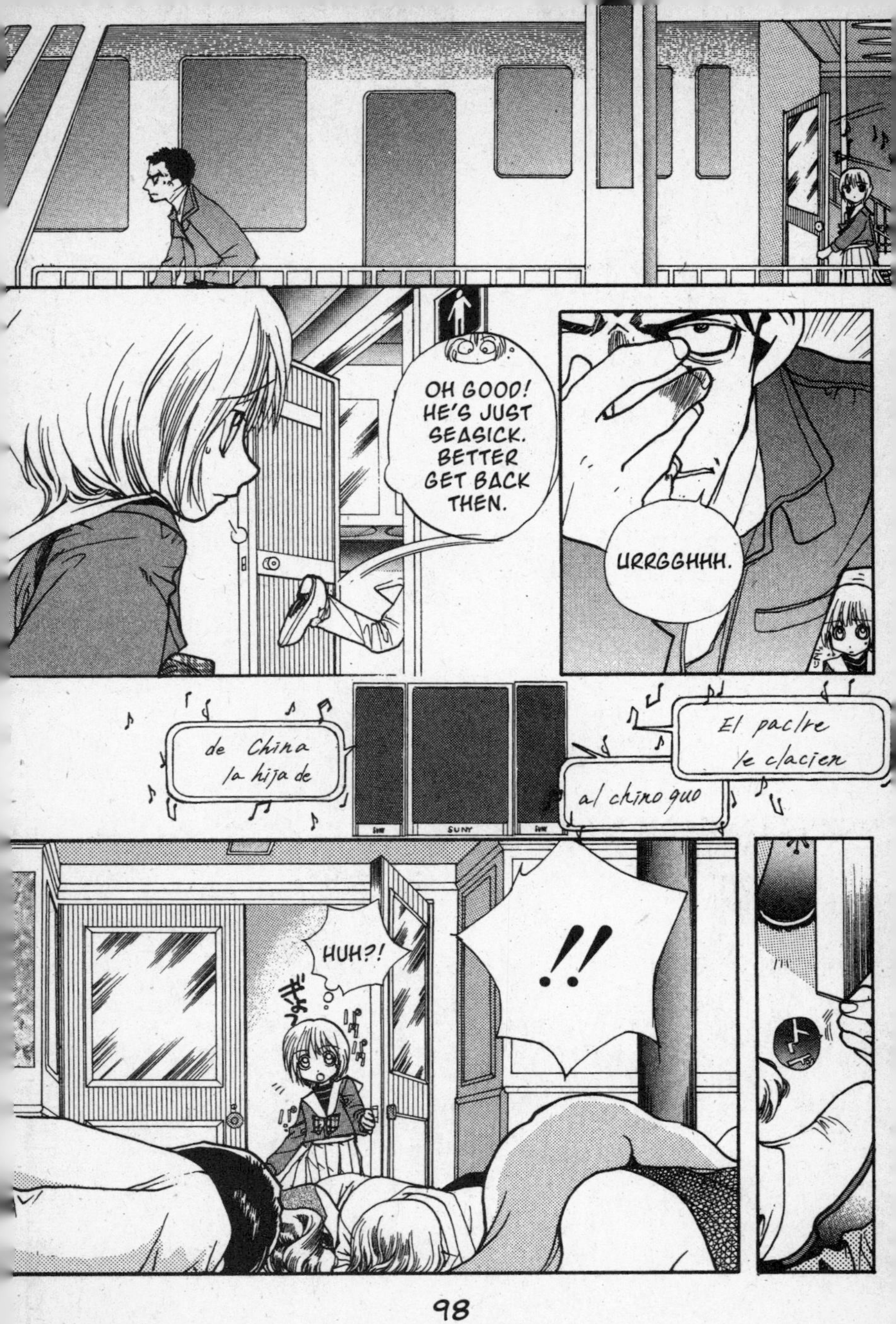
URRGGHHH.
OH GOOD! HE'S JUST SEASICK. BETTER GET BACK THEN.
El padre le dacien
al chino guo
de China la hija de
!!
HUH?!
ぎょっ

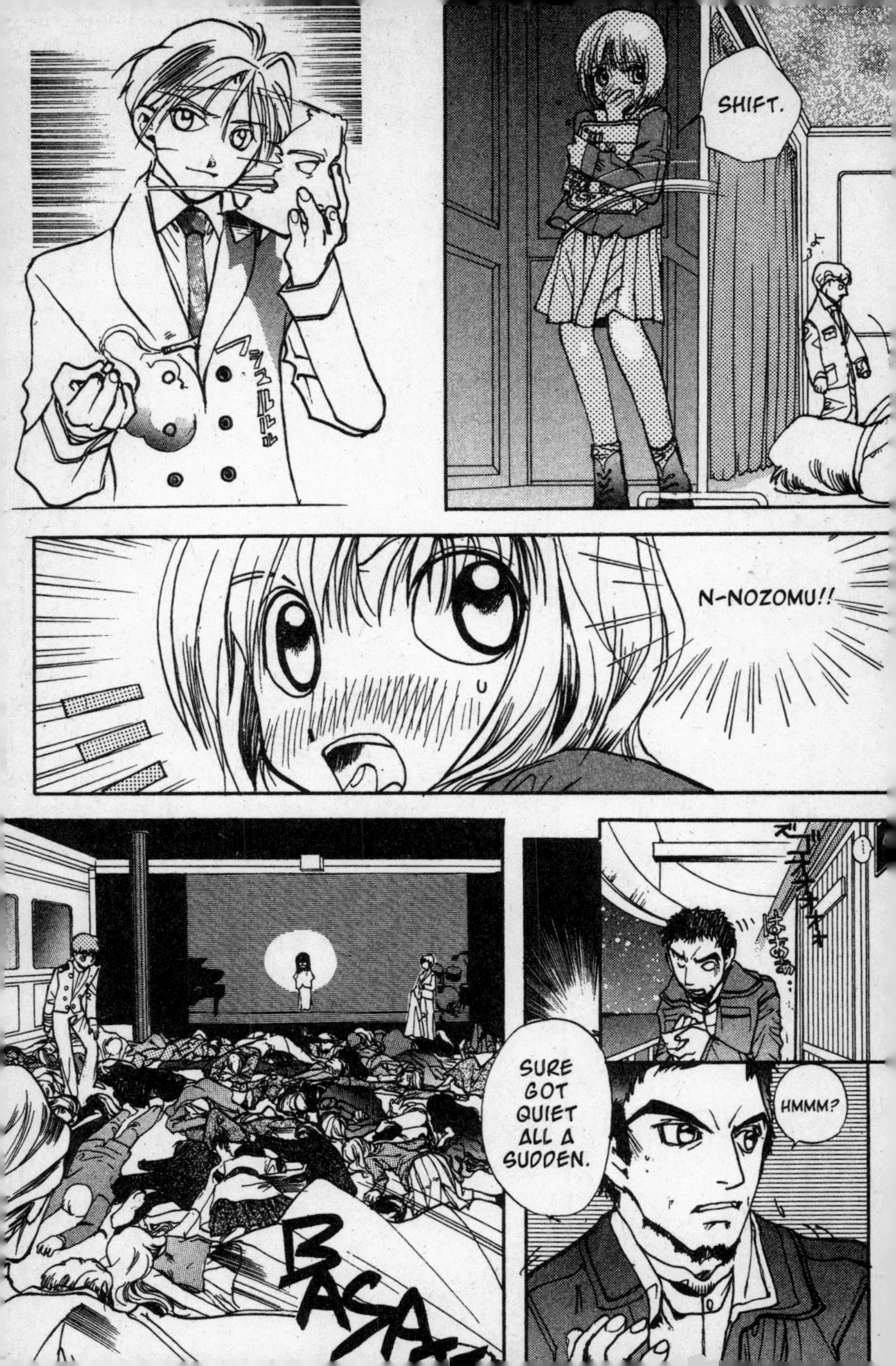
SHIFT.
N-NOZOMU!!
HMMM?
SURE GOT QUIET ALL A SUDDEN.
BACA

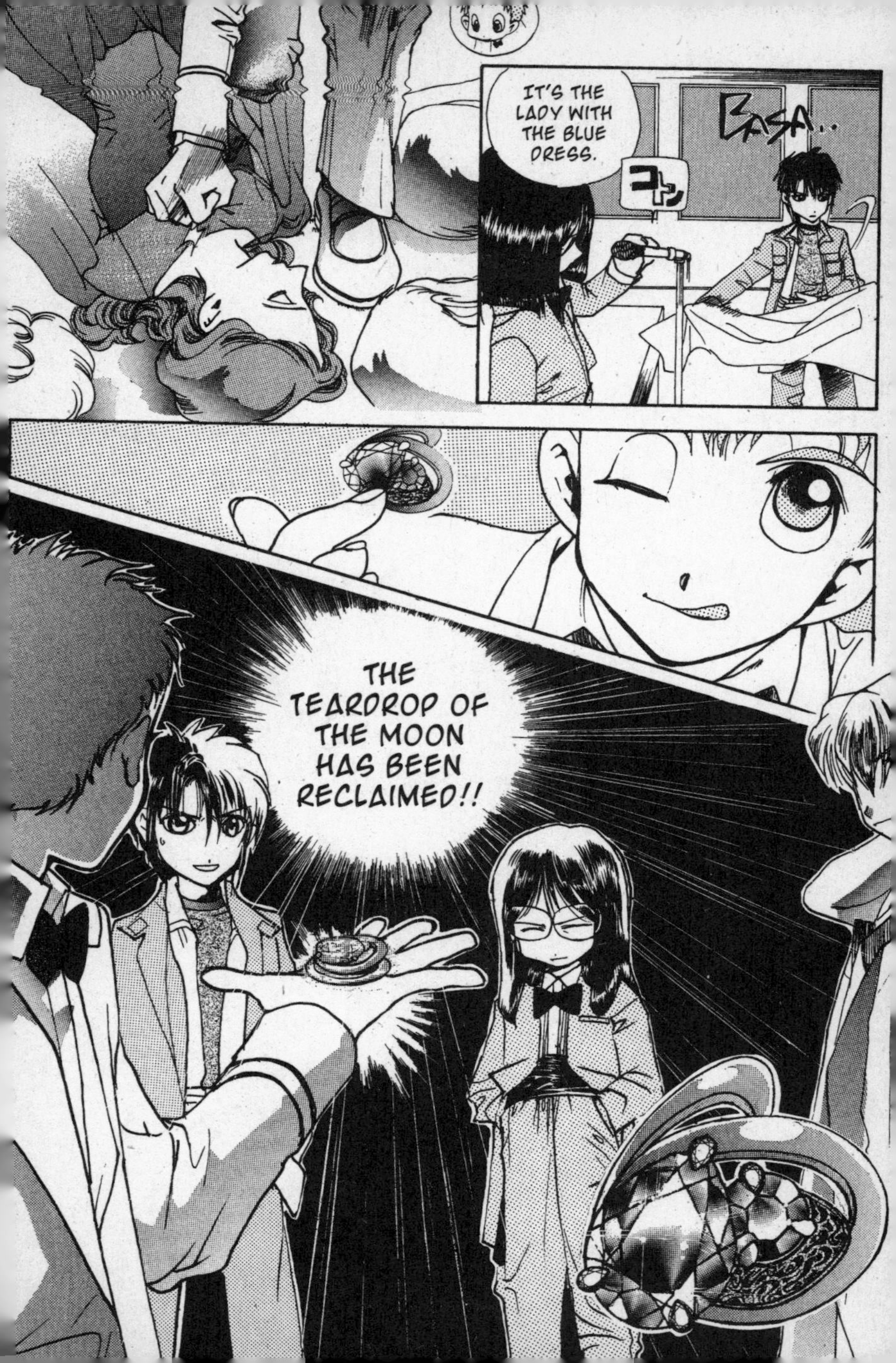
BASA..
IT'S THE LADY WITH THE BLUE DRESS.
コトン
THE TEARDROP OF THE MOON HAS BEEN RECLAIMED!!

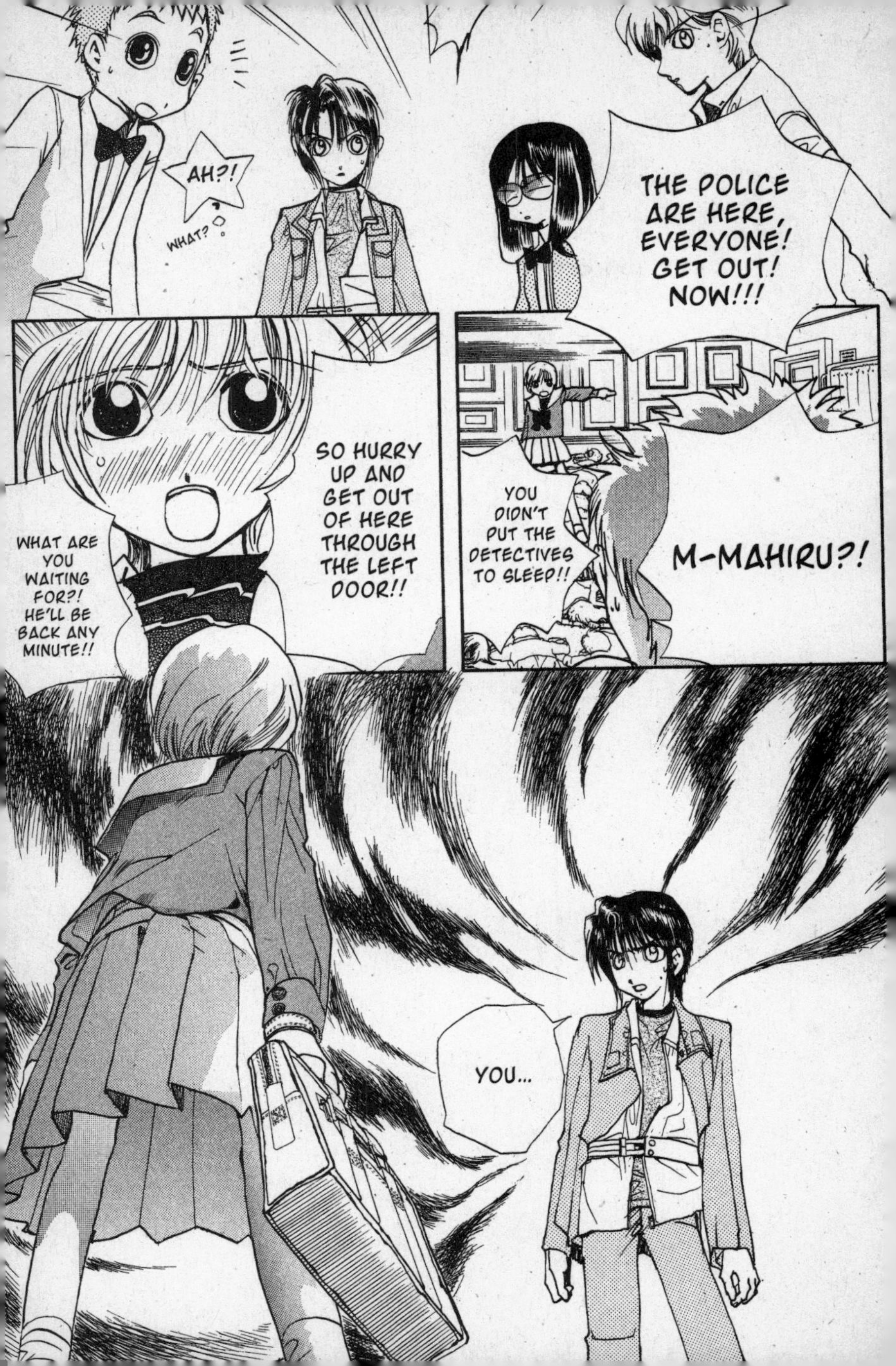
THE POLICE ARE HERE, EVERYONE! GET OUT! NOW!!!
AH?!
WHAT?
M-MAHIRU?!
YOU DIDN'T PUT THE DETECTIVES TO SLEEP!!
SO HURRY UP AND GET OUT OF HERE THROUGH THE LEFT DOOR!!
WHAT ARE YOU WAITING FOR?! HE'LL BE BACK ANY MINUTE!!
YOU...

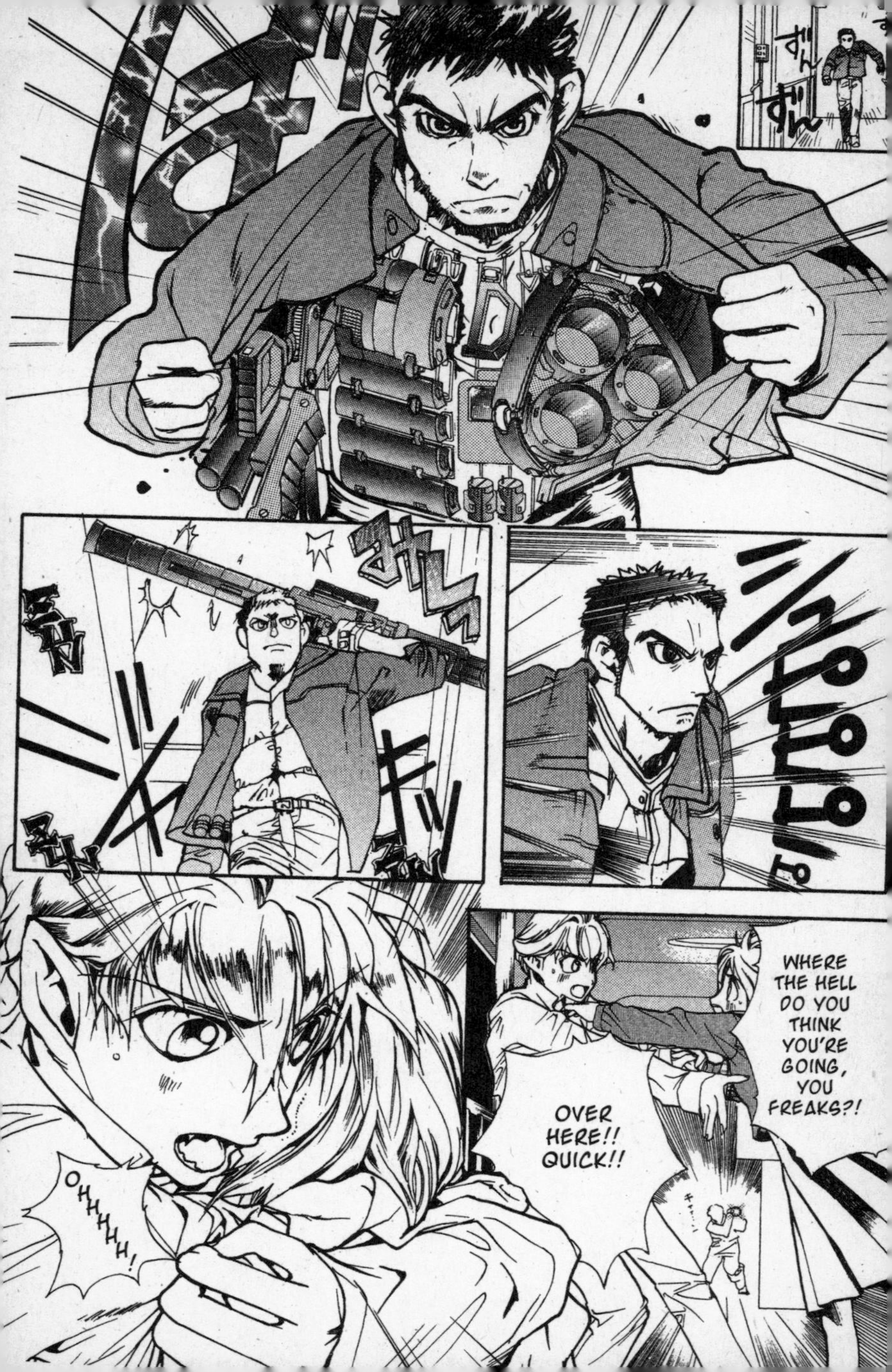
ずん
ずん
WHERE THE HELL DO YOU THINK YOU'RE GOING, YOU FREAKS?!
OVER HERE!! QUICK!!
OHHHHH!

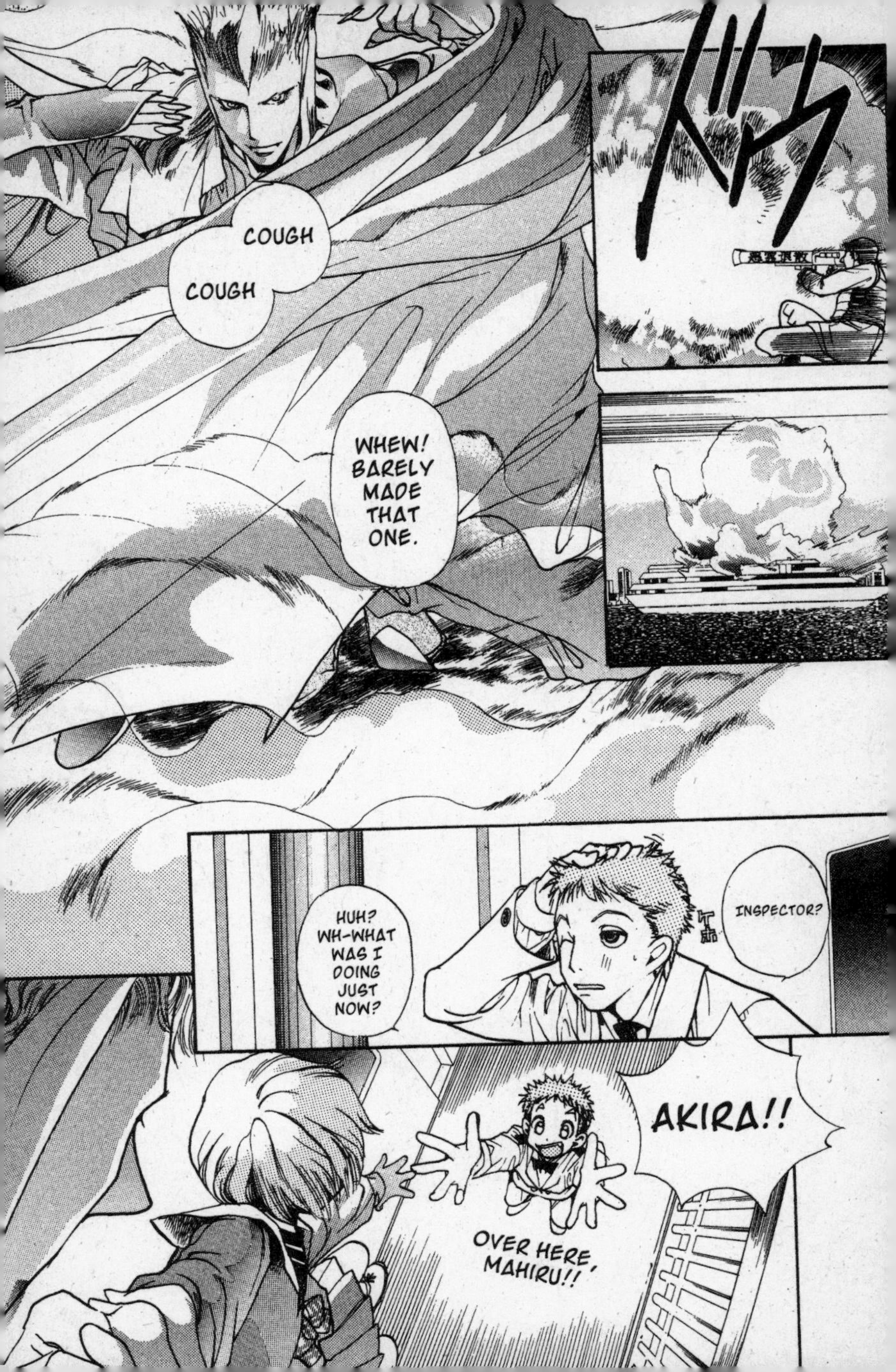
COUGH
COUGH
WHEW! BARELY MADE THAT ONE.
INSPECTOR?
HUH? WH-WHAT WAS I DOING JUST NOW?
AKIRA!!
OVER HERE, MAHIRU!!

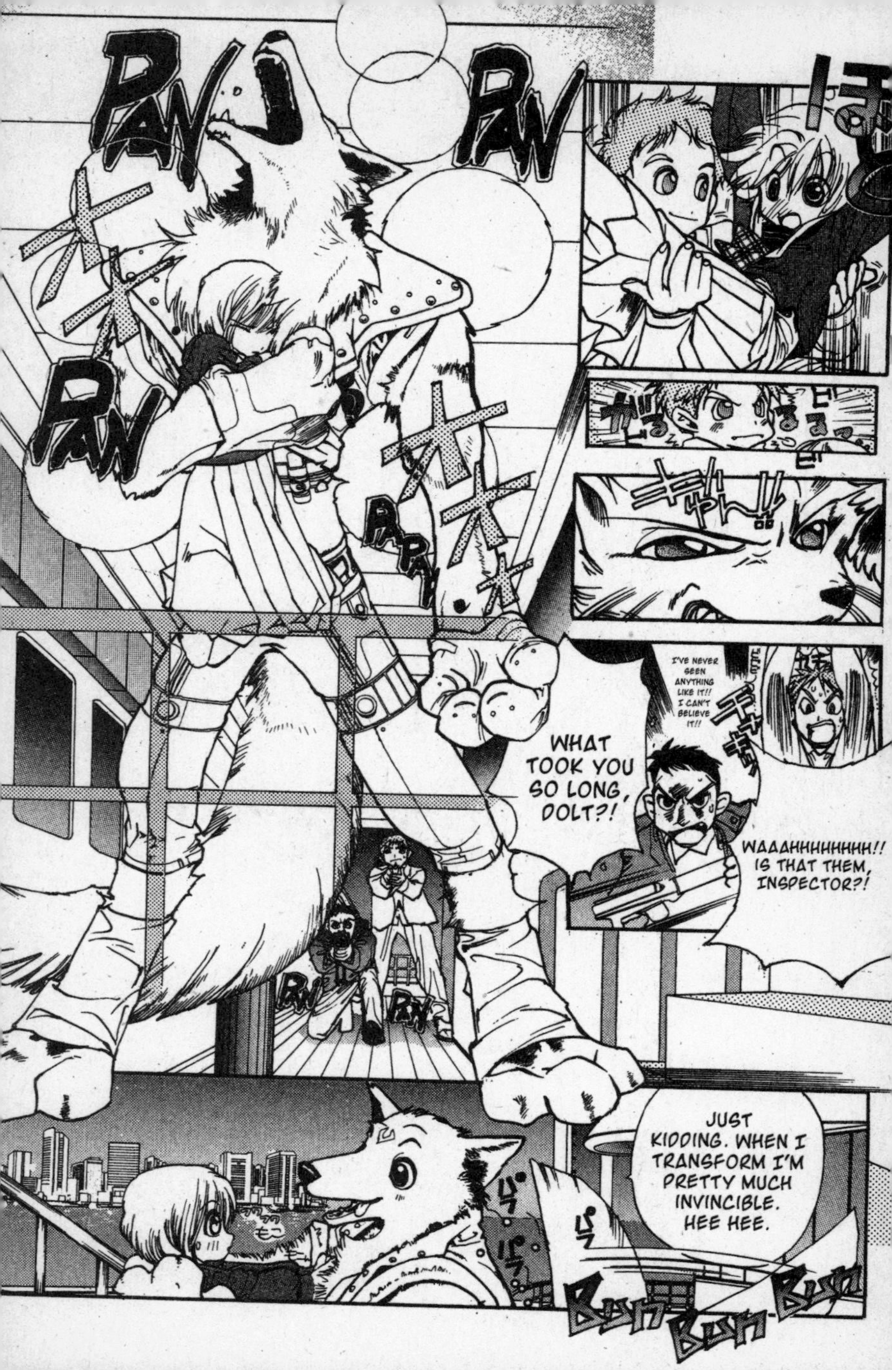

I'VE NEVER SEEN ANYTHING LIKE IT!! I CAN'T BELIEVE IT!!
WHAT TOOK YOU SO LONG, DOLT?!
WAAAHHHHHHHH!! IS THAT THEM, INSPECTOR?!
PAW
PAW
PAW
PAPAW
PAW
PAW
JUST KIDDING. WHEN I TRANSFORM I'M PRETTY MUCH INVINCIBLE. HEE HEE.
BUSH BUSH BUSH

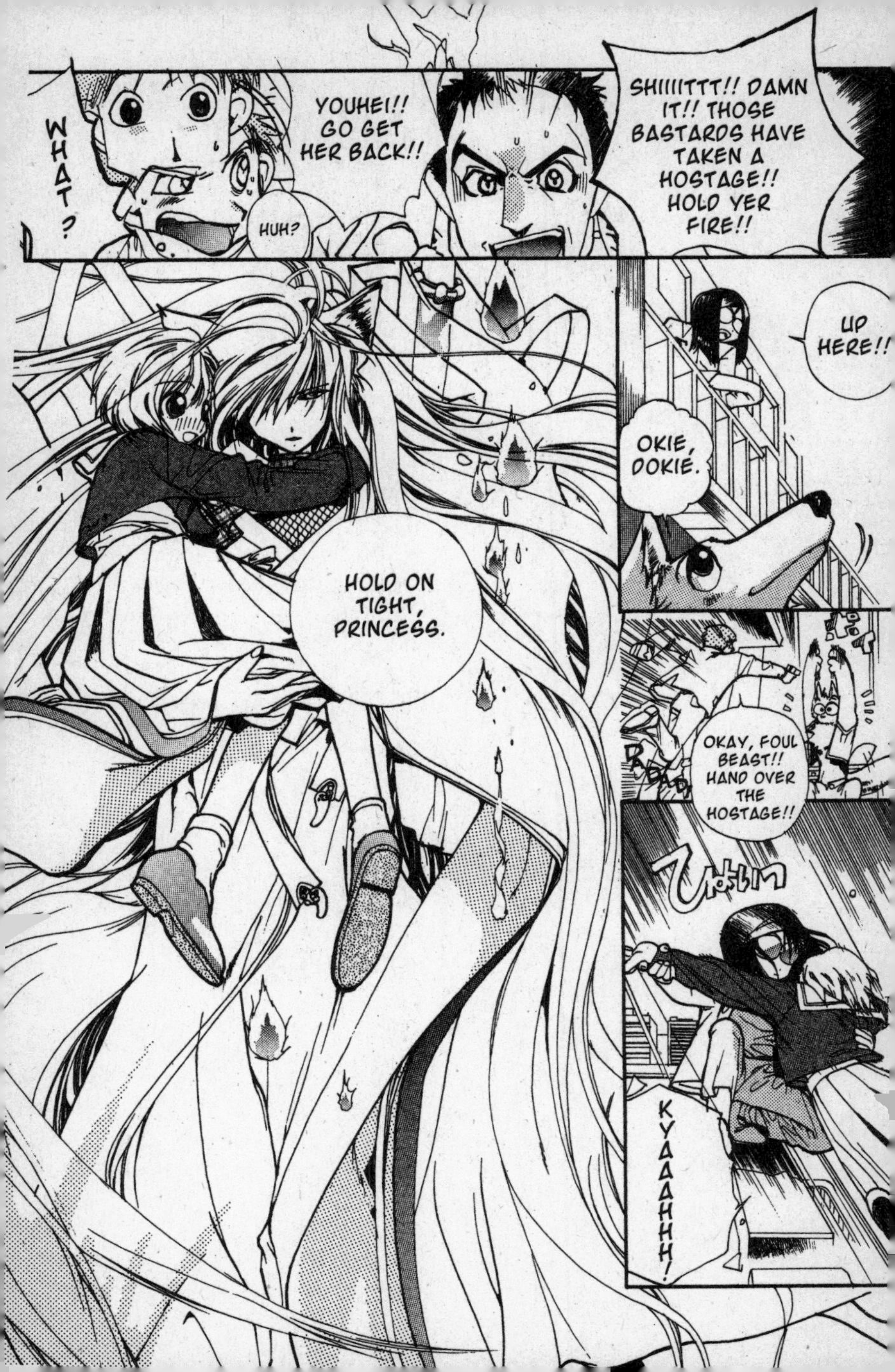
SHIIIITTT!! DAMN IT!! THOSE BASTARDS HAVE TAKEN A HOSTAGE!! HOLD YER FIRE!!
YOUHEI!! GO GET HER BACK!!
HUH?
WHAT?
UP HERE!!
OKIE, DOKIE.
OKAY, FOUL BEAST!! HAND OVER THE HOSTAGE!!
KYAAAHHH!
HOLD ON TIGHT, PRINCESS.

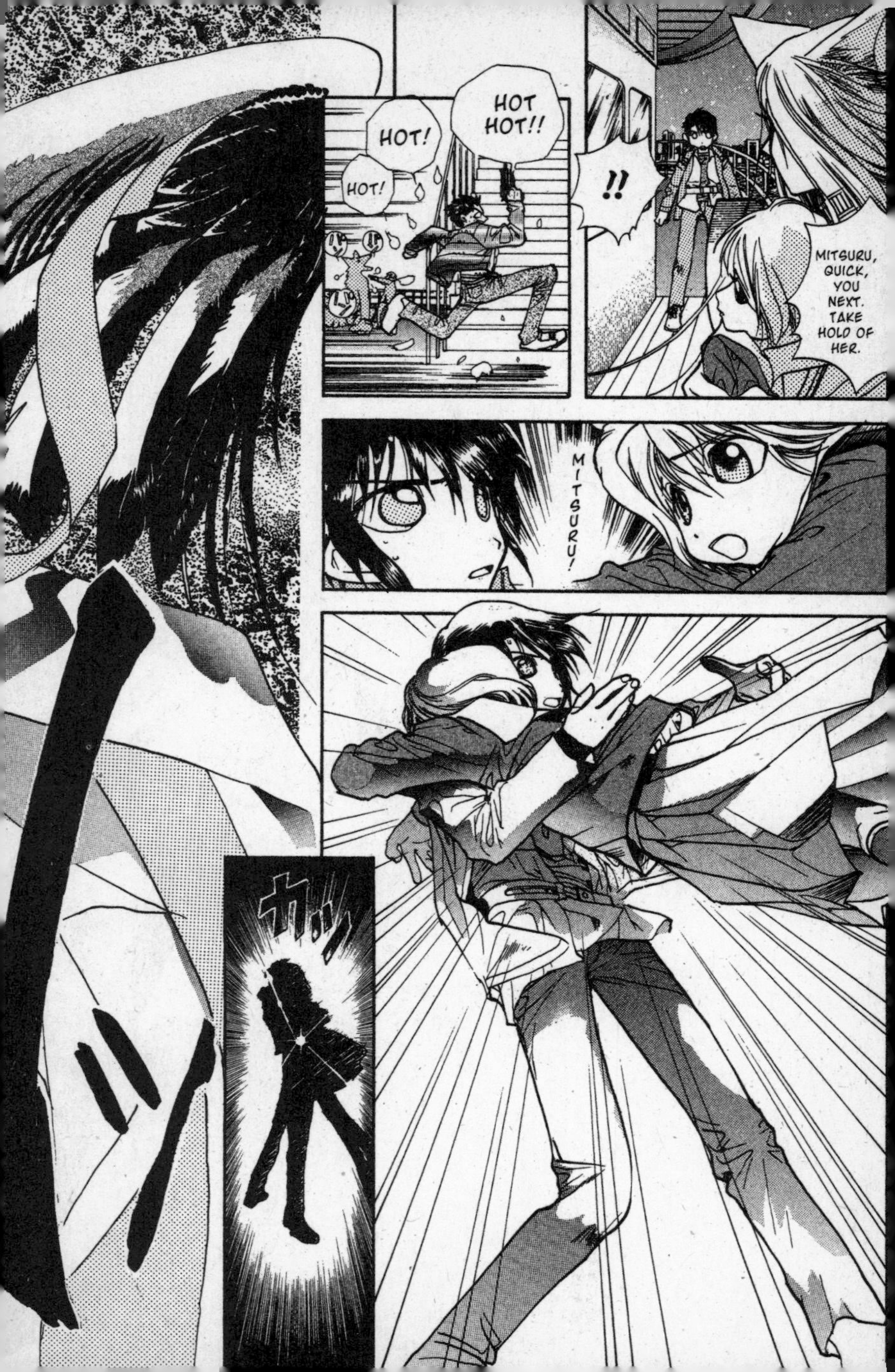
MITSURU, QUICK, YOU NEXT. TAKE HOLD OF HER.
!!
HOT HOT!!
HOT!
HOT!
MITSURU!
カッ

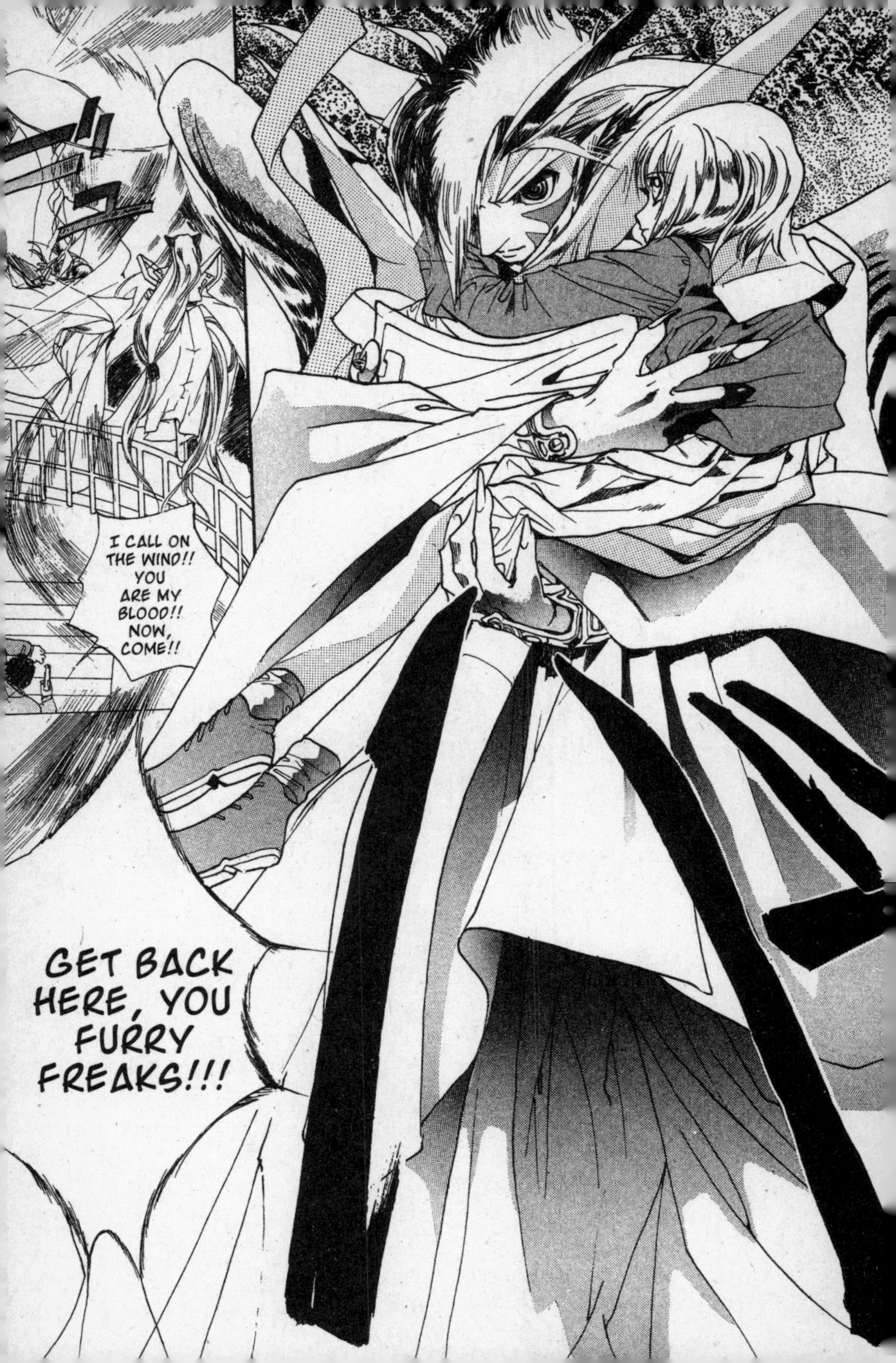
I CALL ON THE WIND!! YOU ARE MY BLOOD!! NOW, COME!!
GET BACK HERE, YOU FURRY FREAKS!!!

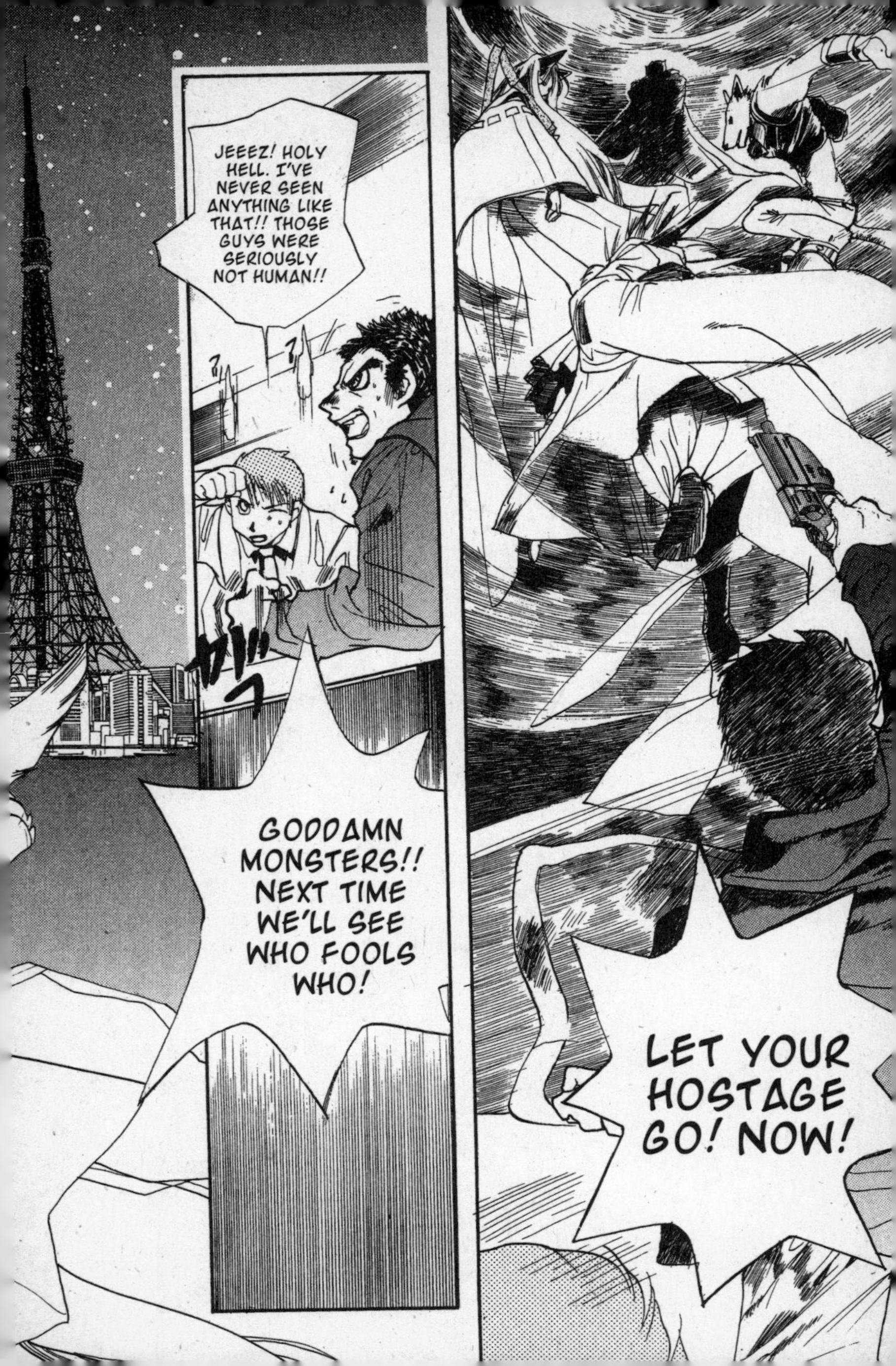
LET YOUR HOSTAGE GO! NOW!
JEEEZ! HOLY HELL. I'VE NEVER SEEN ANYTHING LIKE THAT!! THOSE GUYS WERE SERIOUSLY NOT HUMAN!!
GODDAMN MONSTERS!! NEXT TIME WE'LL SEE WHO FOOLS WHO!

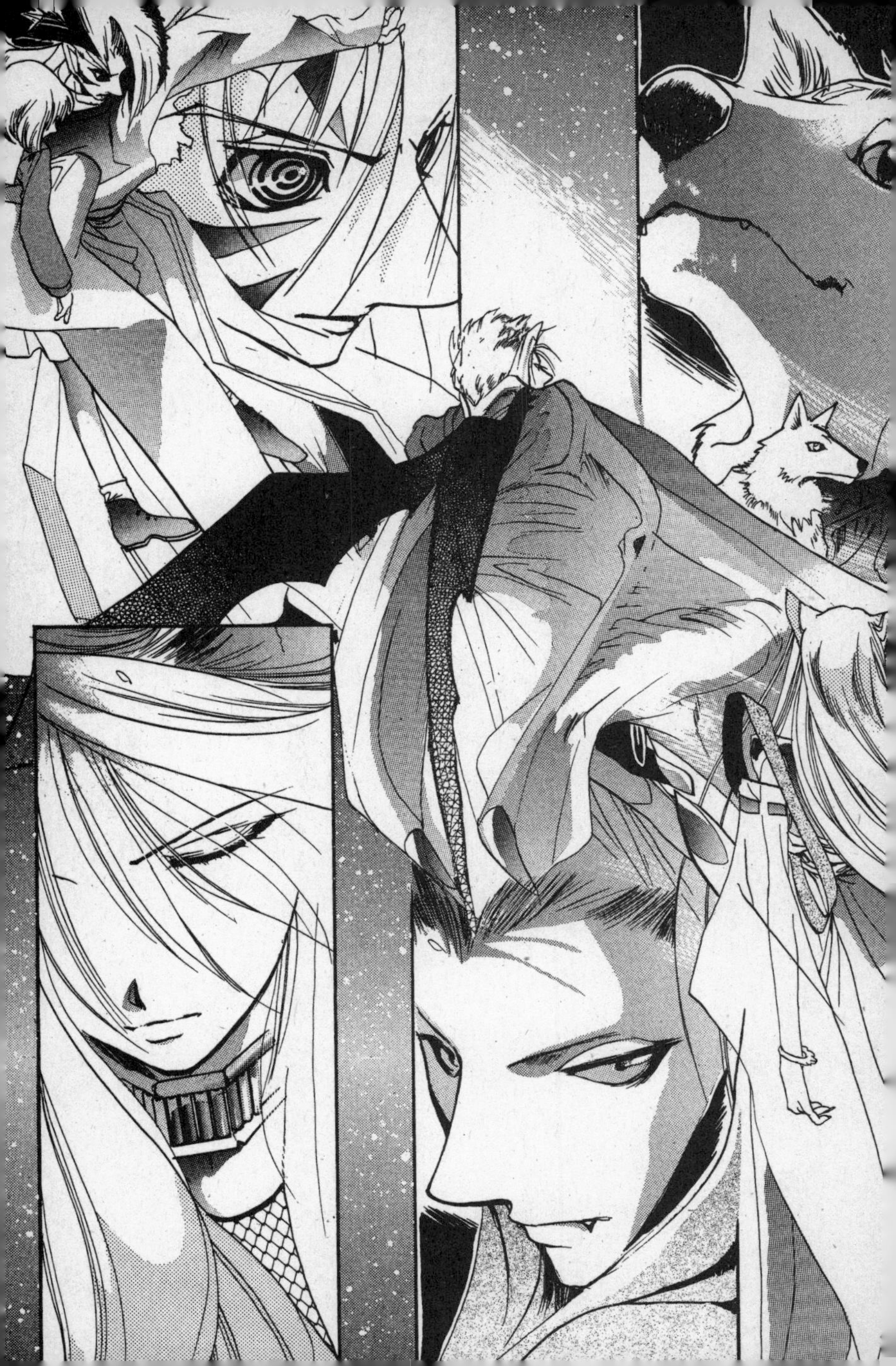

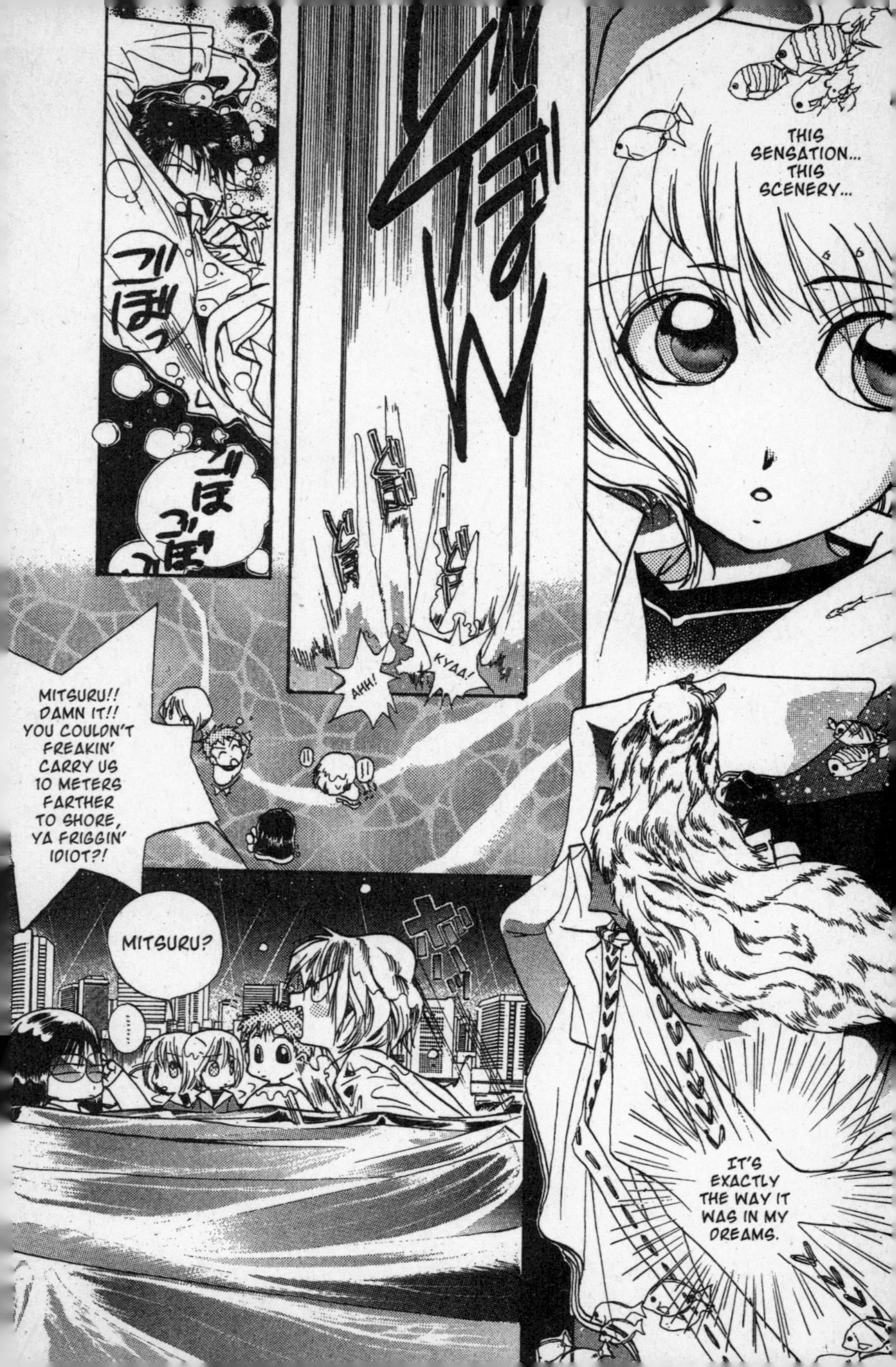
THIS SENSATION... THIS SCENERY...
IT'S EXACTLY THE WAY IT WAS IN MY DREAMS.
KYAA!
AHH!
MITSURU!! DAMN IT!! YOU COULDN'T FREAKIN' CARRY US 10 METERS FARTHER TO SHORE, YA FRIGGIN' IDIOT?!
MITSURU?
......

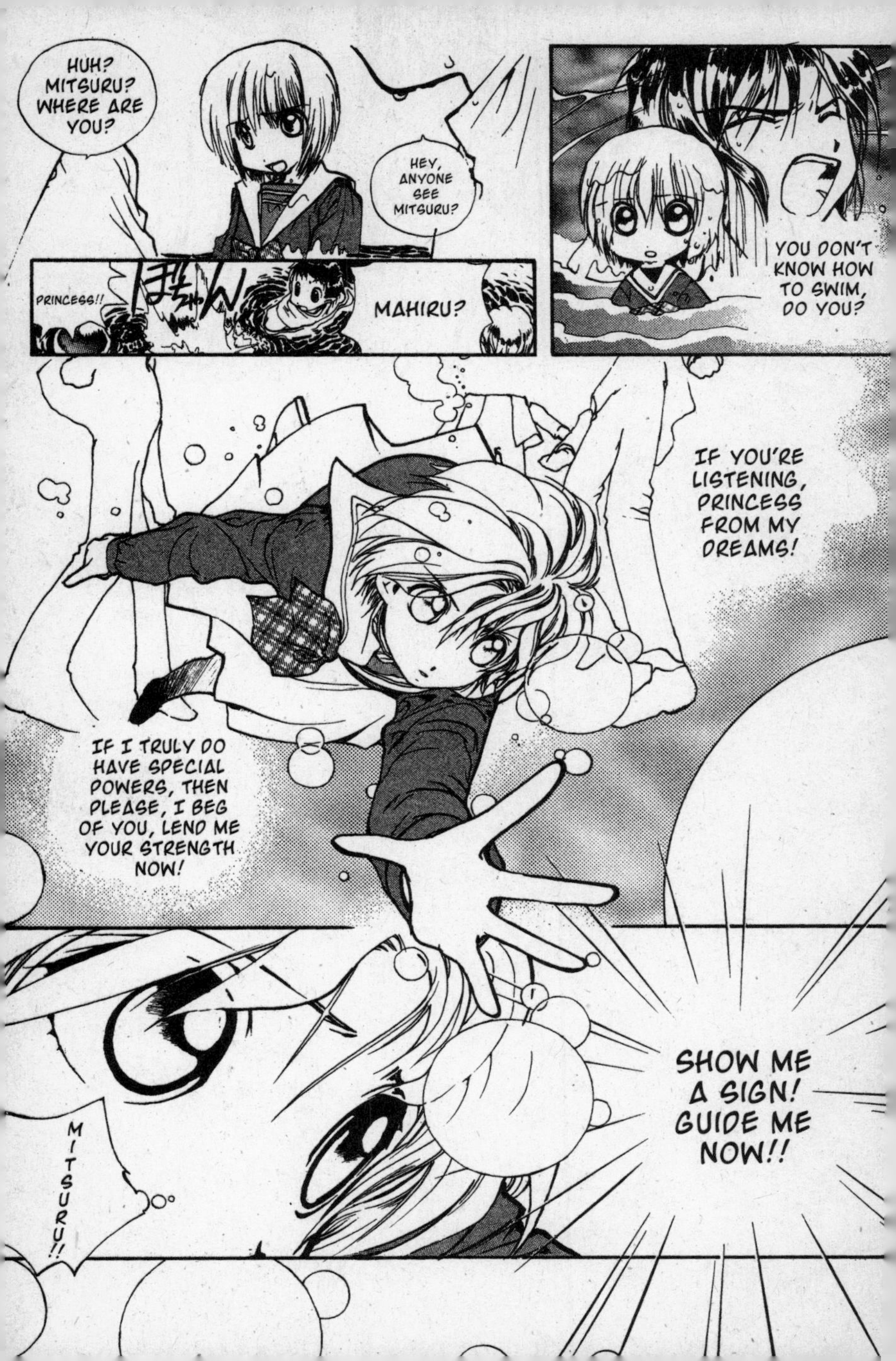
YOU DON'T KNOW HOW TO SWIM, DO YOU?
HEY, ANYONE SEE MITSURU?
HUH? MITSURU? WHERE ARE YOU?
MAHIRU?
ぼちゃん
PRINCESS!!
IF YOU'RE LISTENING, PRINCESS FROM MY DREAMS!
IF I TRULY DO HAVE SPECIAL POWERS, THEN PLEASE, I BEG OF YOU, LEND ME YOUR STRENGTH NOW!
SHOW ME A SIGN! GUIDE ME NOW!!
MITSURU!!

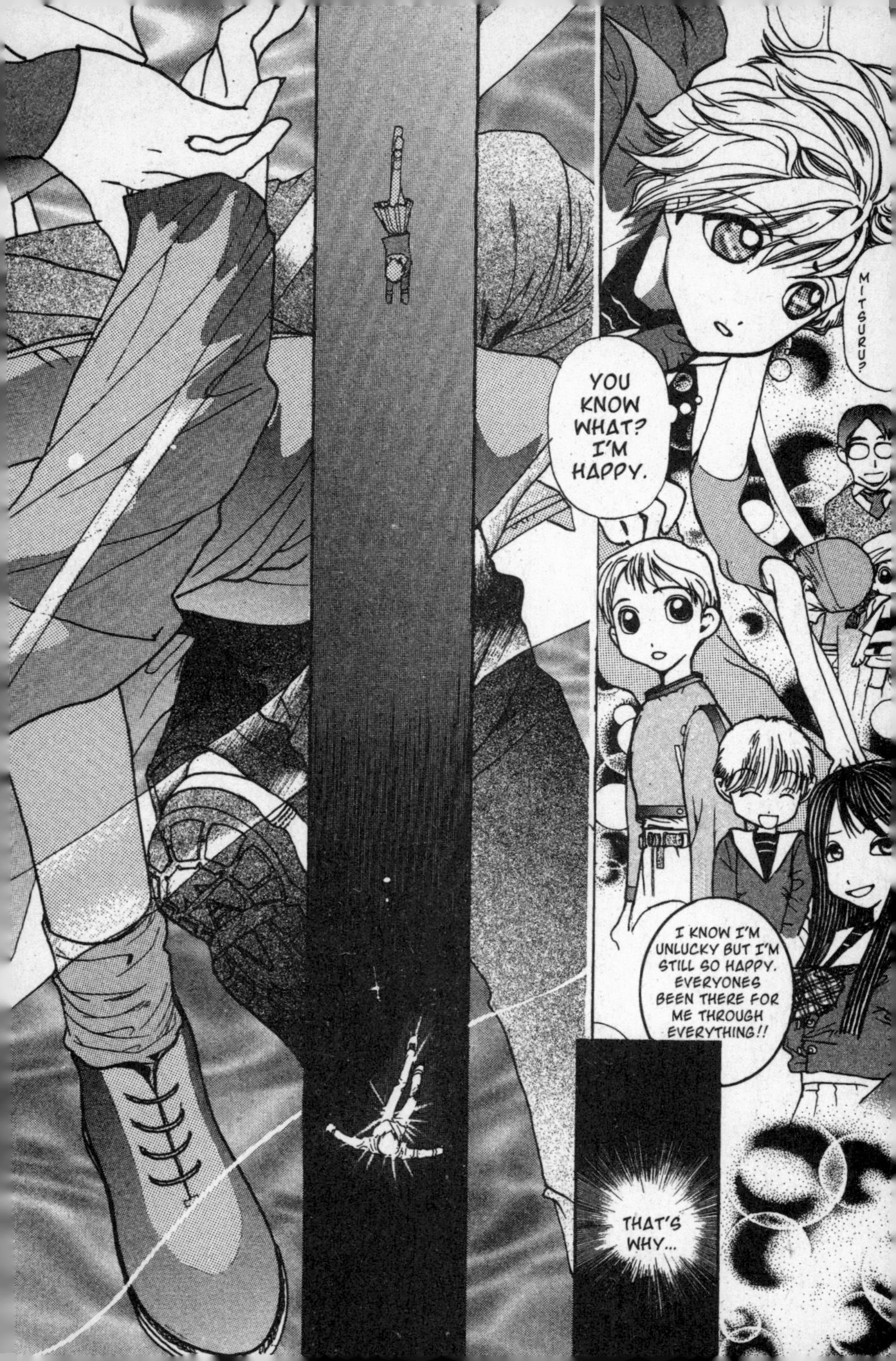
MITSURU?
YOU KNOW WHAT? I'M HAPPY.
I KNOW I'M UNLUCKY BUT I'M STILL SO HAPPY. EVERYONES BEEN THERE FOR ME THROUGH EVERYTHING!!
THAT'S WHY...

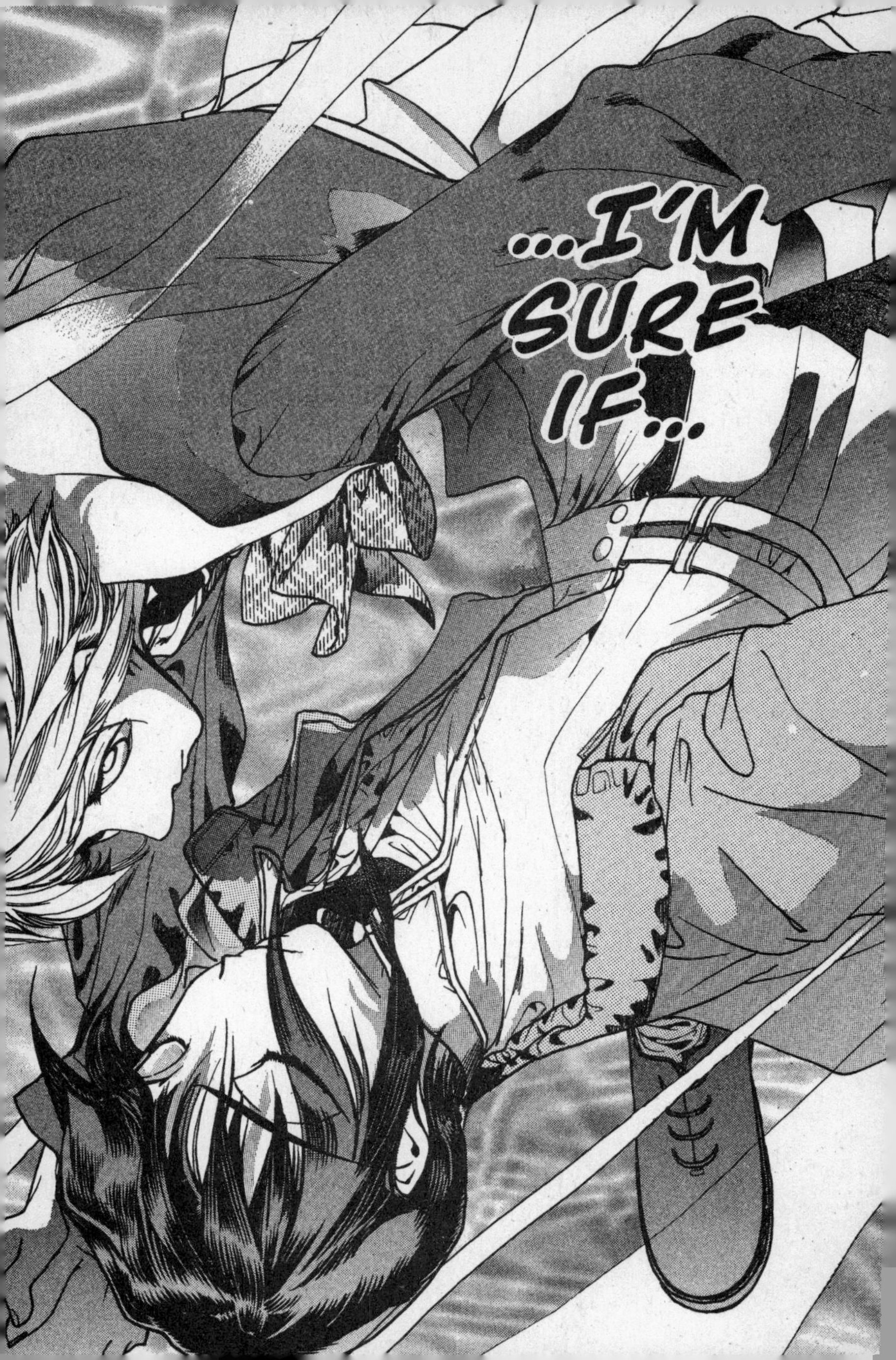
...I'M SURE IF...

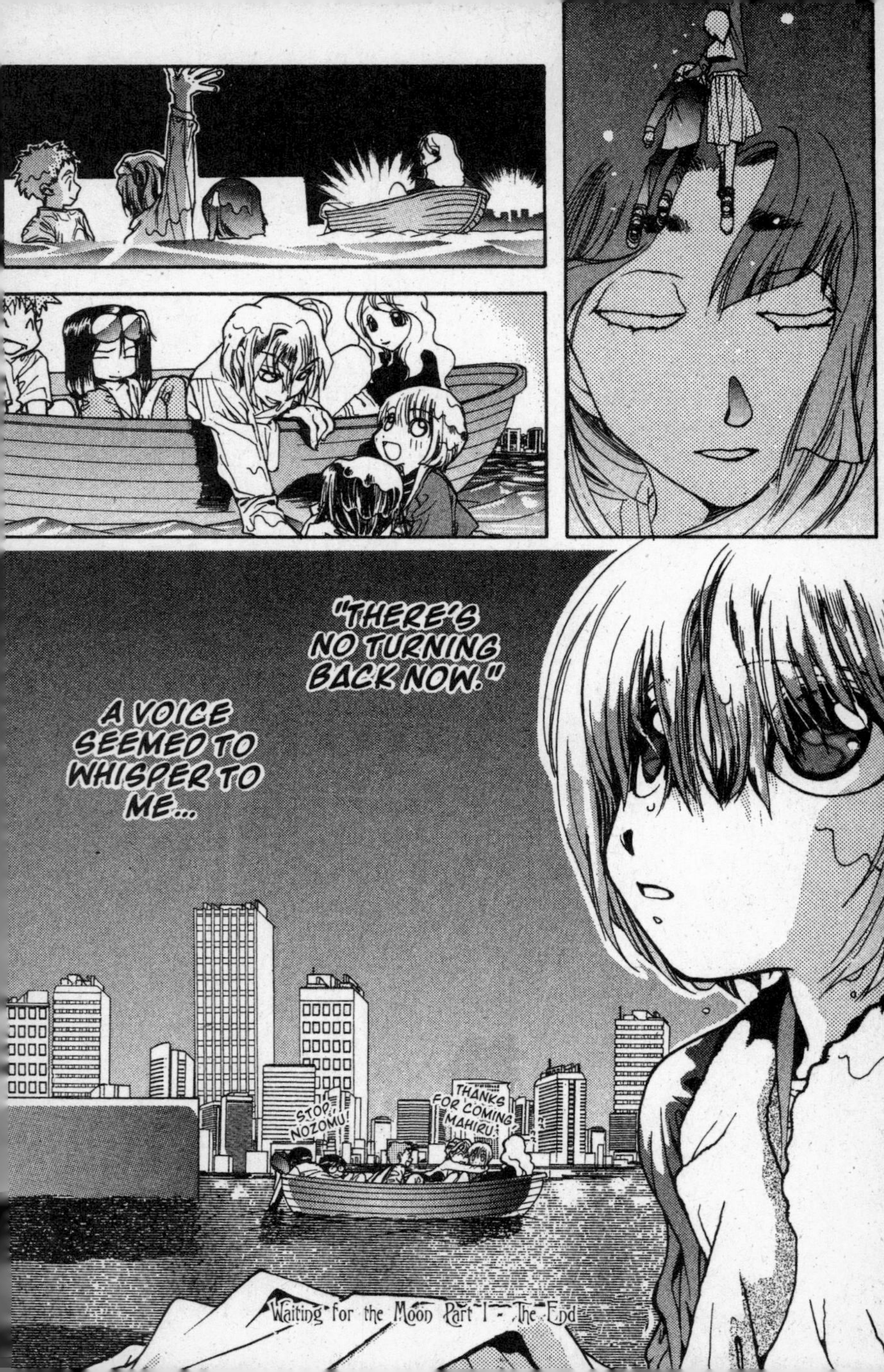
"THERE'S NO TURNING BACK NOW."
A VOICE SEEMED TO WHISPER TO ME...
THANKS FOR COMING MAHIRU!
STOP, NOZOMU!
Waiting for the Moon Part I - The End

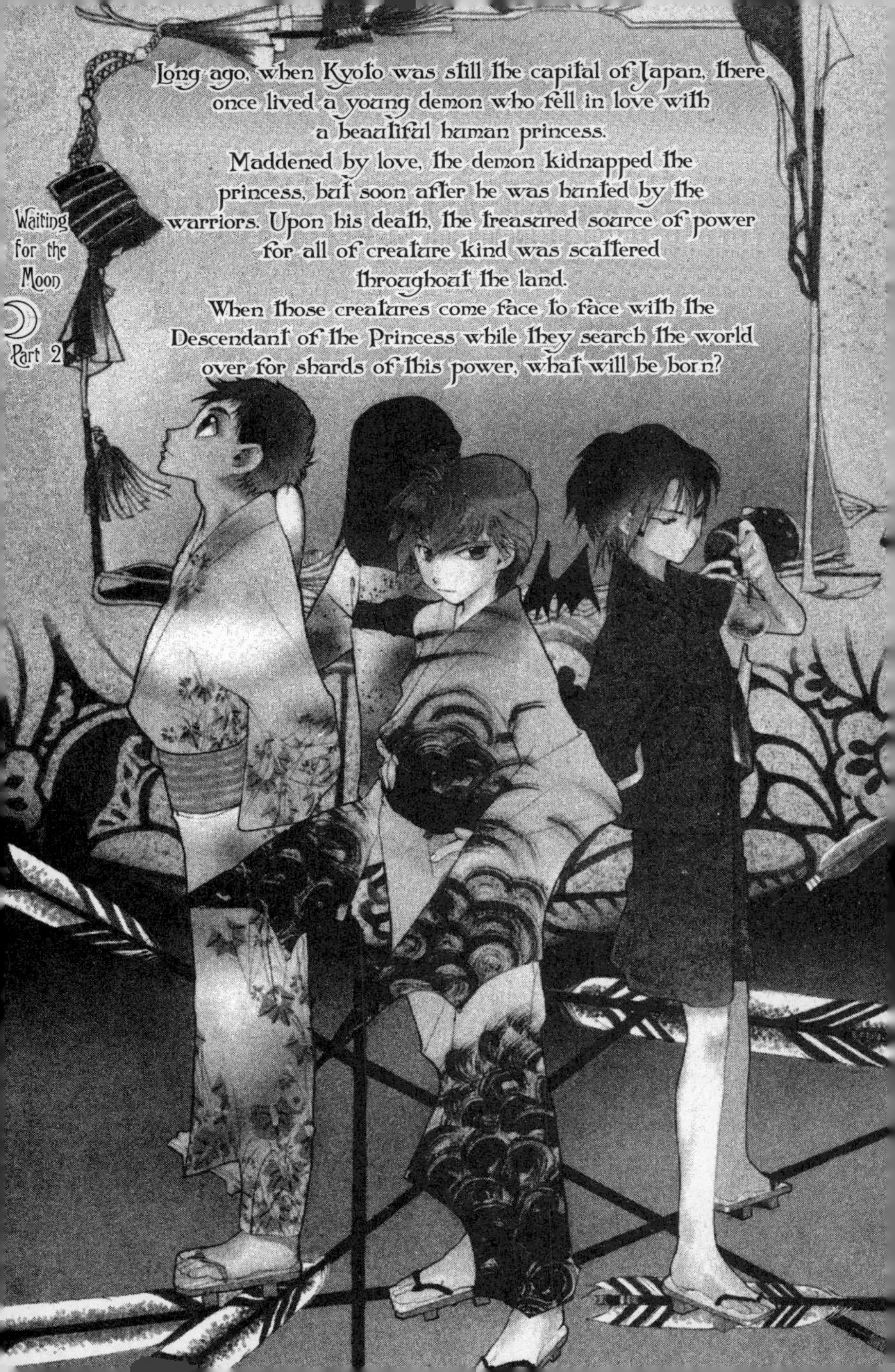
Waiting for the Moon Part 2
Long ago, when Kyoto was still the capital of Japan, there once lived a young demon who fell in love with a beautiful human princess.
Maddened by love, the demon kidnapped the princess, but soon after he was hunted by the warriors. Upon his death, the treasured source of power for all of creature kind was scattered throughout the land.
When those creatures come face to face with the Descendant of the Princess while they search the world over for shards of this power, what will be born?

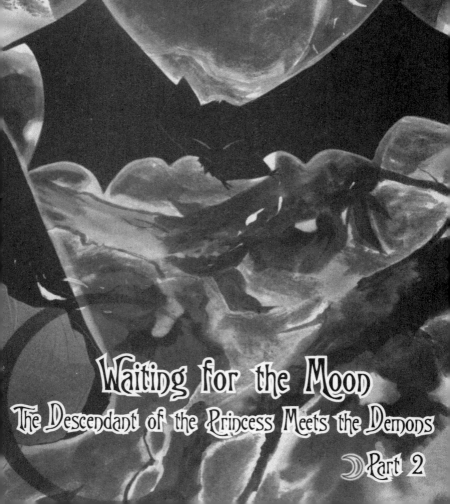

Waiting for the Moon
The Descendant of the Princess Meets the Demons

Part 2

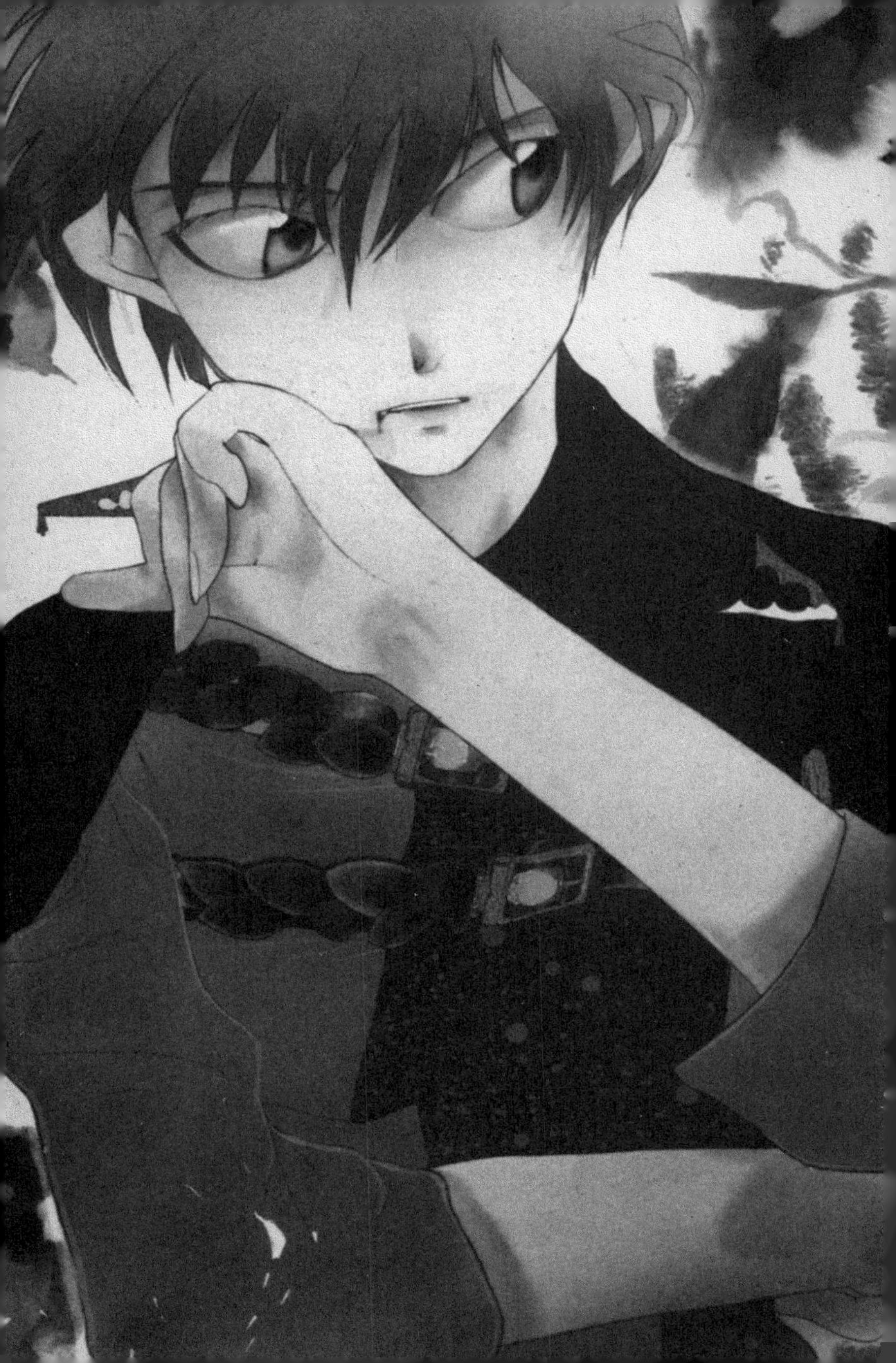

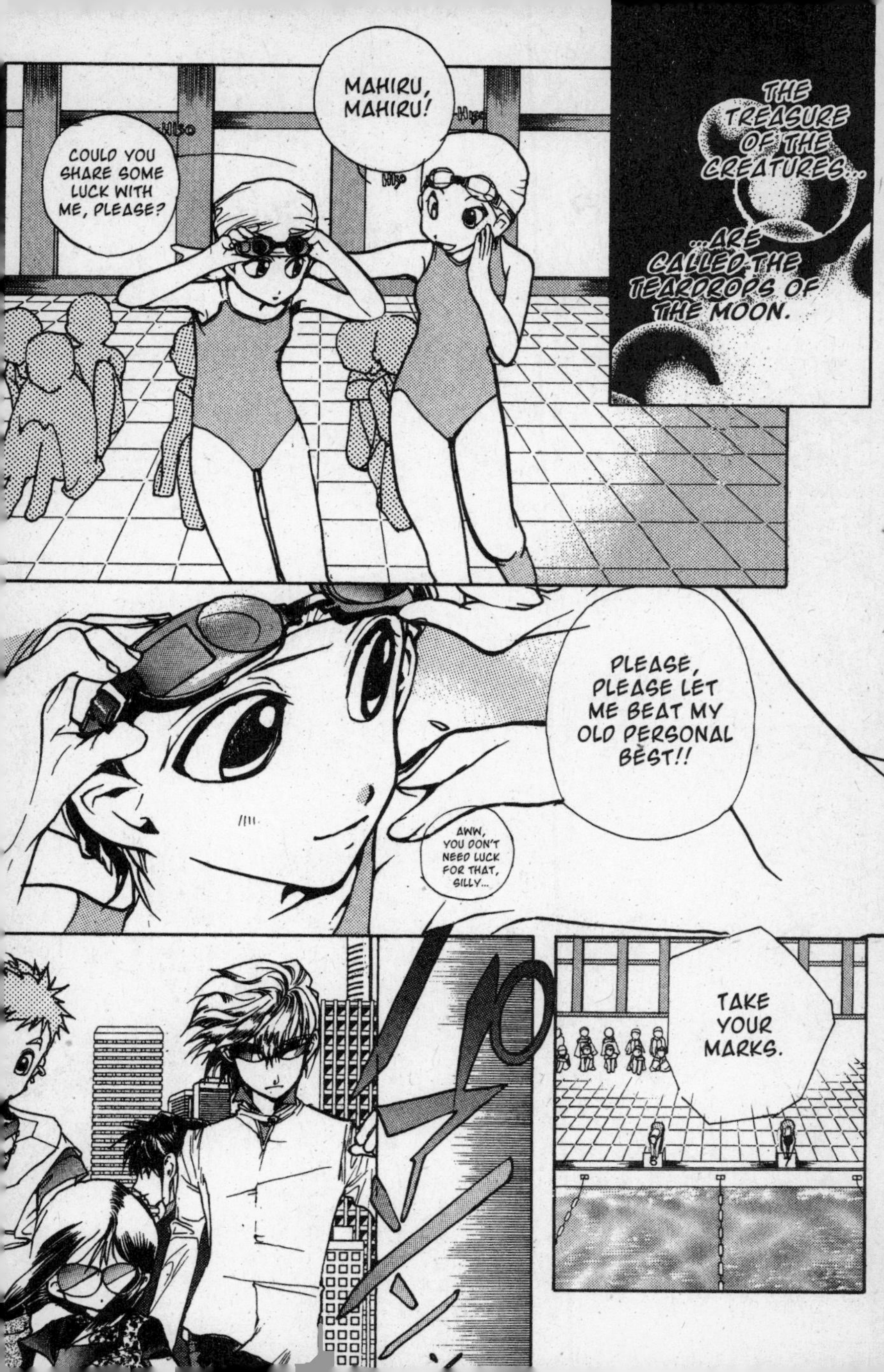
THE TREASURE OF THE CREATURES...
...ARE CALLED THE TEARDROPS OF THE MOON.
MAHIRU, MAHIRU!
COULD YOU SHARE SOME LUCK WITH ME, PLEASE?
PLEASE, PLEASE LET ME BEAT MY OLD PERSONAL BEST!!
AWW, YOU DON'T NEED LUCK FOR THAT, SILLY...
TAKE YOUR MARKS.

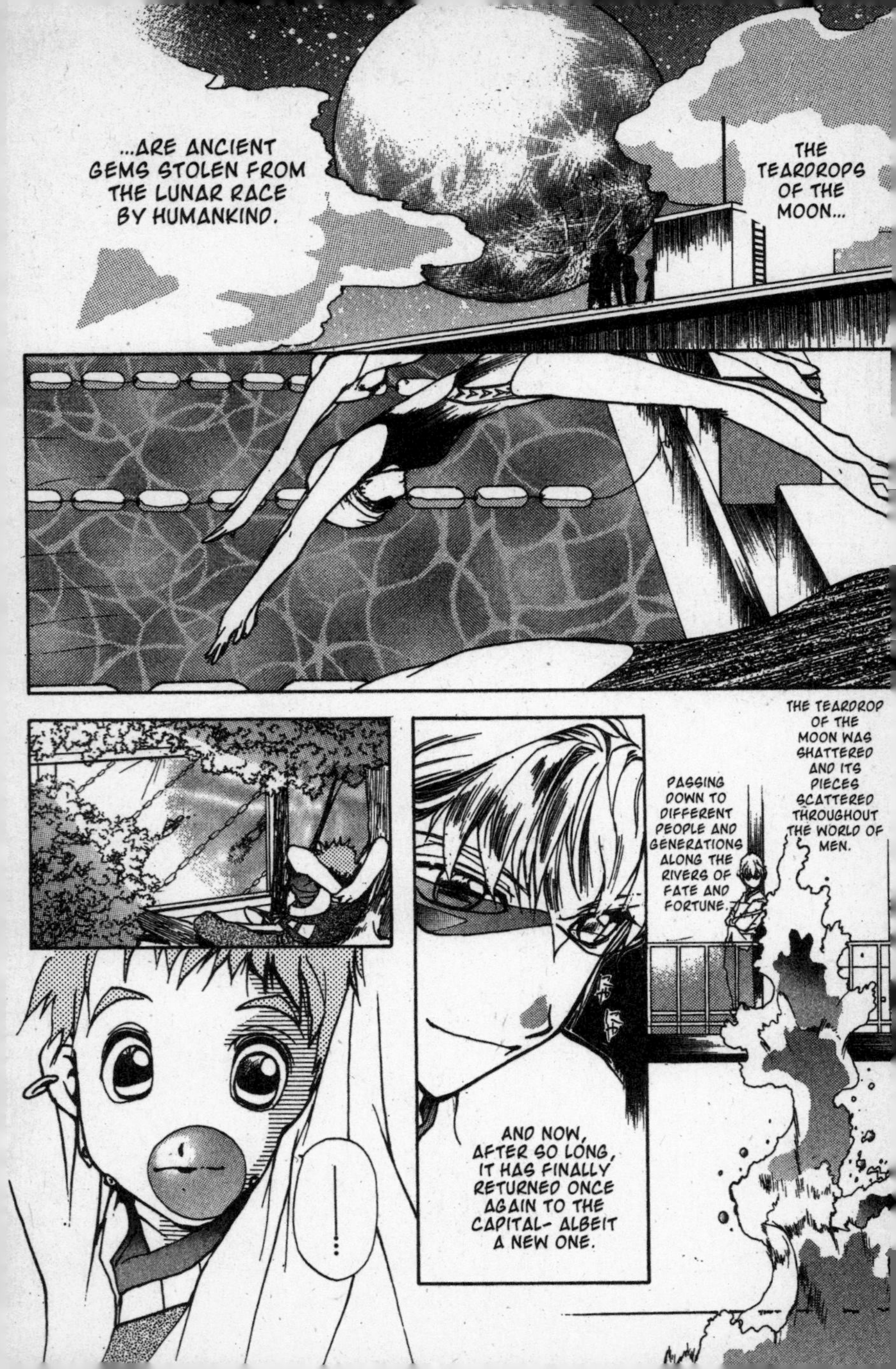
THE TEARDROPS OF THE MOON...
...ARE ANCIENT GEMS STOLEN FROM THE LUNAR RACE BY HUMANKIND.
THE TEARDROP OF THE MOON WAS SHATTERED AND ITS PIECES SCATTERED THROUGHOUT THE WORLD OF MEN.
PASSING DOWN TO DIFFERENT PEOPLE AND GENERATIONS ALONG THE RIVERS OF FATE AND FORTUNE.
AND NOW, AFTER SO LONG, IT HAS FINALLY RETURNED ONCE AGAIN TO THE CAPITAL- ALBEIT A NEW ONE.
......

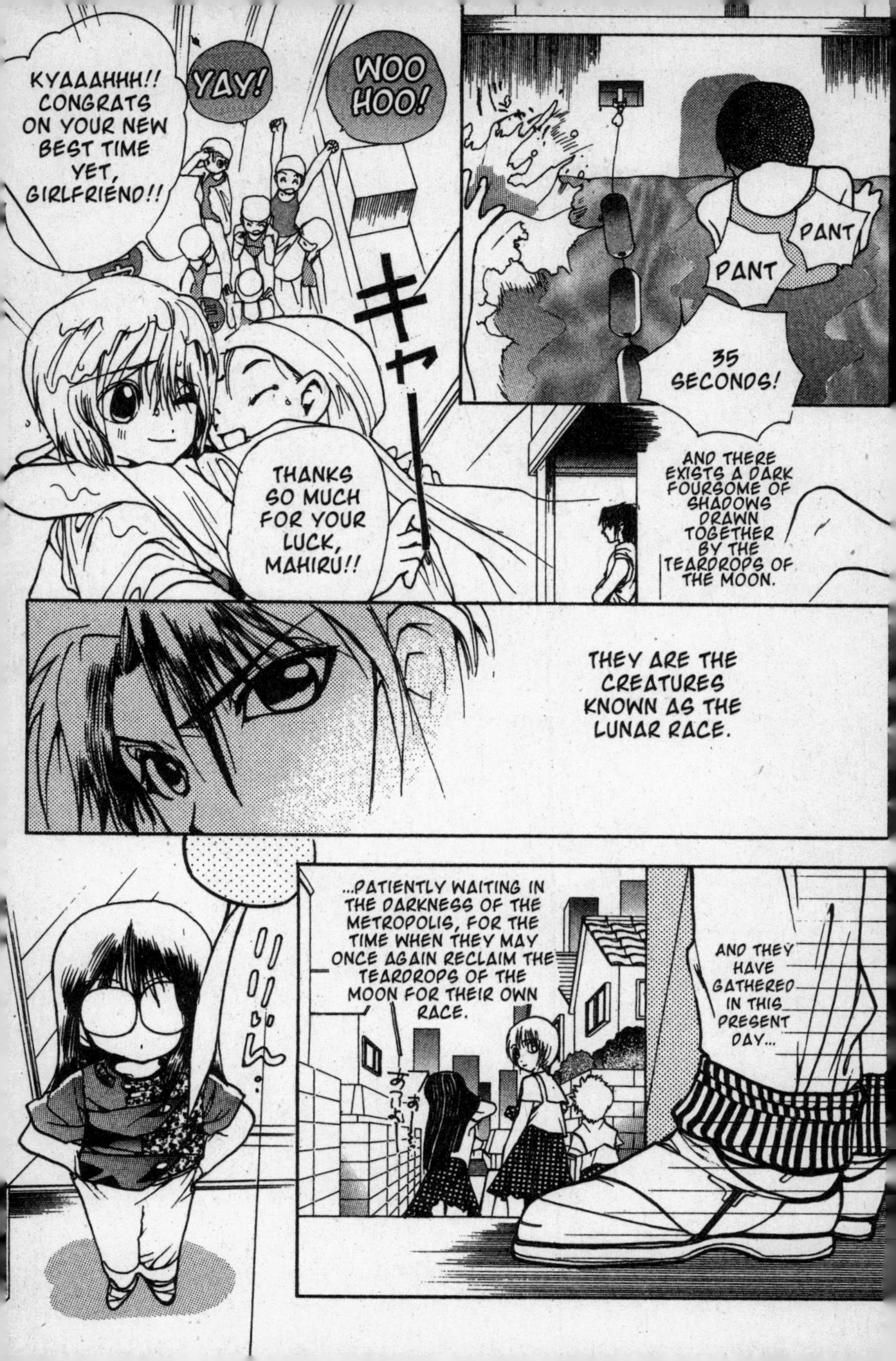

PANT
PANT
35 SECONDS!
AND THERE EXISTS A DARK FOURSOME OF SHADOWS DRAWN TOGETHER BY THE TEARDROPS OF THE MOON.
WOO HOO!
YAY!
KYAAAHHH!! CONGRATS ON YOUR NEW BEST TIME YET, GIRLFRIEND!!
キャー
THANKS SO MUCH FOR YOUR LUCK, MAHIRU!!
THEY ARE THE CREATURES KNOWN AS THE LUNAR RACE.
AND THEY HAVE GATHERED IN THIS PRESENT DAY...
...PATIENTLY WAITING IN THE DARKNESS OF THE METROPOLIS, FOR THE TIME WHEN THEY MAY ONCE AGAIN RECLAIM THE TEARDROPS OF THE MOON FOR THEIR OWN RACE.

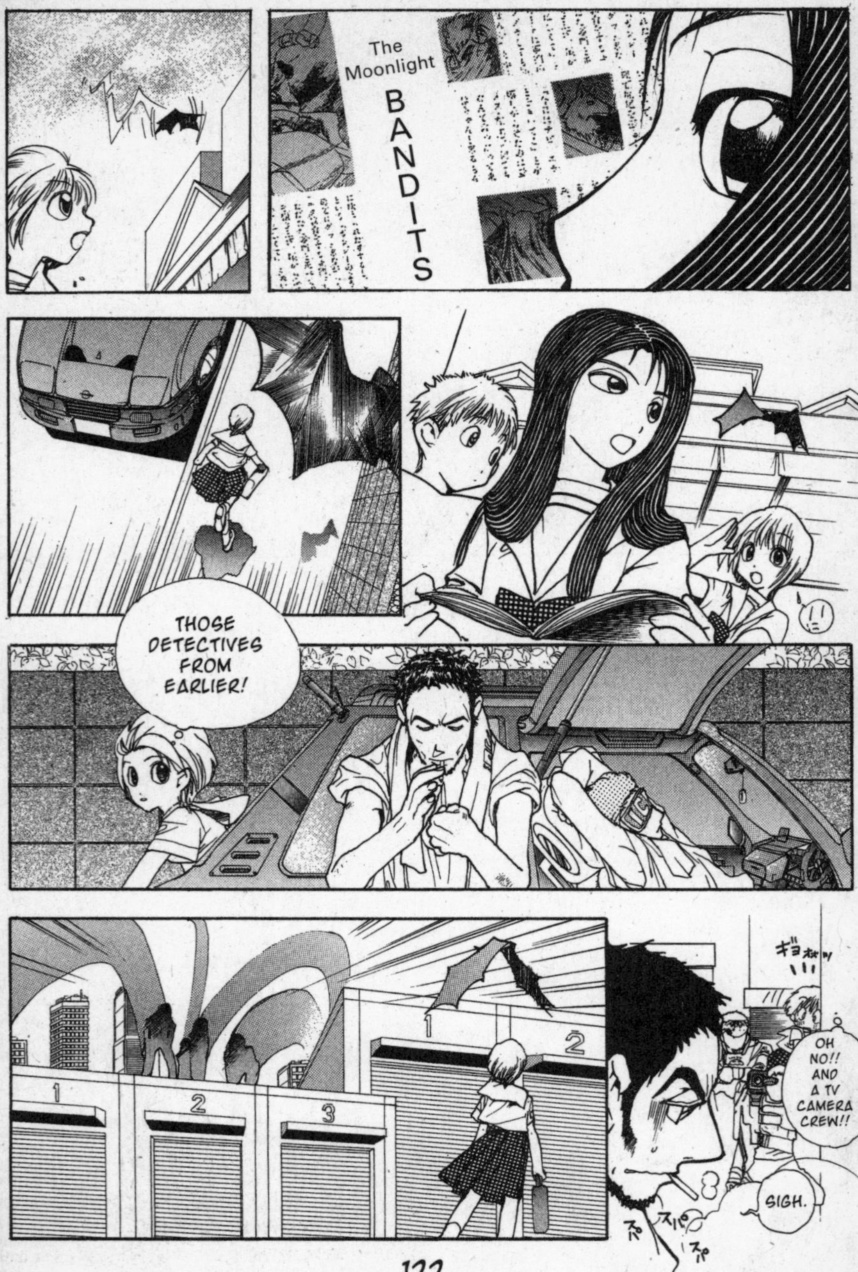
The Moonlight
BANDITS
THOSE DETECTIVES FROM EARLIER!
OH NO!! AND A TV CAMERA CREW!!
SIGH.

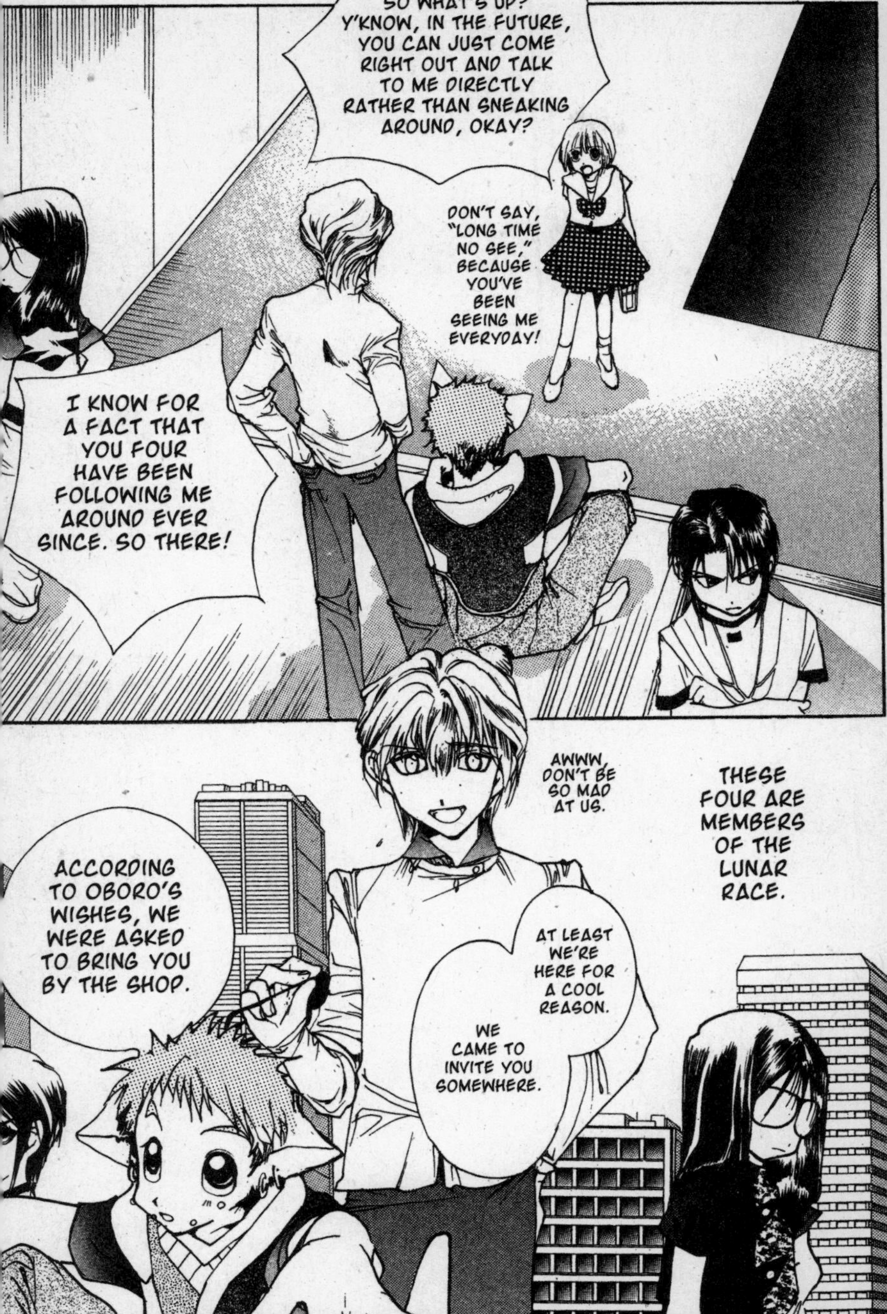
SO WHAT'S UP? Y'KNOW, IN THE FUTURE, YOU CAN JUST COME RIGHT OUT AND TALK TO ME DIRECTLY RATHER THAN SNEAKING AROUND, OKAY?
DON'T SAY, "LONG TIME NO SEE," BECAUSE YOU'VE BEEN SEEING ME EVERYDAY!
I KNOW FOR A FACT THAT YOU FOUR HAVE BEEN FOLLOWING ME AROUND EVER SINCE. SO THERE!
THESE FOUR ARE MEMBERS OF THE LUNAR RACE.
AWWW, DON'T BE SO MAD AT US.
AT LEAST WE'RE HERE FOR A COOL REASON.
WE CAME TO INVITE YOU SOMEWHERE.
ACCORDING TO OBORO'S WISHES, WE WERE ASKED TO BRING YOU BY THE SHOP.

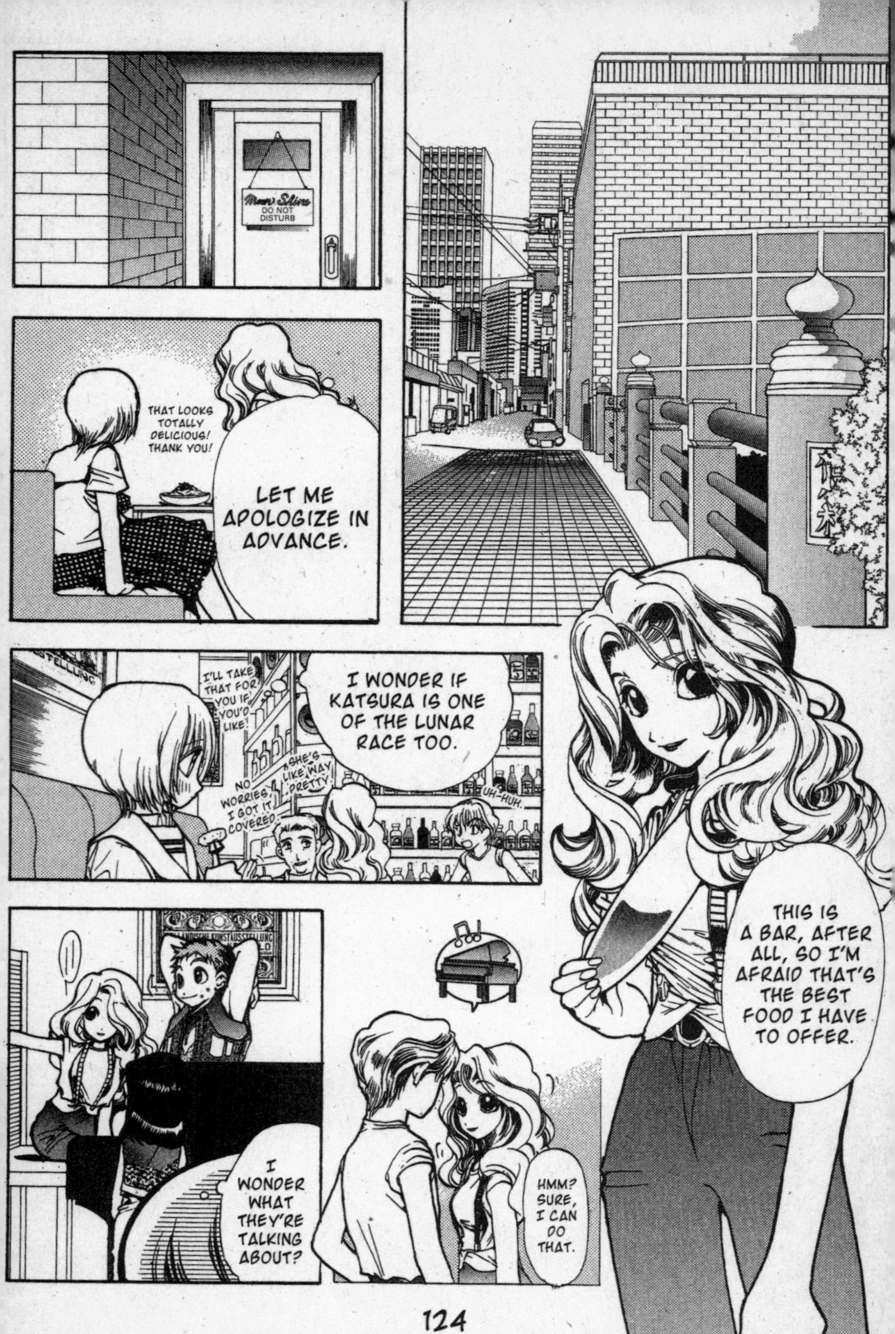

Moon Shine
DO NOT DISTURB
LET ME APOLOGIZE IN ADVANCE.
THAT LOOKS TOTALLY DELICIOUS! THANK YOU!
THIS IS A BAR, AFTER ALL, SO I'M AFRAID THAT'S THE BEST FOOD I HAVE TO OFFER.
I WONDER IF KATSURA IS ONE OF THE LUNAR RACE TOO.
UH-HUH.
SHE'S LIKE WAY PRETTY
I'LL TAKE THAT FOR YOU IF YOU'D LIKE!
NO WORRIES, I GOT IT COVERED.
HMM? SURE, I CAN DO THAT.
I WONDER WHAT THEY'RE TALKING ABOUT?

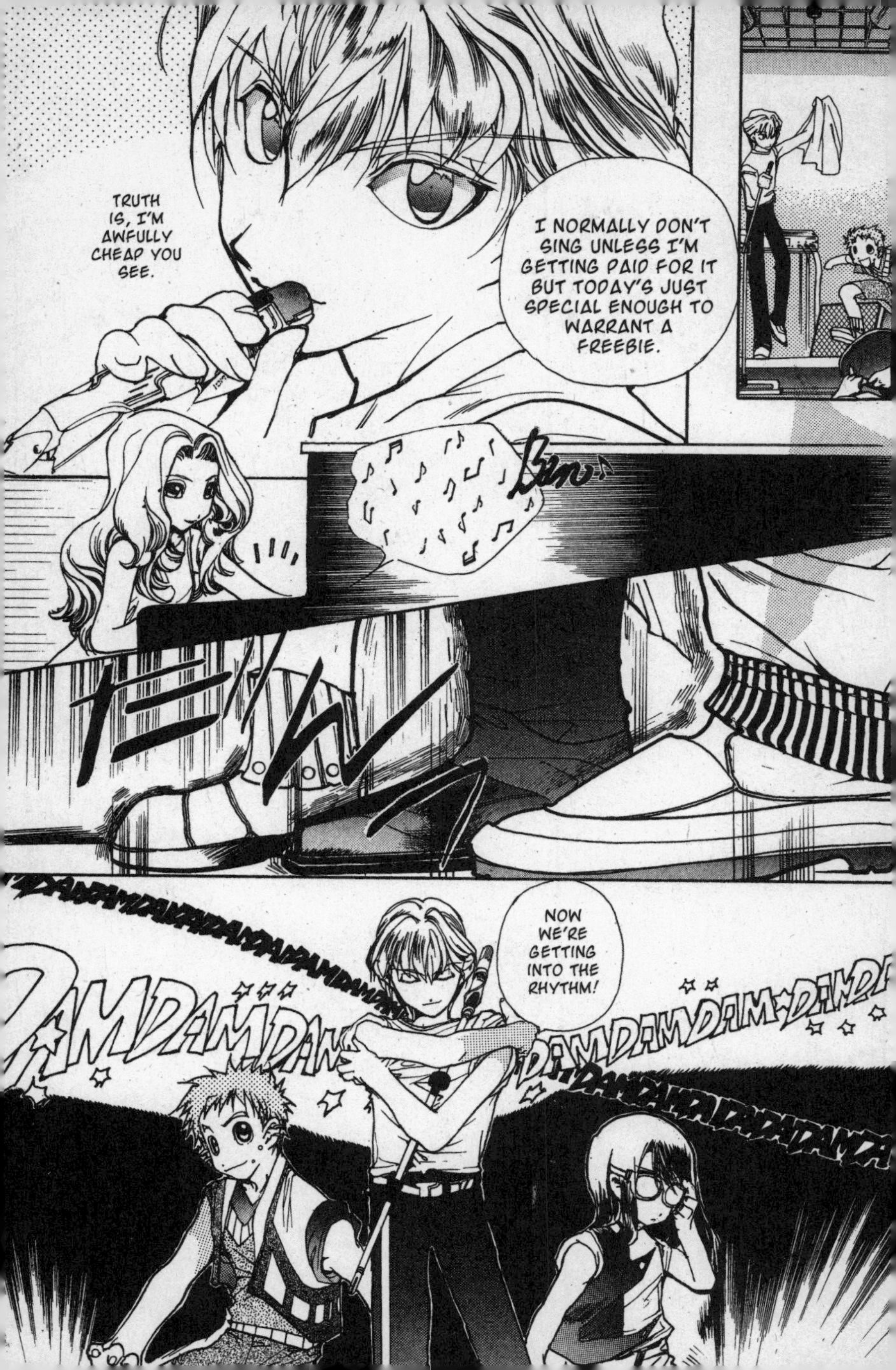
I NORMALLY DON'T SING UNLESS I'M GETTING PAID FOR IT BUT TODAY'S JUST SPECIAL ENOUGH TO WARRANT A FREEBIE.
TRUTH IS, I'M AWFULLY CHEAP YOU SEE.
Ben♪
NOW WE'RE GETTING INTO THE RHYTHM!
DAMDAMDAM-DAMDAMDAM-DAM
DAMDAMDAN

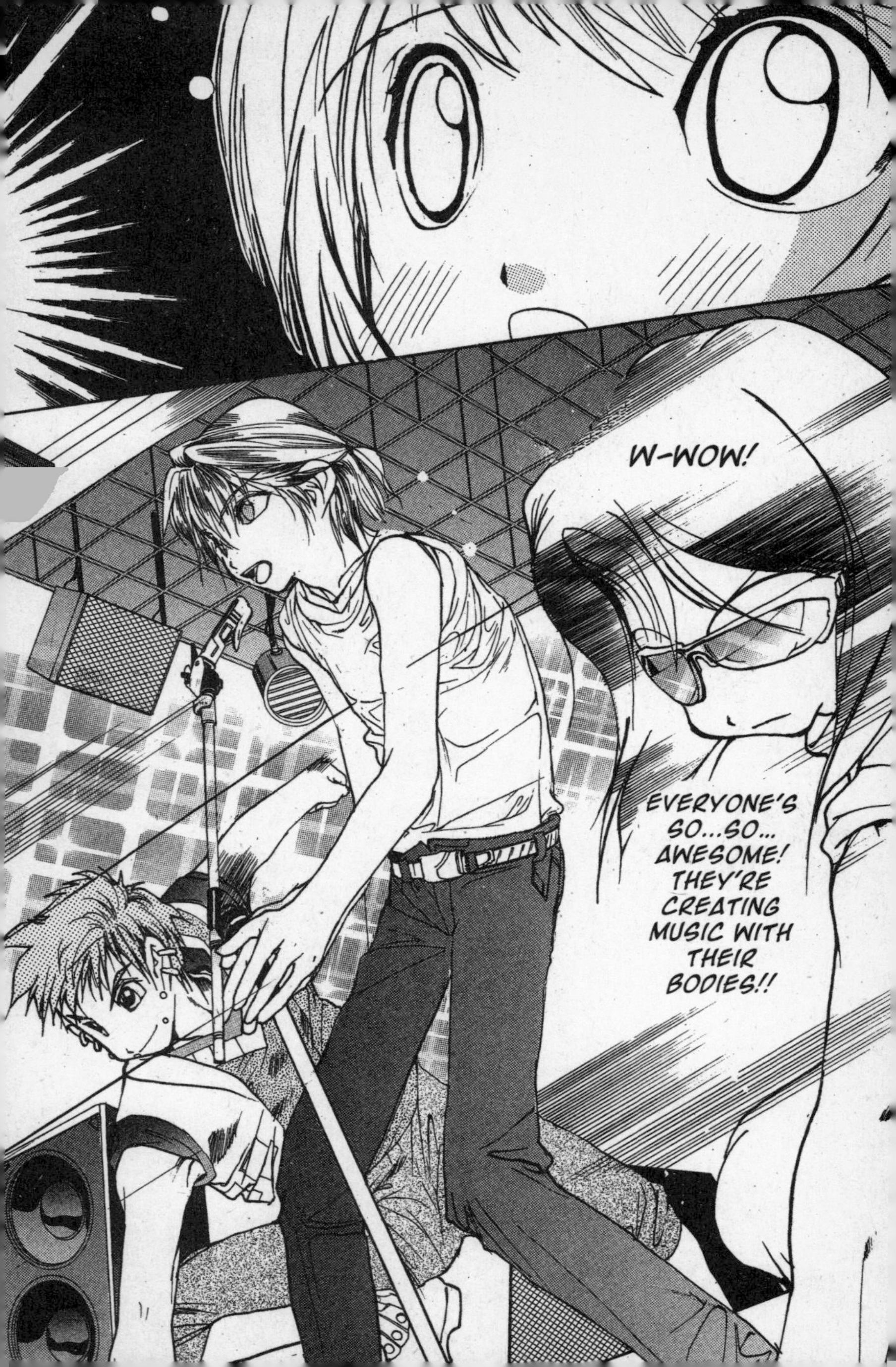
W-WOW!
EVERYONE'S SO...SO... AWESOME! THEY'RE CREATING MUSIC WITH THEIR BODIES!!

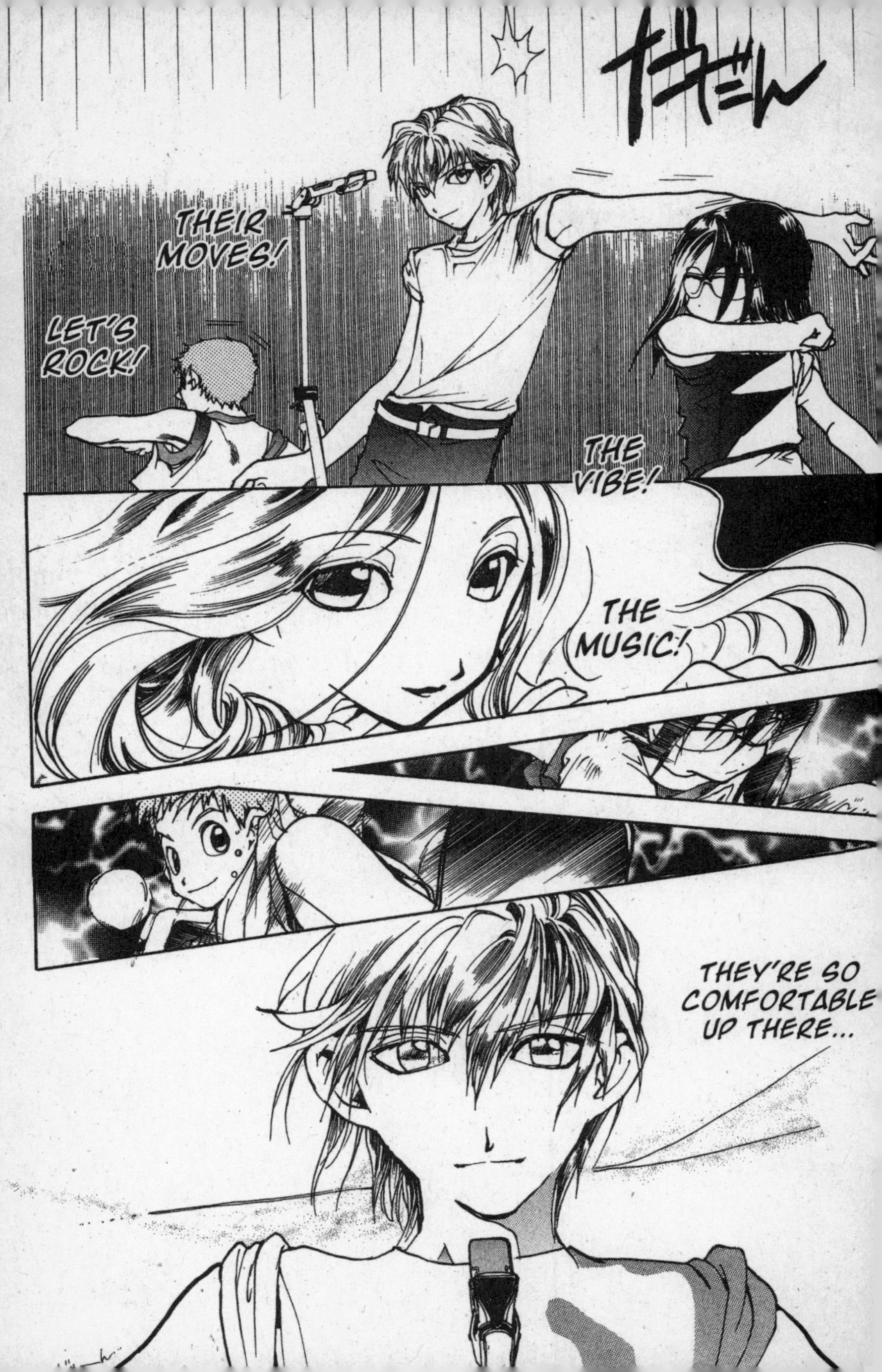
THEIR MOVES!
LET'S ROCK!
THE VIBE!
THE MUSIC!
THEY'RE SO COMFORTABLE UP THERE...

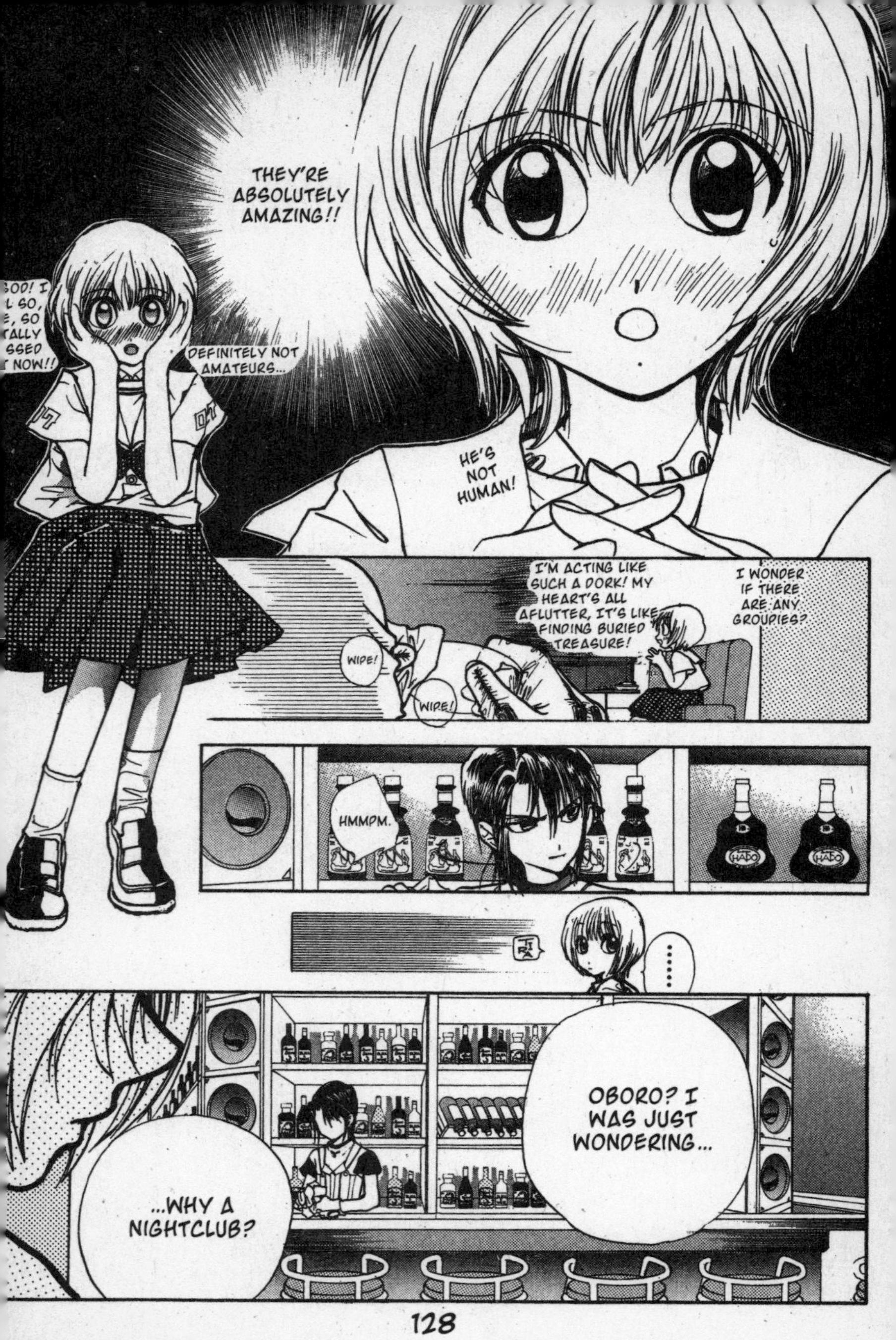
THEY'RE ABSOLUTELY AMAZING!!
HE'S NOT HUMAN!
DEFINITELY NOT AMATEURS...
I WONDER IF THERE ARE ANY GROUPIES?
I'M ACTING LIKE SUCH A DORK! MY HEART'S ALL AFLUTTER, IT'S LIKE FINDING BURIED TREASURE!
WIPE!
WIPE!
HMMPM.
......
OBORO? I WAS JUST WONDERING...
...WHY A NIGHTCLUB?

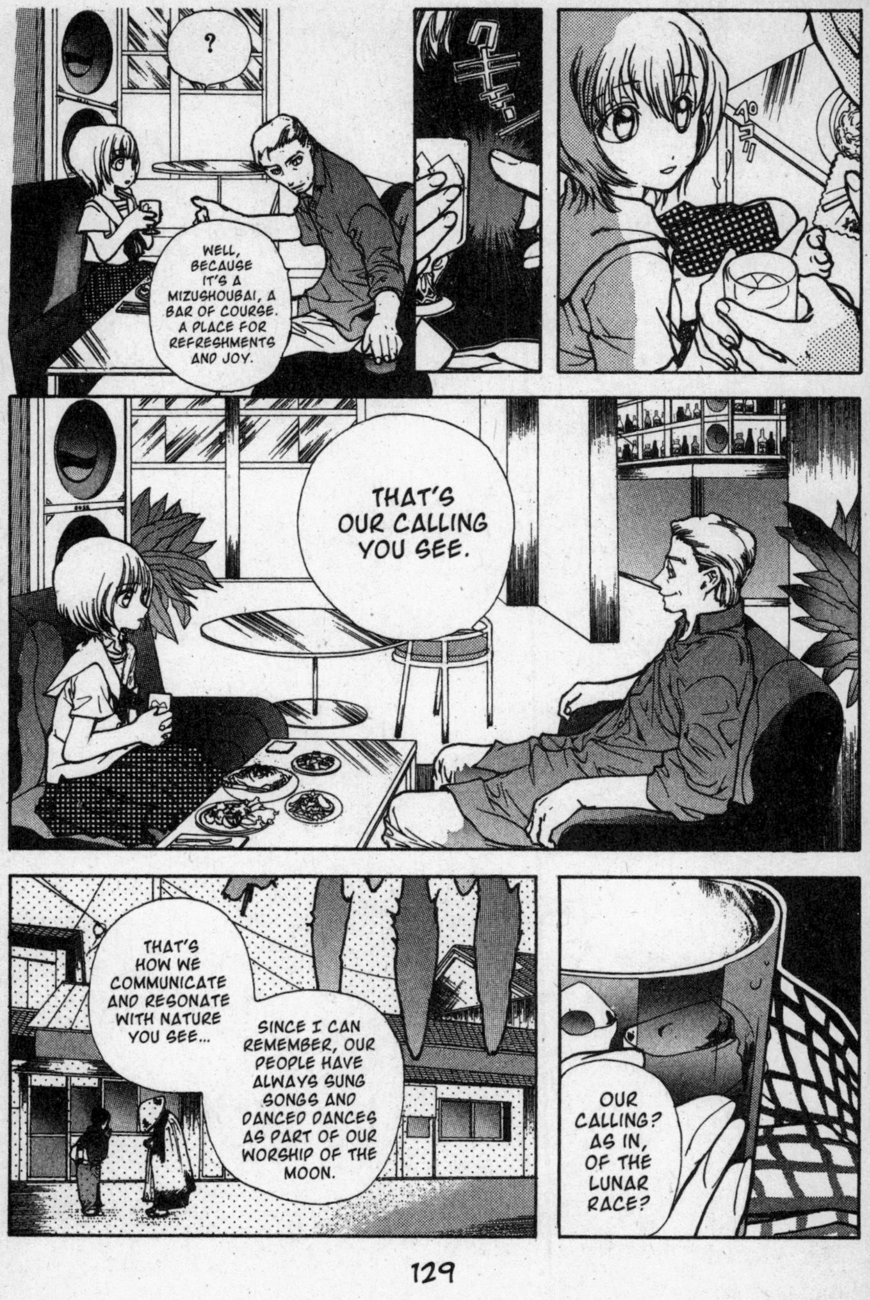
?
WELL, BECAUSE IT'S A MIZUSHOUBAI, A BAR OF COURSE. A PLACE FOR REFRESHMENTS AND JOY.
THAT'S OUR CALLING YOU SEE.
OUR CALLING? AS IN, OF THE LUNAR RACE?
SINCE I CAN REMEMBER, OUR PEOPLE HAVE ALWAYS SUNG SONGS AND DANCED DANCES AS PART OF OUR WORSHIP OF THE MOON.
THAT'S HOW WE COMMUNICATE AND RESONATE WITH NATURE YOU SEE...

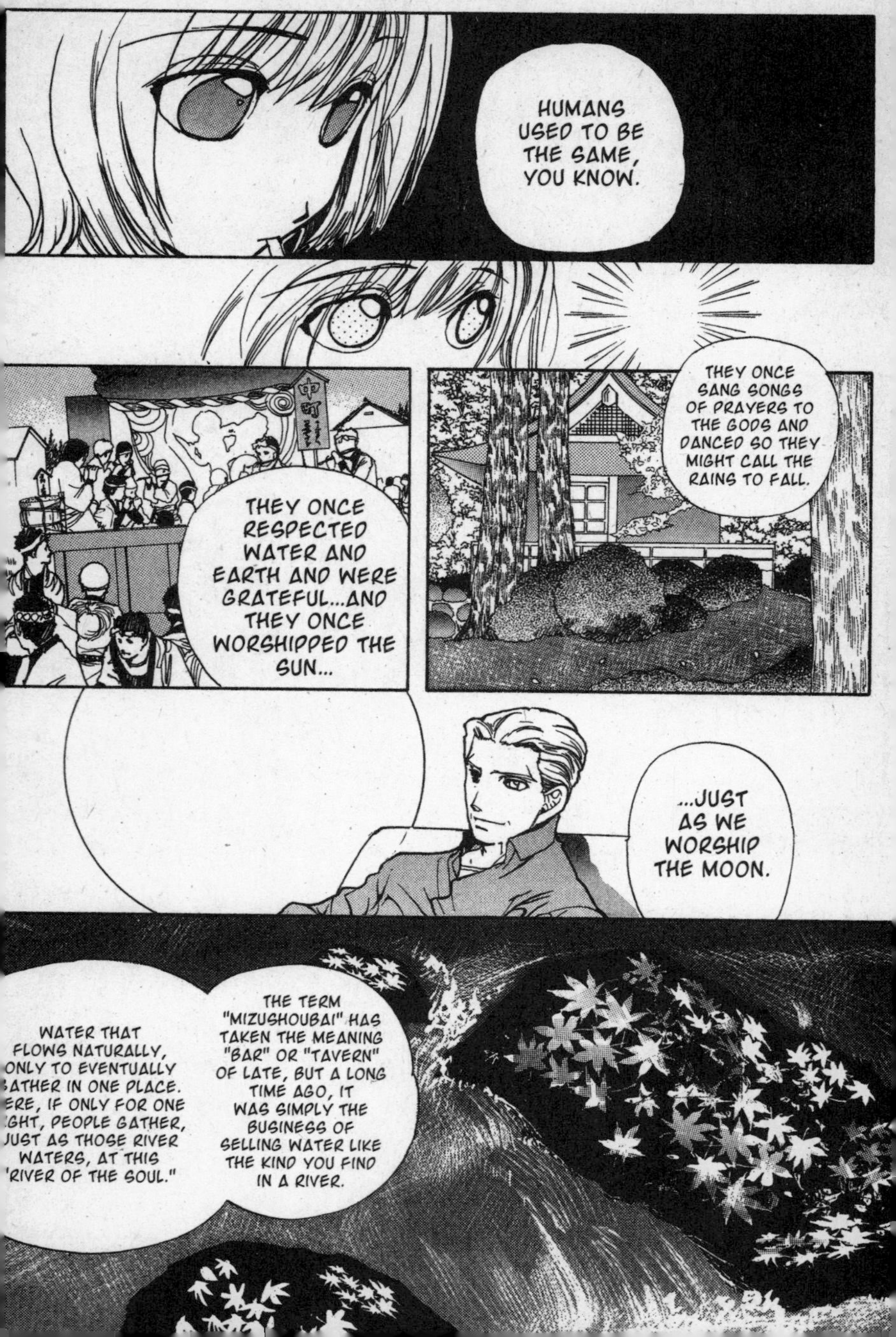
HUMANS USED TO BE THE SAME, YOU KNOW.
THEY ONCE SANG SONGS OF PRAYERS TO THE GODS AND DANCED SO THEY MIGHT CALL THE RAINS TO FALL.
THEY ONCE RESPECTED WATER AND EARTH AND WERE GRATEFUL...AND THEY ONCE WORSHIPPED THE SUN...
...JUST AS WE WORSHIP THE MOON.
THE TERM "MIZUSHOUBAI" HAS TAKEN THE MEANING "BAR" OR "TAVERN" OF LATE, BUT A LONG TIME AGO, IT WAS SIMPLY THE BUSINESS OF SELLING WATER LIKE THE KIND YOU FIND IN A RIVER.
WATER THAT FLOWS NATURALLY, ONLY TO EVENTUALLY ATHER IN ONE PLACE. ERE, IF ONLY FOR ONE GHT, PEOPLE GATHER, JUST AS THOSE RIVER WATERS, AT THIS "RIVER OF THE SOUL."

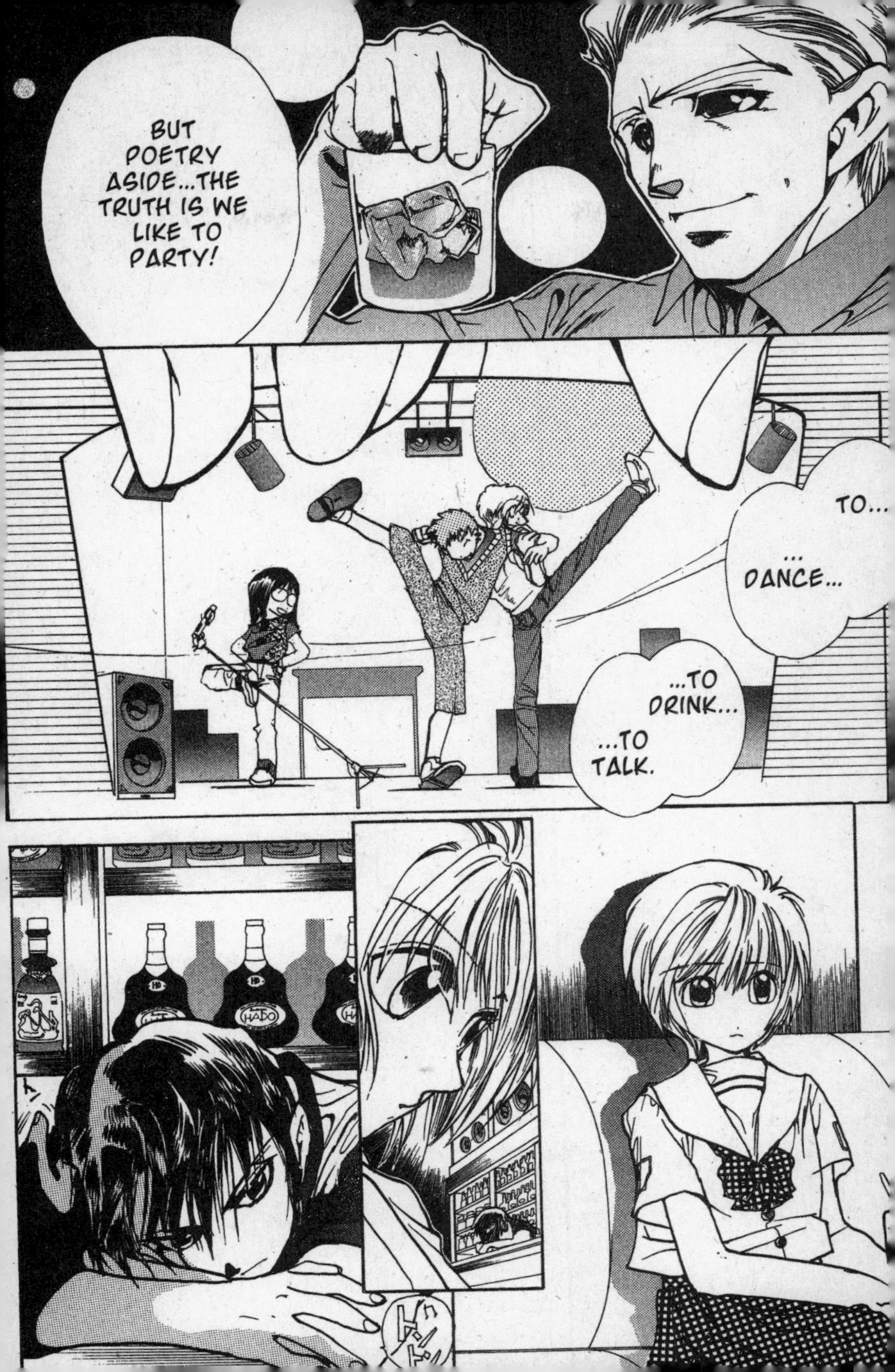
BUT POETRY ASIDE...THE TRUTH IS WE LIKE TO PARTY!
TO... ...DANCE...
...TO DRINK...
...TO TALK.

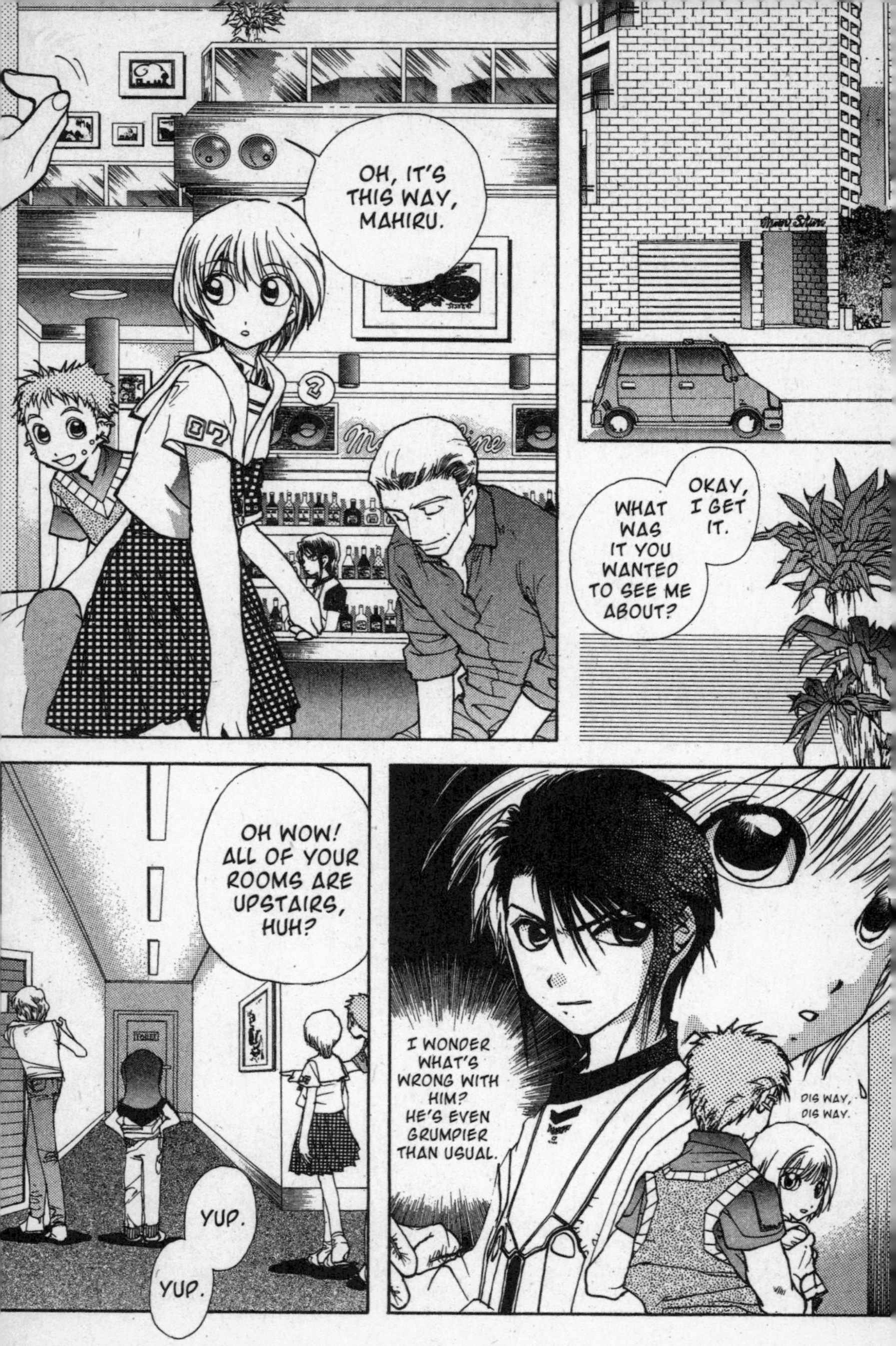
OKAY, I GET IT. WHAT WAS IT YOU WANTED TO SEE ME ABOUT?
OH, IT'S THIS WAY, MAHIRU.
I WONDER WHAT'S WRONG WITH HIM? HE'S EVEN GRUMPIER THAN USUAL.
DIS WAY, DIS WAY.
OH WOW! ALL OF YOUR ROOMS ARE UPSTAIRS, HUH?
YUP.
YUP.

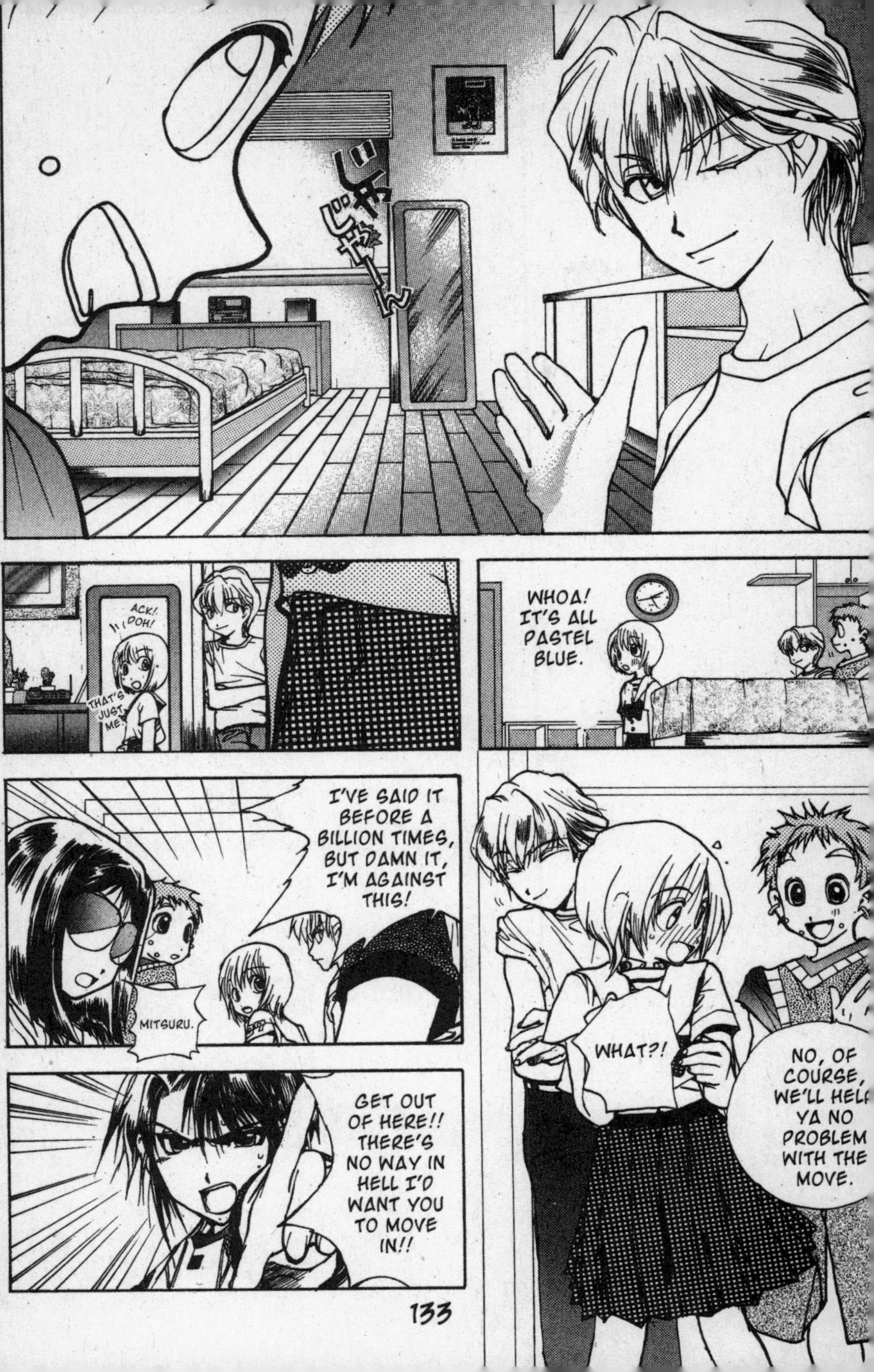
WHOA! IT'S ALL PASTEL BLUE.
ACK! DOH!
THAT'S JUST ME.
NO, OF COURSE, WE'LL HELP YA NO PROBLEM WITH THE MOVE.
WHAT?!
I'VE SAID IT BEFORE A BILLION TIMES, BUT DAMN IT, I'M AGAINST THIS!
MITSURU.
GET OUT OF HERE!! THERE'S NO WAY IN HELL I'D WANT YOU TO MOVE IN!!

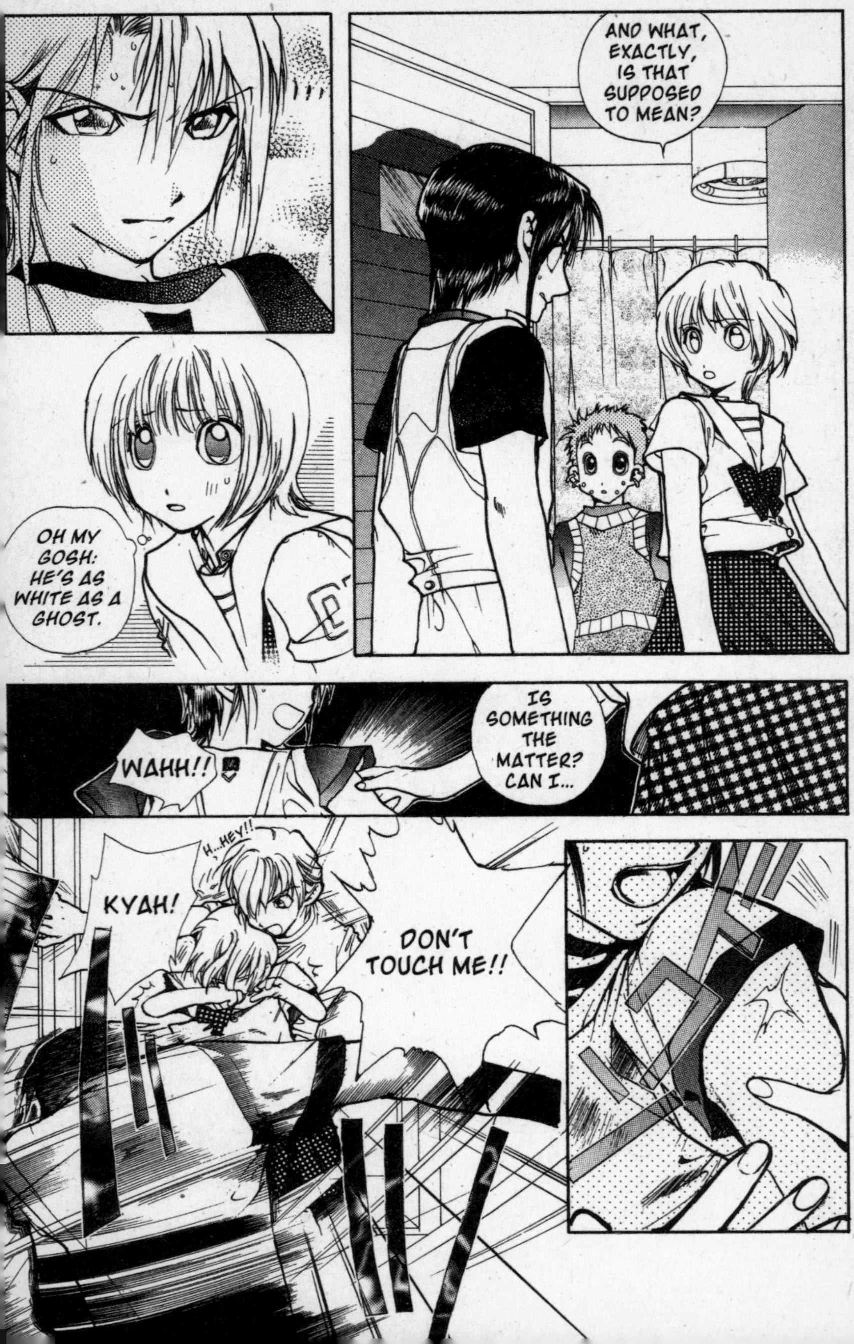
AND WHAT, EXACTLY, IS THAT SUPPOSED TO MEAN?
OH MY GOSH: HE'S AS WHITE AS A GHOST.
IS SOMETHING THE MATTER? CAN I...
WAHH!!
H...HEY!!
KYAH!
DON'T TOUCH ME!!

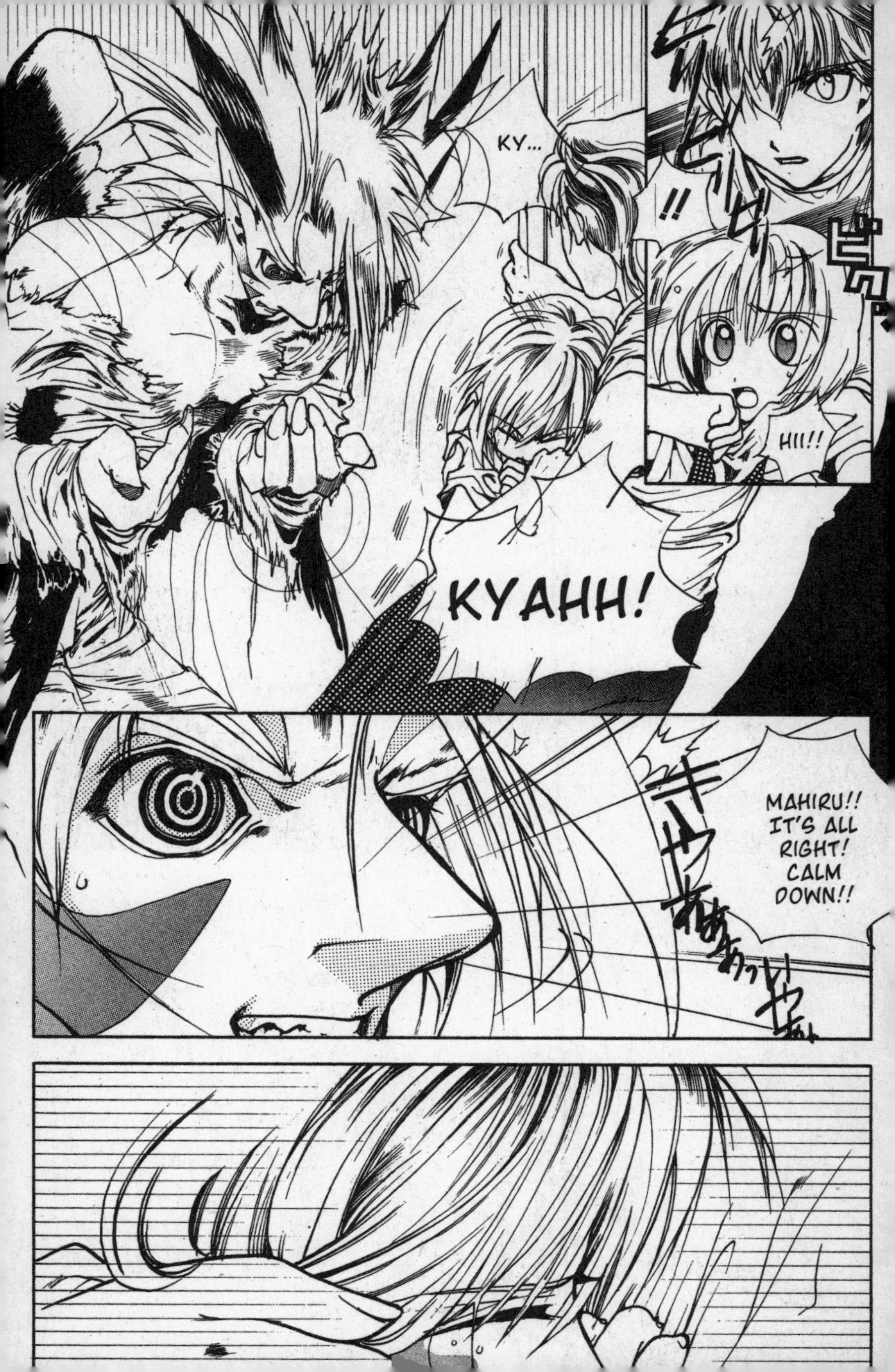
!!
HII!!
KY...
KYAHH!
MAHIRU!! IT'S ALL RIGHT! CALM DOWN!!

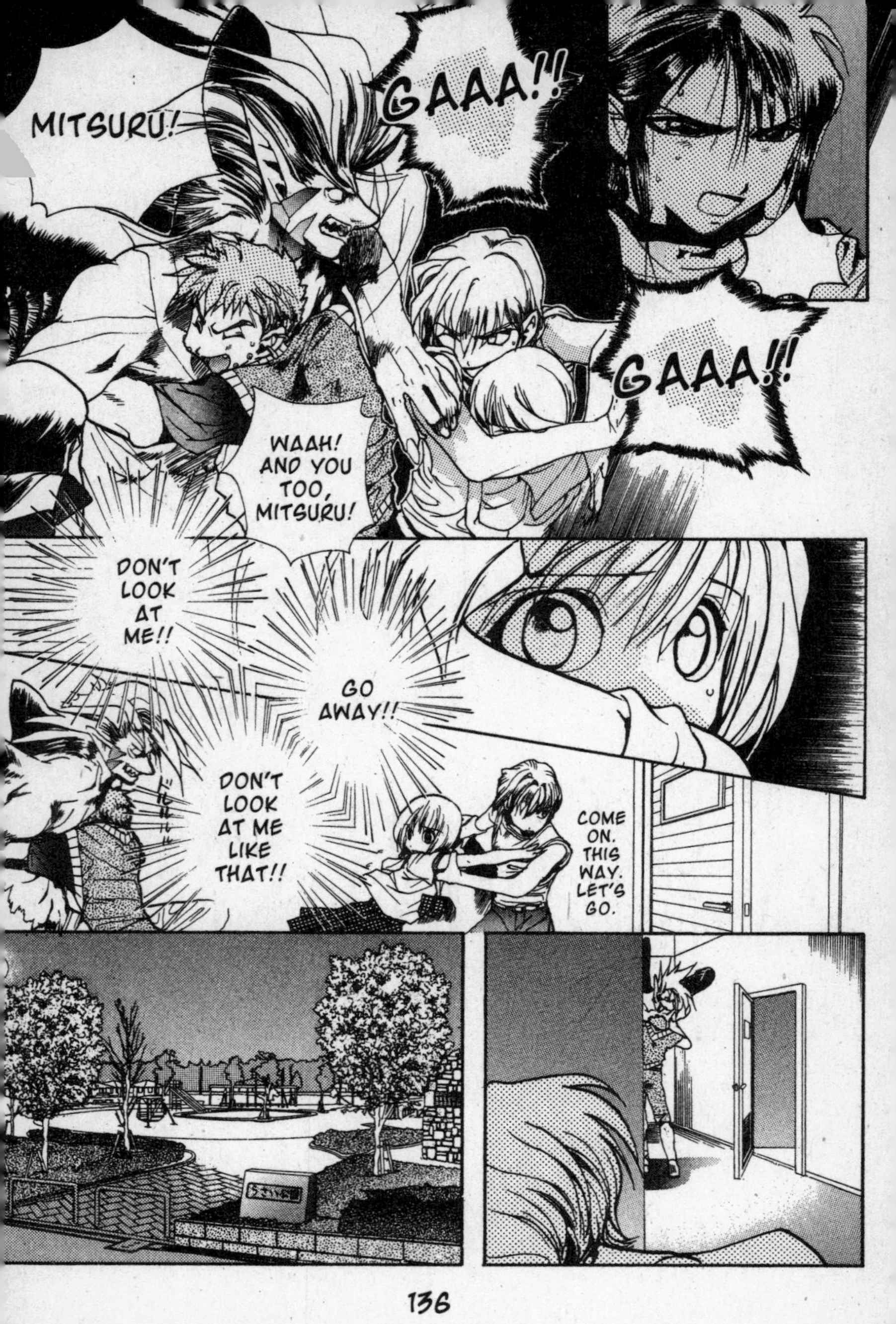
GAAA!!
GAAA!!
MITSURU!
WAAH! AND YOU TOO, MITSURU!
DON'T LOOK AT ME!!
GO AWAY!!
DON'T LOOK AT ME LIKE THAT!!
COME ON. THIS WAY. LET'S GO.

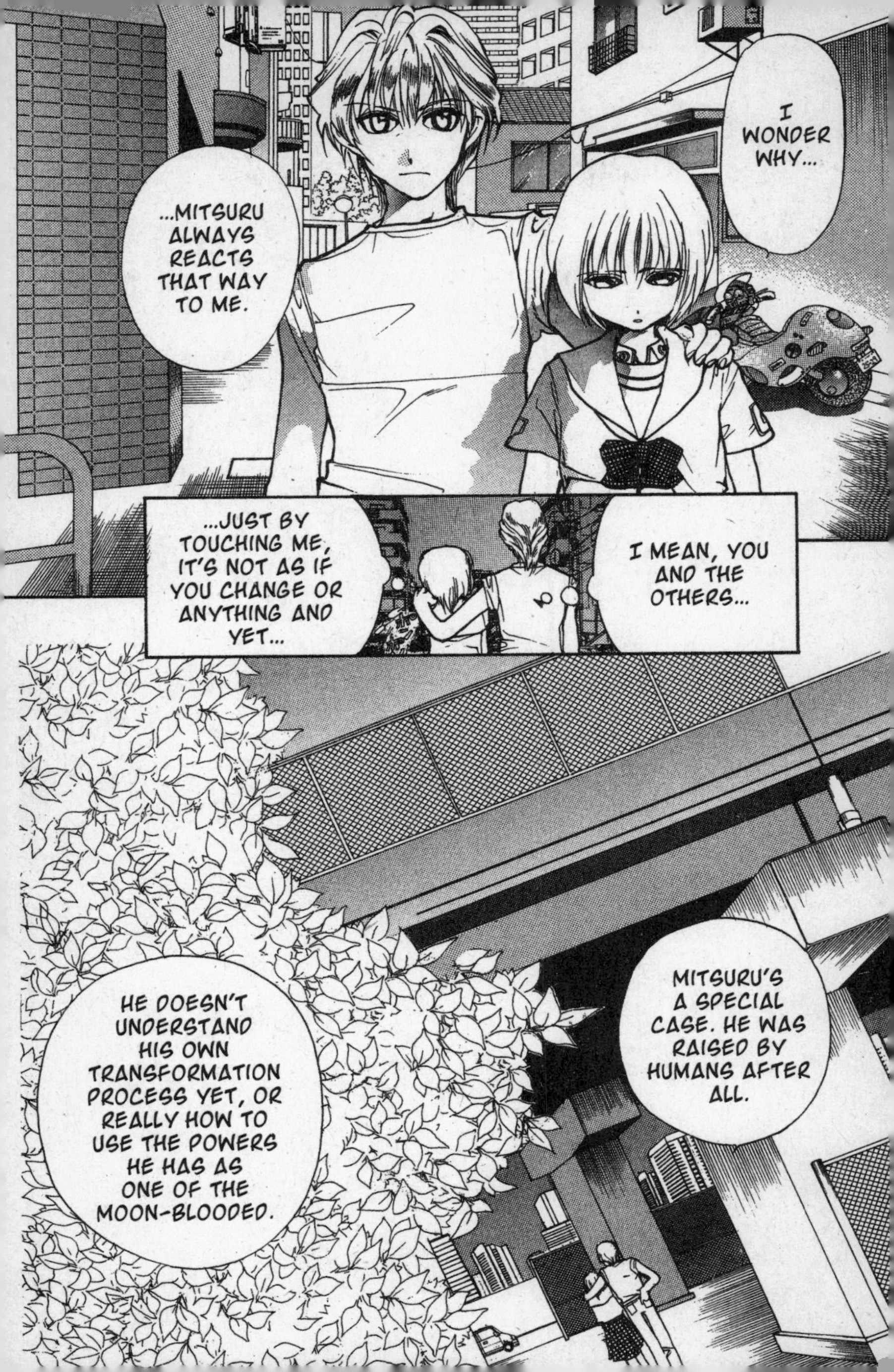
I WONDER WHY...
...MITSURU ALWAYS REACTS THAT WAY TO ME.
I MEAN, YOU AND THE OTHERS...
...JUST BY TOUCHING ME, IT'S NOT AS IF YOU CHANGE OR ANYTHING AND YET...
MITSURU'S A SPECIAL CASE. HE WAS RAISED BY HUMANS AFTER ALL.
HE DOESN'T UNDERSTAND HIS OWN TRANSFORMATION PROCESS YET, OR REALLY HOW TO USE THE POWERS HE HAS AS ONE OF THE MOON-BLOODED.

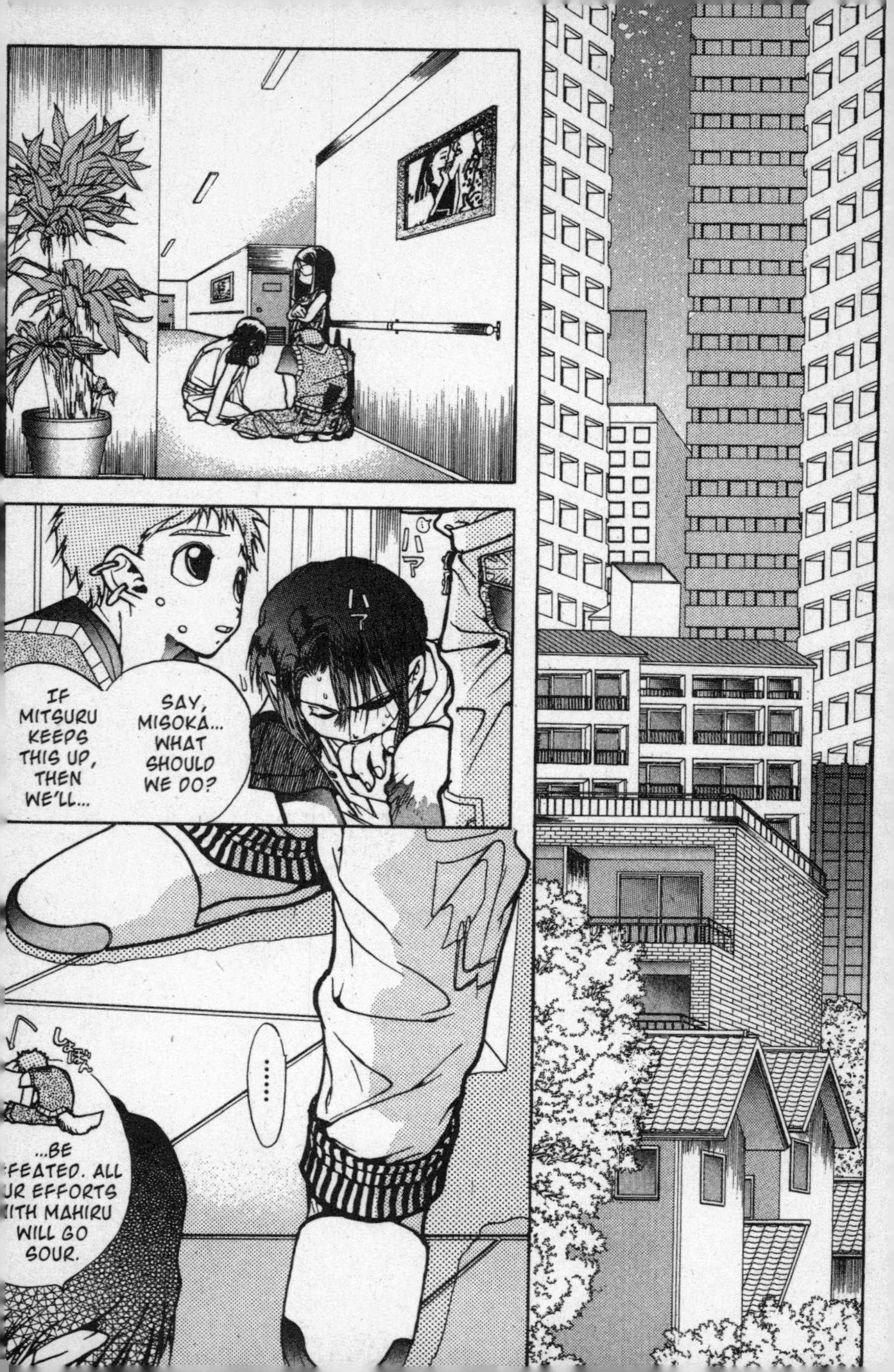
ハァ
ハァ
SAY, MISOKA... WHAT SHOULD WE DO?
IF MITSURU KEEPS THIS UP, THEN WE'LL...
......
...BE EFEATED. ALL UR EFFORTS ITH MAHIRU WILL GO SOUR.

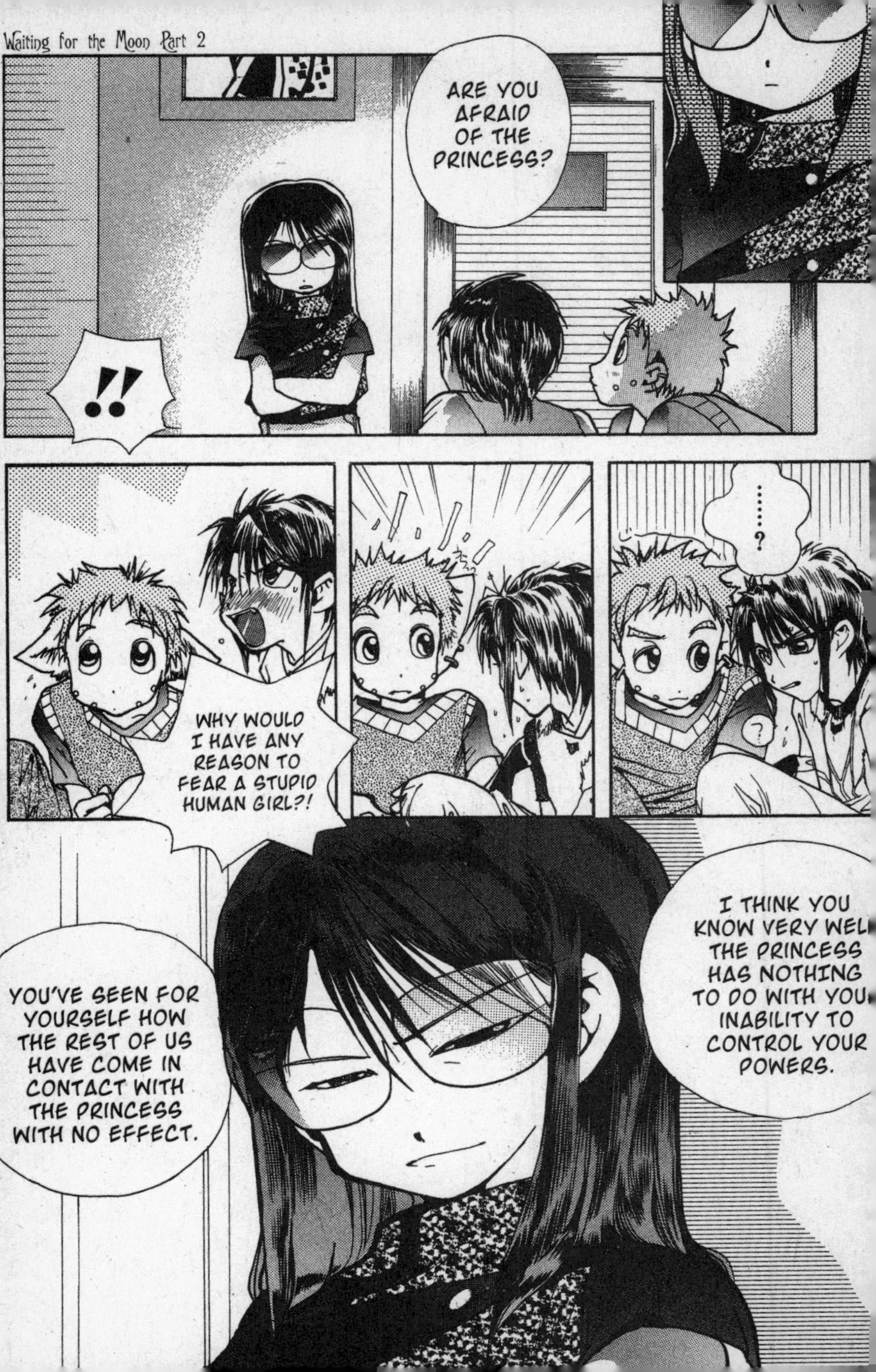
ARE YOU AFRAID OF THE PRINCESS?
!!
......?
WHY WOULD I HAVE ANY REASON TO FEAR A STUPID HUMAN GIRL?!
I THINK YOU KNOW VERY WEL THE PRINCESS HAS NOTHING TO DO WITH YOU INABILITY TO CONTROL YOUR POWERS.
YOU'VE SEEN FOR YOURSELF HOW THE REST OF US HAVE COME IN CONTACT WITH THE PRINCESS WITH NO EFFECT.

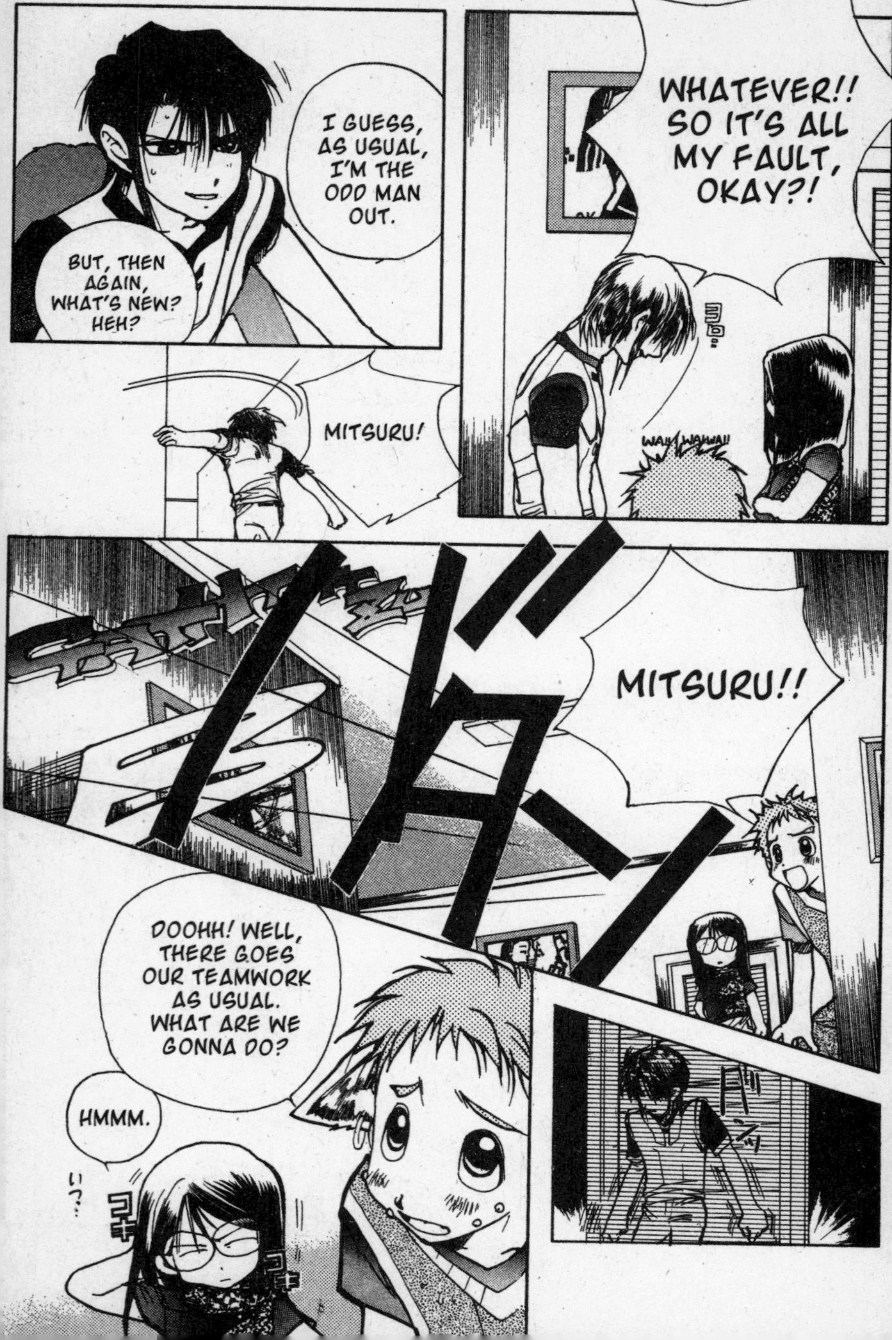
WHATEVER!! SO IT'S ALL MY FAULT, OKAY?!
WA!! WAWA!!
I GUESS, AS USUAL, I'M THE ODD MAN OUT.
BUT, THEN AGAIN, WHAT'S NEW? HEH?
MITSURU!
MITSURU!!
DOOHH! WELL, THERE GOES OUR TEAMWORK AS USUAL. WHAT ARE WE GONNA DO?
HMMM.

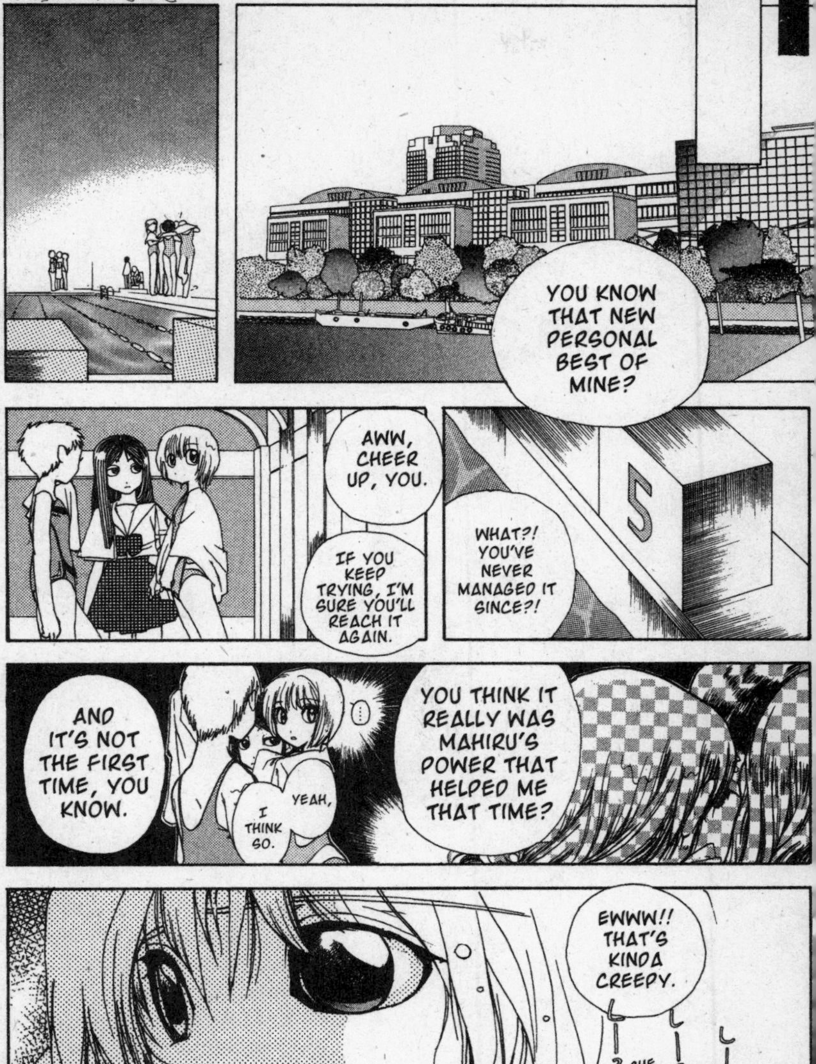
YOU KNOW THAT NEW PERSONAL BEST OF MINE?
WHAT?! YOU'VE NEVER MANAGED IT SINCE?!
AWW, CHEER UP, YOU.
IF YOU KEEP TRYING, I'M SURE YOU'LL REACH IT AGAIN.
YOU THINK IT REALLY WAS MAHIRU'S POWER THAT HELPED ME THAT TIME?
…
YEAH, I THINK SO.
AND IT'S NOT THE FIRST TIME, YOU KNOW.
EWWW!! THAT'S KINDA CREEPY.
SHH!
SHE CAN HEAR YOU!

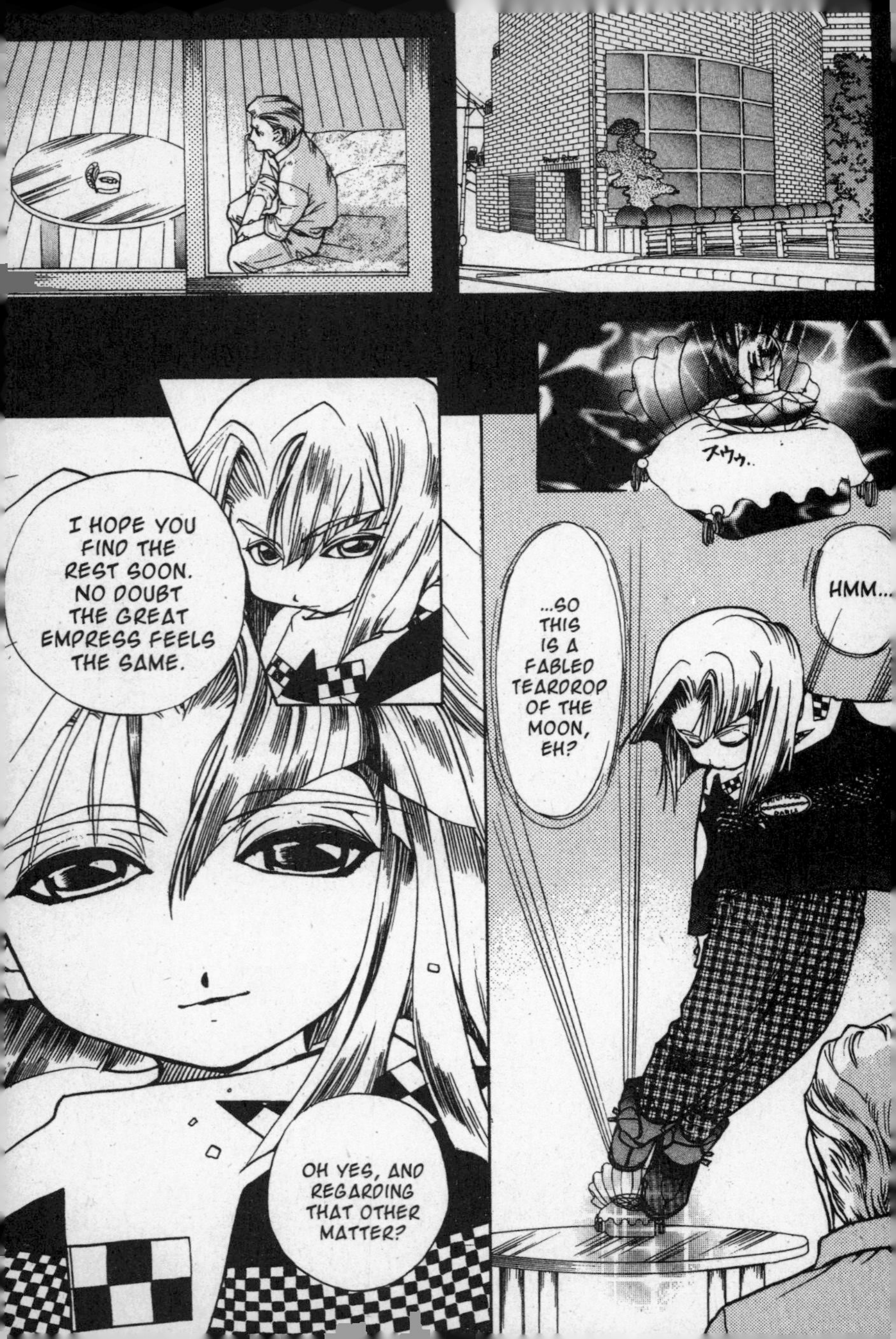
HMM...
...SO THIS IS A FABLED TEARDROP OF THE MOON, EH?
I HOPE YOU FIND THE REST SOON. NO DOUBT THE GREAT EMPRESS FEELS THE SAME.
OH YES, AND REGARDING THAT OTHER MATTER?

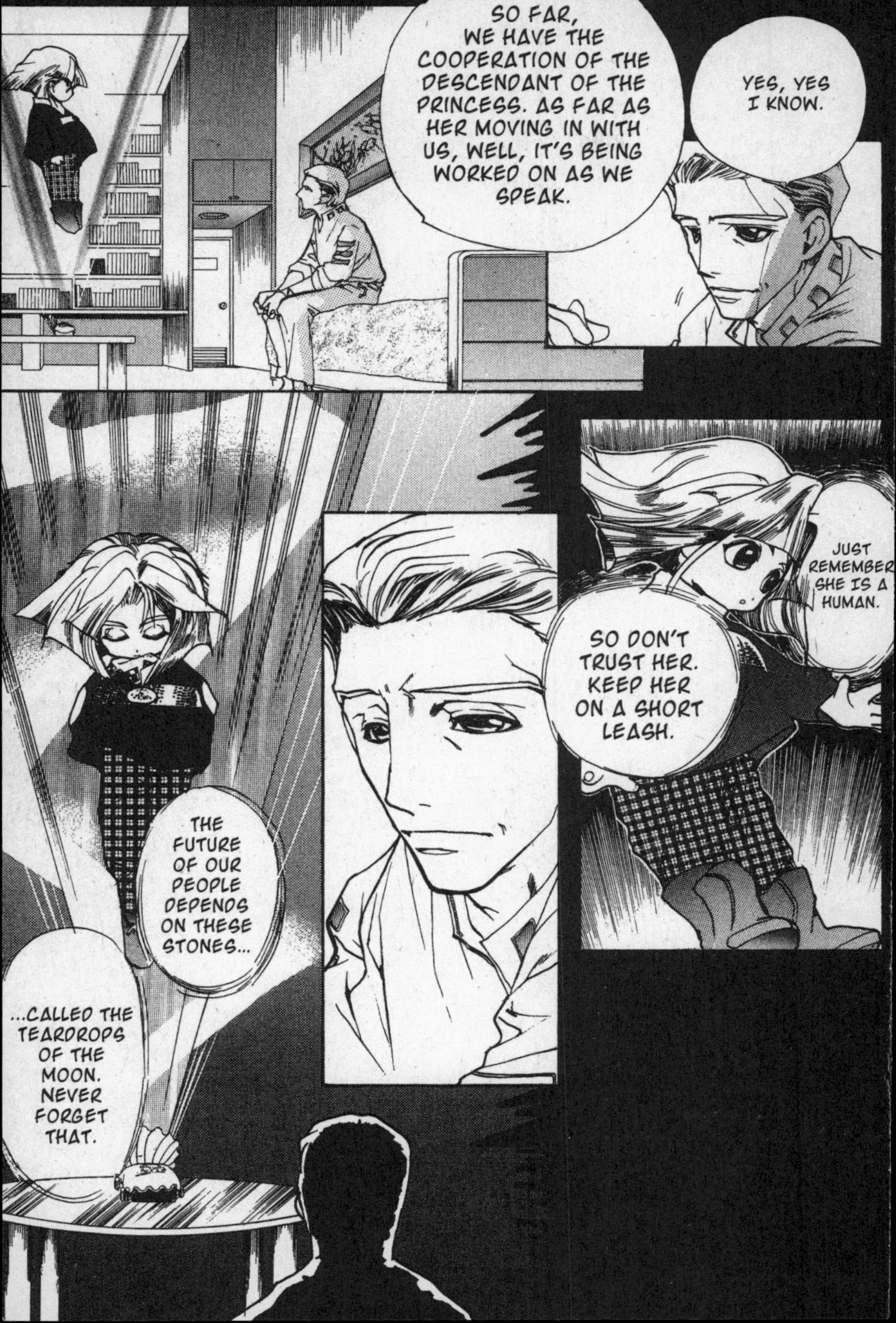
SO FAR, WE HAVE THE COOPERATION OF THE DESCENDANT OF THE PRINCESS. AS FAR AS HER MOVING IN WITH US, WELL, IT'S BEING WORKED ON AS WE SPEAK.
YES, YES I KNOW.
JUST REMEMBER SHE IS A HUMAN.
SO DON'T TRUST HER. KEEP HER ON A SHORT LEASH.
THE FUTURE OF OUR PEOPLE DEPENDS ON THESE STONES...
...CALLED THE TEARDROPS OF THE MOON. NEVER FORGET THAT.

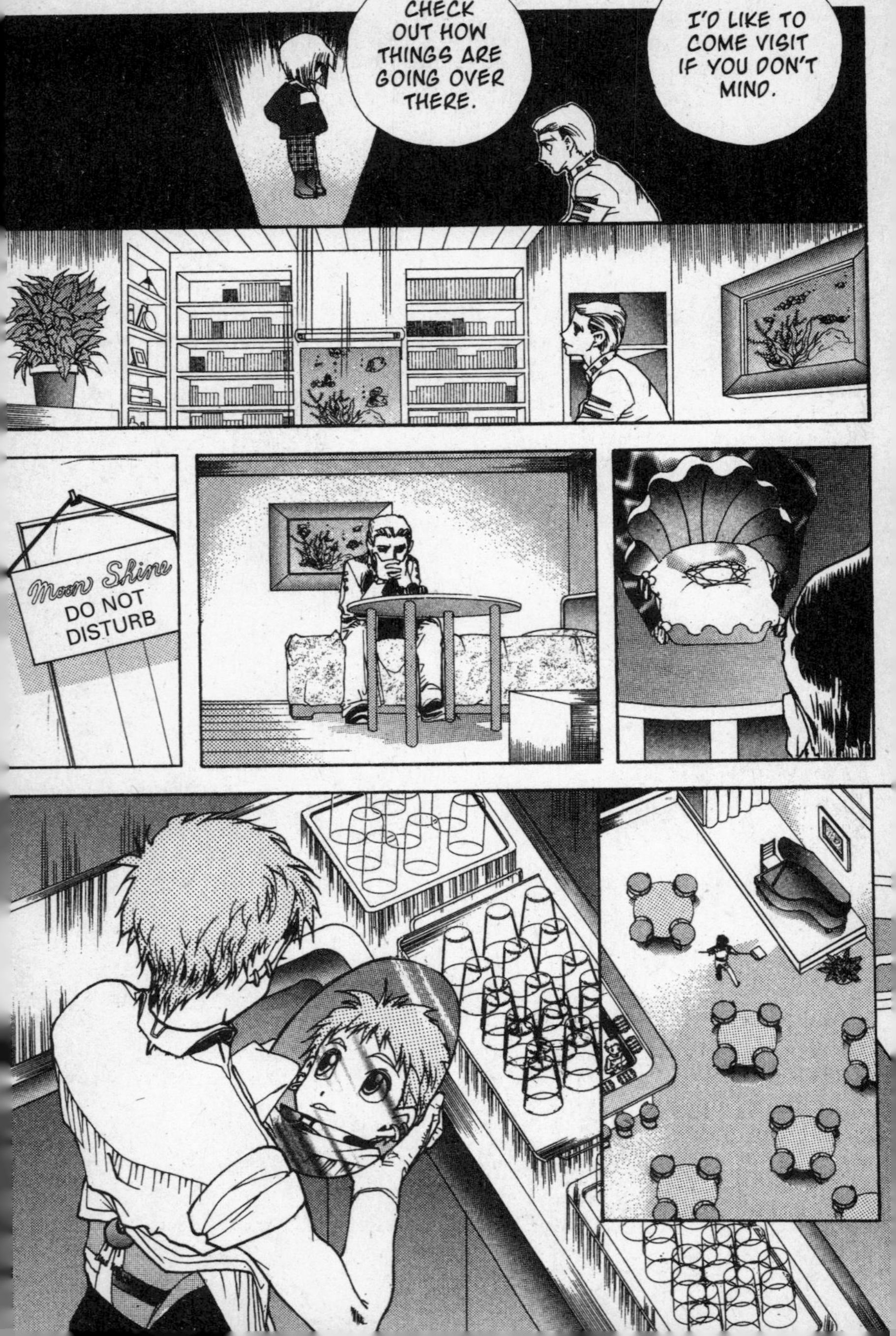
I'D LIKE TO COME VISIT IF YOU DON'T MIND.
CHECK OUT HOW THINGS ARE GOING OVER THERE.
Moon Shine
DO NOT DISTURB

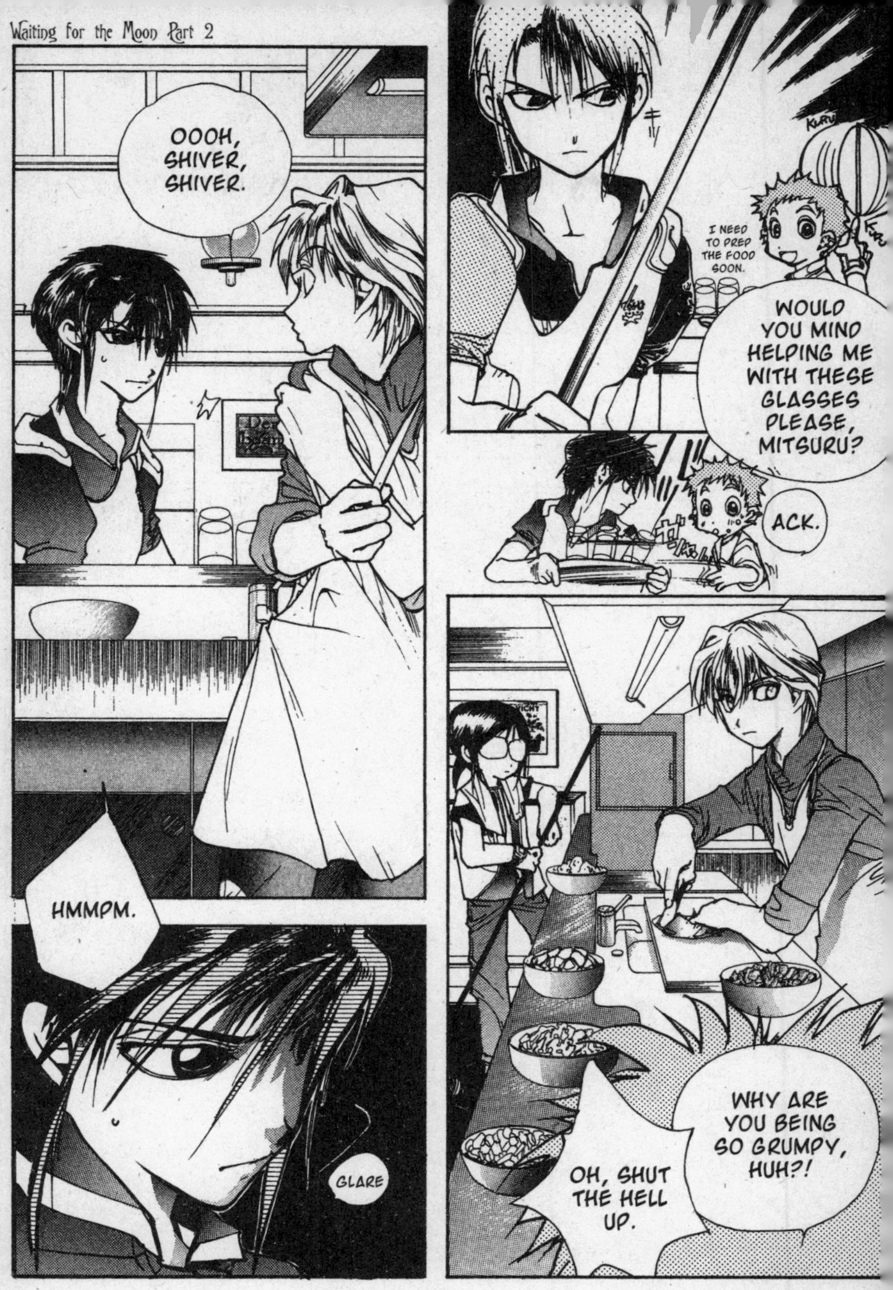
KURU
KURU
I NEED TO PREP THE FOOD SOON.
WOULD YOU MIND HELPING ME WITH THESE GLASSES PLEASE, MITSURU?
ACK.
WHY ARE YOU BEING SO GRUMPY, HUH?!
OH, SHUT THE HELL UP.
OOOH, SHIVER, SHIVER.
HMMPM.
GLARE

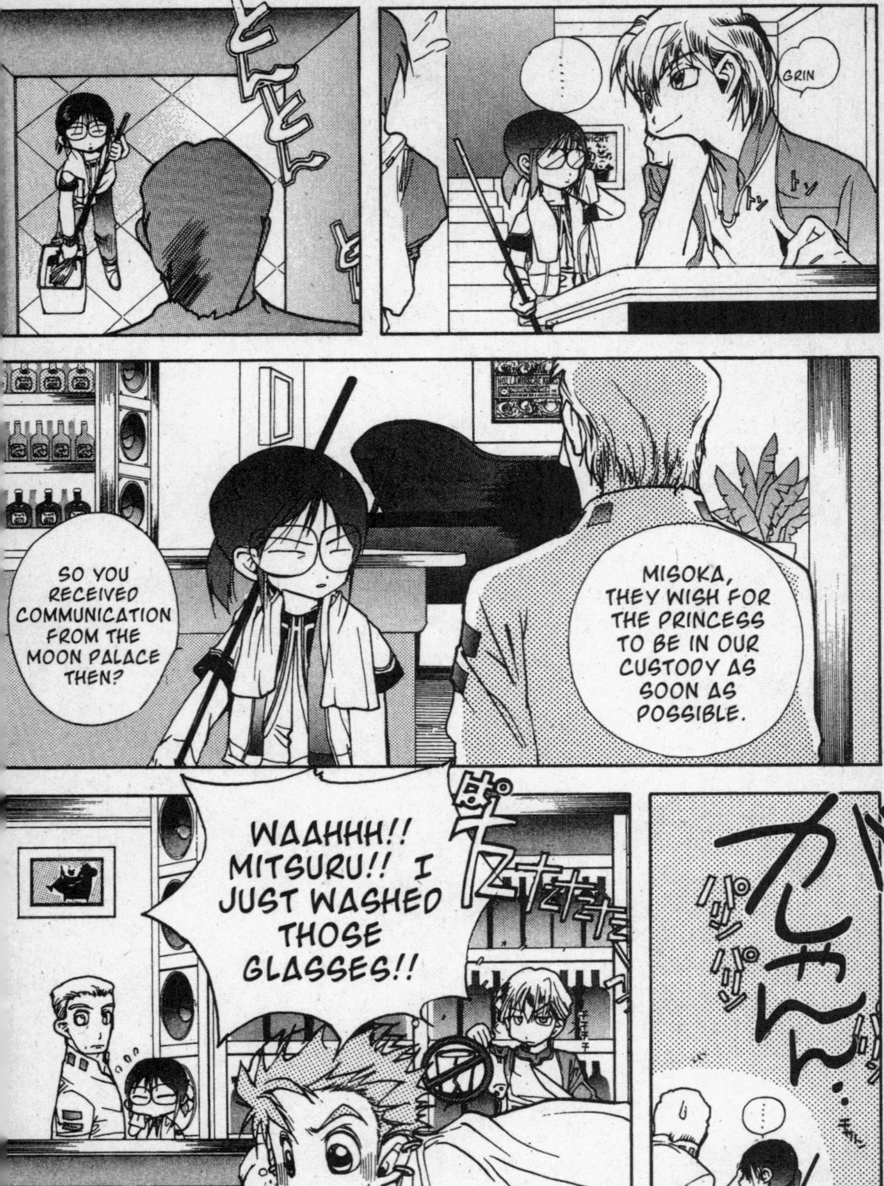
GRIN
...
MISOKA, THEY WISH FOR THE PRINCESS TO BE IN OUR CUSTODY AS SOON AS POSSIBLE.
SO YOU RECEIVED COMMUNICATION FROM THE MOON PALACE THEN?
...
WAAHHH!! MITSURU!! I JUST WASHED THOSE GLASSES!!

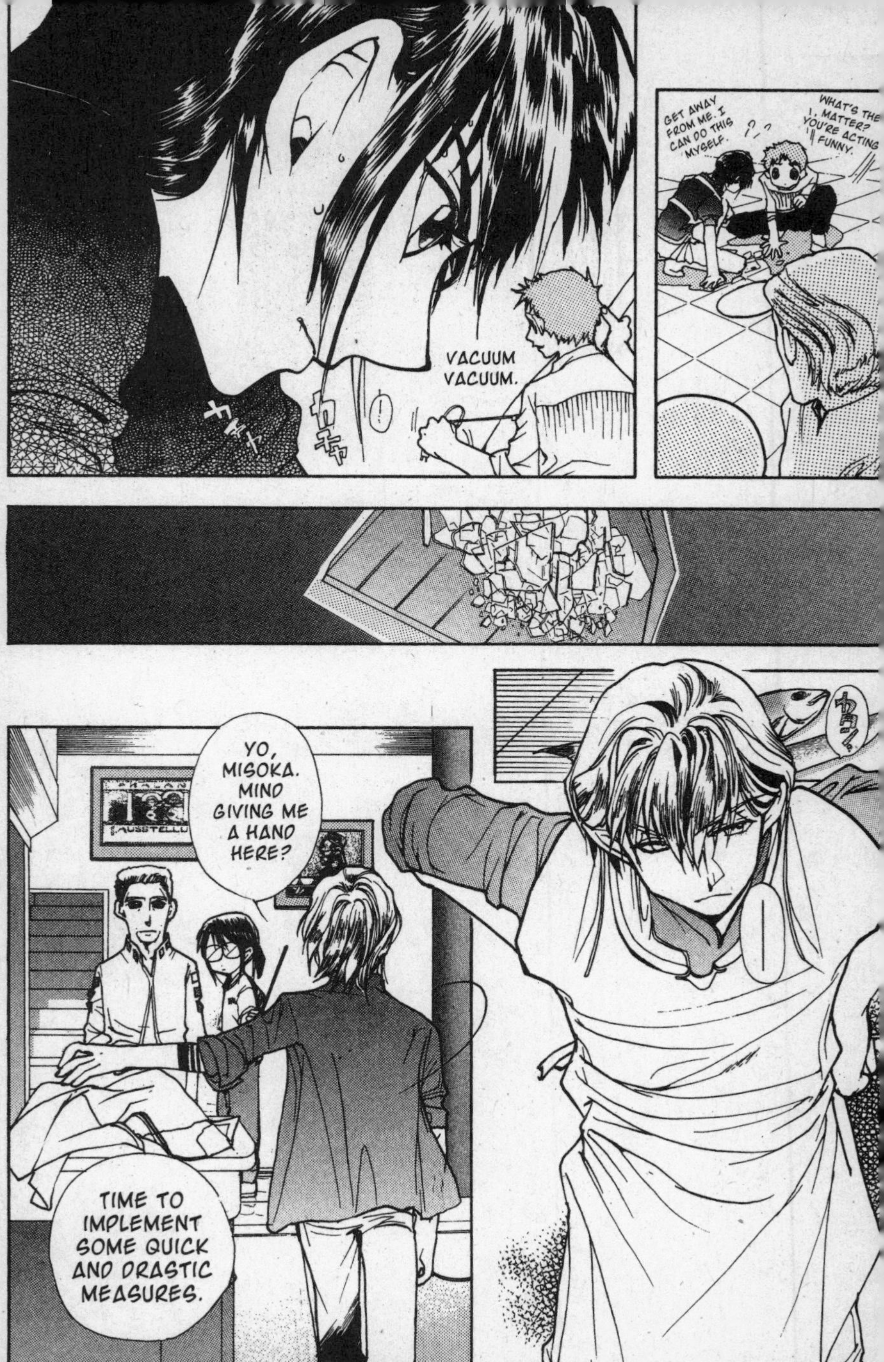
WHAT'S THE MATTER? YOU'RE ACTING FUNNY.
GET AWAY FROM ME. I CAN DO THIS MYSELF.
VACUUM VACUUM.
YO, MISOKA. MIND GIVING ME A HAND HERE?
TIME TO IMPLEMENT SOME QUICK AND DRASTIC MEASURES.

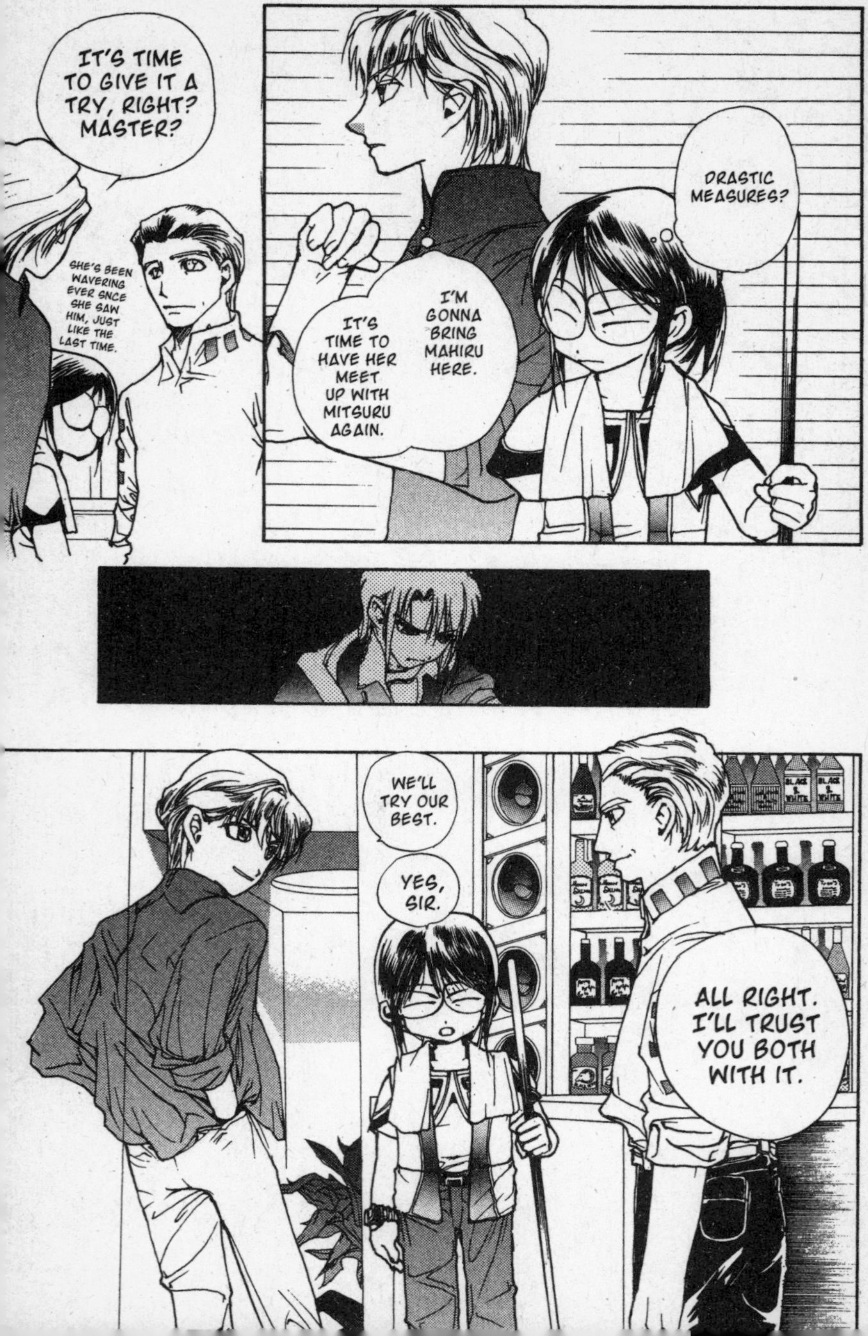
DRASTIC MEASURES?
I'M GONNA BRING MAHIRU HERE.
IT'S TIME TO HAVE HER MEET UP WITH MITSURU AGAIN.
IT'S TIME TO GIVE IT A TRY, RIGHT? MASTER?
SHE'S BEEN WAVERING EVER SNCE SHE SAW HIM, JUST LIKE THE LAST TIME.
ALL RIGHT. I'LL TRUST YOU BOTH WITH IT.
WE'LL TRY OUR BEST.
YES, SIR.

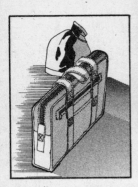

COULD WE REQUEST YOUR PRESENCE AT THE STORE?

SORRY, I CAN'T. NOT NOW.

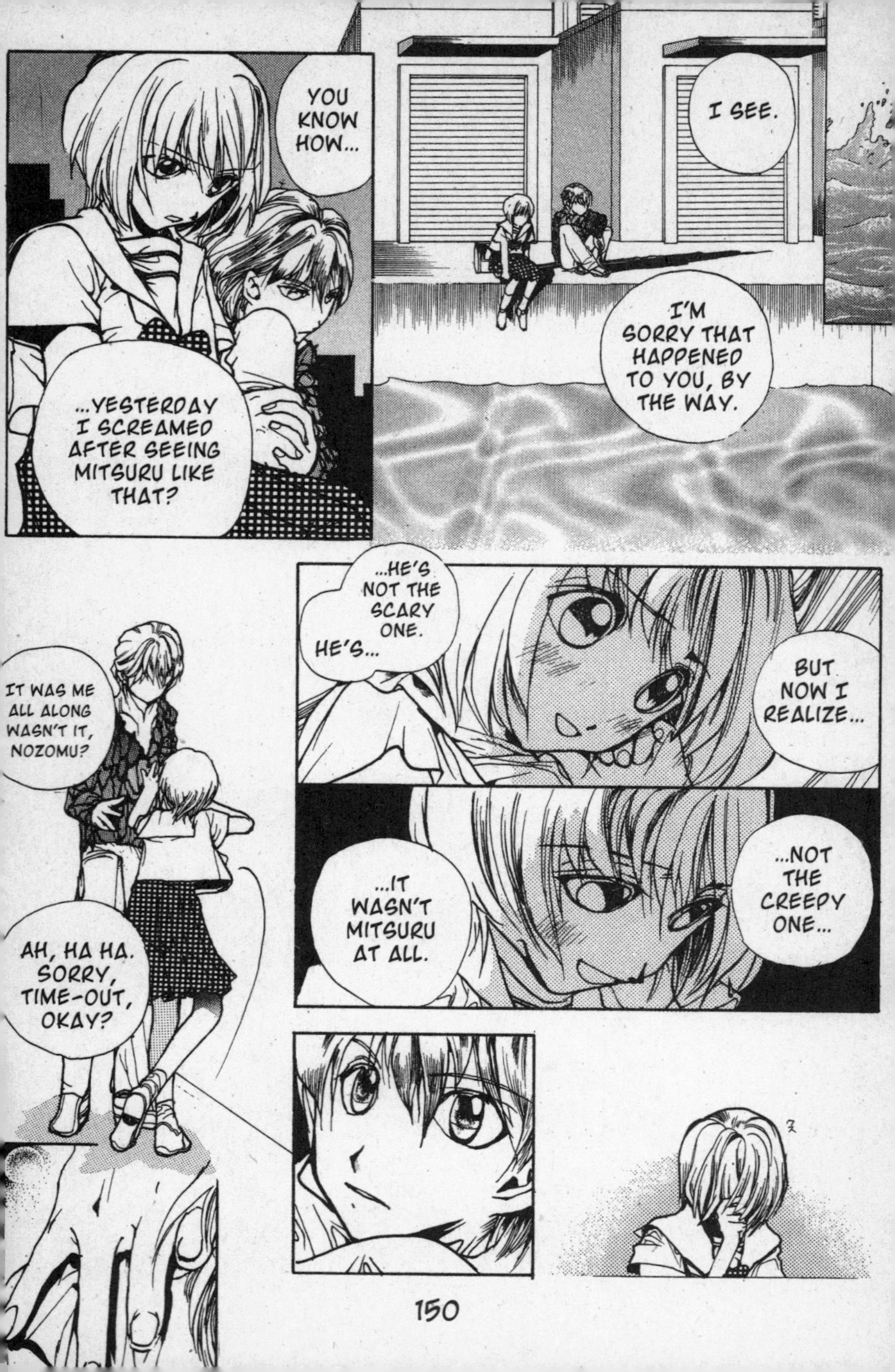
I SEE.
I'M SORRY THAT HAPPENED TO YOU, BY THE WAY.
YOU KNOW HOW...
...YESTERDAY I SCREAMED AFTER SEEING MITSURU LIKE THAT?
BUT NOW I REALIZE...
...HE'S NOT THE SCARY ONE. HE'S...
...NOT THE CREEPY ONE...
...IT WASN'T MITSURU AT ALL.
IT WAS ME ALL ALONG WASN'T IT, NOZOMU?
AH, HA HA. SORRY, TIME-OUT, OKAY?

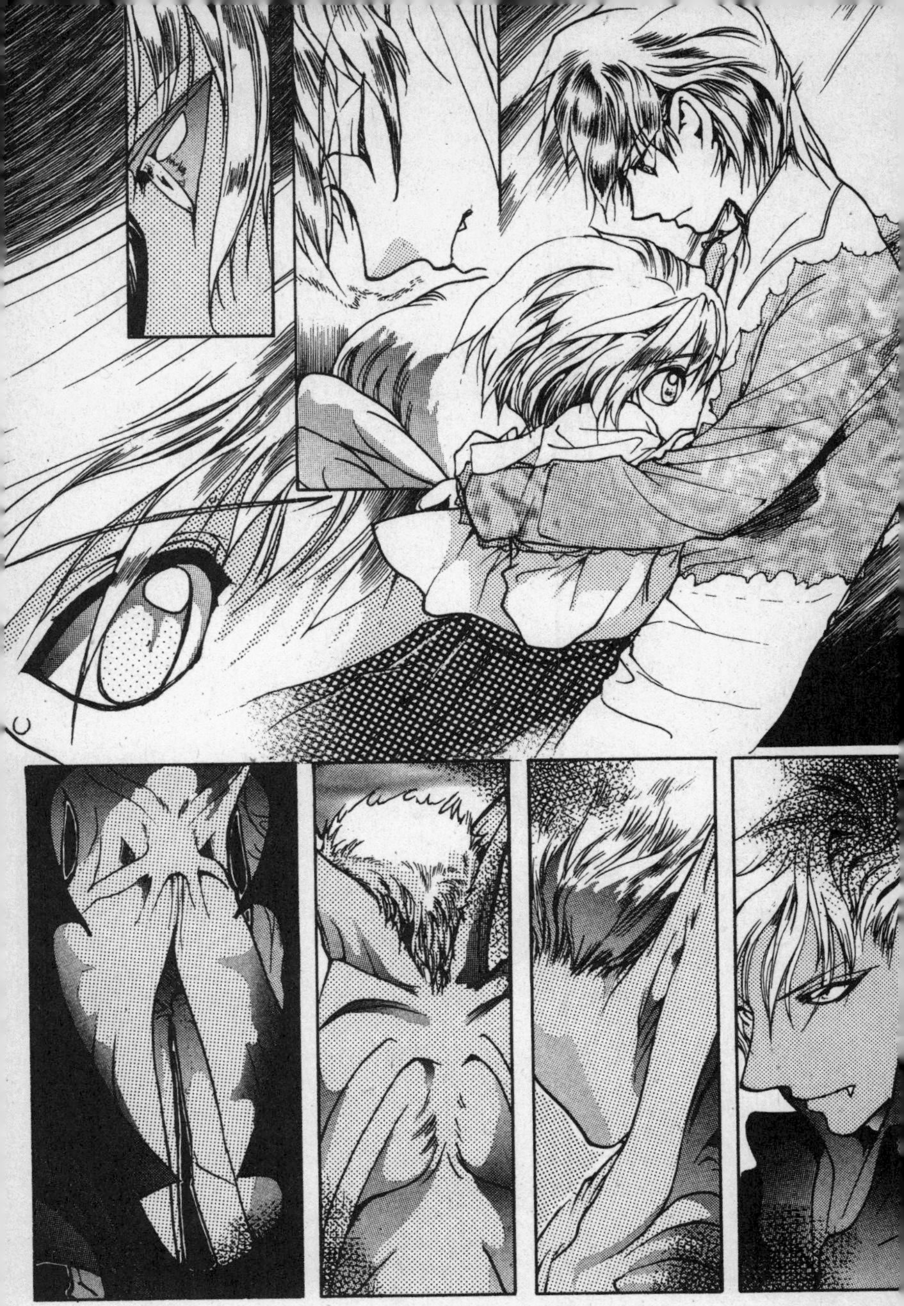

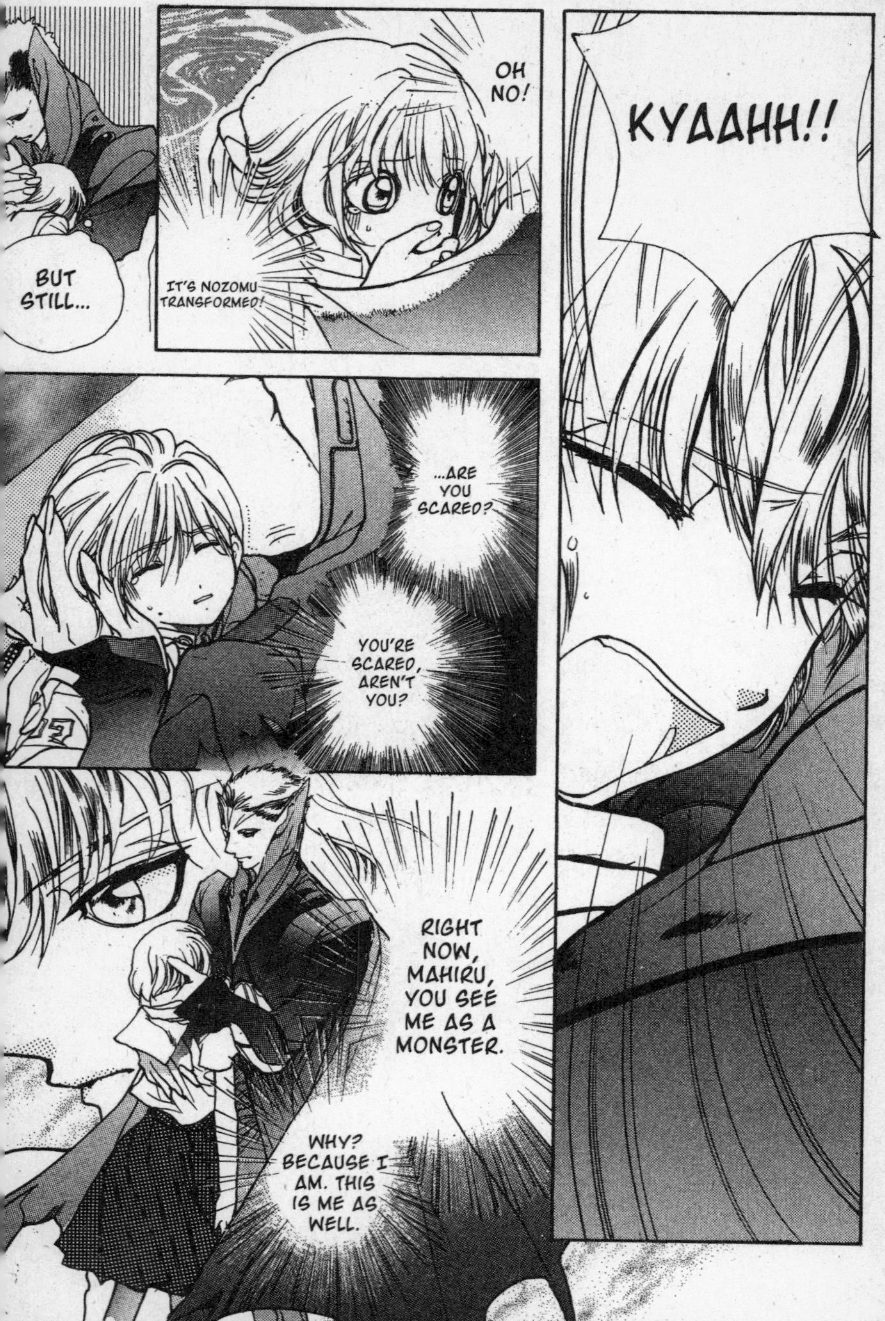
KYAAHH!!
OH NO!
IT'S NOZOMU TRANSFORMED!
BUT STILL...
...ARE YOU SCARED?
YOU'RE SCARED, AREN'T YOU?
RIGHT NOW, MAHIRU, YOU SEE ME AS A MONSTER.
WHY? BECAUSE I AM. THIS IS ME AS WELL.

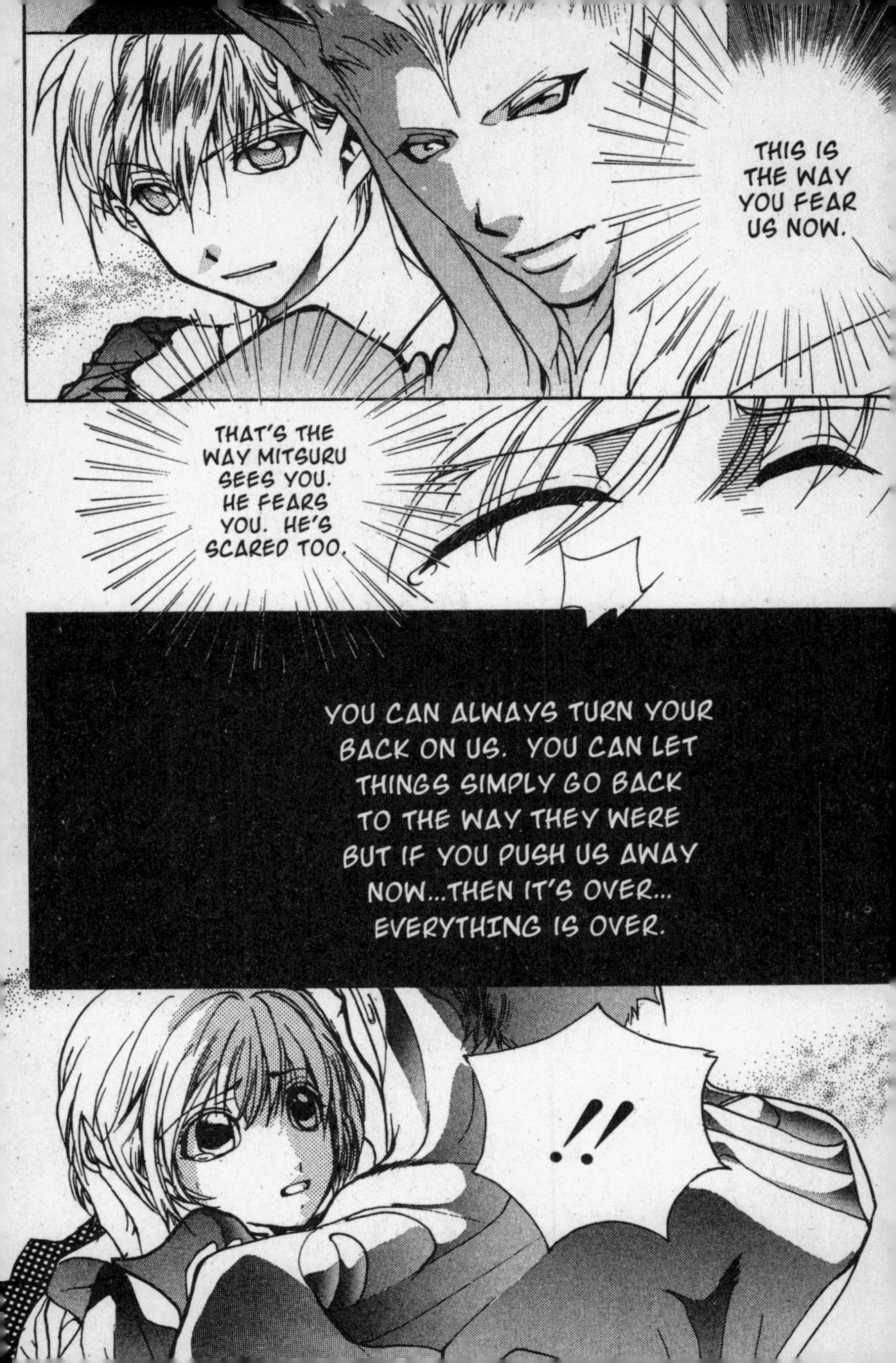
THIS IS THE WAY YOU FEAR US NOW.
THAT'S THE WAY MITSURU SEES YOU. HE FEARS YOU. HE'S SCARED TOO.
YOU CAN ALWAYS TURN YOUR BACK ON US. YOU CAN LET THINGS SIMPLY GO BACK TO THE WAY THEY WERE BUT IF YOU PUSH US AWAY NOW...THEN IT'S OVER... EVERYTHING IS OVER.
!!

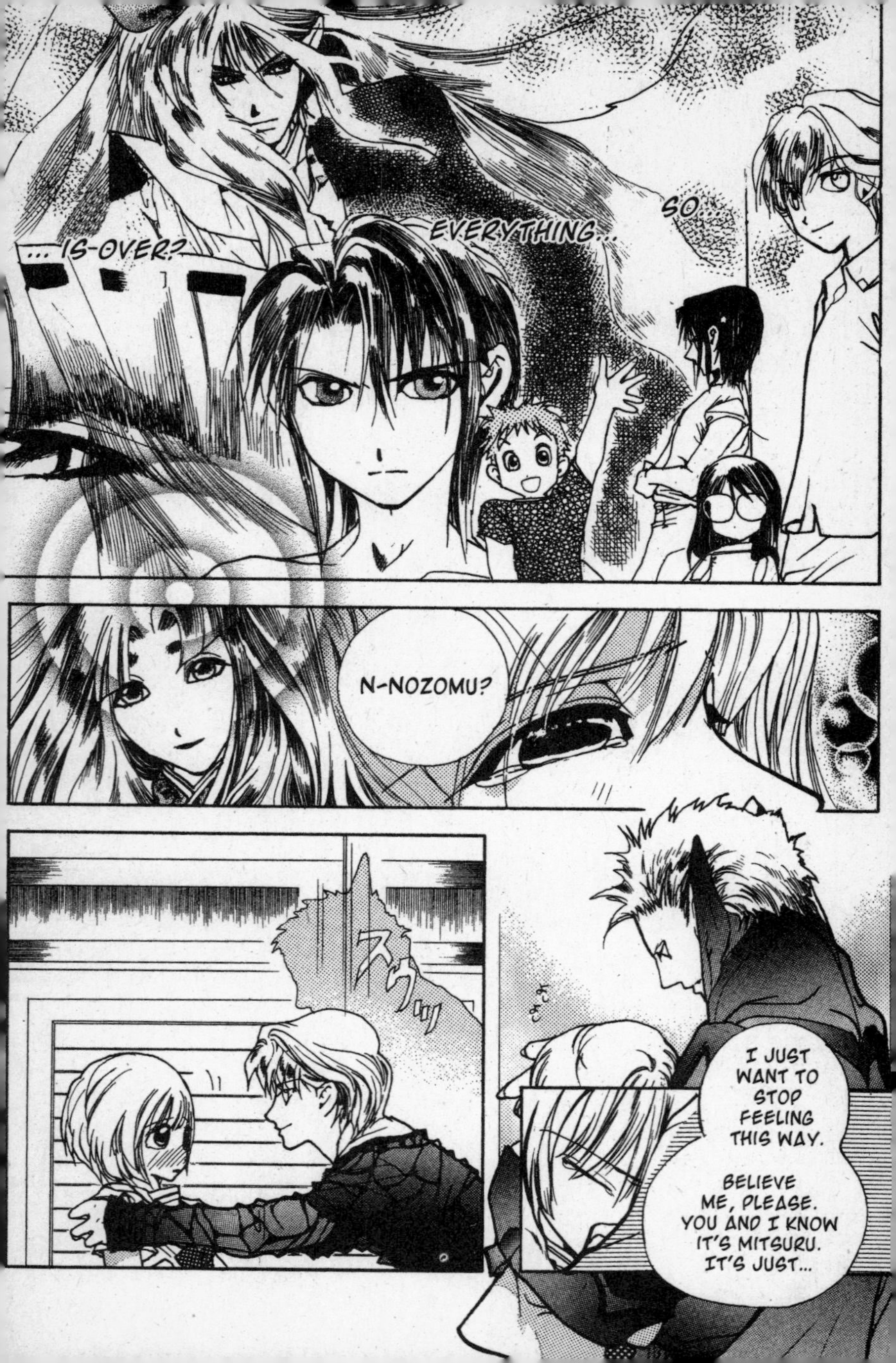
SO...
EVERYTHING...
...IS OVER?
N-NOZOMU?
I JUST WANT TO STOP FEELING THIS WAY.
BELIEVE ME, PLEASE. YOU AND I KNOW IT'S MITSURU. IT'S JUST...

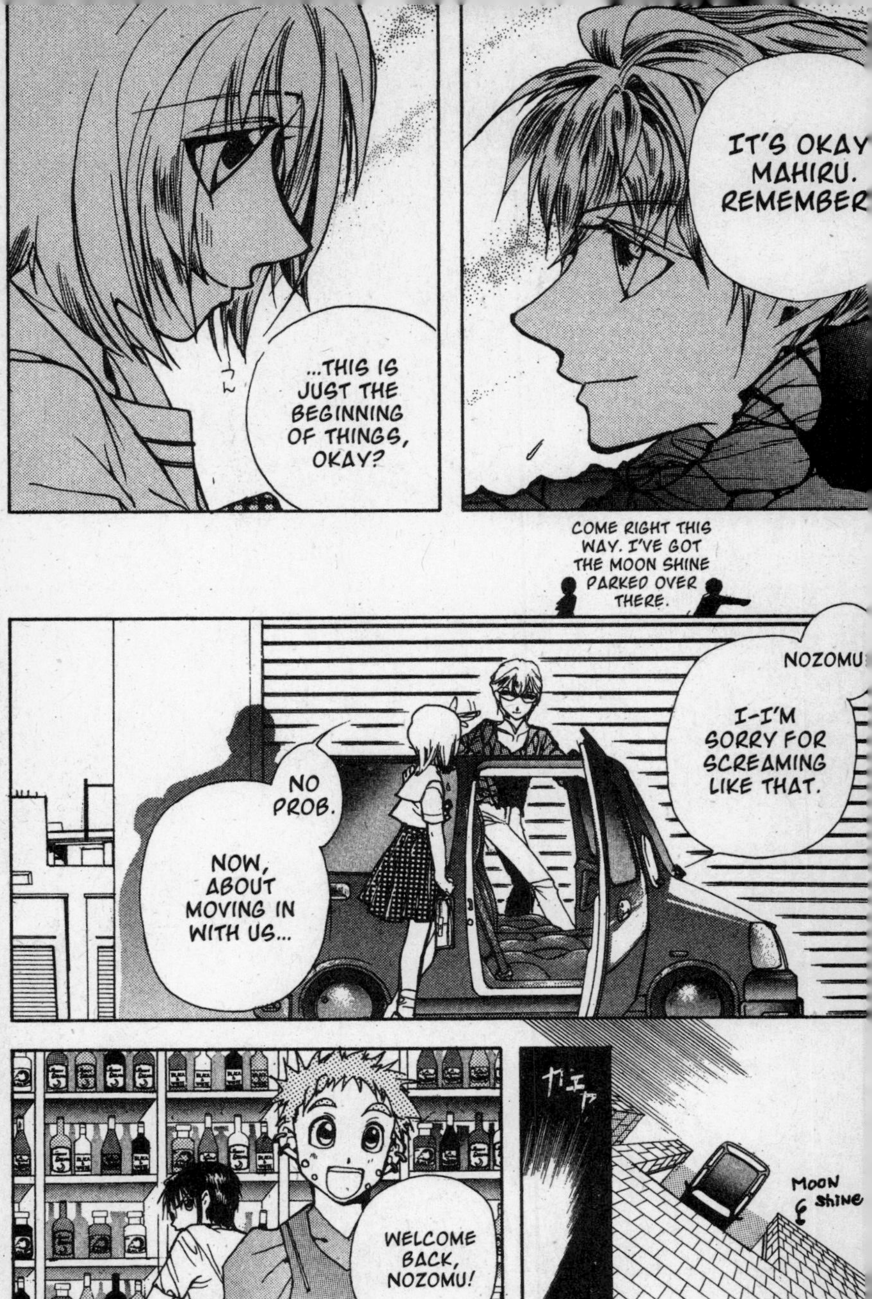
IT'S OKAY MAHIRU. REMEMBER
...THIS IS JUST THE BEGINNING OF THINGS, OKAY?
COME RIGHT THIS WAY. I'VE GOT THE MOON SHINE PARKED OVER THERE.
NOZOMU
I-I'M SORRY FOR SCREAMING LIKE THAT.
NO PROB.
NOW, ABOUT MOVING IN WITH US...
MOON SHINE
WELCOME BACK, NOZOMU!

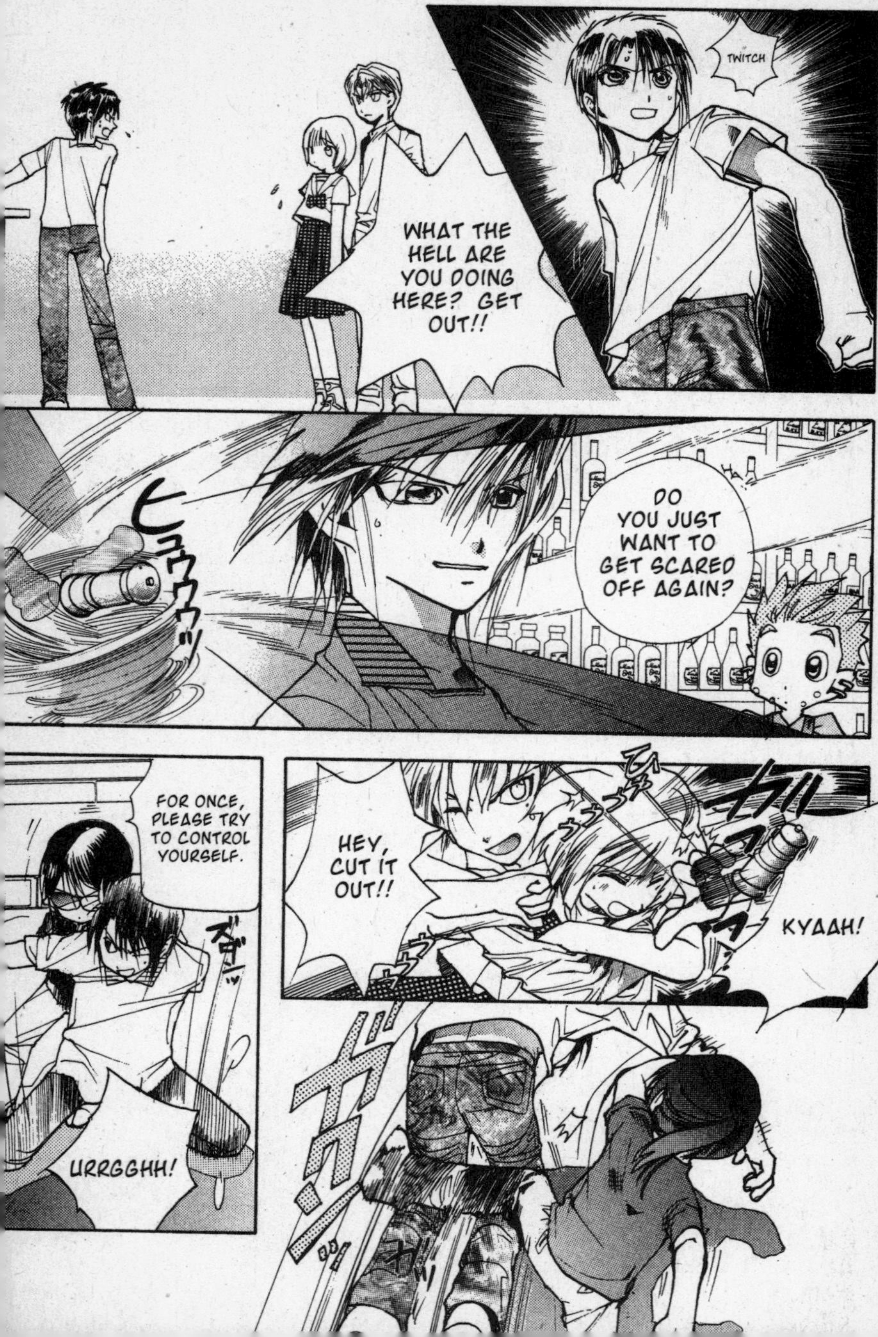
TWITCH
WHAT THE HELL ARE YOU DOING HERE? GET OUT!!
DO YOU JUST WANT TO GET SCARED OFF AGAIN?
HEY, CUT IT OUT!!
KYAAH!
FOR ONCE, PLEASE TRY TO CONTROL YOURSELF.
URRGGHH!

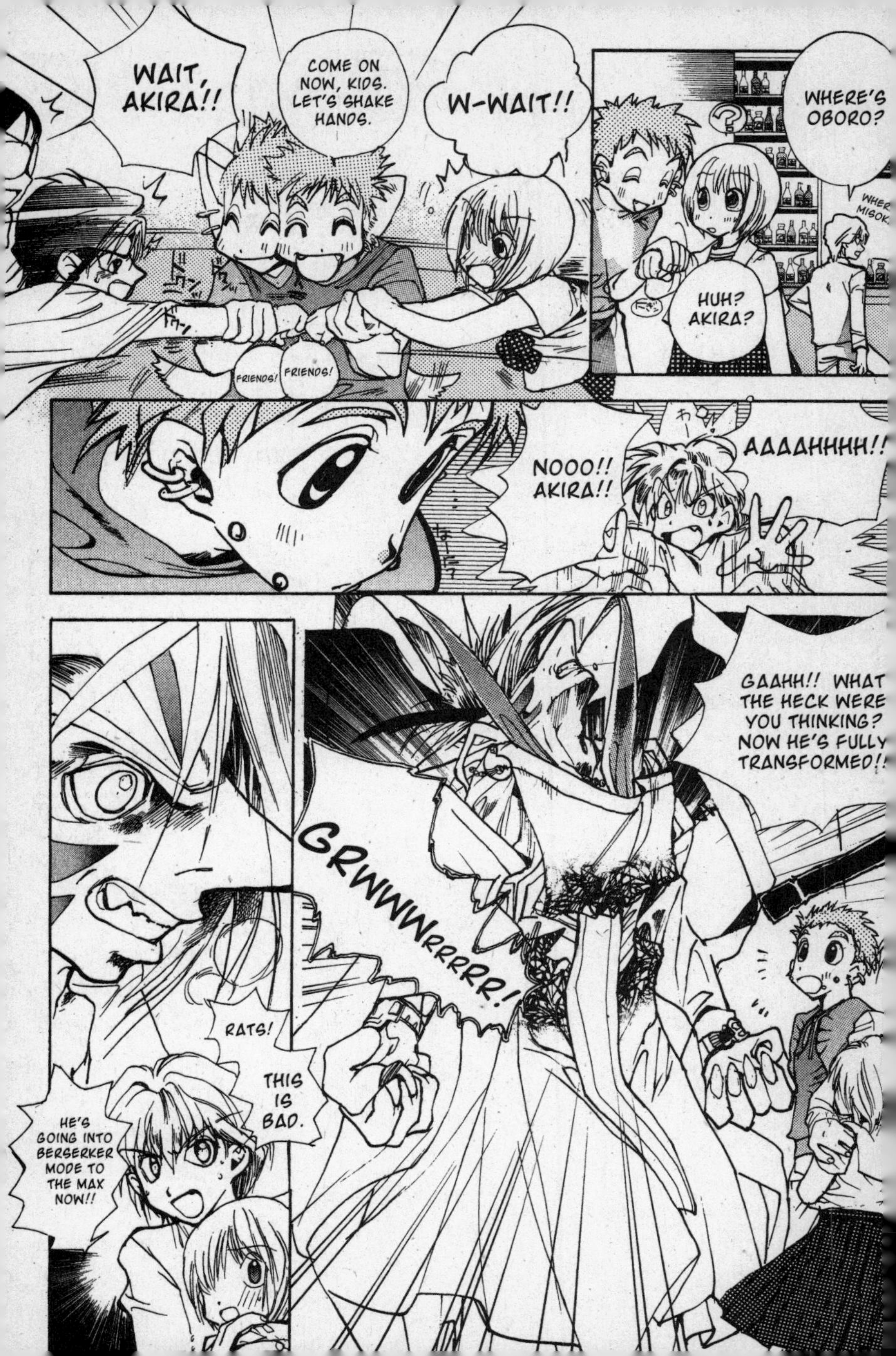
WHERE'S OBORO?
HUH? AKIRA?
W-WAIT!!
COME ON NOW, KIDS. LET'S SHAKE HANDS.
WAIT, AKIRA!!
FRIENDS!
FRIENDS!
AAAAHHHH!!
NOOO!! AKIRA!!
GAAHH!! WHAT THE HECK WERE YOU THINKING? NOW HE'S FULLY TRANSFORMED!!
GRWWWWRRRRR!
RATS!
THIS IS BAD.
HE'S GOING INTO BERSERKER MODE TO THE MAX NOW!!

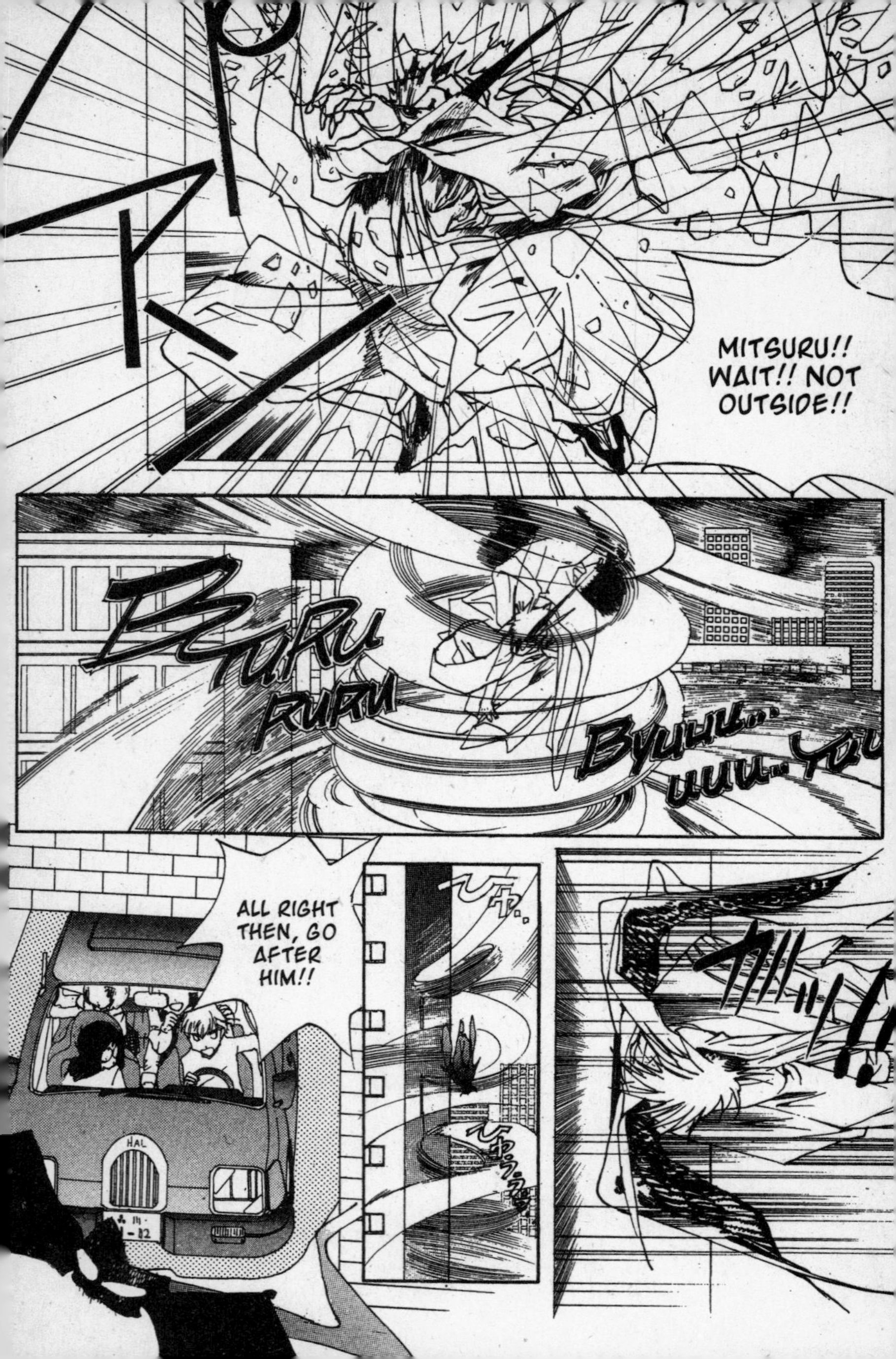
MITSURU!! WAIT!! NOT OUTSIDE!!
BURURU
RURU
Byuuu...
ALL RIGHT THEN, GO AFTER HIM!!

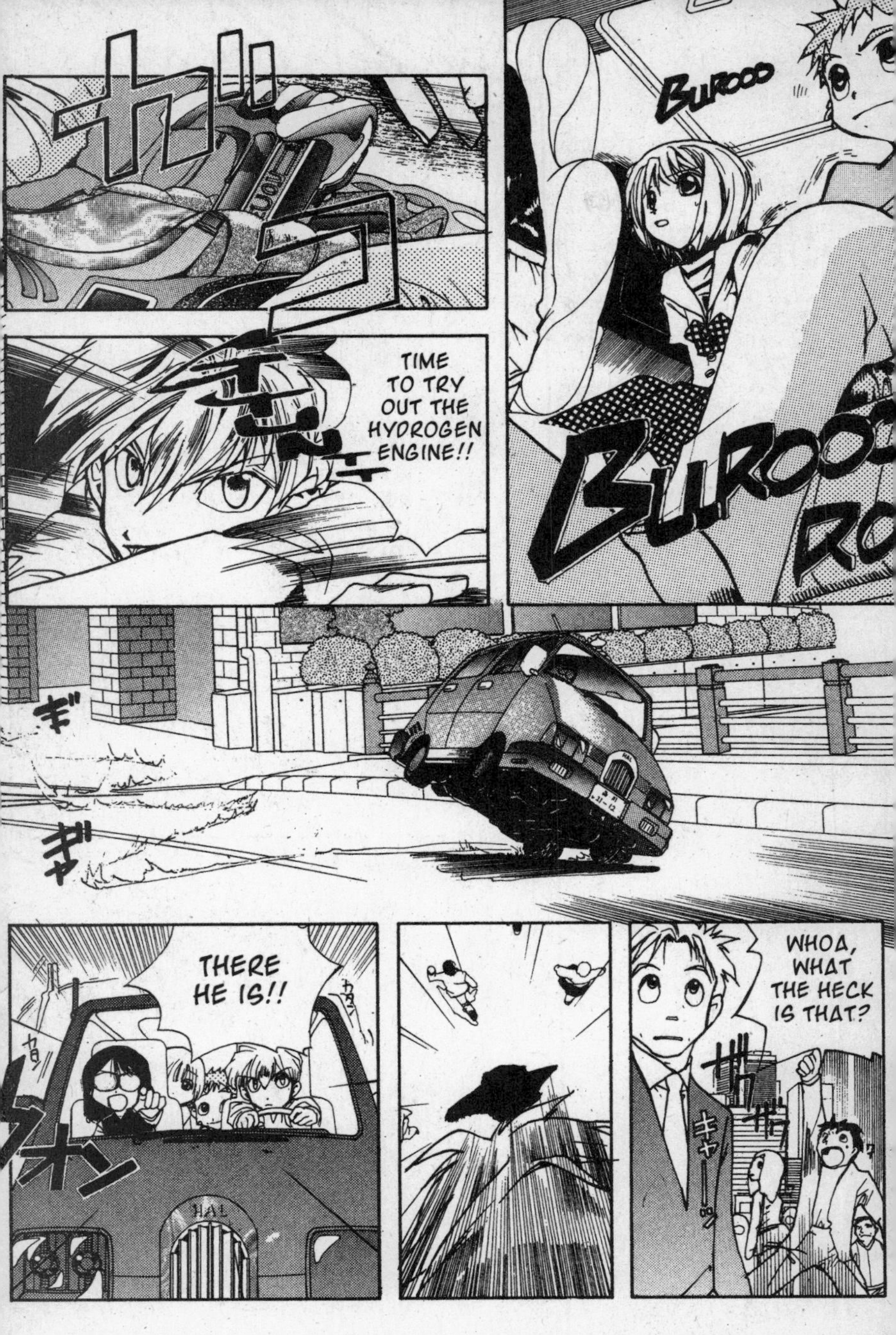
BUROOO
TIME TO TRY OUT THE HYDROGEN ENGINE!!
WHOA, WHAT THE HECK IS THAT?
THERE HE IS!!

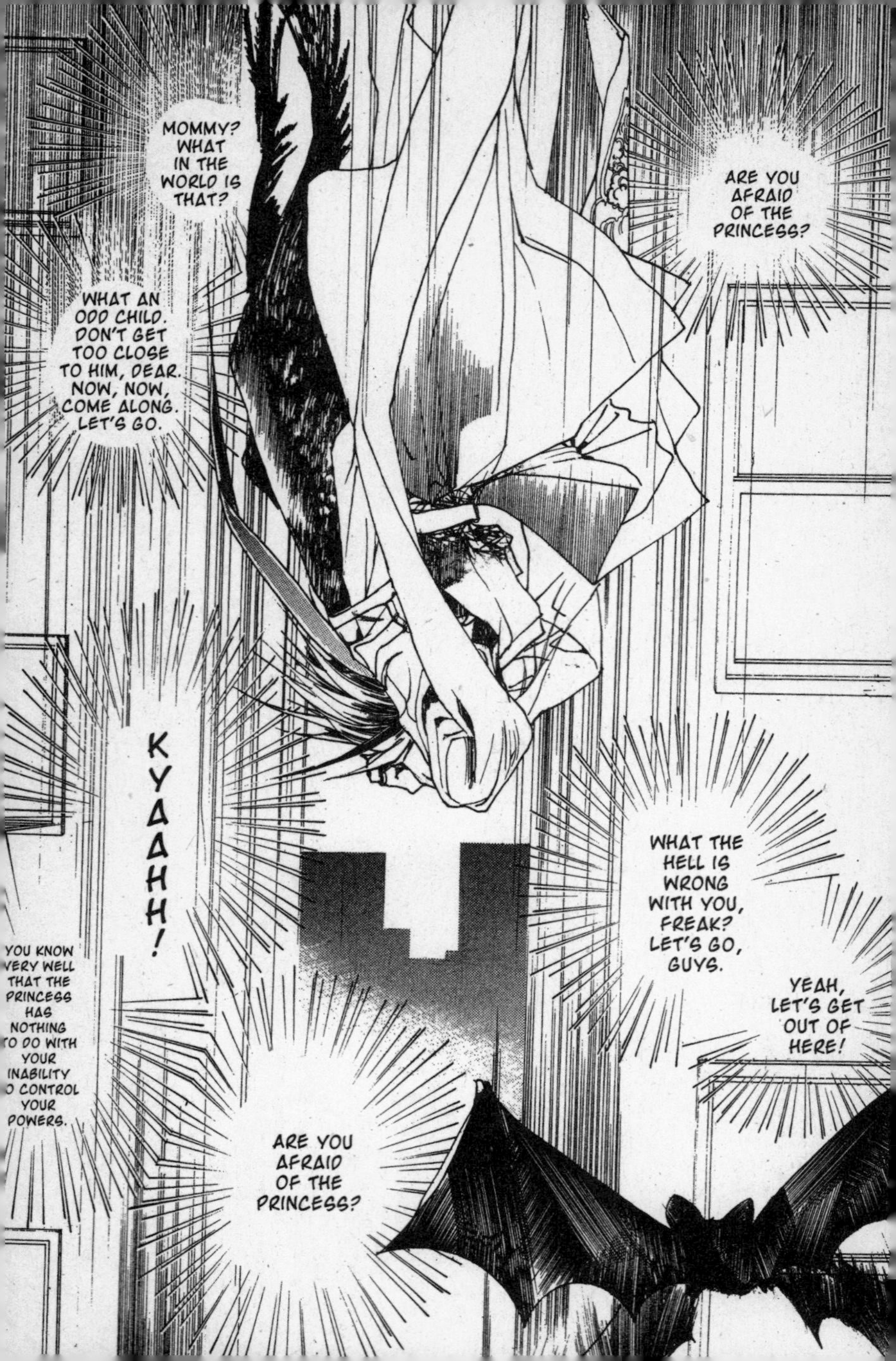
ARE YOU AFRAID OF THE PRINCESS?
MOMMY? WHAT IN THE WORLD IS THAT?
WHAT AN ODD CHILD. DON'T GET TOO CLOSE TO HIM, DEAR. NOW, NOW, COME ALONG. LET'S GO.
WHAT THE HELL IS WRONG WITH YOU, FREAK? LET'S GO, GUYS.
YEAH, LET'S GET OUT OF HERE!
KYAAHH!
ARE YOU AFRAID OF THE PRINCESS?
YOU KNOW VERY WELL THAT THE PRINCESS HAS NOTHING TO DO WITH YOUR INABILITY TO CONTROL YOUR POWERS.

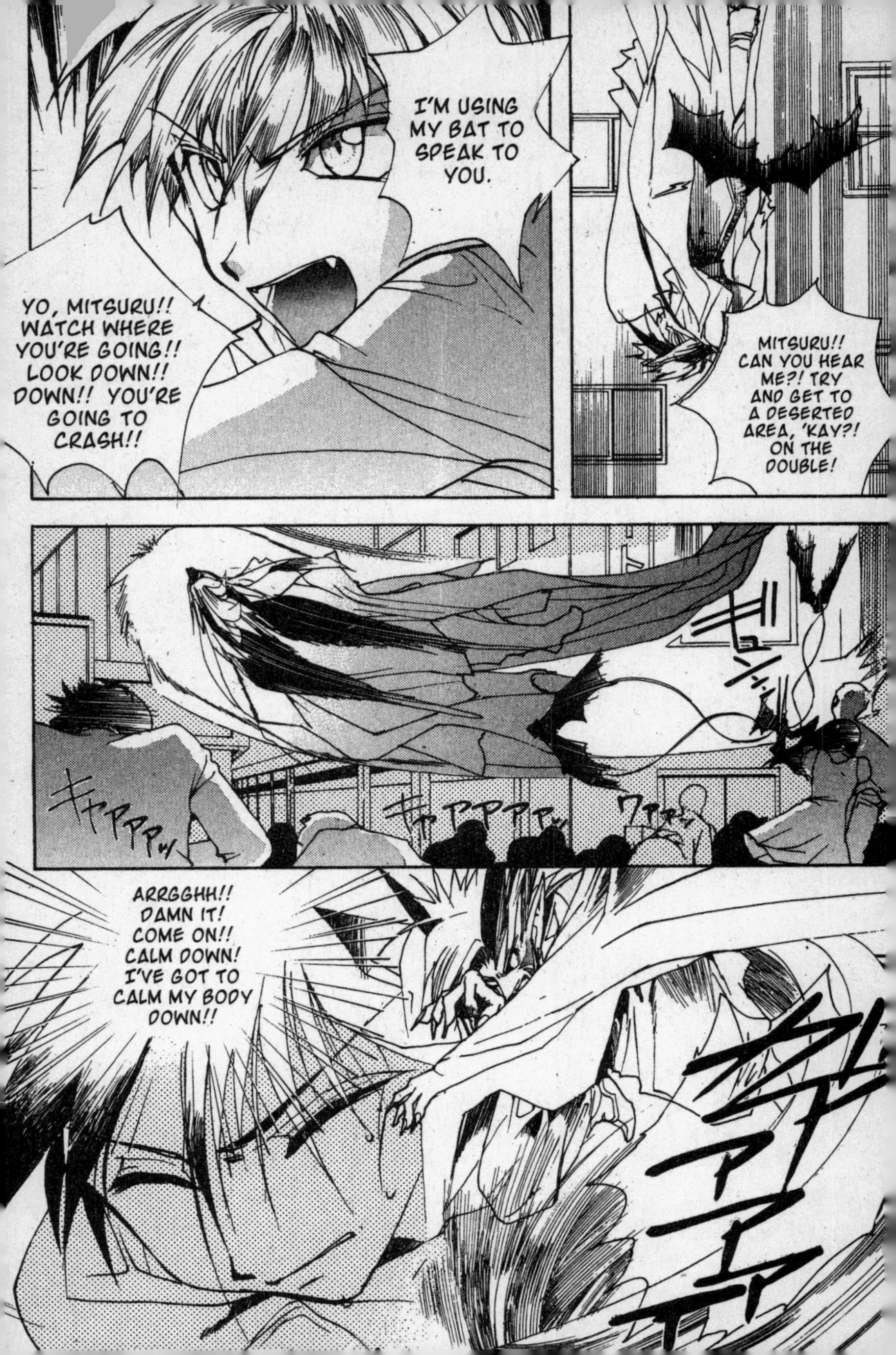
MITSURU!! CAN YOU HEAR ME?! TRY AND GET TO A DESERTED AREA, 'KAY?! ON THE DOUBLE!
I'M USING MY BAT TO SPEAK TO YOU.
YO, MITSURU!! WATCH WHERE YOU'RE GOING!! LOOK DOWN!! DOWN!! YOU'RE GOING TO CRASH!!
ARRGGHH!! DAMN IT! COME ON!! CALM DOWN! I'VE GOT TO CALM MY BODY DOWN!!

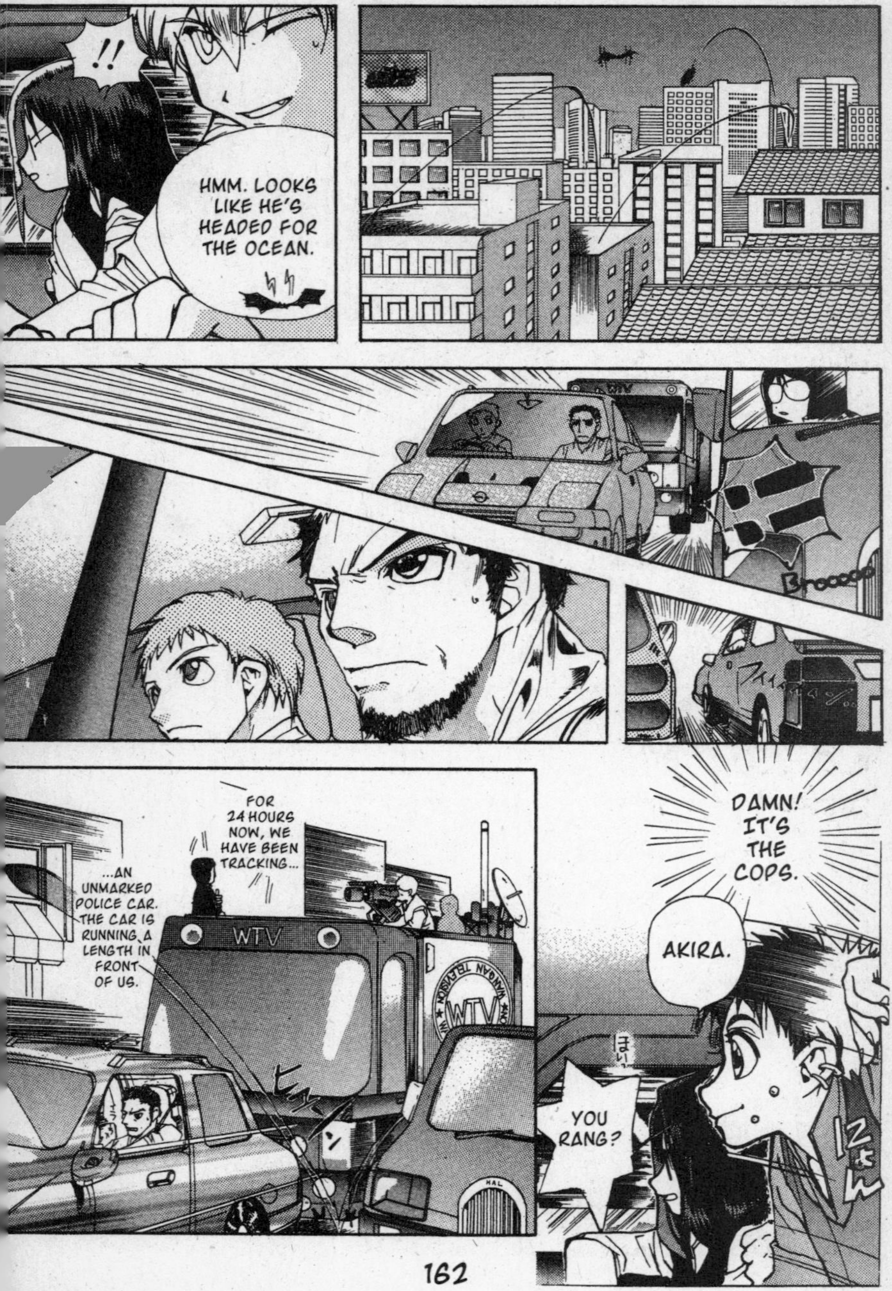
!!
HMM. LOOKS LIKE HE'S HEADED FOR THE OCEAN.
DAMN! IT'S THE COPS.
AKIRA.
YOU RANG?
FOR 24 HOURS NOW, WE HAVE BEEN TRACKING...
...AN UNMARKED POLICE CAR. THE CAR IS RUNNING A LENGTH IN FRONT OF US.
WTV

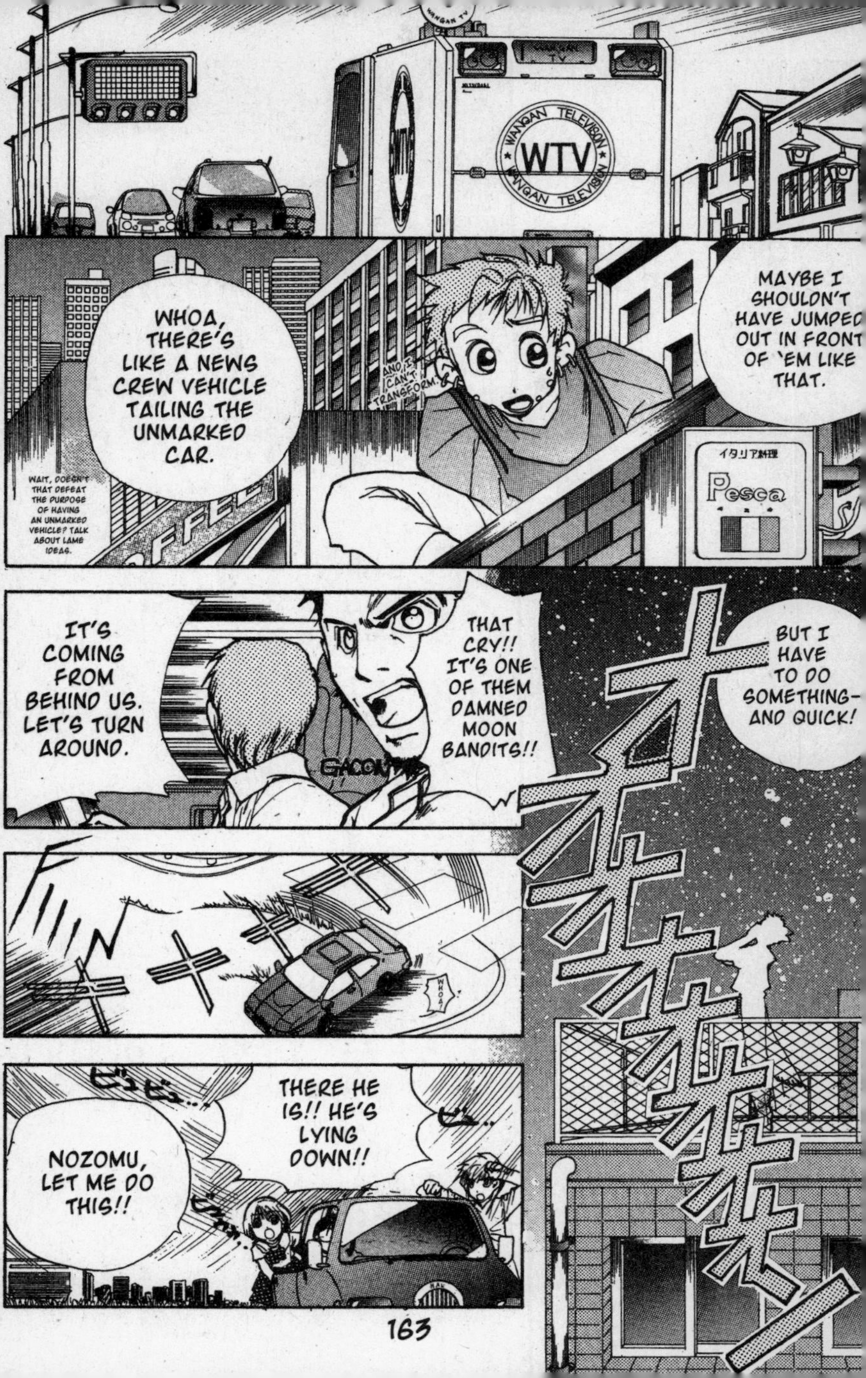
WANGAN TV
WANGAN TELEVISION
WTV
MAYBE I SHOULDN'T HAVE JUMPED OUT IN FRONT OF 'EM LIKE THAT.
AND, I CAN'T TRANSFORM.
WHOA, THERE'S LIKE A NEWS CREW VEHICLE TAILING THE UNMARKED CAR.
WAIT, DOESN'T THAT DEFEAT THE PURPOSE OF HAVING AN UNMARKED VEHICLE? TALK ABOUT LAME IDEAS.
イタリア料理
Pesca
BUT I HAVE TO DO SOMETHING- AND QUICK!
THAT CRY!! IT'S ONE OF THEM DAMNED MOON BANDITS!!
IT'S COMING FROM BEHIND US. LET'S TURN AROUND.
GACON
FIIIN
WHOA!
THERE HE IS!! HE'S LYING DOWN!!
NOZOMU, LET ME DO THIS!!

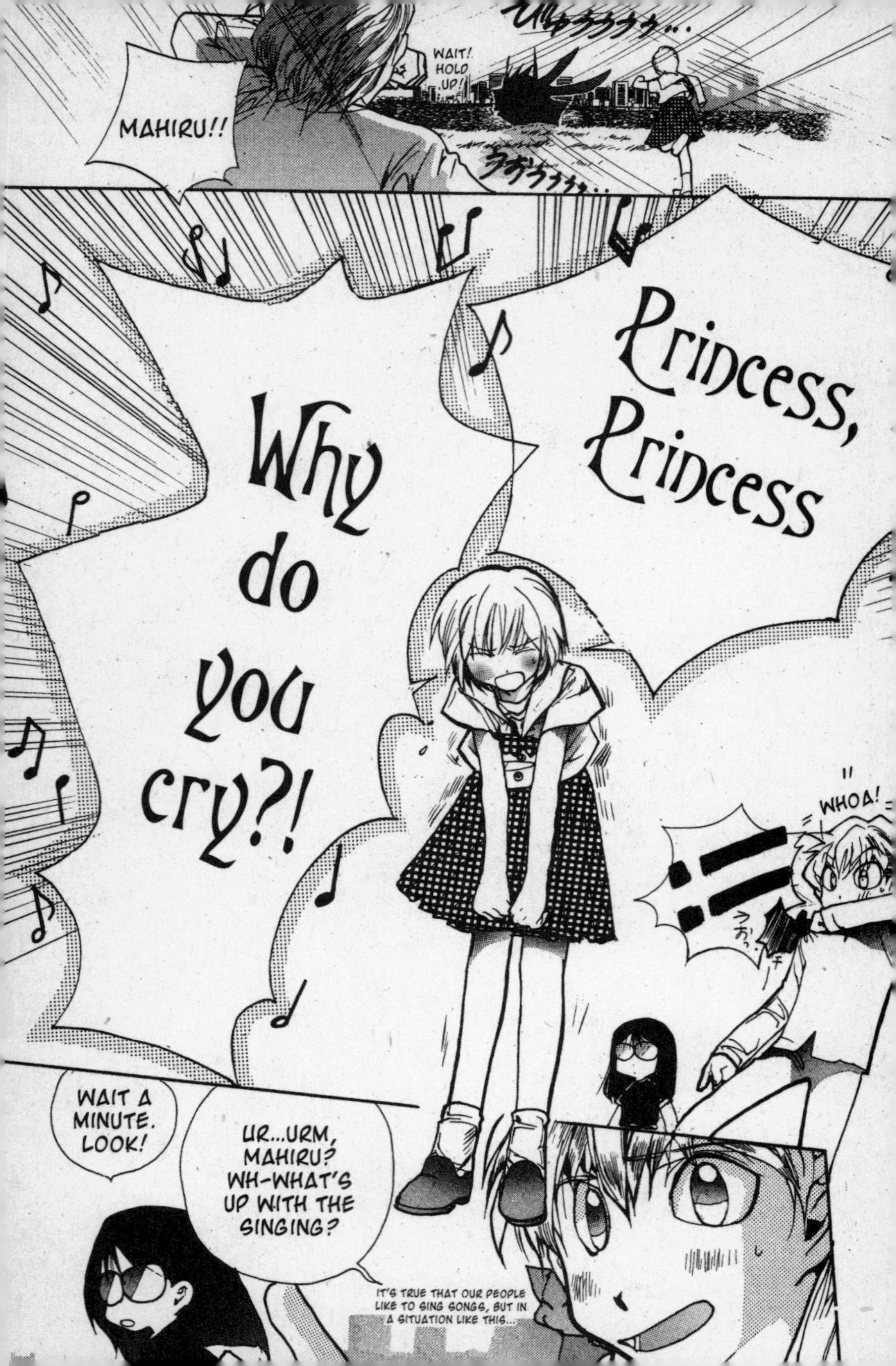
WAIT! HOLD UP!
MAHIRU!!
Princess, Princess
Why do you cry?!
WHOA!
UR...URM, MAHIRU? WH-WHAT'S UP WITH THE SINGING?
WAIT A MINUTE. LOOK!
IT'S TRUE THAT OUR PEOPLE LIKE TO SING SONGS, BUT IN A SITUATION LIKE THIS...

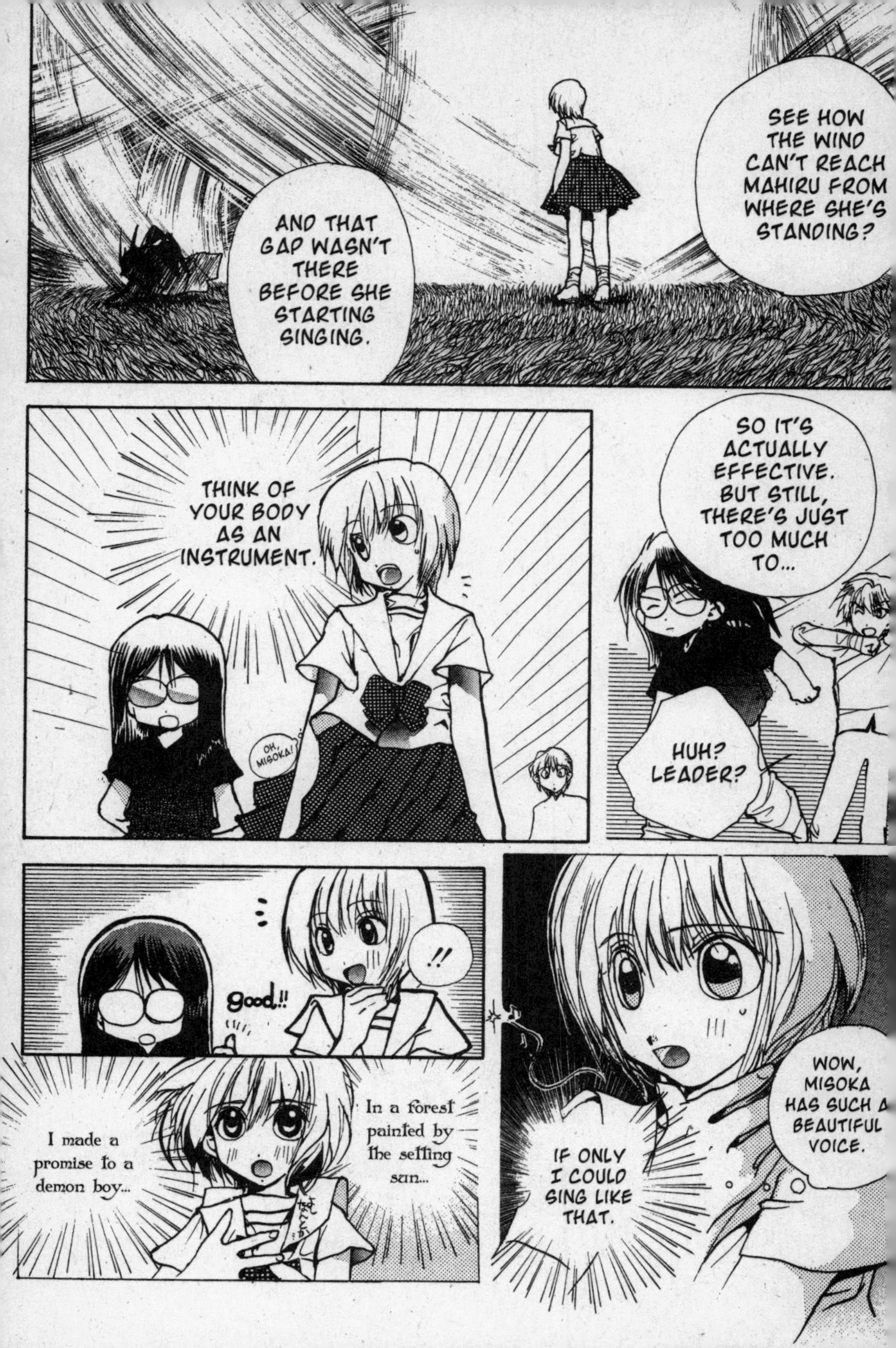
SEE HOW THE WIND CAN'T REACH MAHIRU FROM WHERE SHE'S STANDING?
AND THAT GAP WASN'T THERE BEFORE SHE STARTING SINGING.
SO IT'S ACTUALLY EFFECTIVE. BUT STILL, THERE'S JUST TOO MUCH TO...
HUH? LEADER?
THINK OF YOUR BODY AS AN INSTRUMENT.
OH, MISOKA!
WOW, MISOKA HAS SUCH A BEAUTIFUL VOICE.
IF ONLY I COULD SING LIKE THAT.
!!
good.!!
In a forest painted by the setting sun...
I made a promise to a demon boy...

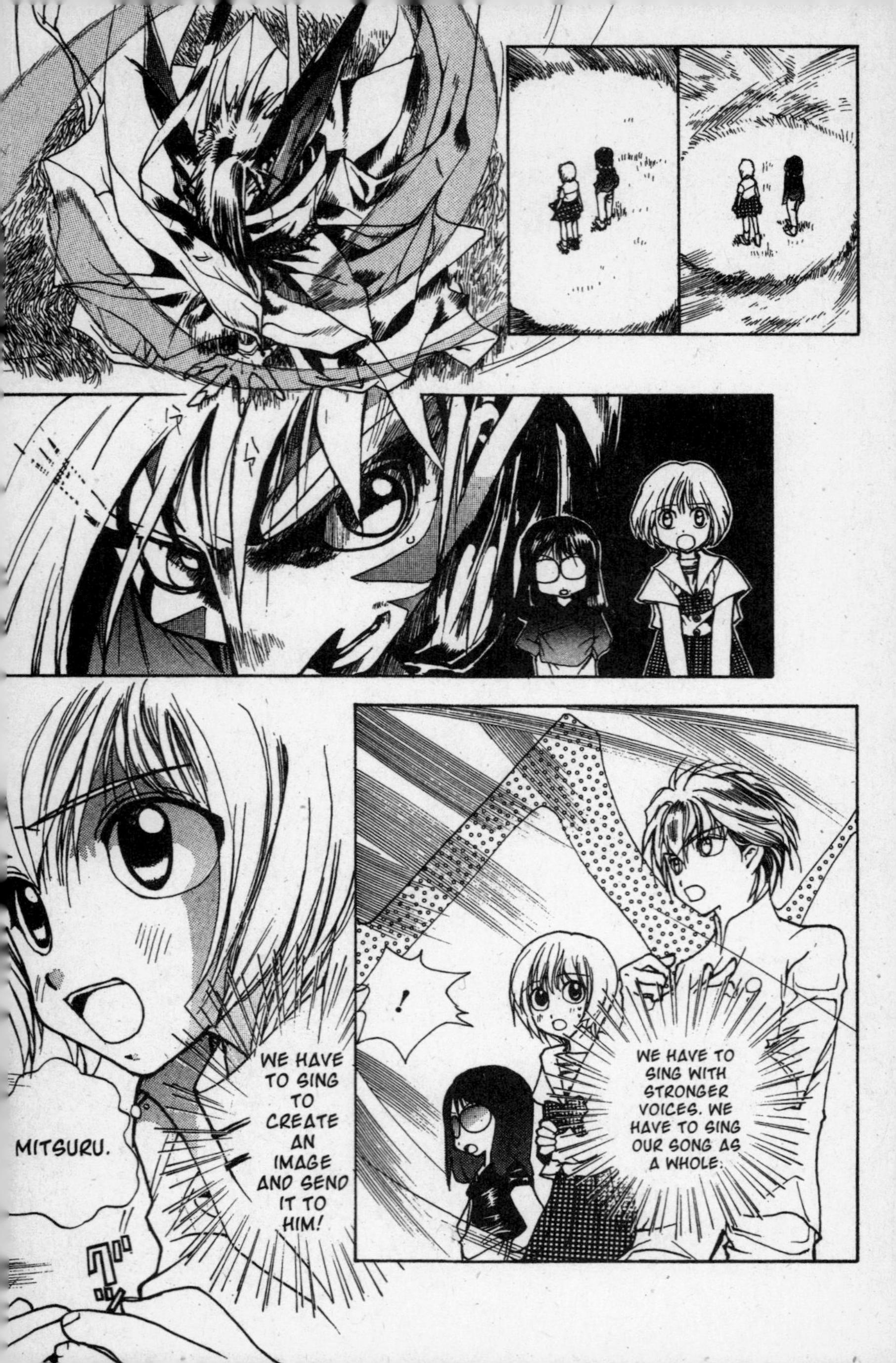
WE HAVE TO SING WITH STRONGER VOICES. WE HAVE TO SING OUR SONG AS A WHOLE.
!
WE HAVE TO SING TO CREATE AN IMAGE AND SEND IT TO HIM!
MITSURU.

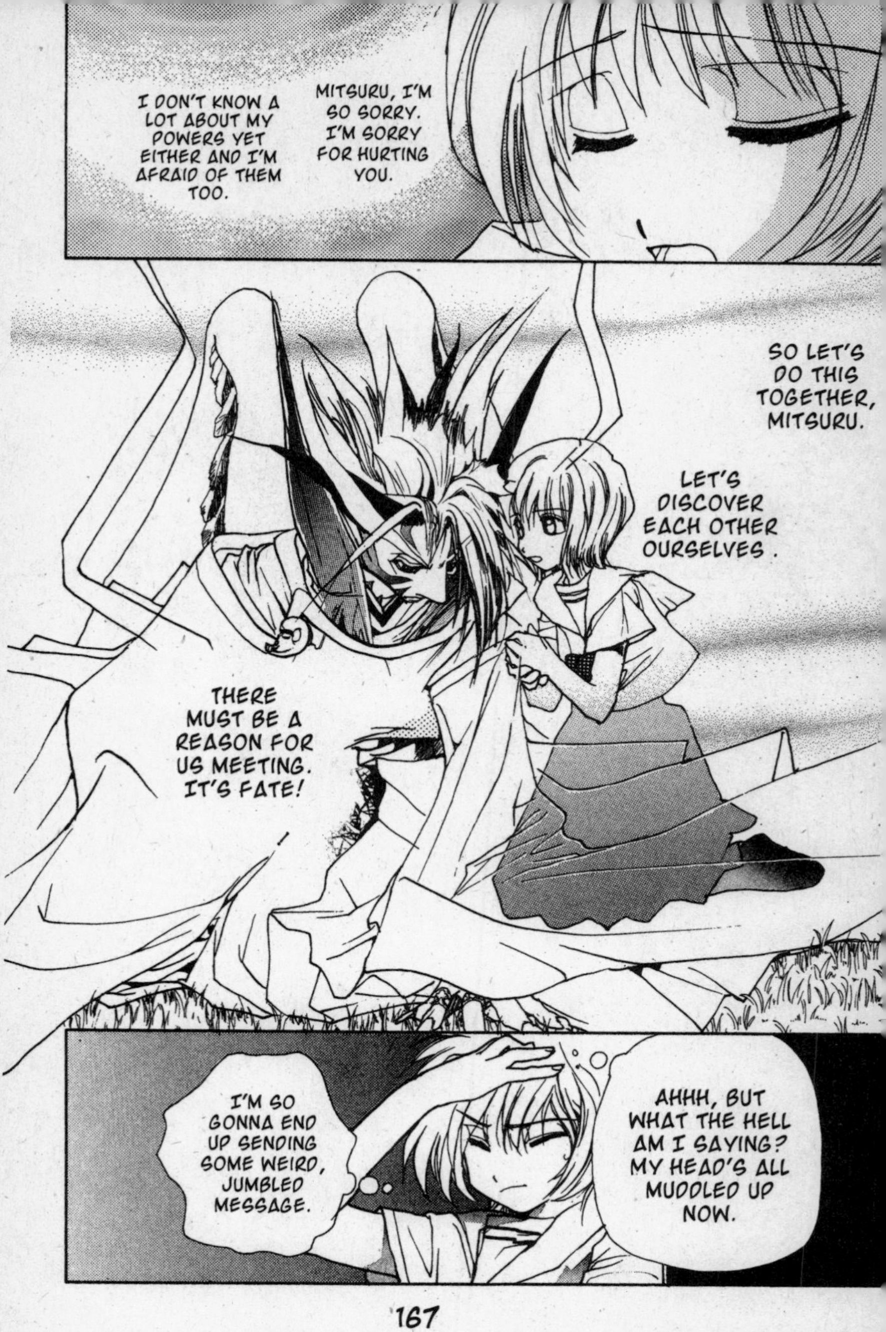
MITSURU, I'M SO SORRY. I'M SORRY FOR HURTING YOU.
I DON'T KNOW A LOT ABOUT MY POWERS YET EITHER AND I'M AFRAID OF THEM TOO.
SO LET'S DO THIS TOGETHER, MITSURU.
LET'S DISCOVER EACH OTHER OURSELVES.
THERE MUST BE A REASON FOR US MEETING. IT'S FATE!
AHHH, BUT WHAT THE HELL AM I SAYING? MY HEAD'S ALL MUDDLED UP NOW.
I'M SO GONNA END UP SENDING SOME WEIRD, JUMBLED MESSAGE.

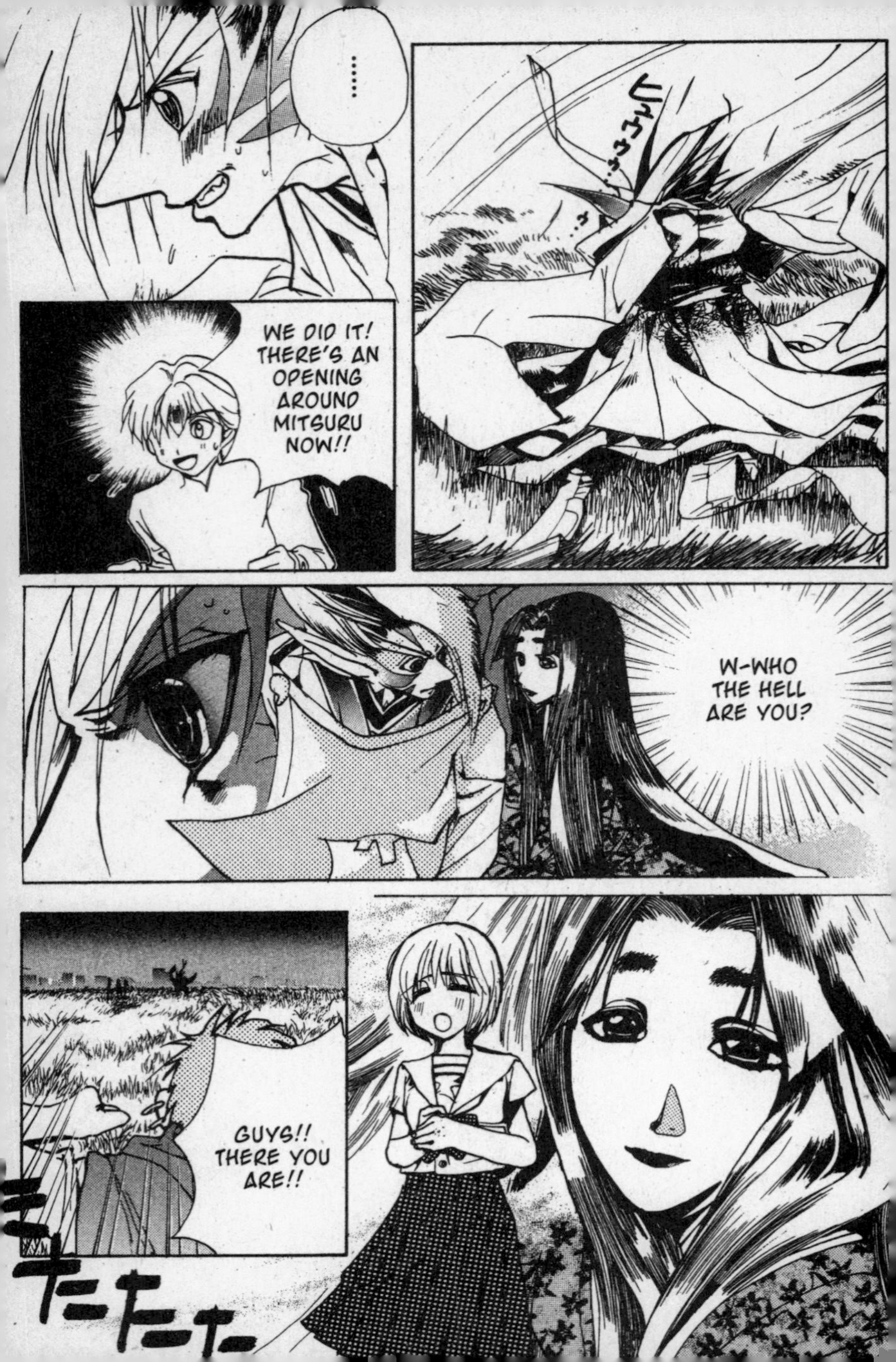
......
WE DID IT! THERE'S AN OPENING AROUND MITSURU NOW!!
W-WHO THE HELL ARE YOU?
GUYS!! THERE YOU ARE!!

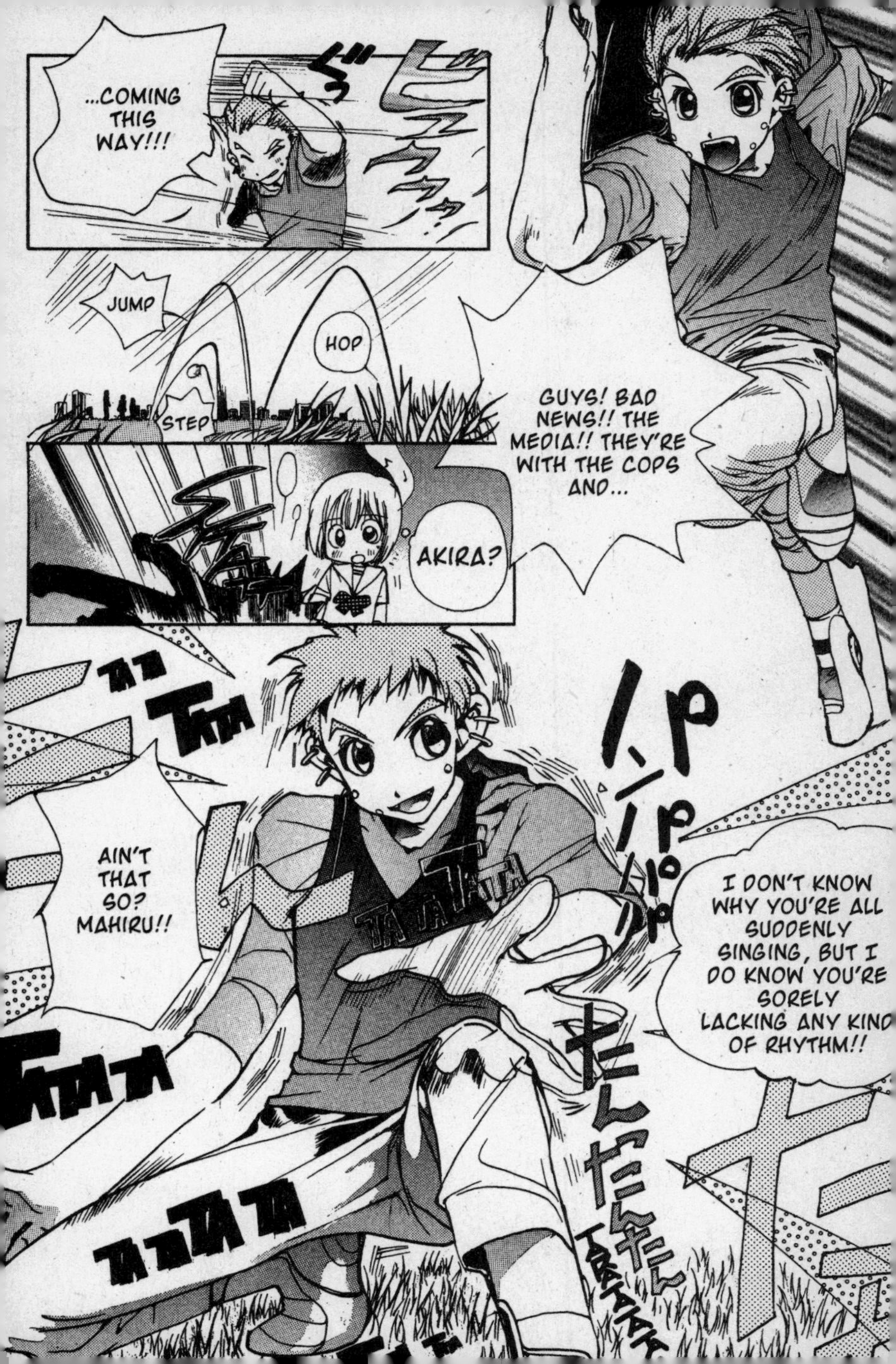
GUYS! BAD NEWS!! THE MEDIA!! THEY'RE WITH THE COPS AND...
...COMING THIS WAY!!!
HOP
JUMP
STEP
AKIRA?
AIN'T THAT SO? MAHIRU!!
I DON'T KNOW WHY YOU'RE ALL SUDDENLY SINGING, BUT I DO KNOW YOU'RE SORELY LACKING ANY KIND OF RHYTHM!!

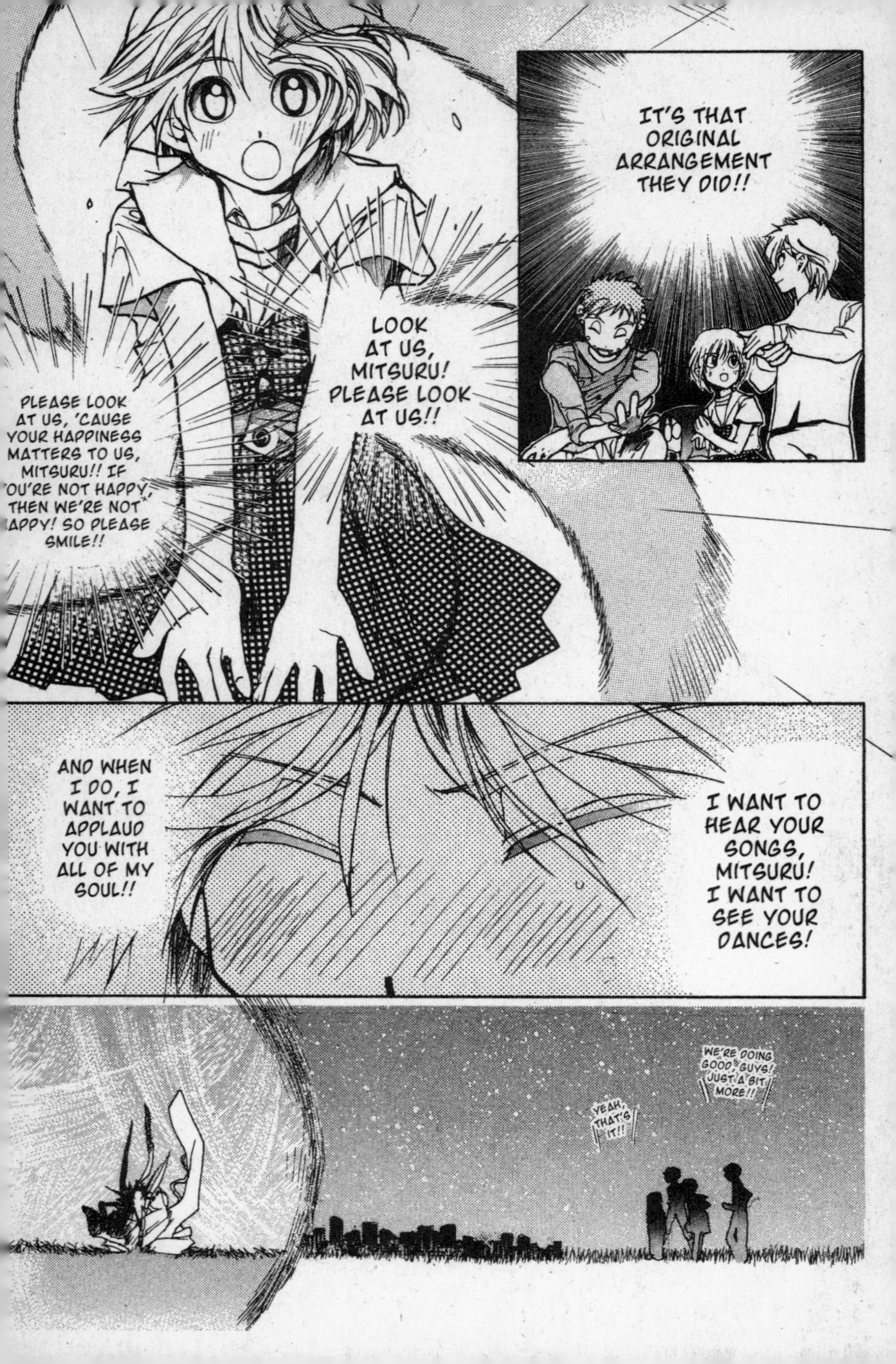
IT'S THAT ORIGINAL ARRANGEMENT THEY DID!!
LOOK AT US, MITSURU! PLEASE LOOK AT US!!
PLEASE LOOK AT US, 'CAUSE YOUR HAPPINESS MATTERS TO US, MITSURU!! IF OU'RE NOT HAPPY, THEN WE'RE NOT APPY! SO PLEASE SMILE!!
I WANT TO HEAR YOUR SONGS, MITSURU! I WANT TO SEE YOUR DANCES!
AND WHEN I DO, I WANT TO APPLAUD YOU WITH ALL OF MY SOUL!!
WE'RE DOING GOOD, GUYS! JUST A BIT MORE!!
YEAH, THAT'S IT!!

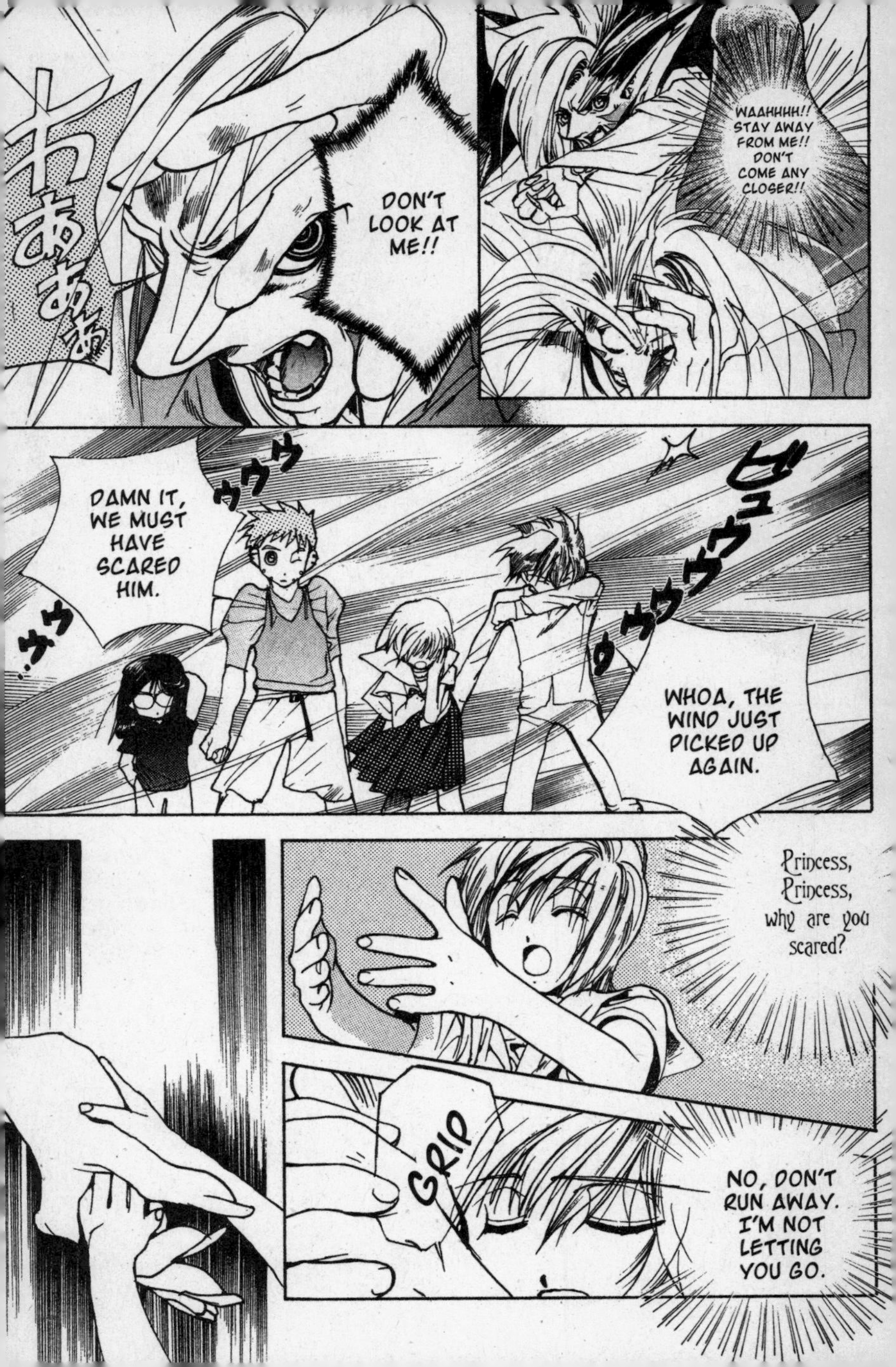
WAAHHHH!! STAY AWAY FROM ME!! DON'T COME ANY CLOSER!!
DON'T LOOK AT ME!!
わあああ
ビュウウウウ
WHOA, THE WIND JUST PICKED UP AGAIN.
ウウウ
DAMN IT, WE MUST HAVE SCARED HIM.
ウウウ
Princess, Princess, why are you scared?
GRIP
NO, DON'T RUN AWAY. I'M NOT LETTING YOU GO.

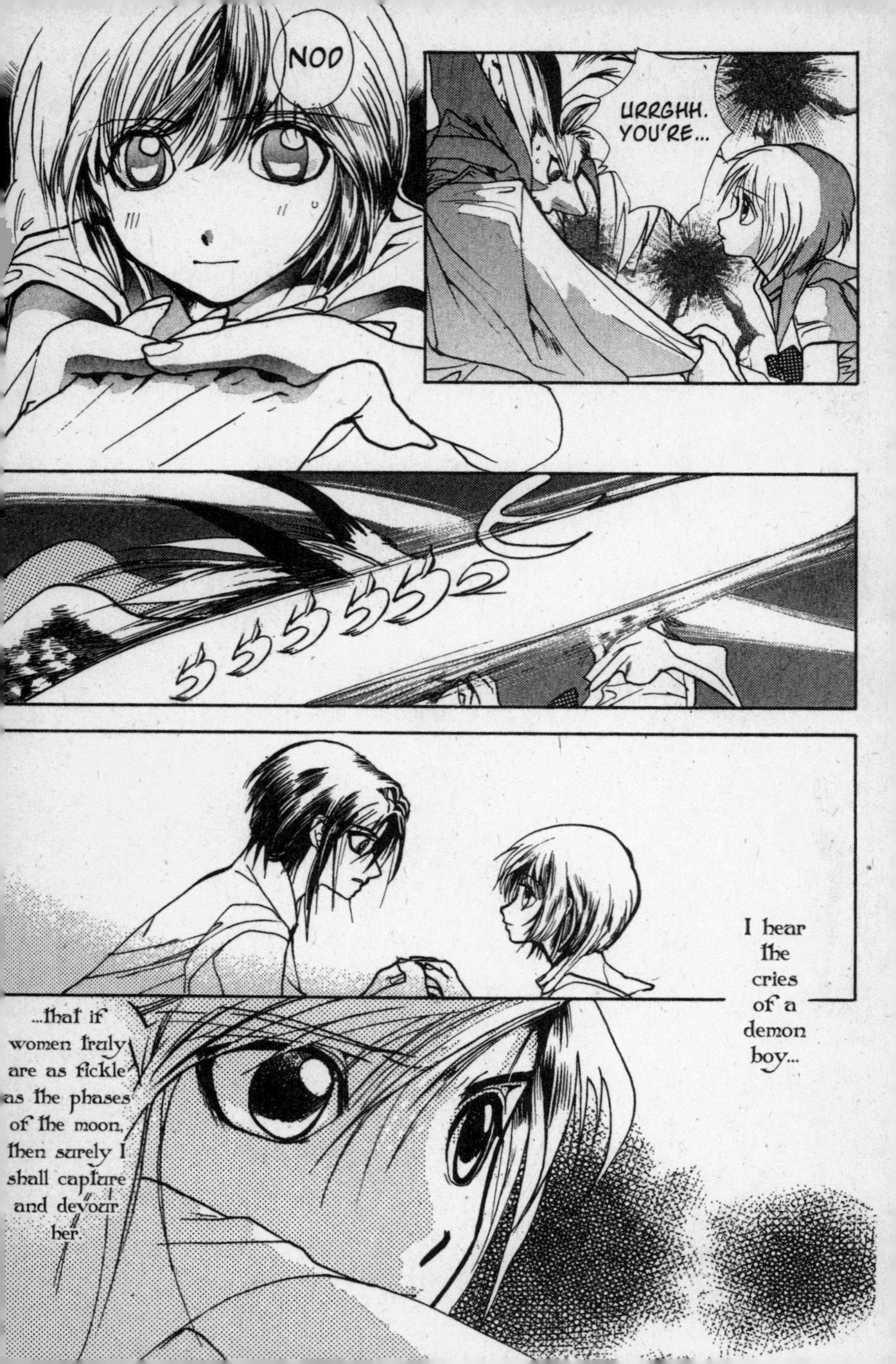
URRGHH. YOU'RE...
NOD
I hear the cries of a demon boy...
...that if women truly are as fickle as the phases of the moon, then surely I shall capture and devour her.

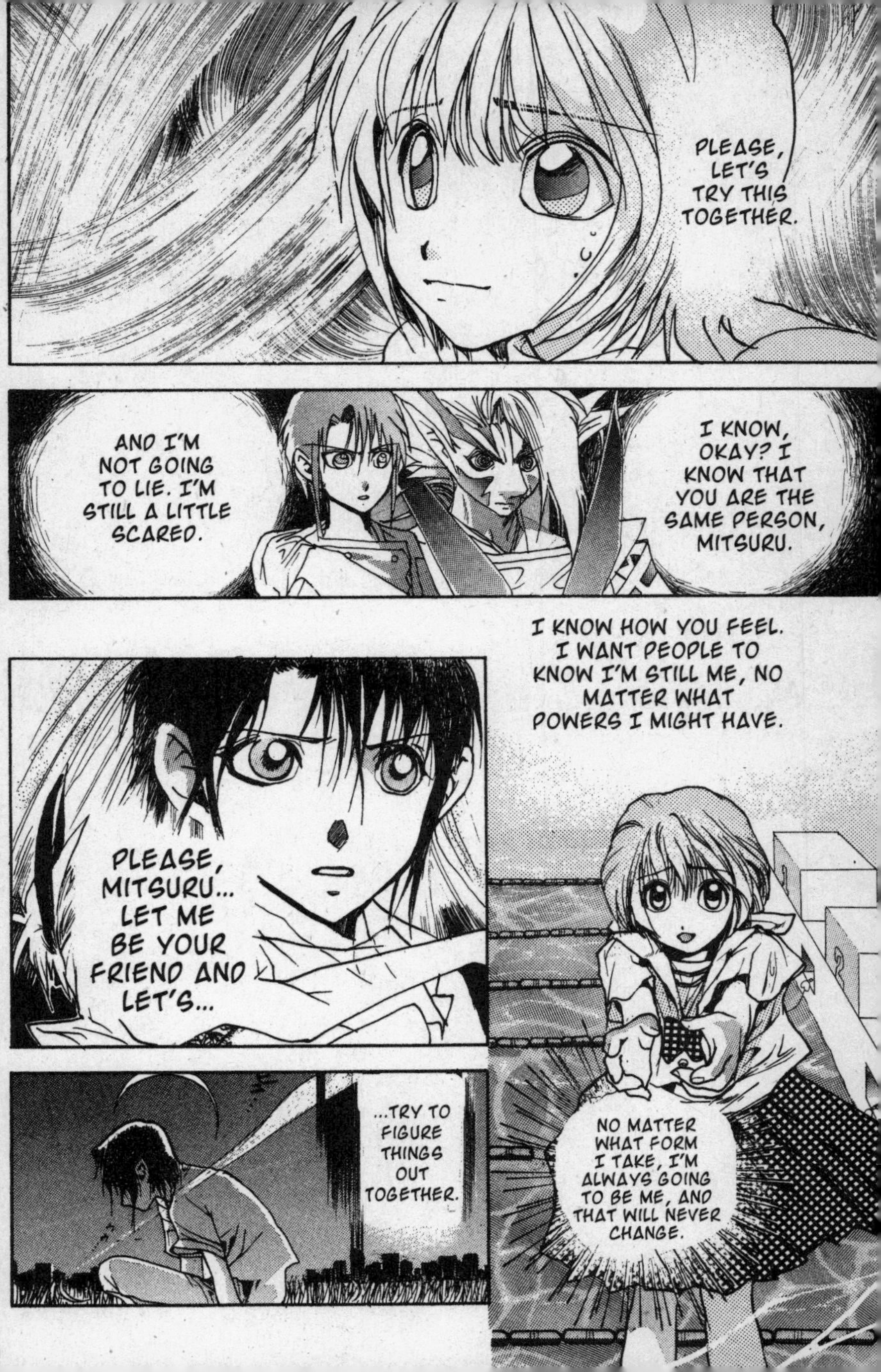
PLEASE, LET'S TRY THIS TOGETHER.
I KNOW, OKAY? I KNOW THAT YOU ARE THE SAME PERSON, MITSURU.
AND I'M NOT GOING TO LIE. I'M STILL A LITTLE SCARED.
I KNOW HOW YOU FEEL. I WANT PEOPLE TO KNOW I'M STILL ME, NO MATTER WHAT POWERS I MIGHT HAVE.
NO MATTER WHAT FORM I TAKE, I'M ALWAYS GOING TO BE ME, AND THAT WILL NEVER CHANGE.
PLEASE, MITSURU... LET ME BE YOUR FRIEND AND LET'S...
...TRY TO FIGURE THINGS OUT TOGETHER.

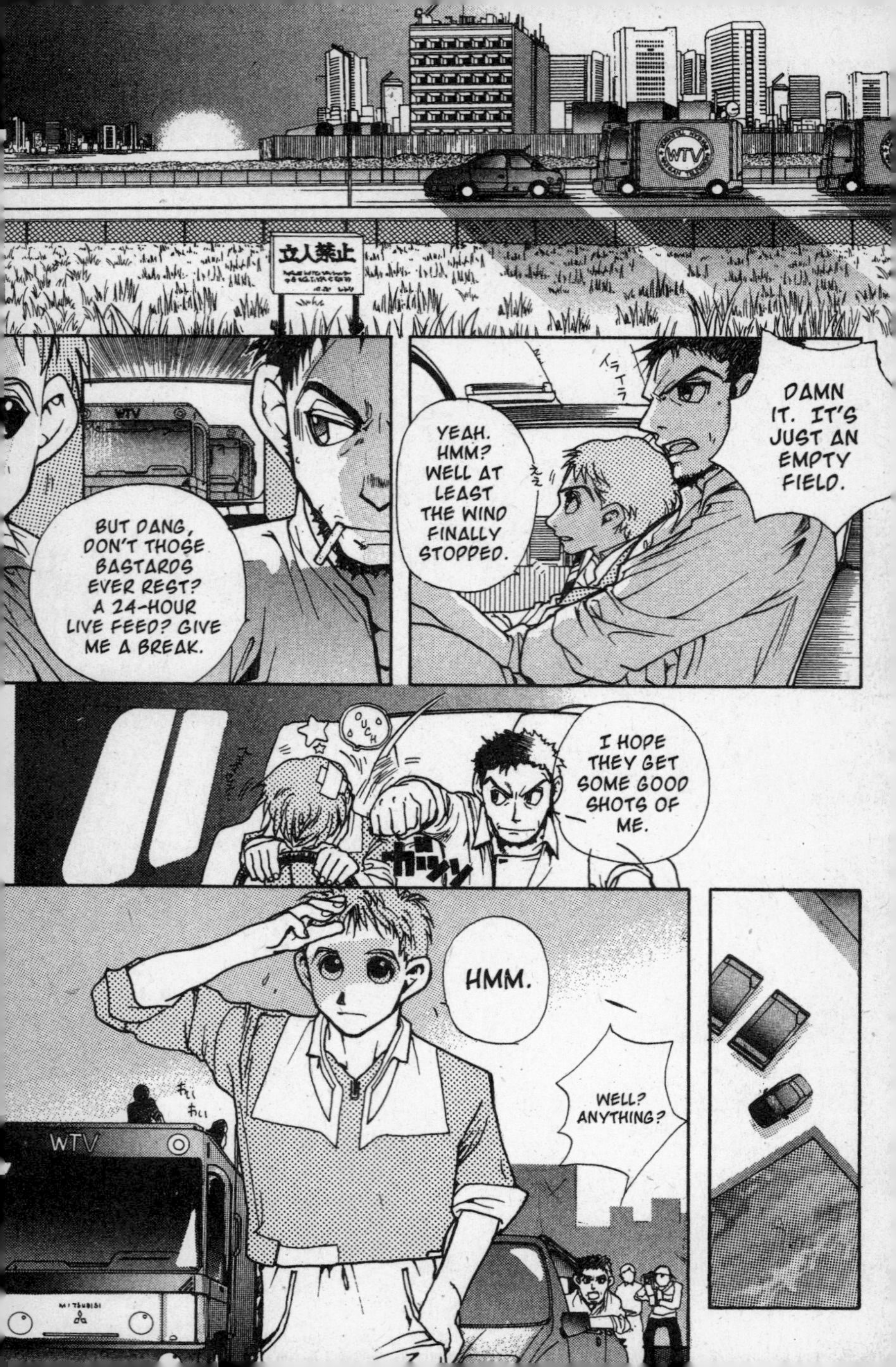
立入禁止
イライラ
DAMN IT. IT'S JUST AN EMPTY FIELD.
YEAH. HMM? WELL AT LEAST THE WIND FINALLY STOPPED.
BUT DANG, DON'T THOSE BASTARDS EVER REST? A 24-HOUR LIVE FEED? GIVE ME A BREAK.
I HOPE THEY GET SOME GOOD SHOTS OF ME.
OUCH
WELL? ANYTHING?
HMM.

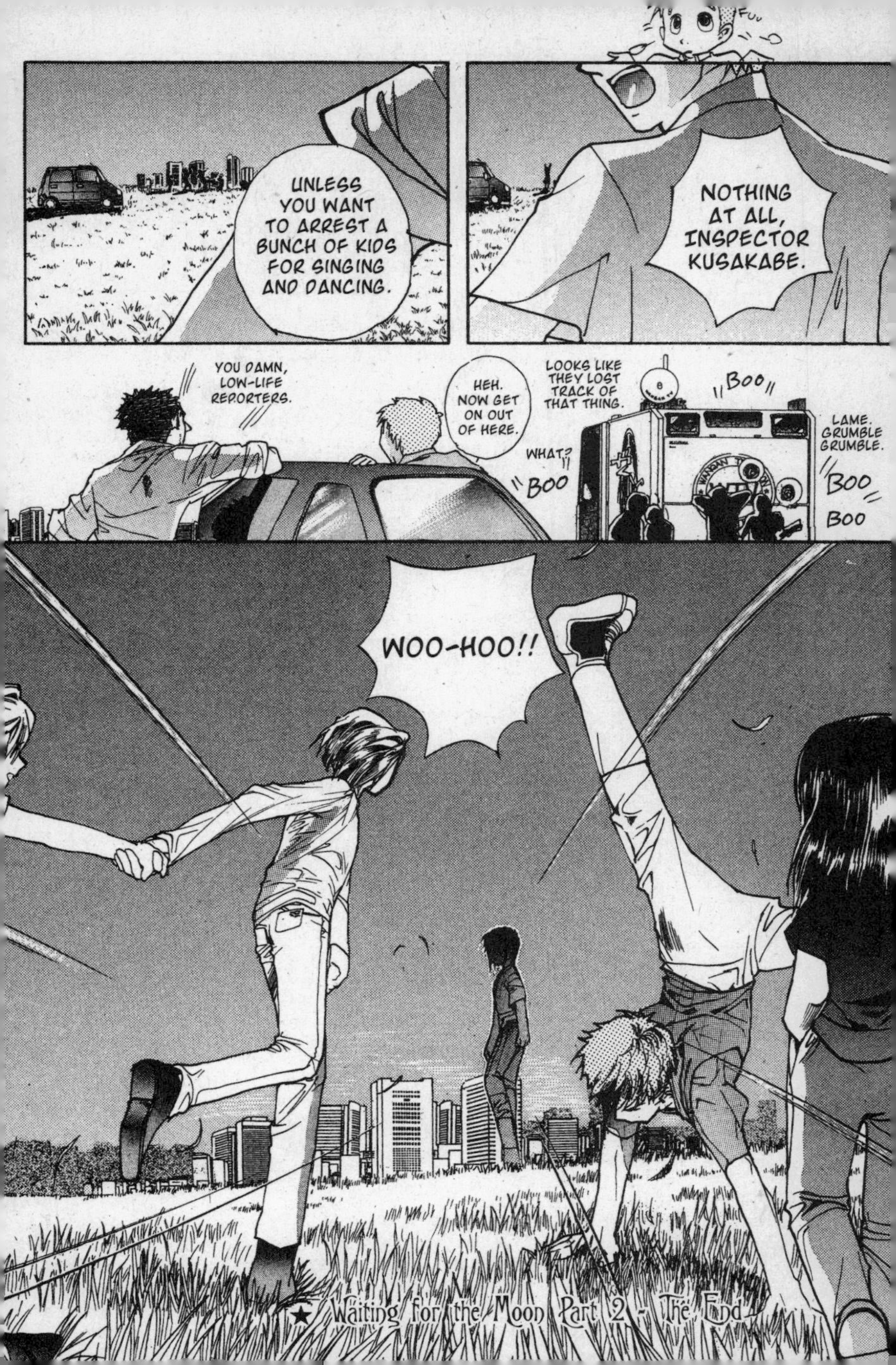
FUU
NOTHING AT ALL, INSPECTOR KUSAKABE.
UNLESS YOU WANT TO ARREST A BUNCH OF KIDS FOR SINGING AND DANCING.
LAME. GRUMBLE GRUMBLE.
BOO
BOO
BOO
LOOKS LIKE THEY LOST TRACK OF THAT THING.
WHAT?!
BOO
HEH. NOW GET ON OUT OF HERE.
YOU DAMN, LOW-LIFE REPORTERS.
WOO-HOO!!
★ Waiting for the Moon Part 2 - The End

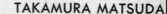

TAKAMURA MATSUDA

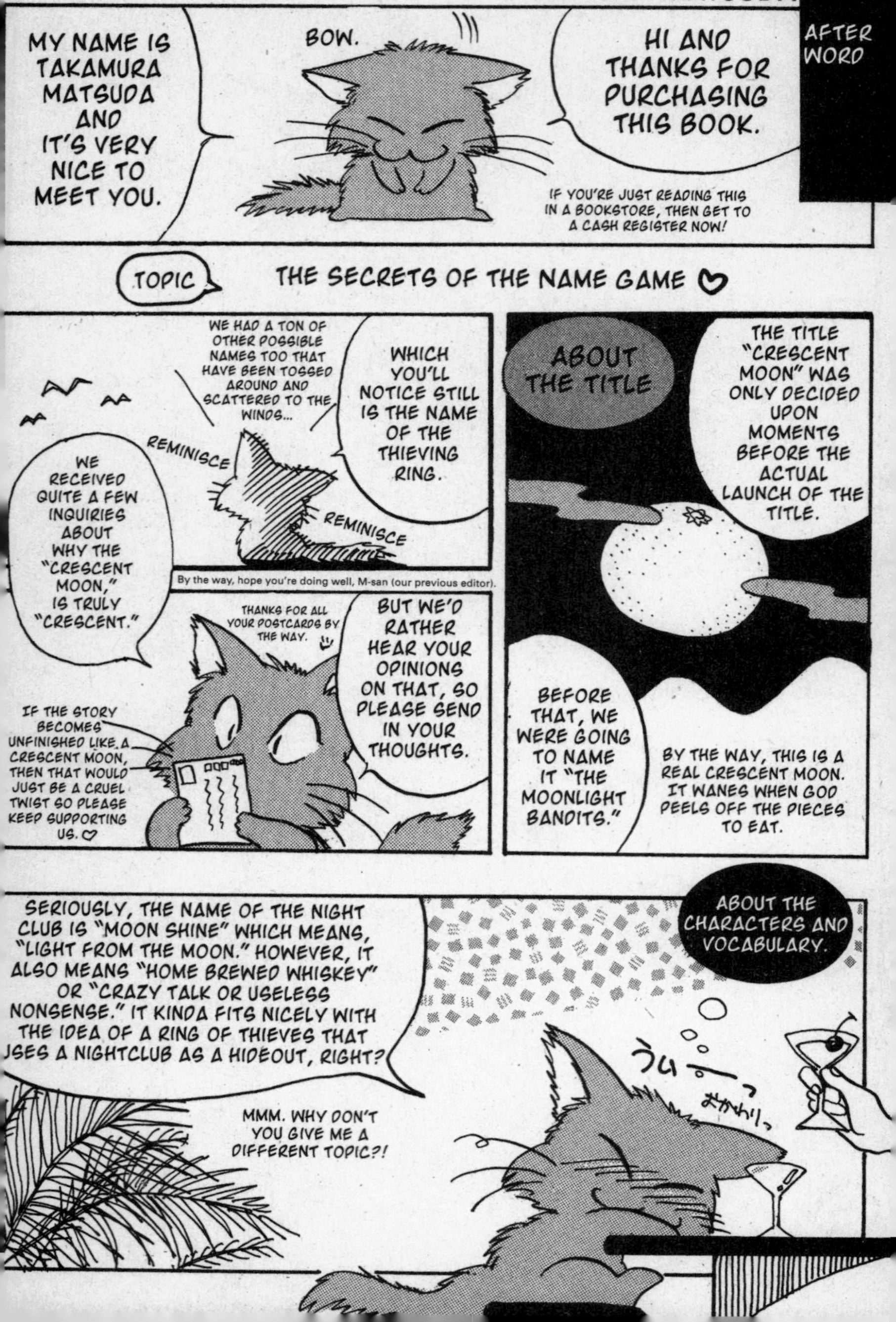
AFTER WORD
HI AND THANKS FOR PURCHASING THIS BOOK.
BOW.
MY NAME IS TAKAMURA MATSUDA AND IT'S VERY NICE TO MEET YOU.
IF YOU'RE JUST READING THIS IN A BOOKSTORE, THEN GET TO A CASH REGISTER NOW!
TOPIC
THE SECRETS OF THE NAME GAME ♡
ABOUT THE TITLE
THE TITLE "CRESCENT MOON" WAS ONLY DECIDED UPON MOMENTS BEFORE THE ACTUAL LAUNCH OF THE TITLE.
BEFORE THAT, WE WERE GOING TO NAME IT "THE MOONLIGHT BANDITS."
BY THE WAY, THIS IS A REAL CRESCENT MOON. IT WANES WHEN GOD PEELS OFF THE PIECES TO EAT.
WHICH YOU'LL NOTICE STILL IS THE NAME OF THE THIEVING RING.
WE HAD A TON OF OTHER POSSIBLE NAMES TOO THAT HAVE BEEN TOSSED AROUND AND SCATTERED TO THE WINDS...
REMINISCE
REMINISCE
By the way, hope you're doing well, M-san (our previous editor).
WE RECEIVED QUITE A FEW INQUIRIES ABOUT WHY THE "CRESCENT MOON," IS TRULY "CRESCENT."
BUT WE'D RATHER HEAR YOUR OPINIONS ON THAT, SO PLEASE SEND IN YOUR THOUGHTS.
THANKS FOR ALL YOUR POSTCARDS BY THE WAY.
IF THE STORY BECOMES UNFINISHED LIKE A CRESCENT MOON, THEN THAT WOULD JUST BE A CRUEL TWIST SO PLEASE KEEP SUPPORTING US. ♡
ABOUT THE CHARACTERS AND VOCABULARY.
SERIOUSLY, THE NAME OF THE NIGHT CLUB IS "MOON SHINE" WHICH MEANS, "LIGHT FROM THE MOON." HOWEVER, IT ALSO MEANS "HOME BREWED WHISKEY" OR "CRAZY TALK OR USELESS NONSENSE." IT KINDA FITS NICELY WITH THE IDEA OF A RING OF THIEVES THAT USES A NIGHTCLUB AS A HIDEOUT, RIGHT?
うい〜っ
おかわりっ
MMM. WHY DON'T YOU GIVE ME A DIFFERENT TOPIC?!

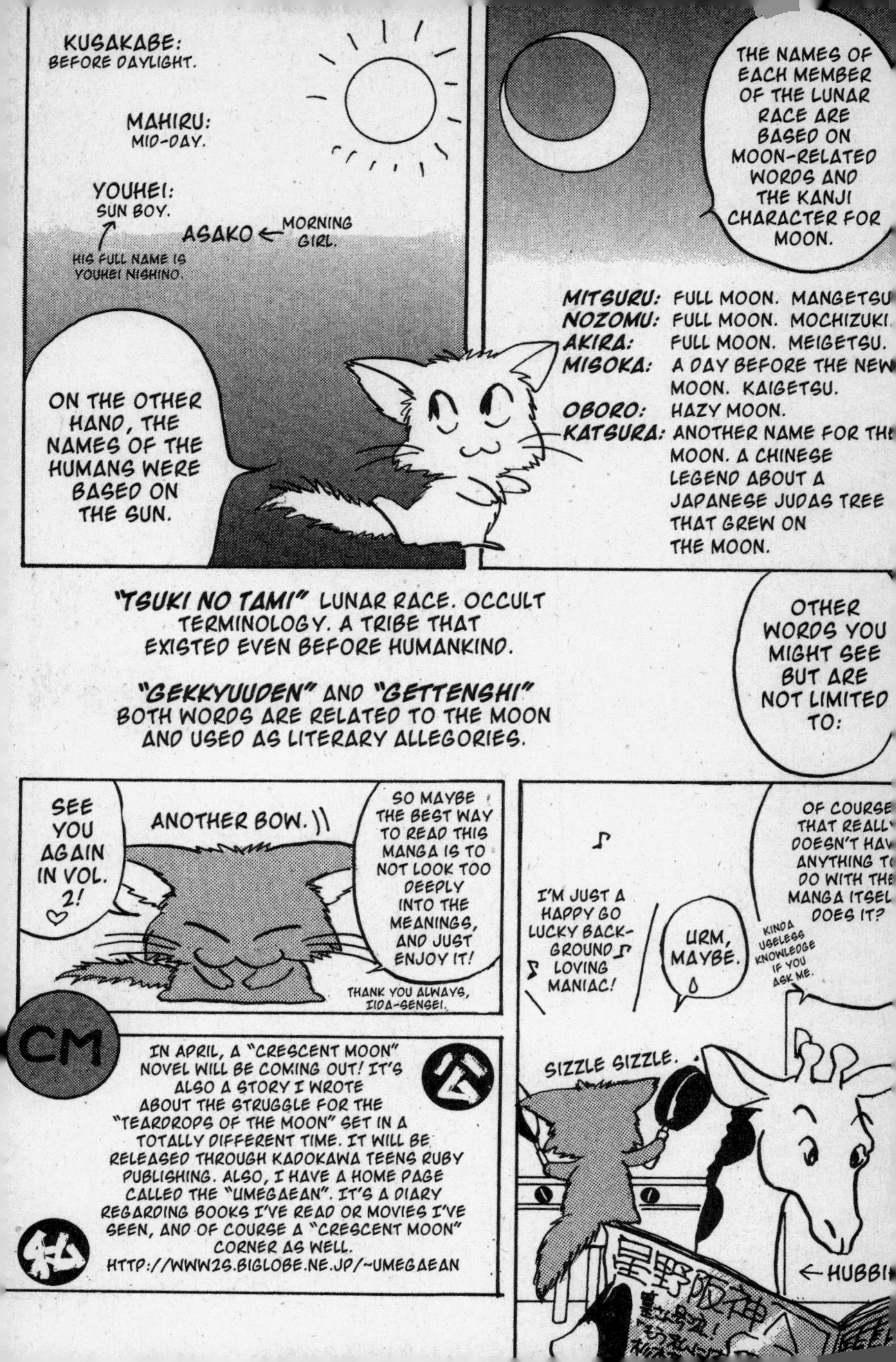

THE NAMES OF EACH MEMBER OF THE LUNAR RACE ARE BASED ON MOON-RELATED WORDS AND THE KANJI CHARACTER FOR MOON.
MITSURU: FULL MOON. MANGETSU
NOZOMU: FULL MOON. MOCHIZUKI.
AKIRA: FULL MOON. MEIGETSU.
MISOKA: A DAY BEFORE THE NEW MOON. KAIGETSU.
OBORO: HAZY MOON.
KATSURA: ANOTHER NAME FOR THE MOON. A CHINESE LEGEND ABOUT A JAPANESE JUDAS TREE THAT GREW ON THE MOON.
KUSAKABE: BEFORE DAYLIGHT.
MAHIRU: MID-DAY.
YOUHEI: SUN BOY.
HIS FULL NAME IS YOUHEI NISHINO.
ASAKO ← MORNING GIRL.
ON THE OTHER HAND, THE NAMES OF THE HUMANS WERE BASED ON THE SUN.
OTHER WORDS YOU MIGHT SEE BUT ARE NOT LIMITED TO:
"TSUKI NO TAMI" LUNAR RACE. OCCULT TERMINOLOGY. A TRIBE THAT EXISTED EVEN BEFORE HUMANKIND.
"GEKKYUUDEN" AND "GETTENSHI" BOTH WORDS ARE RELATED TO THE MOON AND USED AS LITERARY ALLEGORIES.
OF COURSE THAT REALLY DOESN'T HAVE ANYTHING TO DO WITH THE MANGA ITSELF DOES IT?
KINDA USELESS KNOWLEDGE IF YOU ASK ME.
URM, MAYBE.
I'M JUST A HAPPY GO LUCKY BACK-GROUND ♪ LOVING MANIAC!
SIZZLE SIZZLE.
← HUBBI
星野阪神
SO MAYBE THE BEST WAY TO READ THIS MANGA IS TO NOT LOOK TOO DEEPLY INTO THE MEANINGS, AND JUST ENJOY IT!
THANK YOU ALWAYS, IIDA-SENSEI.
ANOTHER BOW.
SEE YOU AGAIN IN VOL. 2! ♡
CM
IN APRIL, A "CRESCENT MOON" NOVEL WILL BE COMING OUT! IT'S ALSO A STORY I WROTE ABOUT THE STRUGGLE FOR THE "TEARDROPS OF THE MOON" SET IN A TOTALLY DIFFERENT TIME. IT WILL BE RELEASED THROUGH KADOKAWA TEENS RUBY PUBLISHING. ALSO, I HAVE A HOME PAGE CALLED THE "UMEGAEAN". IT'S A DIARY REGARDING BOOKS I'VE READ OR MOVIES I'VE SEEN, AND OF COURSE A "CRESCENT MOON" CORNER AS WELL.
HTTP://WWW2S.BIGLOBE.NE.JP/~UMEGAEAN

HARUKO IIDA

VOLUME 1 IS NOW OVER. I AM SO SLEEPY.

YAWN!

SEE YOU NEXT TIME!

CRESCENT MOON

Preview

Don't miss out on the next volume when Mahiru joins the Lunar Race on a rip-roaring heist to reclaim the Teardrops. Things go awry on the night of a full moon when Mitsuru gets caught in a fiery trap set by the police! Will Akira, Misoka and Nozomu rescue Mitsuru before it's too late? And will they be able to save the precious Teardrop from the hands of evil? Find out in Volume 2 if Mahiru's special powers save the day!

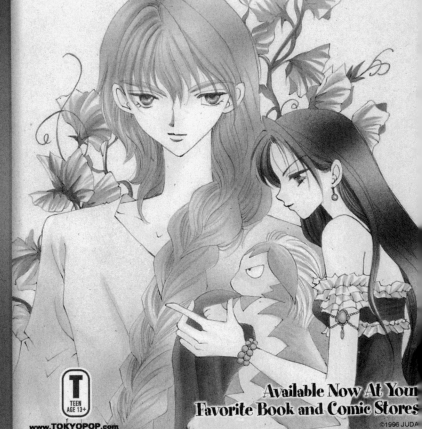

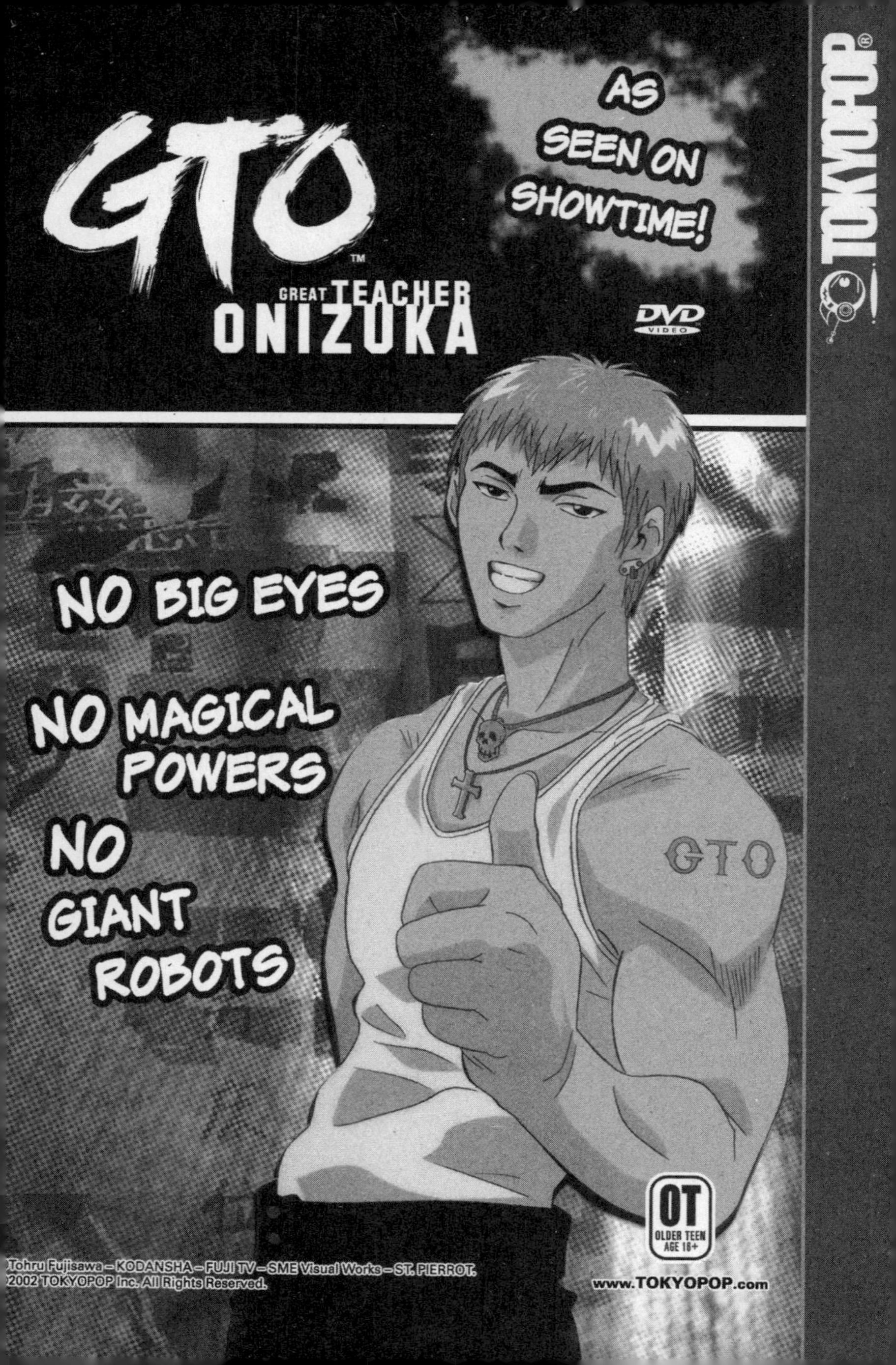
GTO™
GREAT TEACHER ONIZUKA
AS SEEN ON SHOWTIME!
DVD VIDEO
TOKYOPOP®
NO BIG EYES
NO MAGICAL POWERS
NO GIANT ROBOTS
GTO
OT OLDER TEEN AGE 16+
Tohru Fujisawa – KODANSHA – FUJI TV – SME Visual Works – ST. PIERROT.
2002 TOKYOPOP Inc. All Rights Reserved.
www.TOKYOPOP.com

TOKYO
BABYLON™

Welcome to Tokyo.
The city never sleeps.
The dead want it to rest in pieces.

TEEN
AGE 13+

www.TOKYOPOP.com

STOP!

This is the back of the book.
You wouldn't want to spoil a great ending!

This book is printed "manga-style," in the authentic Japanese right-to-left format. Since none of the artwork has been flipped or altered, readers get to experience the story just as the creator intended. You've been asking for it, so TOKYOPOP® delivered: authentic, hot-off-the-press, and far more fun!

DIRECTIONS

If this is your first time reading manga-style, here's a quick guide to help you understand how it works.

It's easy... just start in the top right panel and follow the numbers. Have fun, and look for more 100% authentic manga from TOKYOPOP®!